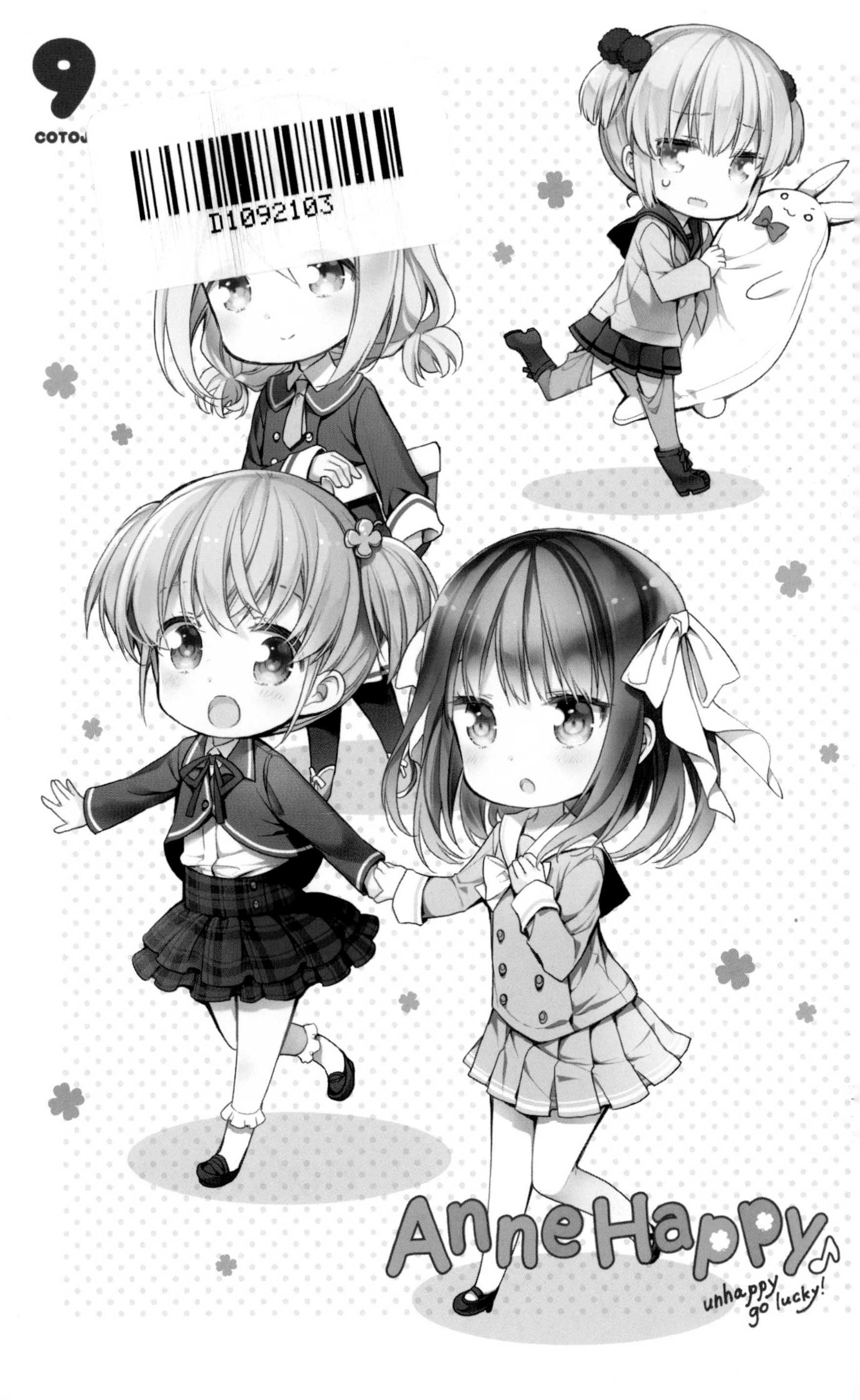
9
COTOJ
Anne Happy
unhappy go lucky!

CONTENTS
ANNE HAPPY
VOLUME NINE
COTOJI

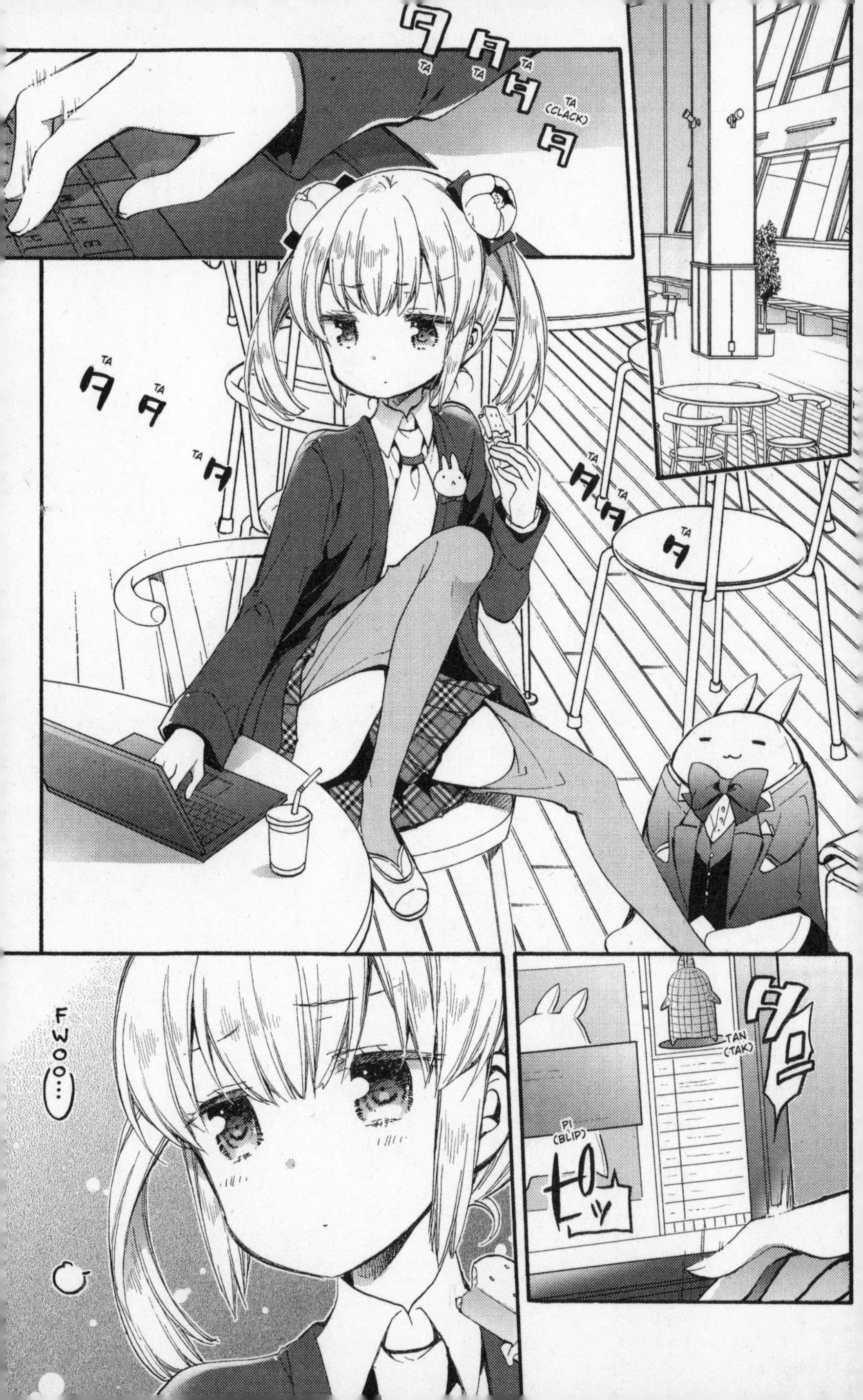

TA TA TA
TA (CLACK)
TA TA TA
TA TA TA
TAN (TAK)
PI (BLIP)
FWOO...

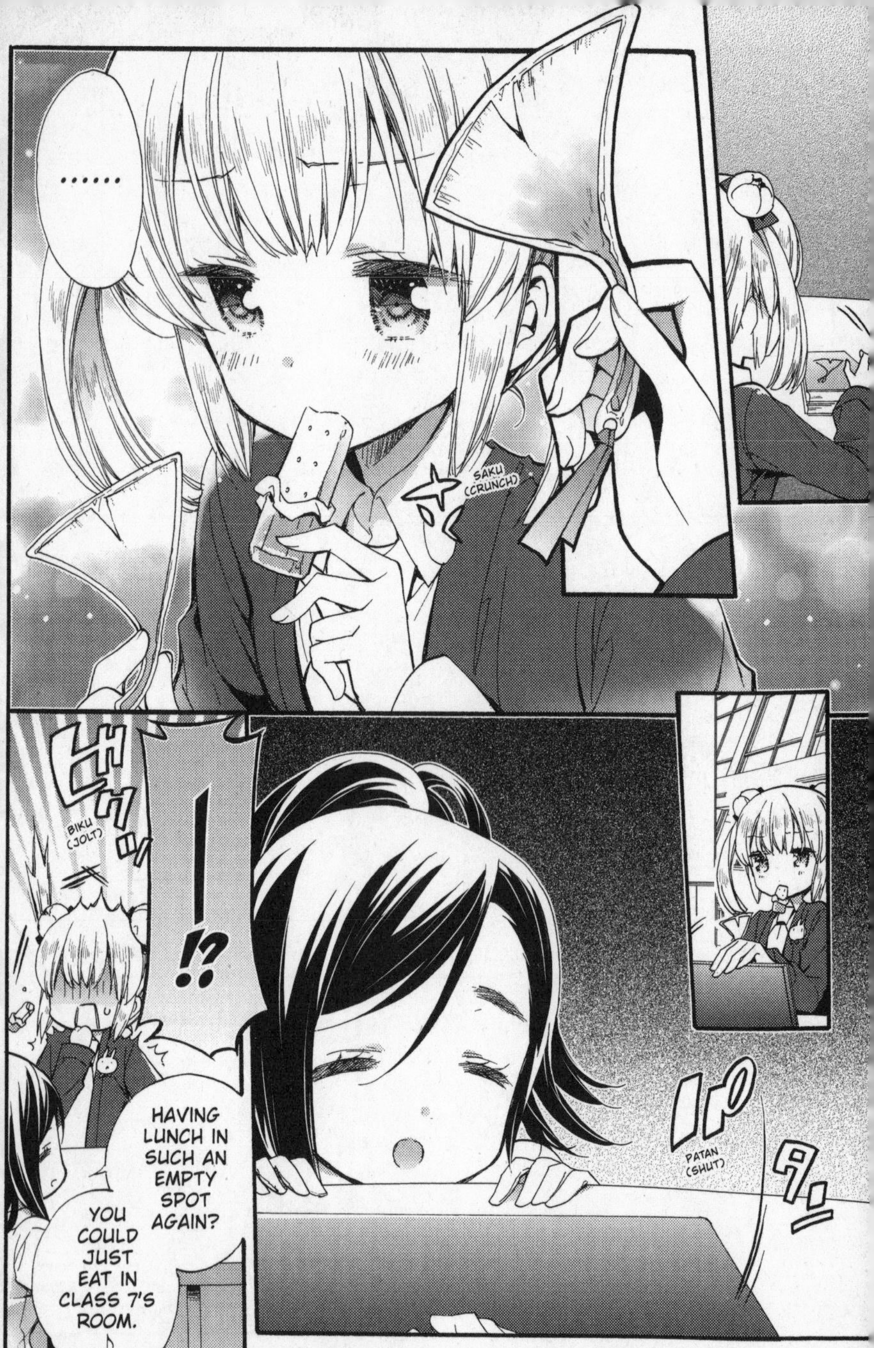
......
SAKU (CRUNCH)
PATAN (SHUT)
!!?
BIKU (JOLT)
HAVING LUNCH IN SUCH AN EMPTY SPOT AGAIN?
YOU COULD JUST EAT IN CLASS 7'S ROOM. ♪

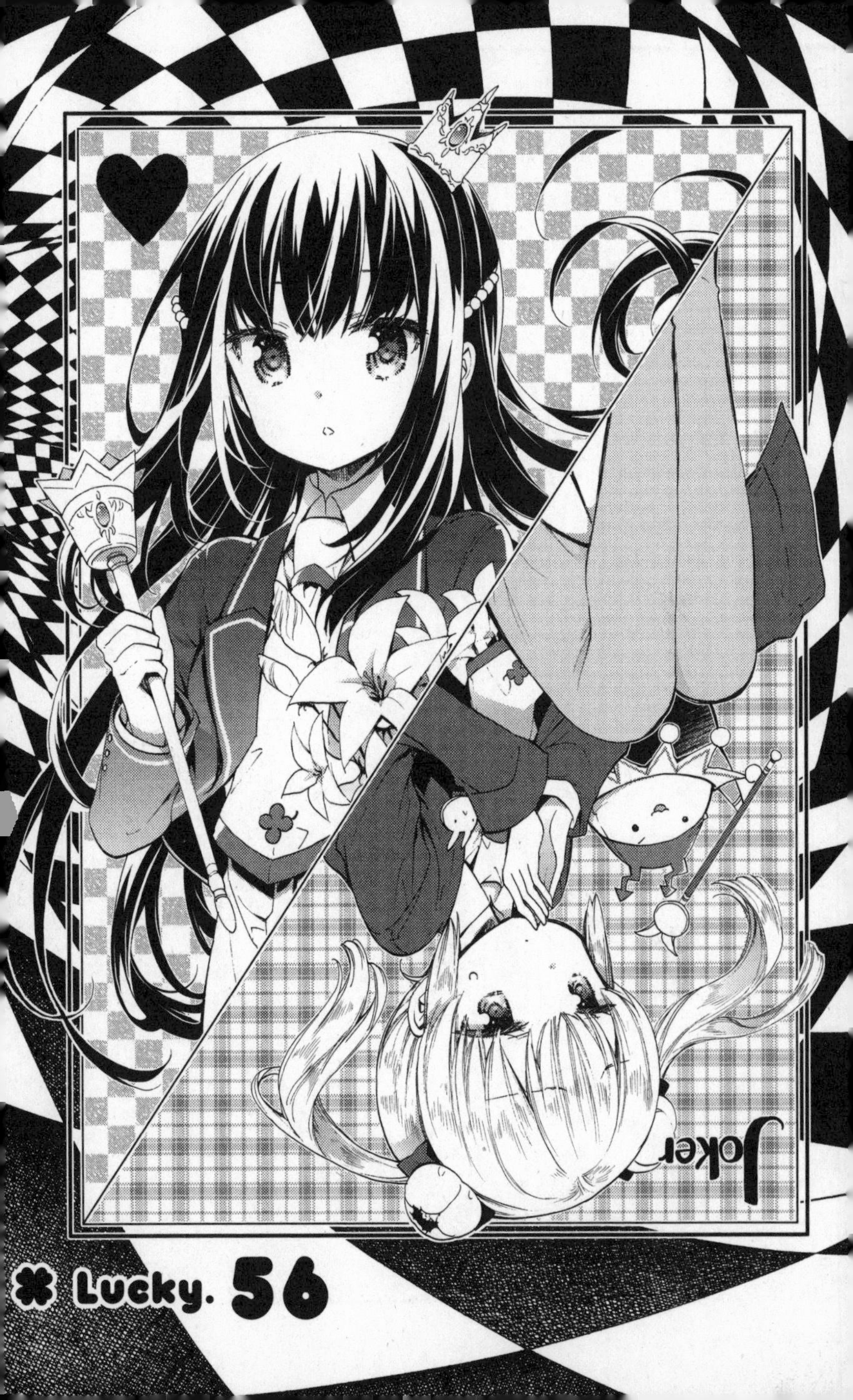
Joker

Lucky. 56

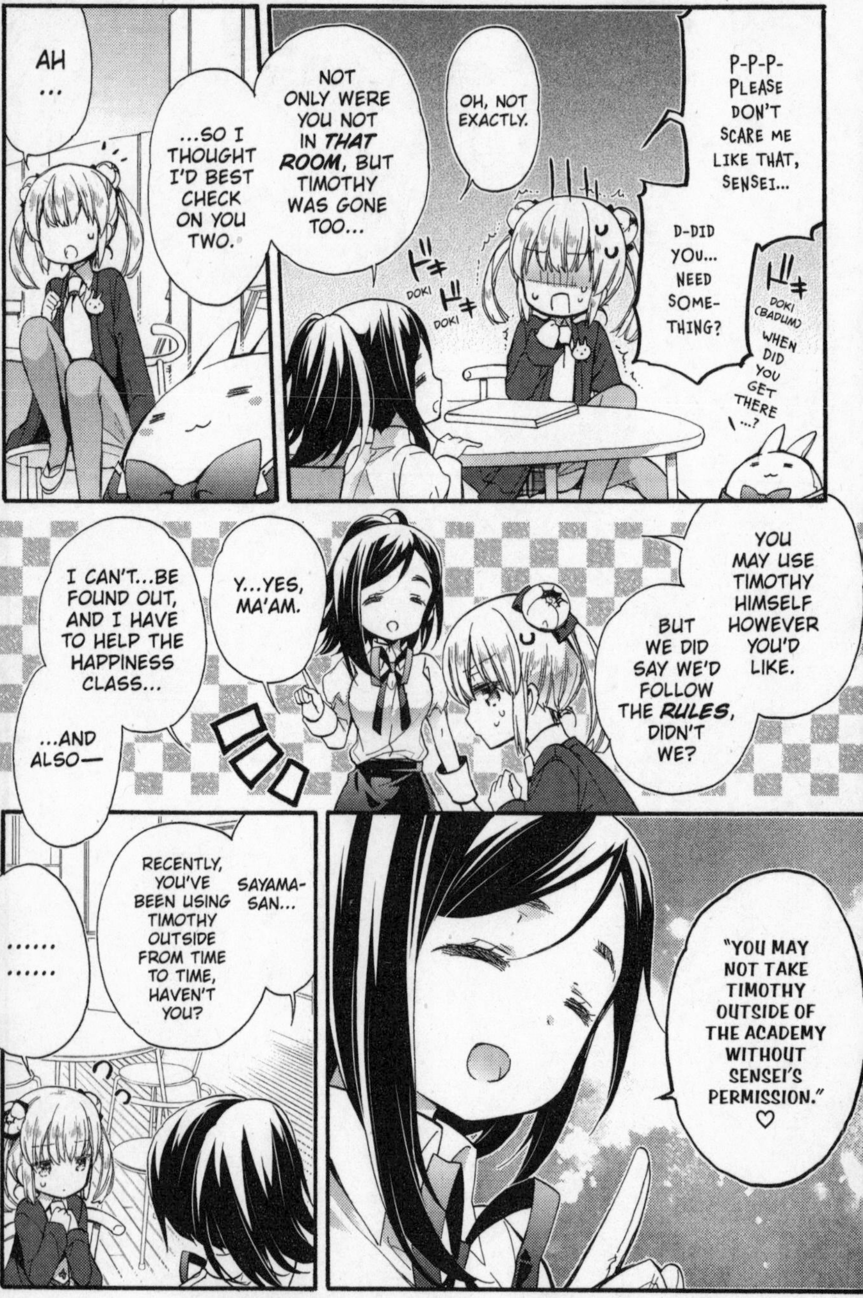
P-P-P-PLEASE DON'T SCARE ME LIKE THAT, SENSEI...
D-DID YOU... NEED SOME-THING?
ドキ DOKI (BADUM)
WHEN DID YOU GET THERE...?
OH, NOT EXACTLY.
NOT ONLY WERE YOU NOT IN ***THAT ROOM***, BUT TIMOTHY WAS GONE TOO...
ドキ DOKI
ドキ DOKI
...SO I THOUGHT I'D BEST CHECK ON YOU TWO.
AH...
YOU MAY USE TIMOTHY HIMSELF HOWEVER YOU'D LIKE.
BUT WE DID SAY WE'D FOLLOW THE ***RULES***, DIDN'T WE?
Y...YES, MA'AM.
I CAN'T...BE FOUND OUT, AND I HAVE TO HELP THE HAPPINESS CLASS...
...AND ALSO—
"YOU MAY NOT TAKE TIMOTHY OUTSIDE OF THE ACADEMY WITHOUT SENSEI'S PERMISSION." ♡
SAYAMA-SAN...
RECENTLY, YOU'VE BEEN USING TIMOTHY OUTSIDE FROM TIME TO TIME, HAVEN'T YOU?
....

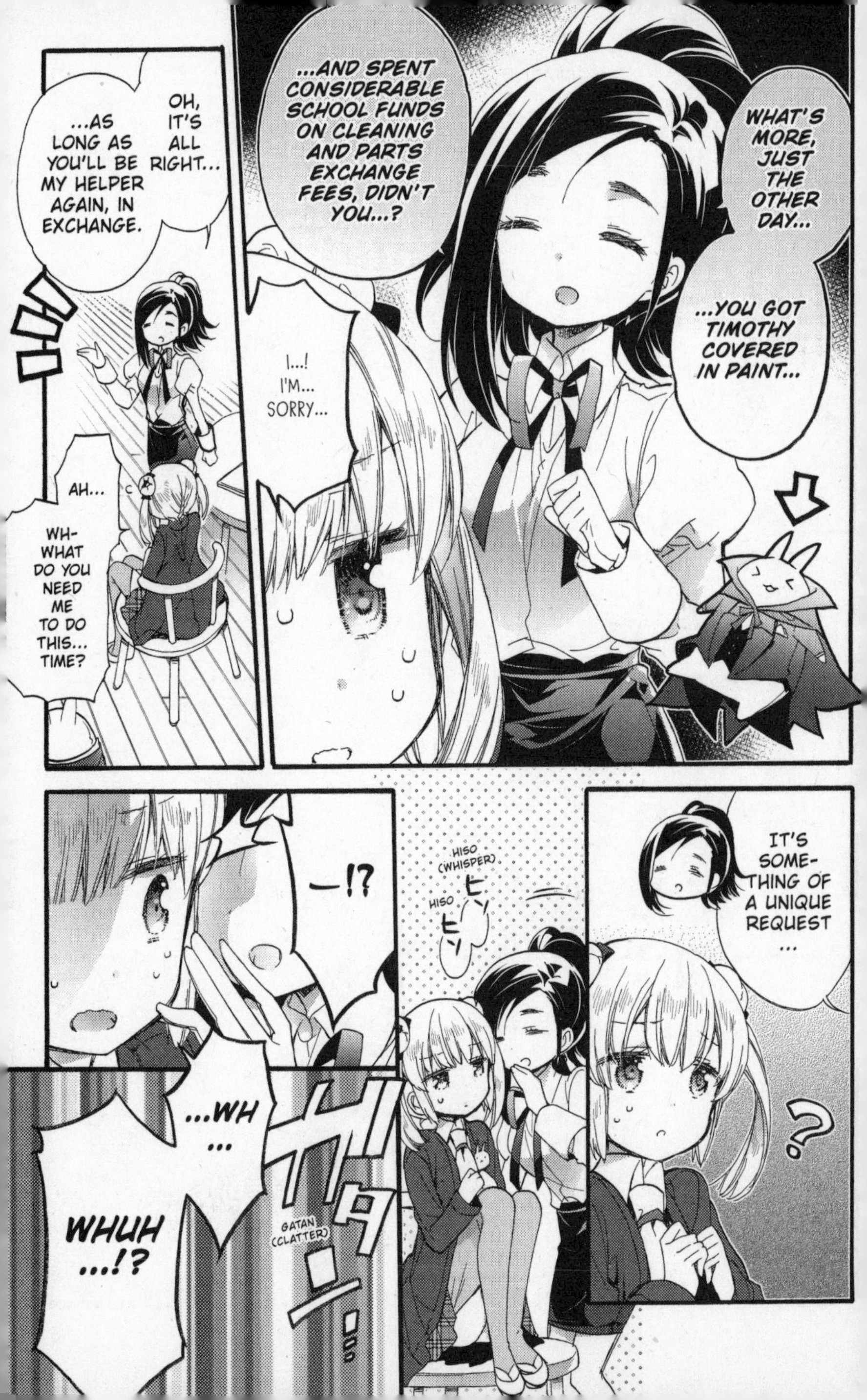
WHAT'S MORE, JUST THE OTHER DAY...
...YOU GOT TIMOTHY COVERED IN PAINT...
...AND SPENT CONSIDERABLE SCHOOL FUNDS ON CLEANING AND PARTS EXCHANGE FEES, DIDN'T YOU...?
I...! I'M... SORRY...
OH, IT'S ALL RIGHT...
...AS LONG AS YOU'LL BE MY HELPER AGAIN, IN EXCHANGE.
AH...
WH-WHAT DO YOU NEED ME TO DO THIS... TIME?
IT'S SOME-THING OF A UNIQUE REQUEST ...
HISO (WHISPER)
HISO
—!?
...WH ...
WHUH ...!?
GATAN (CLATTER)

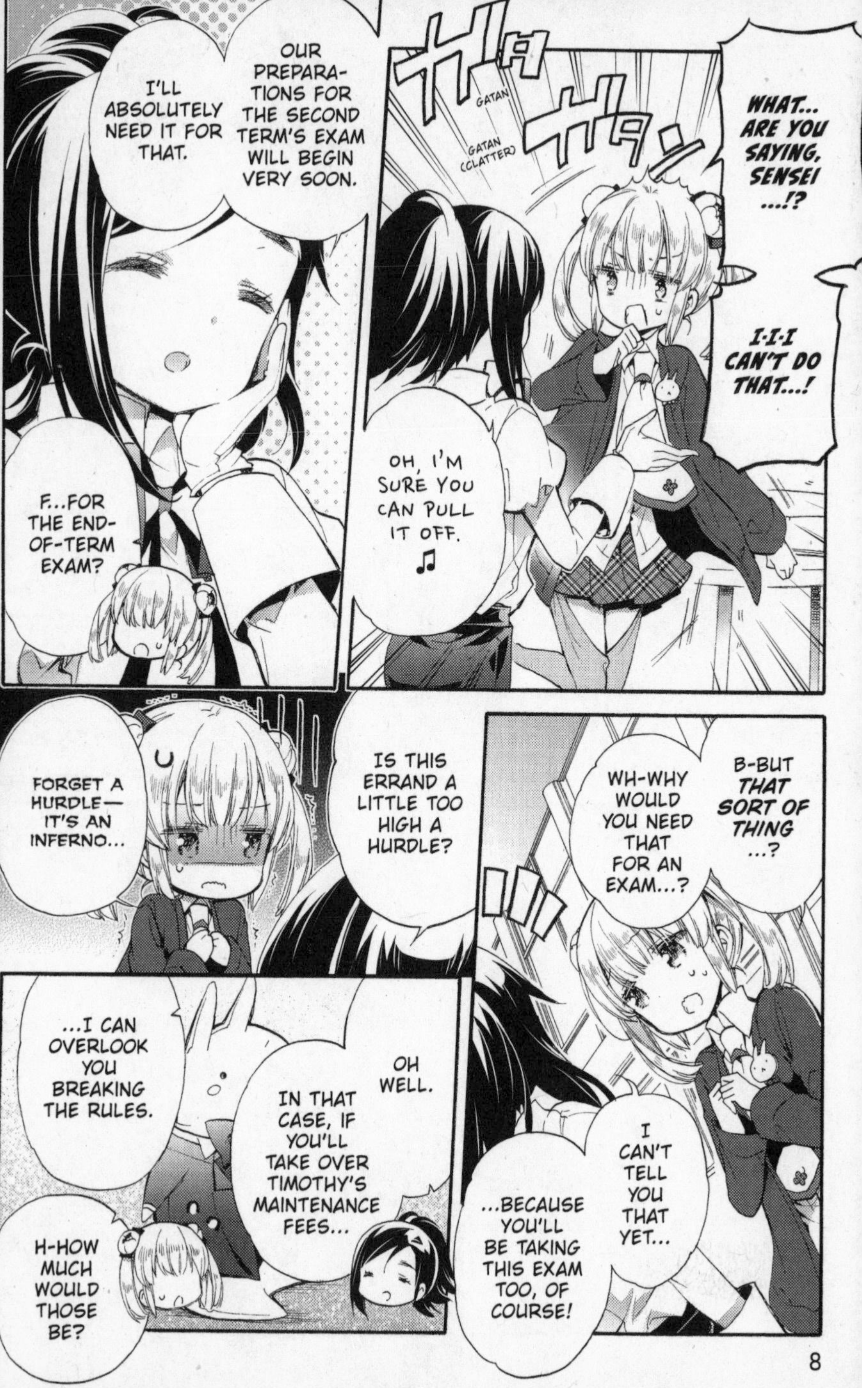
WHAT... ARE YOU SAYING, SENSEI...!?
GATAN
GATAN (CLATTER)
I-I-I CAN'T DO THAT...!
OH, I'M SURE YOU CAN PULL IT OFF. ♫
OUR PREPARATIONS FOR THE SECOND TERM'S EXAM WILL BEGIN VERY SOON.
I'LL ABSOLUTELY NEED IT FOR THAT.
F...FOR THE END-OF-TERM EXAM?
B-BUT THAT SORT OF THING...?
WH-WHY WOULD YOU NEED THAT FOR AN EXAM...?
I CAN'T TELL YOU THAT YET...
...BECAUSE YOU'LL BE TAKING THIS EXAM TOO, OF COURSE!
IS THIS ERRAND A LITTLE TOO HIGH A HURDLE?
FORGET A HURDLE—IT'S AN INFERNO...
OH WELL.
IN THAT CASE, IF YOU'LL TAKE OVER TIMOTHY'S MAINTENANCE FEES...
...I CAN OVERLOOK YOU BREAKING THE RULES.
H-HOW MUCH WOULD THOSE BE?

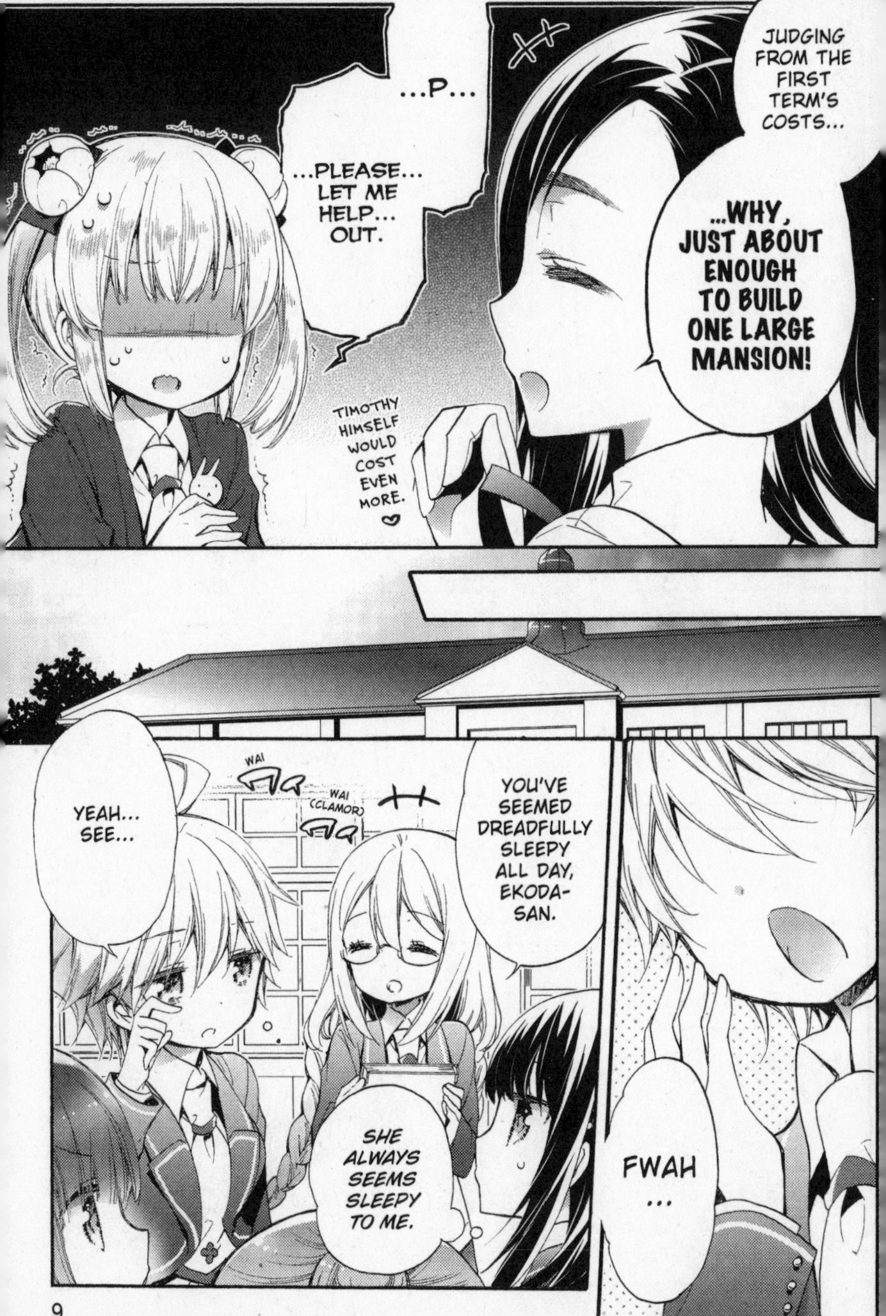
JUDGING FROM THE FIRST TERM'S COSTS...
...WHY, JUST ABOUT ENOUGH TO BUILD ONE LARGE MANSION!
TIMOTHY HIMSELF WOULD COST EVEN MORE.
...P...
...PLEASE... LET ME HELP... OUT.
FWAH ...
YOU'VE SEEMED DREADFULLY SLEEPY ALL DAY, EKODA-SAN.
WAI
WAI (CLAMOR)
YEAH... SEE...
SHE ALWAYS SEEMS SLEEPY TO ME.

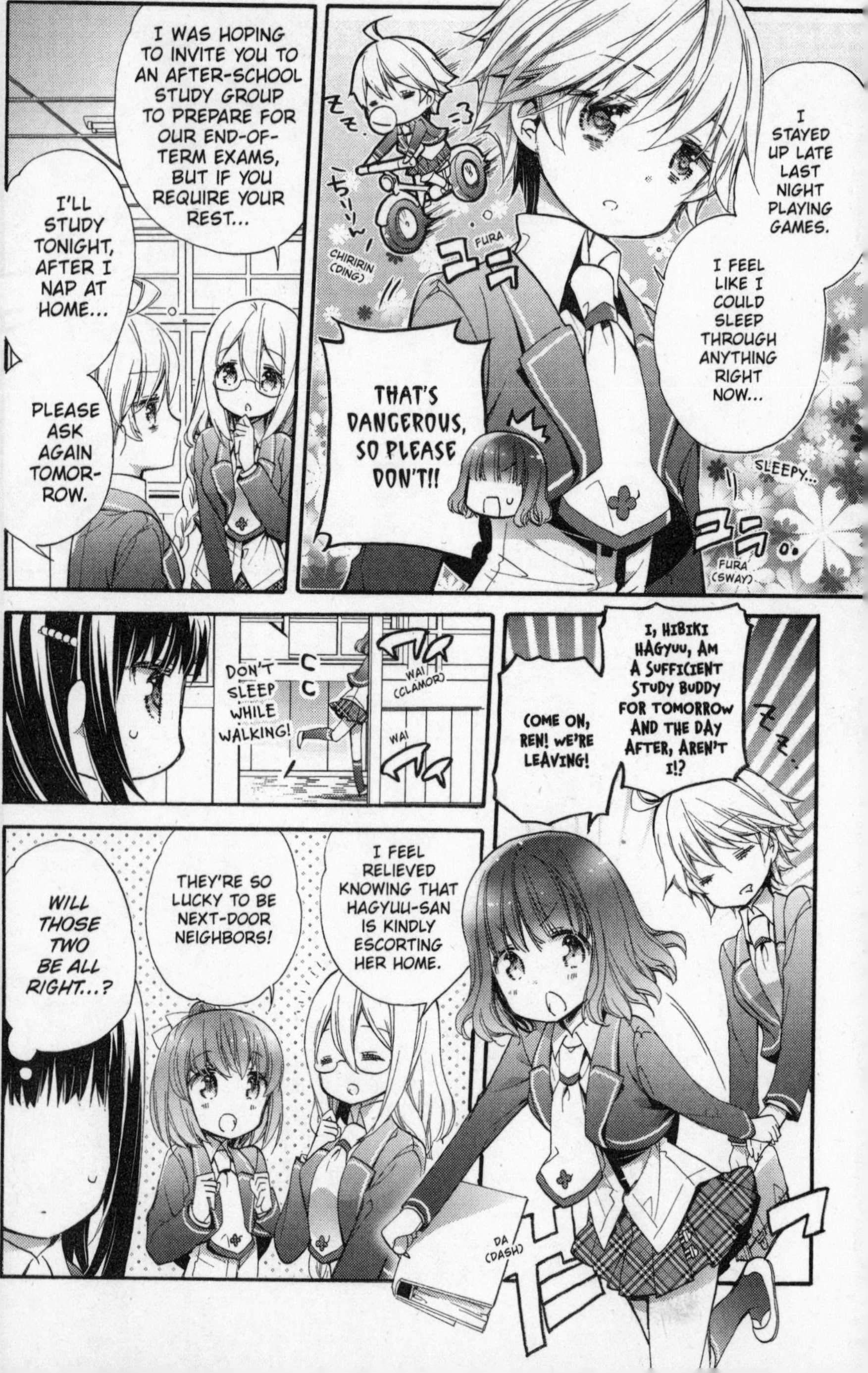
I STAYED UP LATE LAST NIGHT PLAYING GAMES.
I FEEL LIKE I COULD SLEEP THROUGH ANYTHING RIGHT NOW...
SLEEPY...
FURA (SWAY)
FURA
CHIRIRIN (DING)
THAT'S DANGEROUS, SO PLEASE DON'T!!
I WAS HOPING TO INVITE YOU TO AN AFTER-SCHOOL STUDY GROUP TO PREPARE FOR OUR END-OF-TERM EXAMS, BUT IF YOU REQUIRE YOUR REST...
I'LL STUDY TONIGHT, AFTER I NAP AT HOME...
PLEASE ASK AGAIN TOMORROW.
I, HIBIKI HAGYUU, AM A SUFFICIENT STUDY BUDDY FOR TOMORROW AND THE DAY AFTER, AREN'T I!?
COME ON, REN! WE'RE LEAVING!
DA (DASH)
WAI (CLAMOR)
WAI
DON'T SLEEP WHILE WALKING!
I FEEL RELIEVED KNOWING THAT HAGYUU-SAN IS KINDLY ESCORTING HER HOME.
THEY'RE SO LUCKY TO BE NEXT-DOOR NEIGHBORS!
WILL THOSE TWO BE ALL RIGHT...?

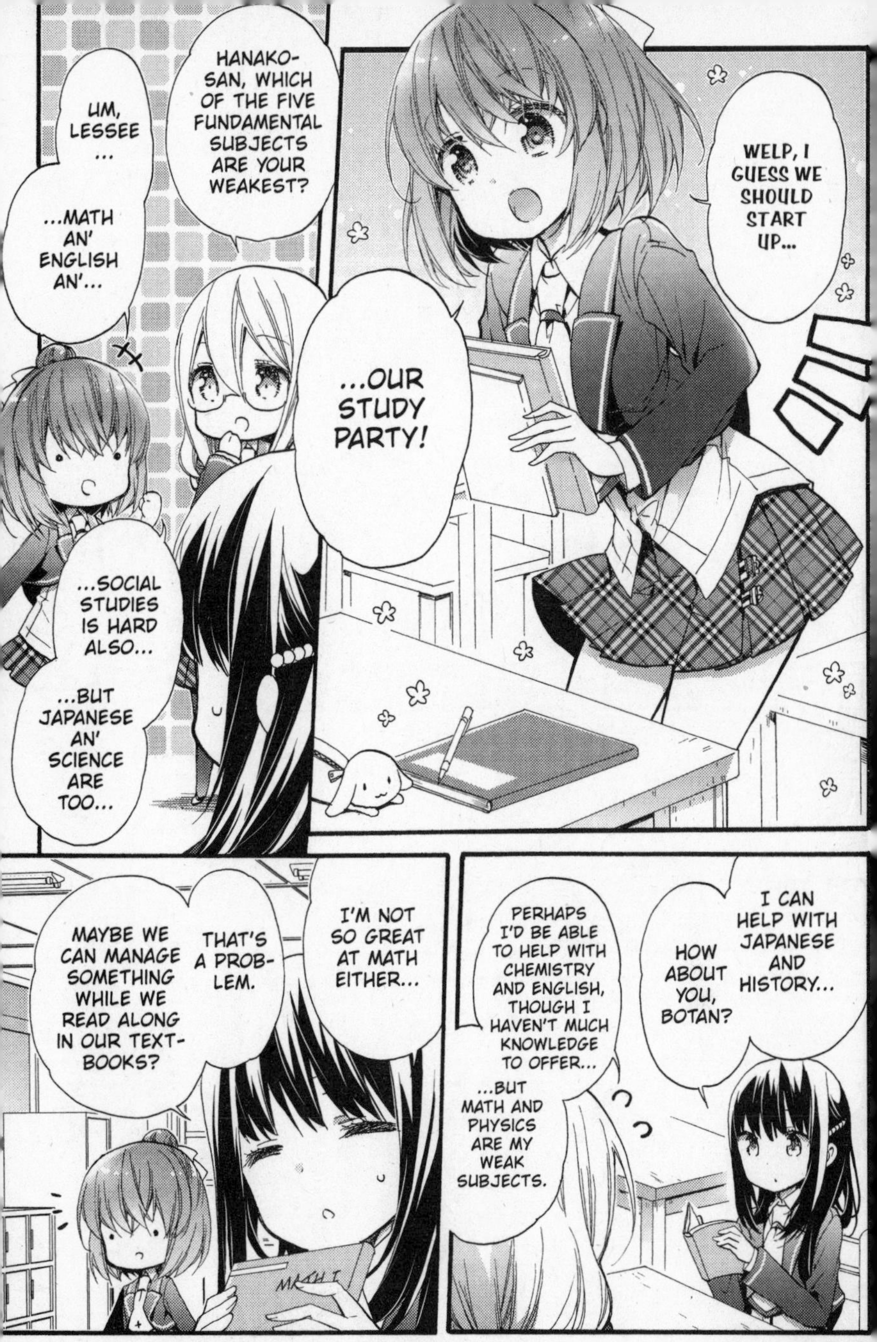
WELP, I GUESS WE SHOULD START UP...
...OUR STUDY PARTY!
HANAKO-SAN, WHICH OF THE FIVE FUNDAMENTAL SUBJECTS ARE YOUR WEAKEST?
UM, LESSEE...
...MATH AN' ENGLISH AN'...
...SOCIAL STUDIES IS HARD ALSO...
...BUT JAPANESE AN' SCIENCE ARE TOO...
I CAN HELP WITH JAPANESE AND HISTORY...
HOW ABOUT YOU, BOTAN?
PERHAPS I'D BE ABLE TO HELP WITH CHEMISTRY AND ENGLISH, THOUGH I HAVEN'T MUCH KNOWLEDGE TO OFFER...
...BUT MATH AND PHYSICS ARE MY WEAK SUBJECTS.
I'M NOT SO GREAT AT MATH EITHER...
THAT'S A PROB-LEM.
MAYBE WE CAN MANAGE SOMETHING WHILE WE READ ALONG IN OUR TEXT-BOOKS?

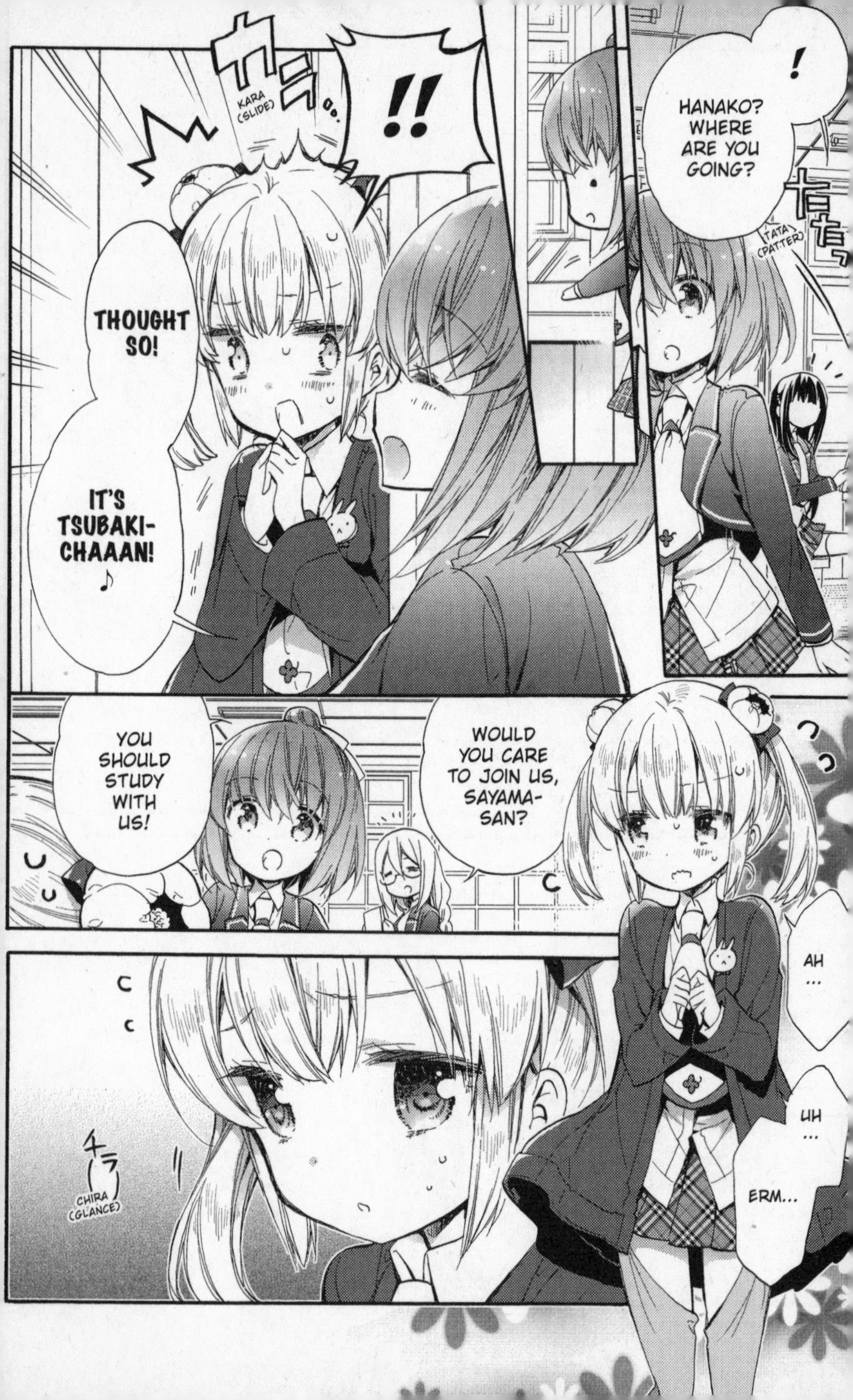
!
HANAKO? WHERE ARE YOU GOING?
TATA (PATTER)
KARA (SLIDE)
!!
THOUGHT SO!
IT'S TSUBAKI-CHAAAN! ♪
WOULD YOU CARE TO JOIN US, SAYAMA-SAN?
YOU SHOULD STUDY WITH US!
AH ...
UH ...
ERM...
CHIRA (GLANCE)

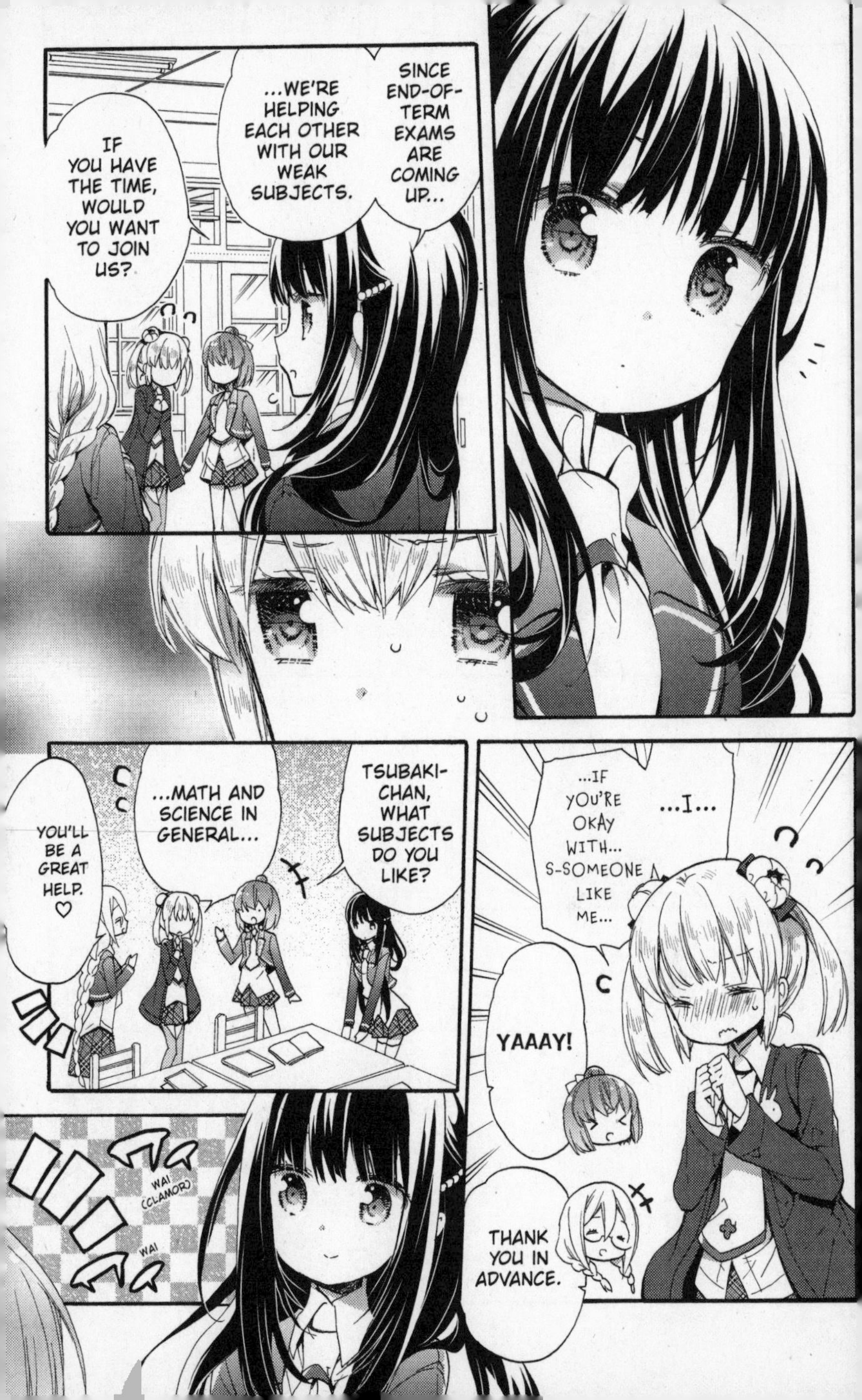
SINCE END-OF-TERM EXAMS ARE COMING UP...
...WE'RE HELPING EACH OTHER WITH OUR WEAK SUBJECTS.
IF YOU HAVE THE TIME, WOULD YOU WANT TO JOIN US?
...I...
...IF YOU'RE OKAY WITH... S-SOMEONE LIKE ME...
YAAAY!
THANK YOU IN ADVANCE.
TSUBAKI-CHAN, WHAT SUBJECTS DO YOU LIKE?
...MATH AND SCIENCE IN GENERAL...
YOU'LL BE A GREAT HELP. ♡
WAI (CLAMOR)
WAI

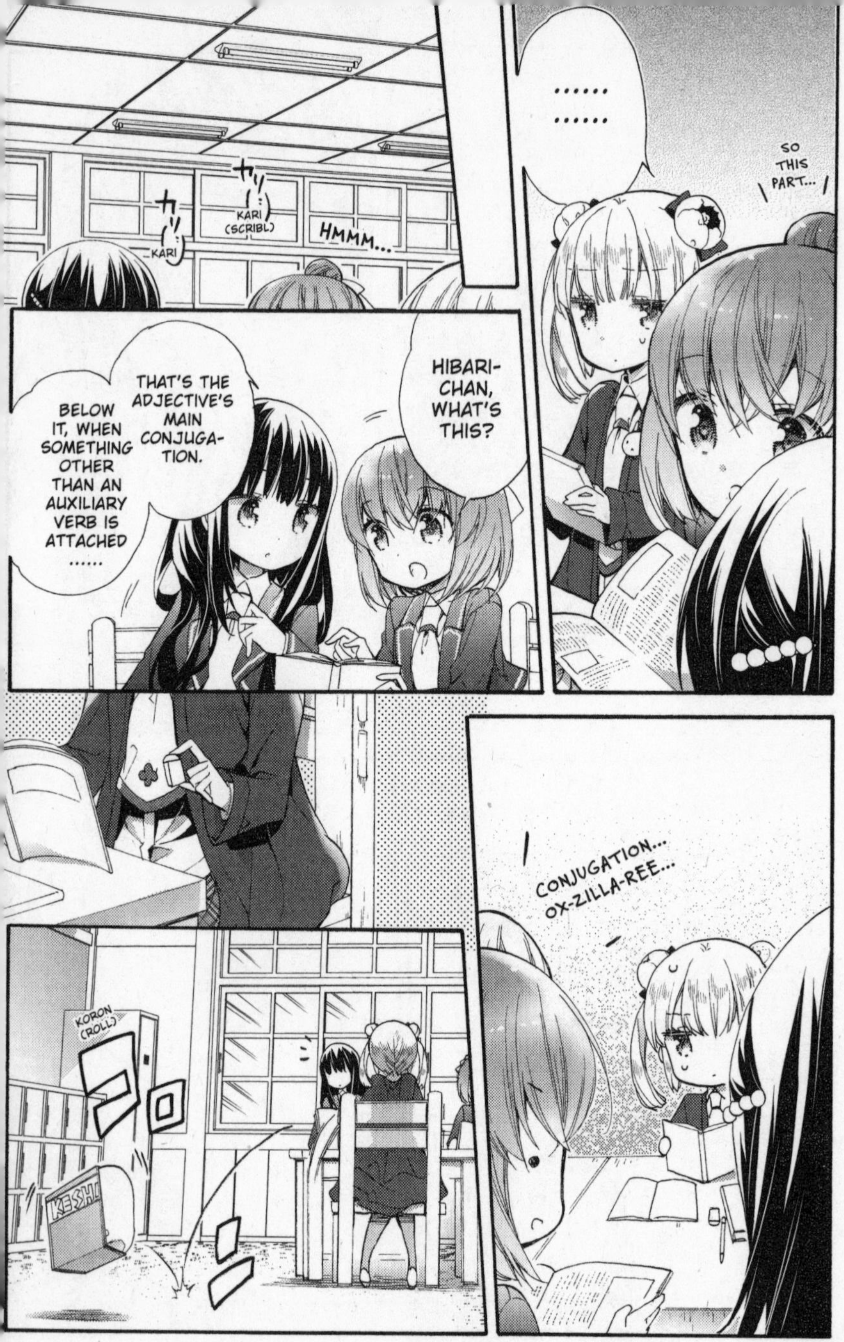
......
......
SO THIS PART...
KARI (SCRIBL)
KARI
HMMM...
HIBARI-CHAN, WHAT'S THIS?
THAT'S THE ADJECTIVE'S MAIN CONJUGATION.
BELOW IT, WHEN SOMETHING OTHER THAN AN AUXILIARY VERB IS ATTACHED ......
CONJUGATION... OX-ZILLA-REE...
KORON (ROLL)
KESHI

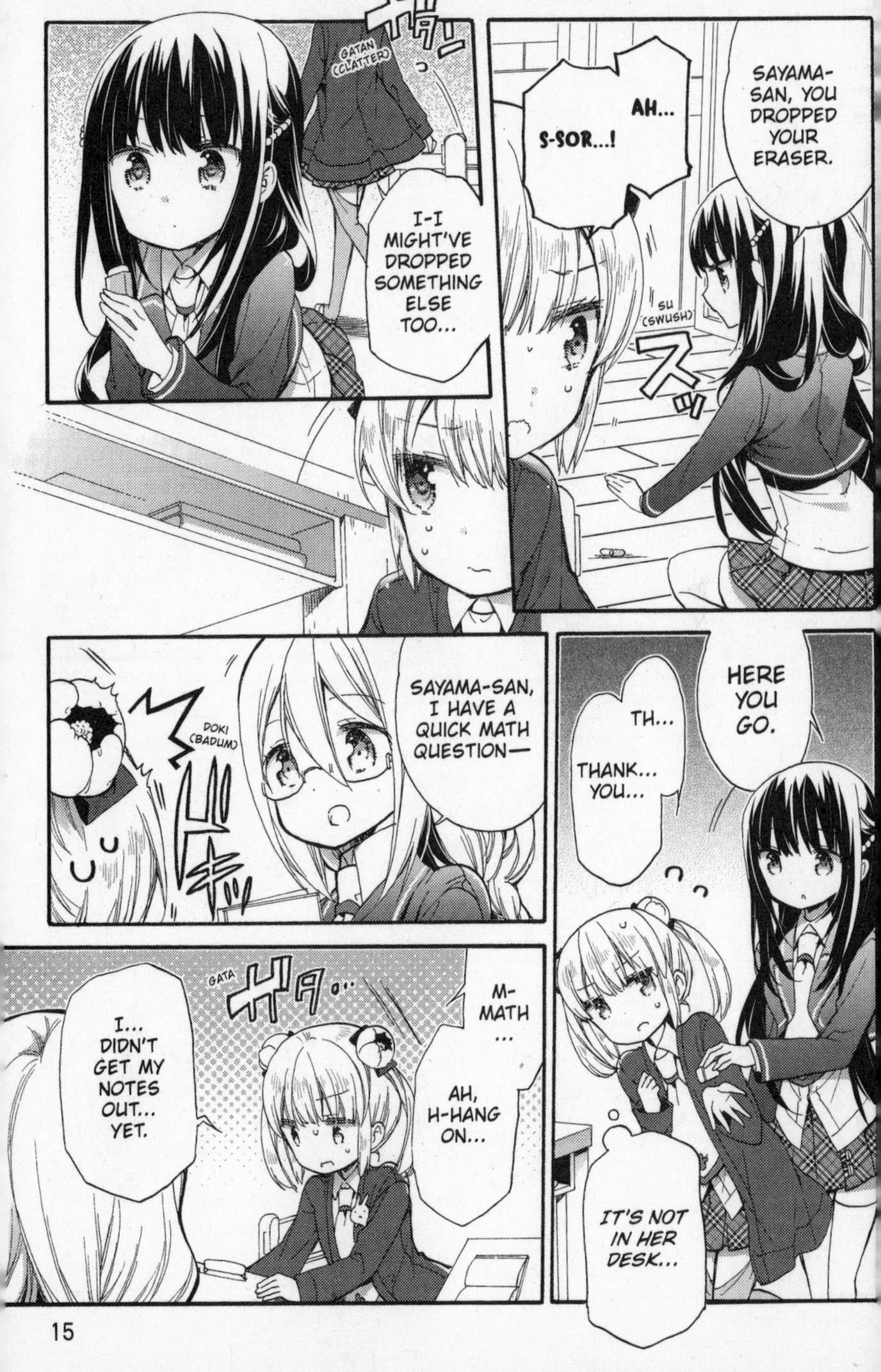
SAYAMA-SAN, YOU DROPPED YOUR ERASER.
AH...
S-SOR...!
SU (SWUSH)
GATAN (CLATTER)
I-I MIGHT'VE DROPPED SOMETHING ELSE TOO...
HERE YOU GO.
TH...
THANK... YOU...
IT'S NOT IN HER DESK...
SAYAMA-SAN, I HAVE A QUICK MATH QUESTION—
DOKI (BADUM)
M-MATH...
AH, H-HANG ON...
GATA
I... DIDN'T GET MY NOTES OUT... YET.

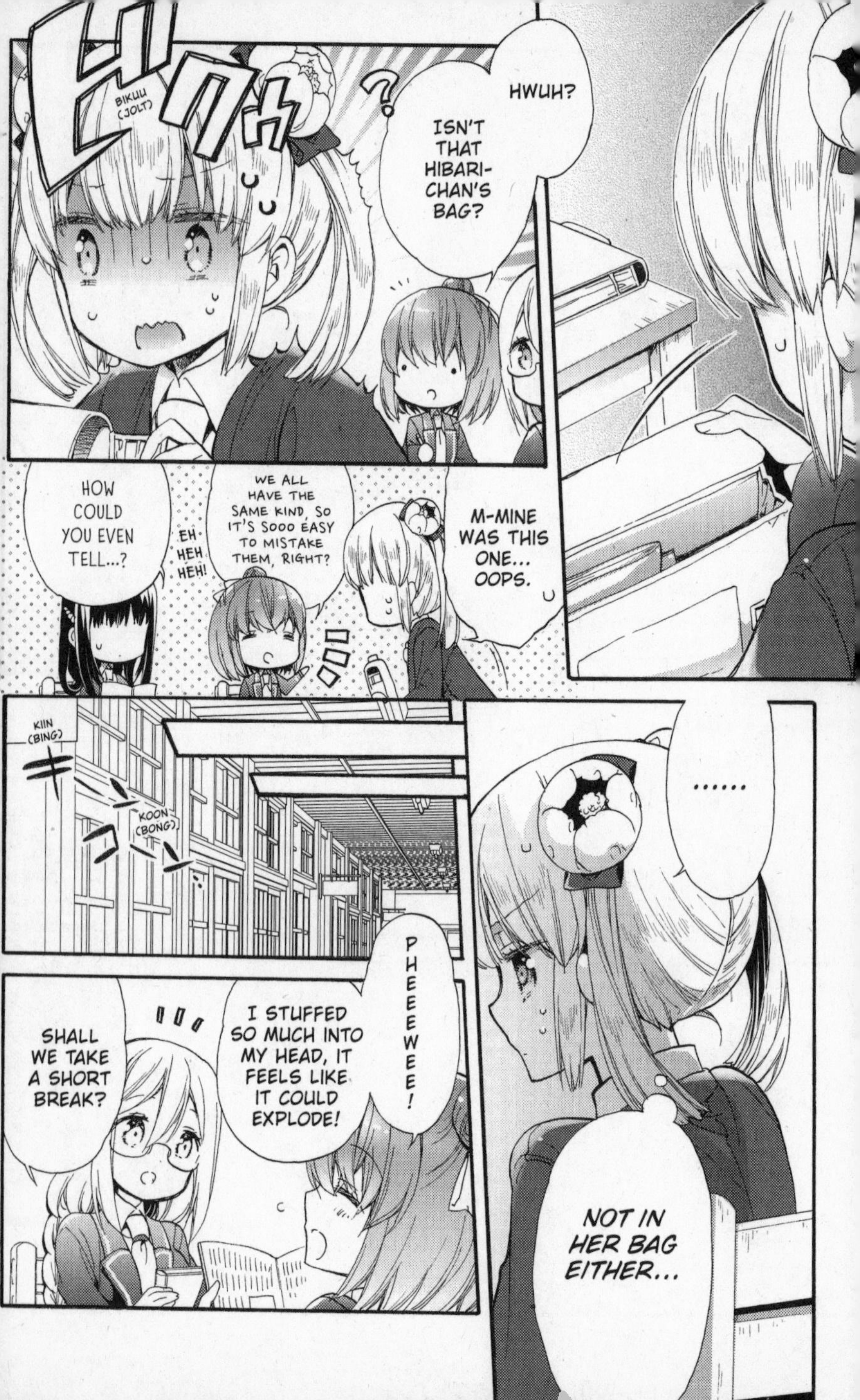
HWUH?
ISN'T THAT HIBARI-CHAN'S BAG?
BIKUU (JOLT)
M-MINE WAS THIS ONE... OOPS.
WE ALL HAVE THE SAME KIND, SO IT'S SOOO EASY TO MISTAKE THEM, RIGHT?
EH HEH HEH!
HOW COULD YOU EVEN TELL...?
......
NOT IN HER BAG EITHER...
KIIN (BING)
KOON (BONG)
PHEEEEWEEE!
I STUFFED SO MUCH INTO MY HEAD, IT FEELS LIKE IT COULD EXPLODE!
SHALL WE TAKE A SHORT BREAK?

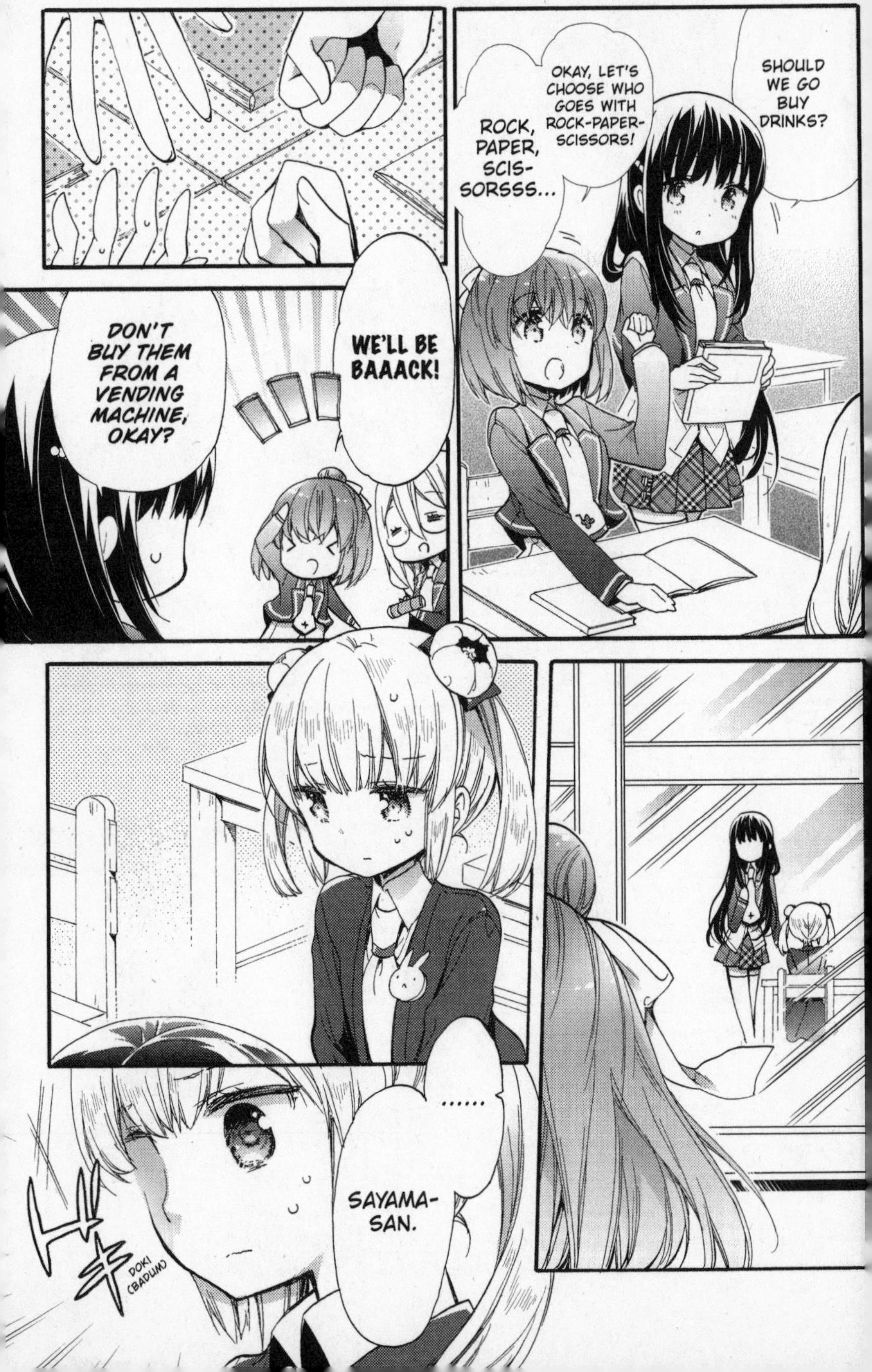
SHOULD WE GO BUY DRINKS?
OKAY, LET'S CHOOSE WHO GOES WITH ROCK-PAPER-SCISSORS!
ROCK, PAPER, SCIS-SORSSS...
WE'LL BE BAAACK!
DON'T BUY THEM FROM A VENDING MACHINE, OKAY?
......
SAYAMA-SAN.
DOKI (BADUM)

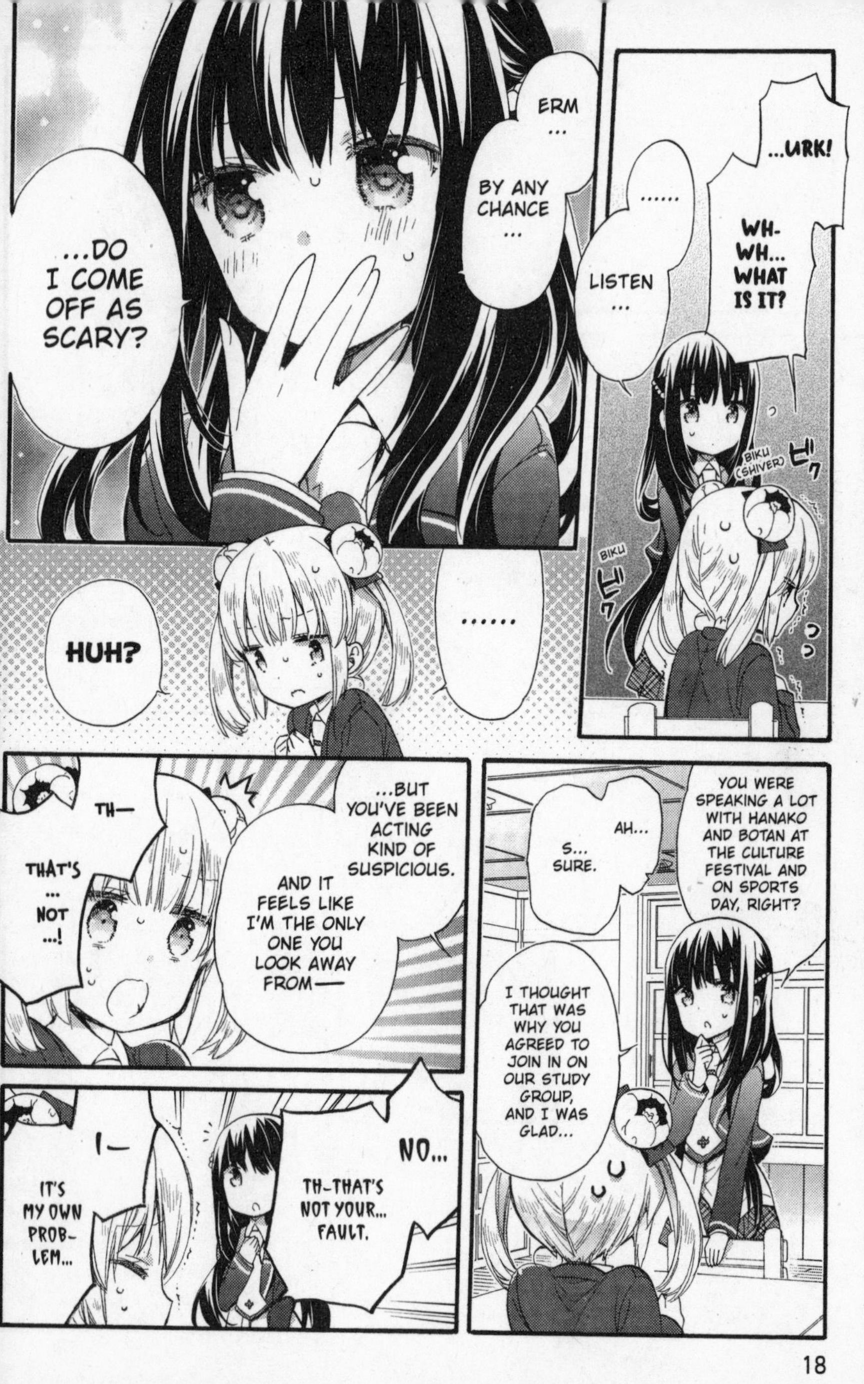
...URK!
WH-WH... WHAT IS IT?
......
LISTEN...
BIKU (SHIVER)
BIKU
ERM...
BY ANY CHANCE...
...DO I COME OFF AS SCARY?
......
HUH?
YOU WERE SPEAKING A LOT WITH HANAKO AND BOTAN AT THE CULTURE FESTIVAL AND ON SPORTS DAY, RIGHT?
AH... S... SURE.
I THOUGHT THAT WAS WHY YOU AGREED TO JOIN IN ON OUR STUDY GROUP, AND I WAS GLAD...
...BUT YOU'VE BEEN ACTING KIND OF SUSPICIOUS.
AND IT FEELS LIKE I'M THE ONLY ONE YOU LOOK AWAY FROM—
TH—
THAT'S ... NOT ...!
NO...
TH-THAT'S NOT YOUR... FAULT.
I—
IT'S MY OWN PROB-LEM...

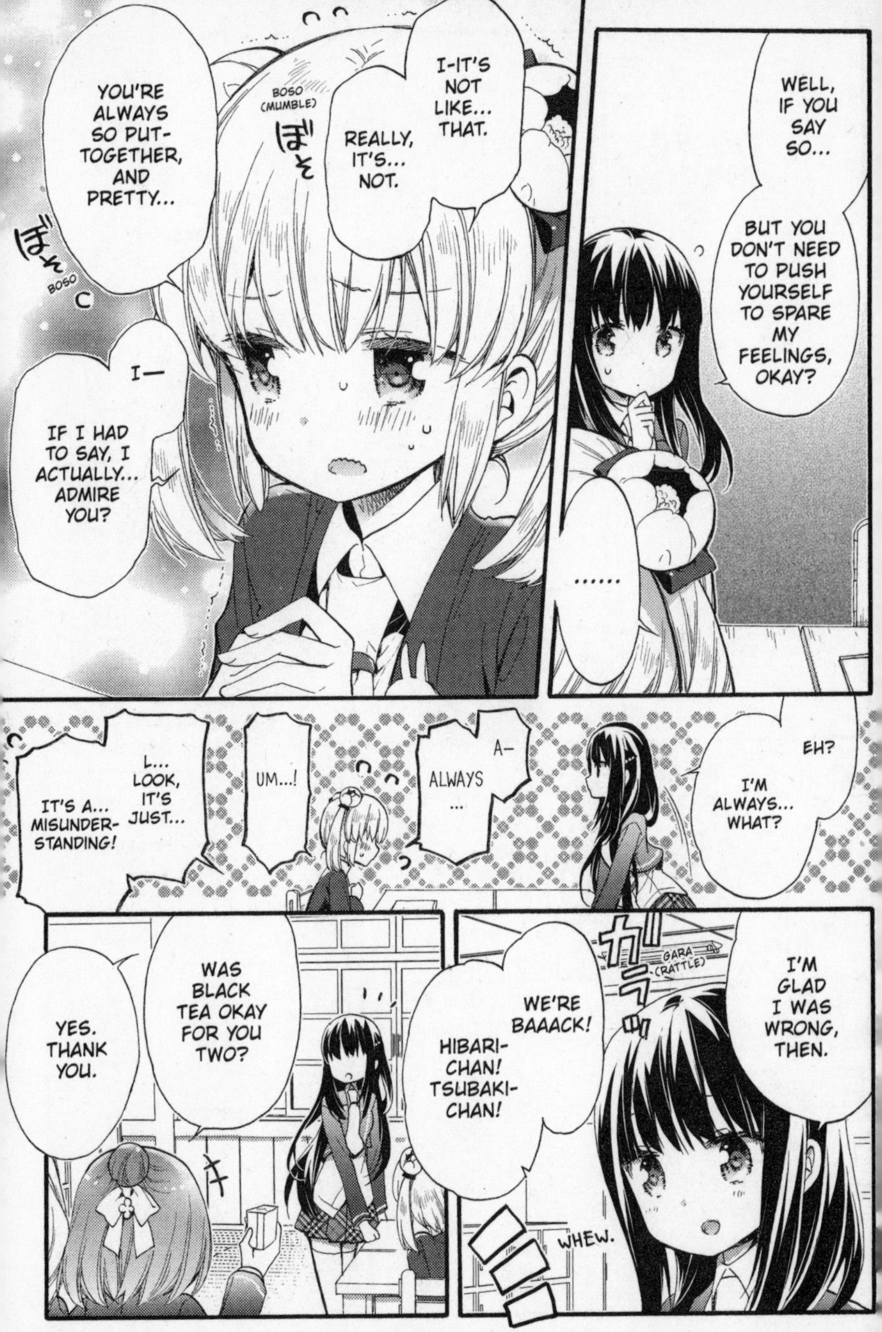
WELL, IF YOU SAY SO...
BUT YOU DON'T NEED TO PUSH YOURSELF TO SPARE MY FEELINGS, OKAY?
......
I-IT'S NOT LIKE... THAT.
REALLY, IT'S... NOT.
BOSO (MUMBLE)
YOU'RE ALWAYS SO PUT-TOGETHER, AND PRETTY...
BOSO
I—
IF I HAD TO SAY, I ACTUALLY... ADMIRE YOU?
EH?
I'M ALWAYS... WHAT?
A- ALWAYS ...
UM...!
L... LOOK, IT'S JUST...
IT'S A... MISUNDER-STANDING!
I'M GLAD I WAS WRONG, THEN.
GARA (RATTLE)
WE'RE BAAACK!
HIBARI-CHAN! TSUBAKI-CHAN!
WHEW.
WAS BLACK TEA OKAY FOR YOU TWO?
YES. THANK YOU.

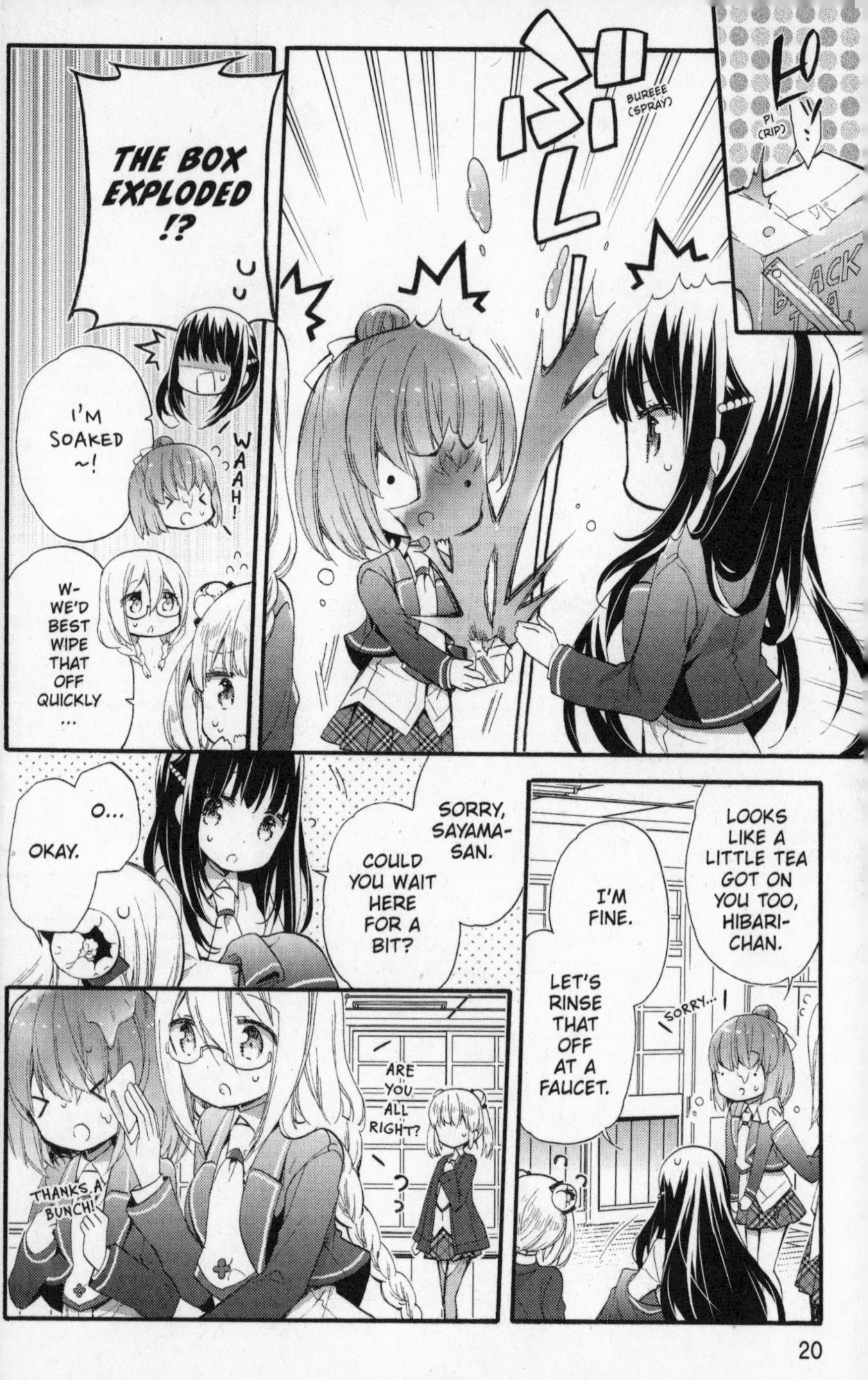
PI (RIP)
BUREEE (SPRAY)
THE BOX EXPLODED!?
I'M SOAKED ~!
WAAAH!
W-WE'D BEST WIPE THAT OFF QUICKLY...
LOOKS LIKE A LITTLE TEA GOT ON YOU TOO, HIBARI-CHAN.
I'M FINE.
LET'S RINSE THAT OFF AT A FAUCET.
SORRY...
SORRY, SAYAMA-SAN.
COULD YOU WAIT HERE FOR A BIT?
O... OKAY.
ARE YOU ALL RIGHT?
THANKS A BUNCH!

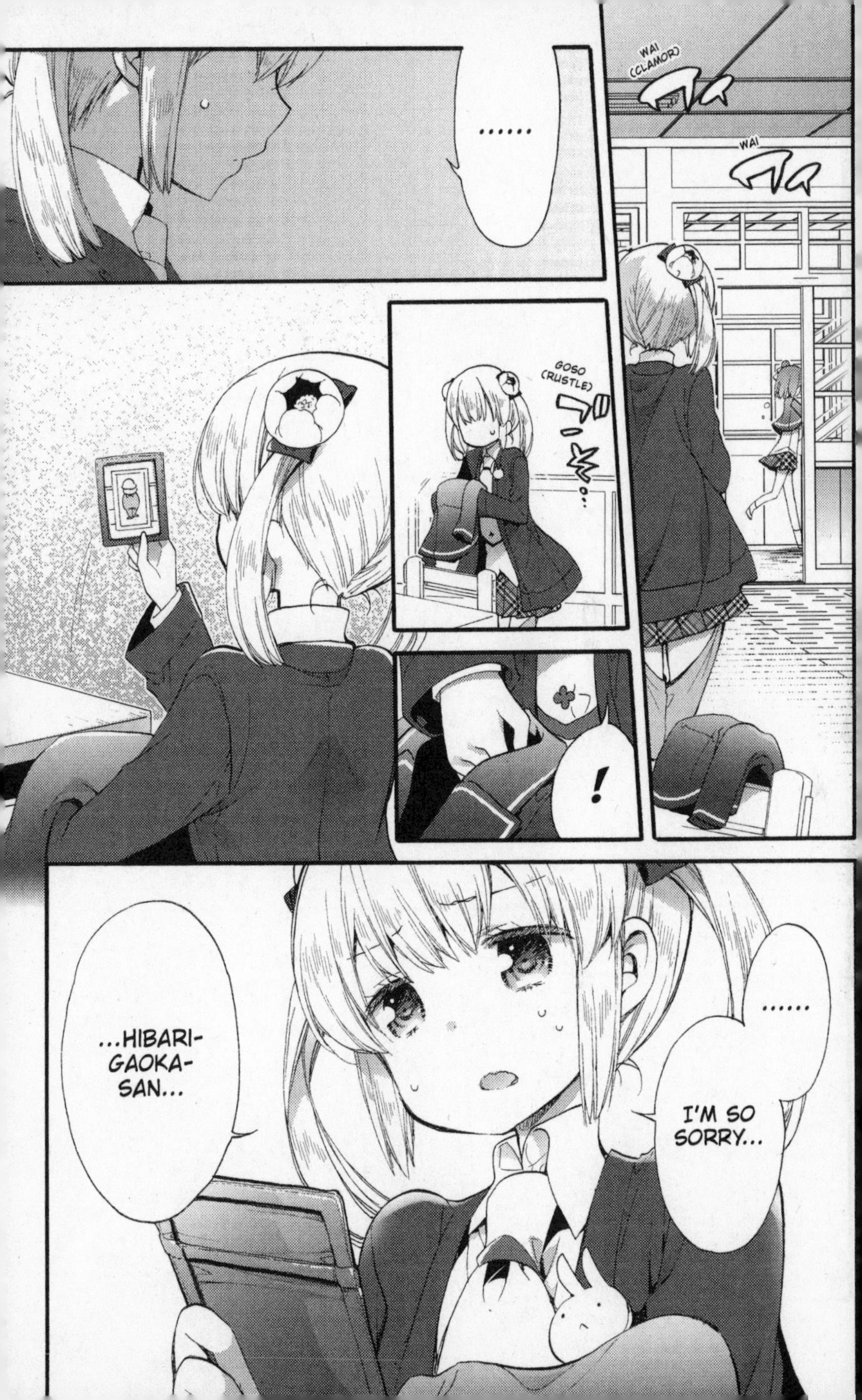
WAI (CLAMOR)
WAI
......
GOSO (RUSTLE)
!
......
I'M SO SORRY...
...HIBARI-GAOKA-SAN...

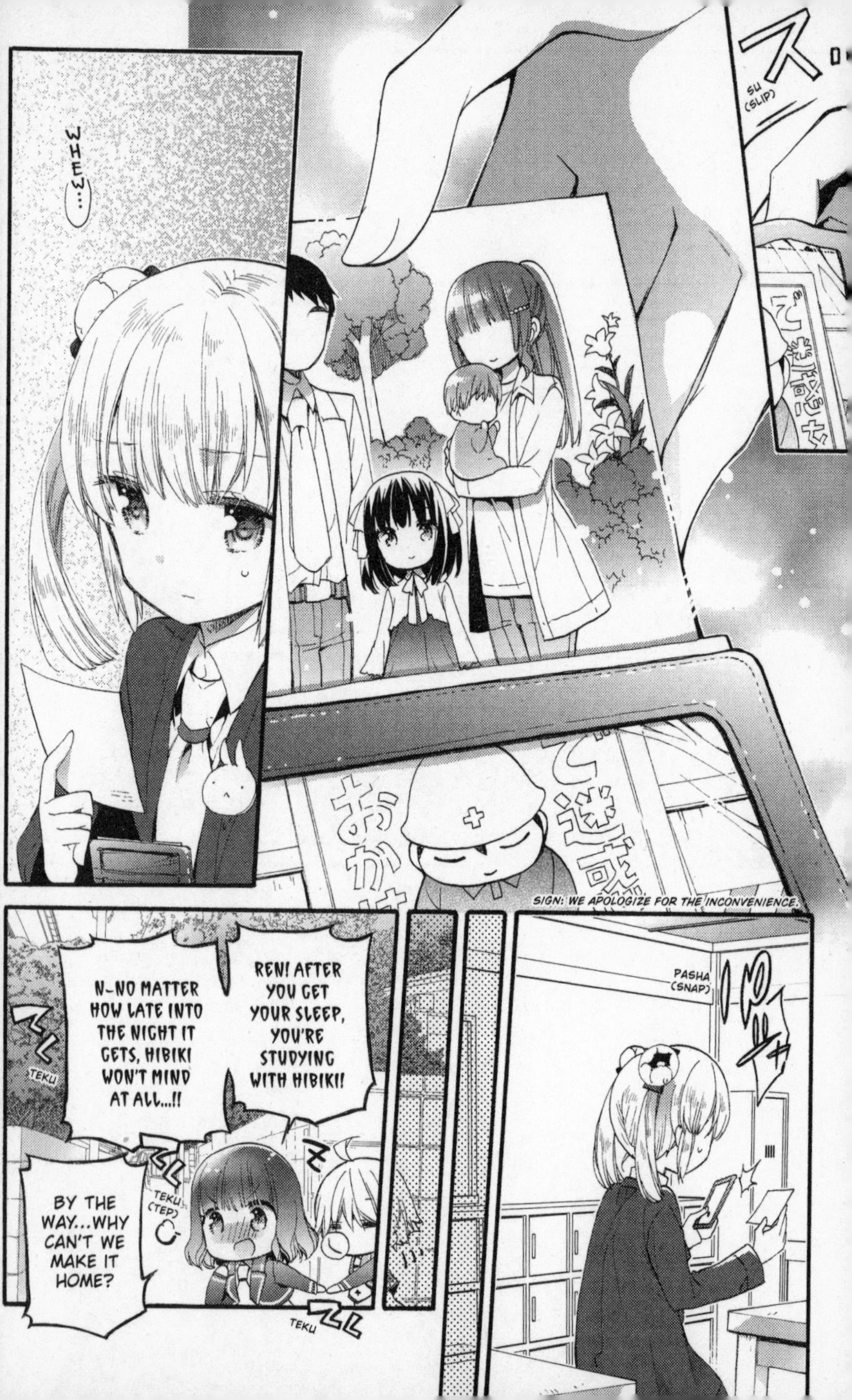

SU (SLIP)
SIGN: WE APOLOGIZE FOR THE INCONVENIENCE.
WHEW...
PASHA (SNAP)
REN! AFTER YOU GET YOUR SLEEP, YOU'RE STUDYING WITH HIBIKI!
N-NO MATTER HOW LATE INTO THE NIGHT IT GETS, HIBIKI WON'T MIND AT ALL...!!
TEKU
TEKU (TEP)
BY THE WAY...WHY CAN'T WE MAKE IT HOME?
TEKU

AnneHappy♪

unhappy go lucky!

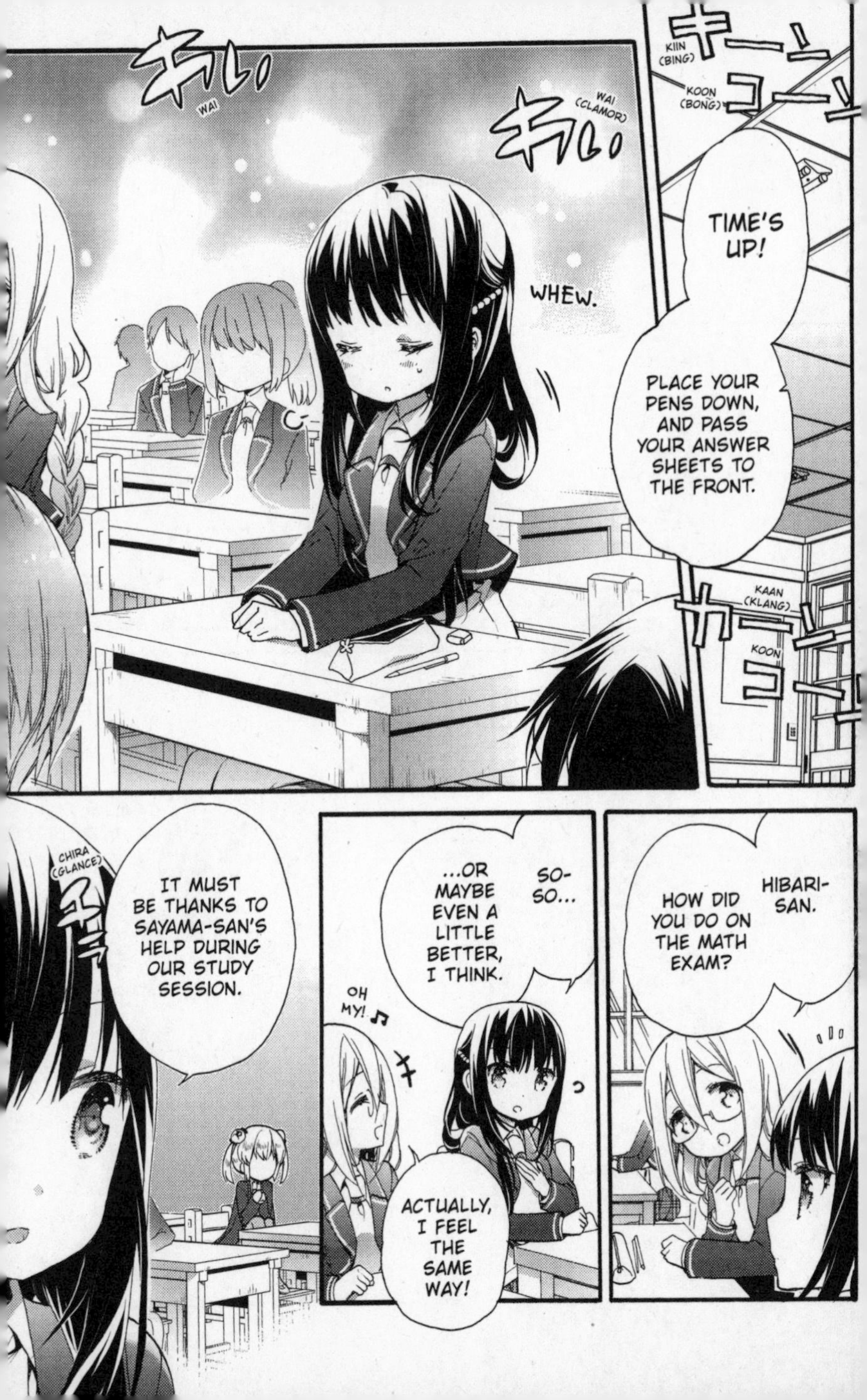
KIIN (BING)
KOON (BONG)
TIME'S UP!
PLACE YOUR PENS DOWN, AND PASS YOUR ANSWER SHEETS TO THE FRONT.
KAAN (KLANG)
KOON
WAI (CLAMOR)
WAI
WHEW.
HIBARI-SAN.
HOW DID YOU DO ON THE MATH EXAM?
SO-SO...
...OR MAYBE EVEN A LITTLE BETTER, I THINK.
OH MY!
ACTUALLY, I FEEL THE SAME WAY!
CHIRA (GLANCE)
IT MUST BE THANKS TO SAYAMA-SAN'S HELP DURING OUR STUDY SESSION.

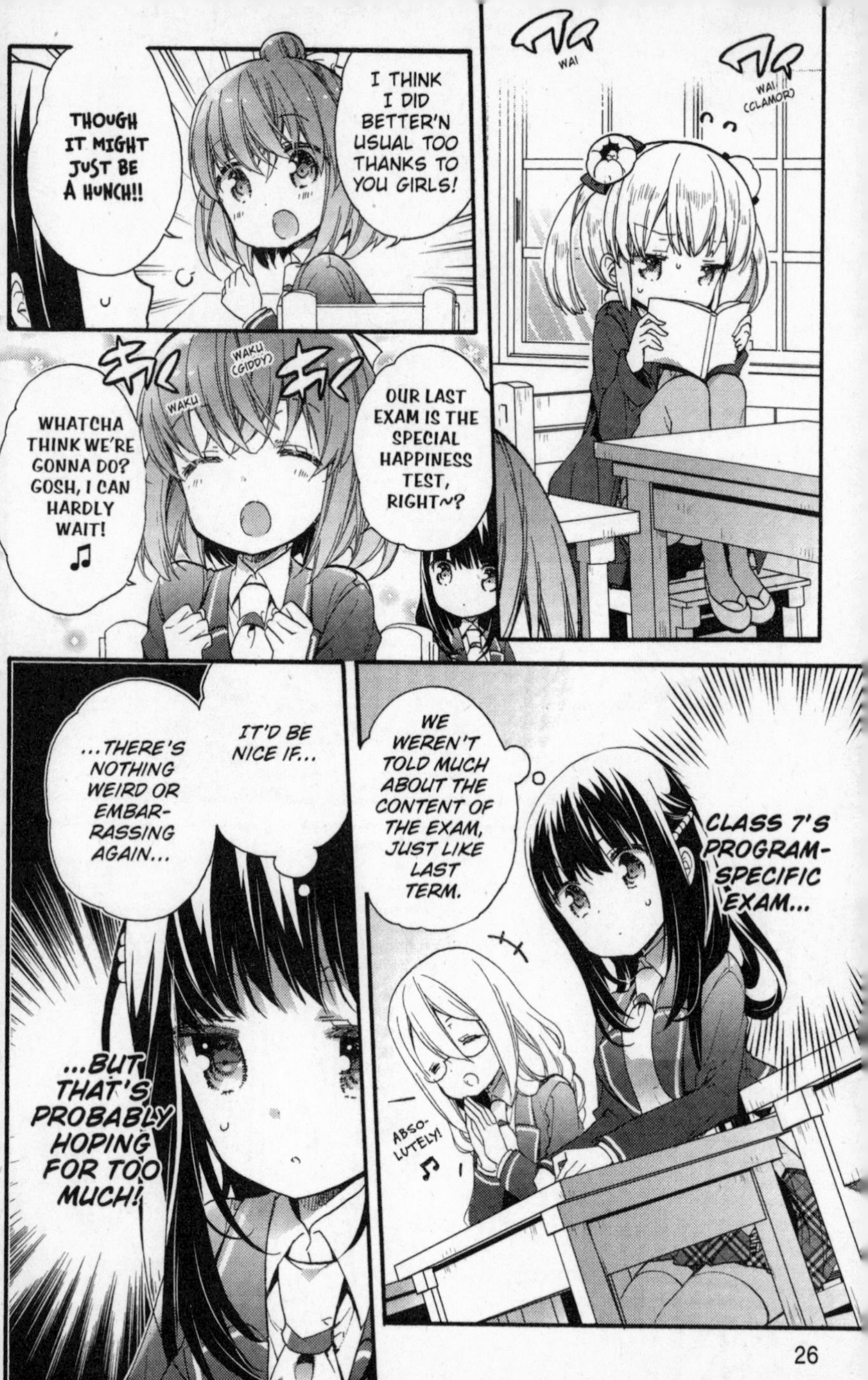
WAI
WAI (CLAMOR)
I THINK I DID BETTER'N USUAL TOO THANKS TO YOU GIRLS!
THOUGH IT MIGHT JUST BE A HUNCH!!
WAKU
WAKU (GIDDY)
OUR LAST EXAM IS THE SPECIAL HAPPINESS TEST, RIGHT~?
WHATCHA THINK WE'RE GONNA DO? GOSH, I CAN HARDLY WAIT! ♫
CLASS 7'S PROGRAM-SPECIFIC EXAM...
WE WEREN'T TOLD MUCH ABOUT THE CONTENT OF THE EXAM, JUST LIKE LAST TERM.
ABSOLUTELY! ♫
IT'D BE NICE IF...
...THERE'S NOTHING WEIRD OR EMBARRASSING AGAIN...
...BUT THAT'S PROBABLY HOPING FOR TOO MUCH!

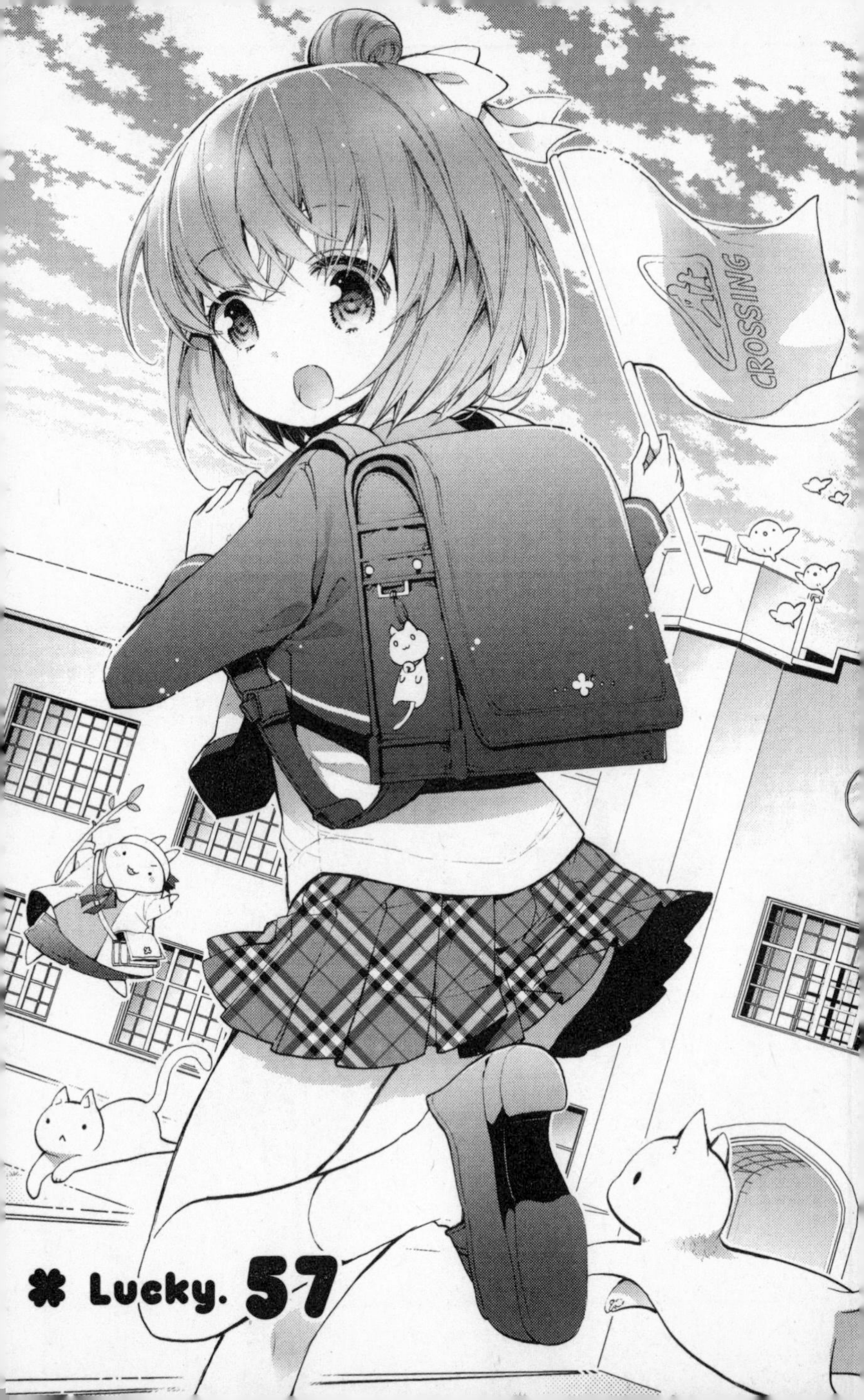
CROSSING
✤ Lucky. 57

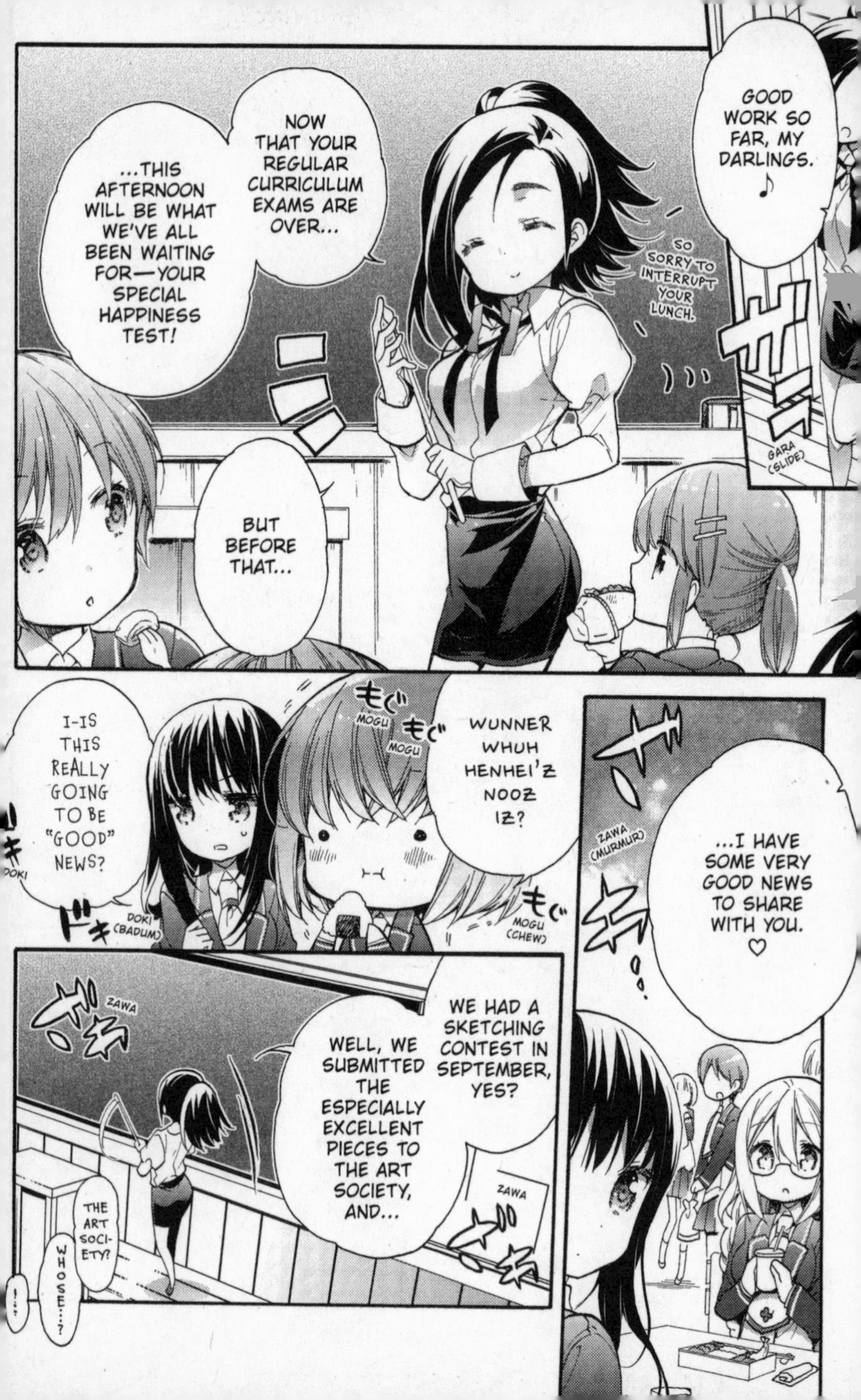

GOOD WORK SO FAR, MY DARLINGS. ♪
GARA (SLIDE)
SO SORRY TO INTERRUPT YOUR LUNCH.
NOW THAT YOUR REGULAR CURRICULUM EXAMS ARE OVER...
...THIS AFTERNOON WILL BE WHAT WE'VE ALL BEEN WAITING FOR—YOUR SPECIAL HAPPINESS TEST!
BUT BEFORE THAT...
ZAWA (MURMUR)
...I HAVE SOME VERY GOOD NEWS TO SHARE WITH YOU. ♡
MOGU
MOGU
WUNNER WHUH HENHEI'Z NOOZ IZ?
MOGU (CHEW)
I-IS THIS REALLY GOING TO BE "GOOD" NEWS?
DOKI (BADUM)
WE HAD A SKETCHING CONTEST IN SEPTEMBER, YES?
WELL, WE SUBMITTED THE ESPECIALLY EXCELLENT PIECES TO THE ART SOCIETY, AND...
ZAWA
ZAWA
THE ART SOCI-ETY?
WHOSE...?
!...?

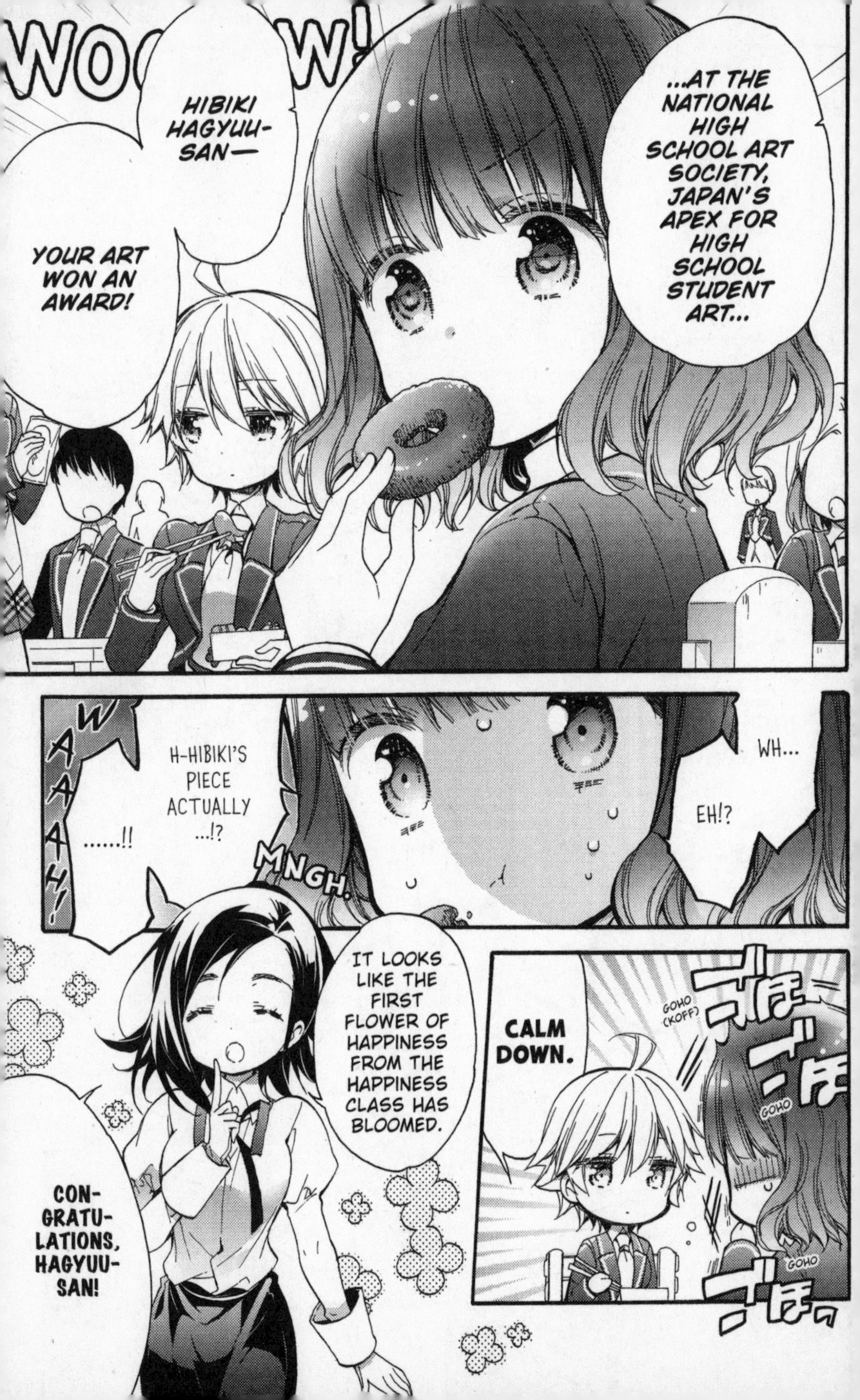
...AT THE NATIONAL HIGH SCHOOL ART SOCIETY, JAPAN'S APEX FOR HIGH SCHOOL STUDENT ART...
HIBIKI HAGYUU-SAN—
YOUR ART WON AN AWARD!
WH...
EH!?
MNGH.
H-HIBIKI'S PIECE ACTUALLY ...!?
......!!
WAAAAH!
GOHO (KOFF)
GOHO
GOHO
CALM DOWN.
IT LOOKS LIKE THE FIRST FLOWER OF HAPPINESS FROM THE HAPPINESS CLASS HAS BLOOMED.
CONGRATULATIONS, HAGYUU-SAN!

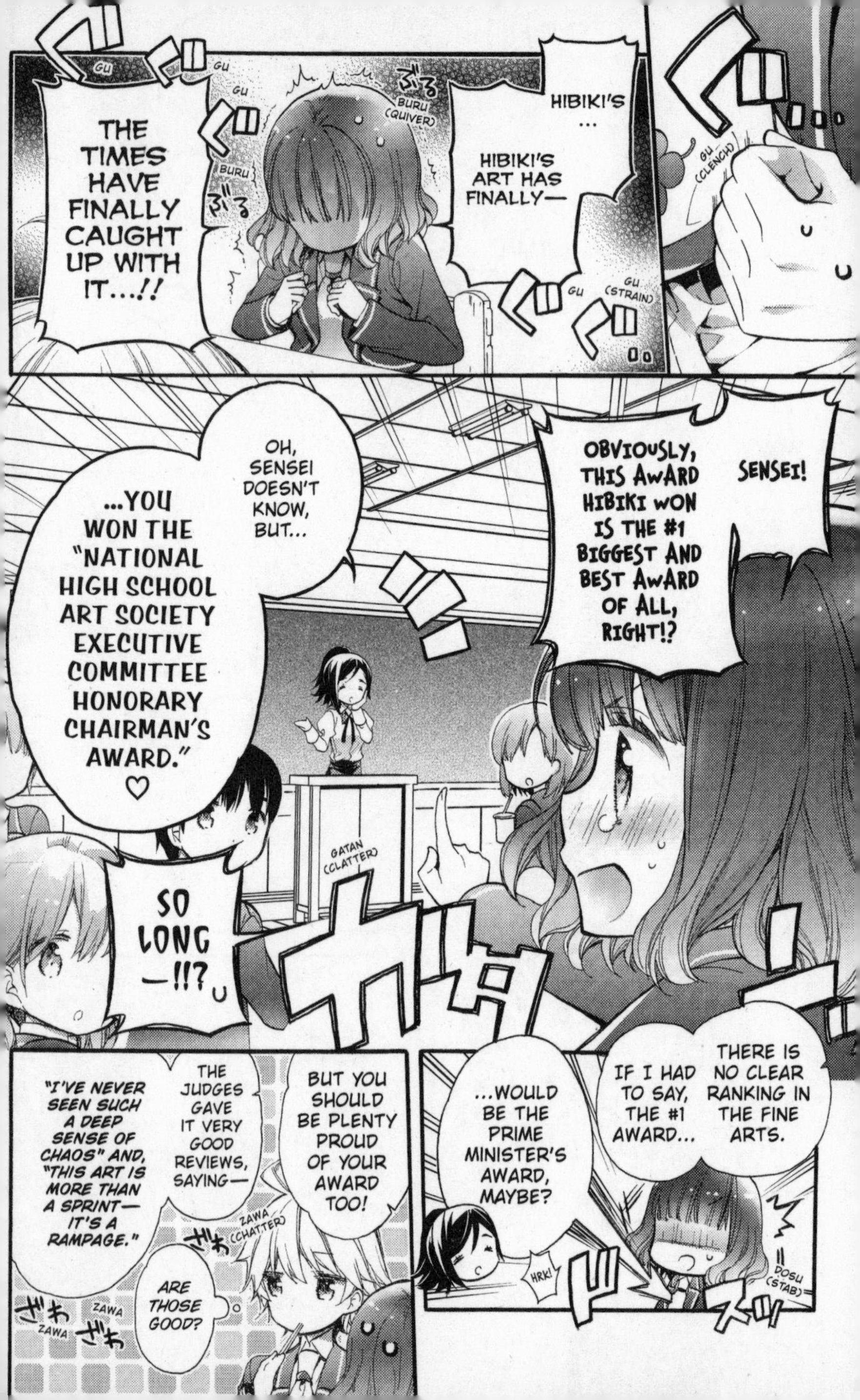
GU (CLENCH)
HIBIKI'S ...
HIBIKI'S ART HAS FINALLY—
BURU (QUIVER)
GU (STRAIN)
GU
GU
GU
THE TIMES HAVE FINALLY CAUGHT UP WITH IT...!!
BURU
SENSEI!
OBVIOUSLY, THIS AWARD HIBIKI WON IS THE #1 BIGGEST AND BEST AWARD OF ALL, RIGHT!?
OH, SENSEI DOESN'T KNOW, BUT...
...YOU WON THE "NATIONAL HIGH SCHOOL ART SOCIETY EXECUTIVE COMMITTEE HONORARY CHAIRMAN'S AWARD." ♡
GATAN (CLATTER)
SO LONG—!!?
THERE IS NO CLEAR RANKING IN THE FINE ARTS.
IF I HAD TO SAY, THE #1 AWARD...
...WOULD BE THE PRIME MINISTER'S AWARD, MAYBE?
DOSU (STAB)
HRK!
BUT YOU SHOULD BE PLENTY PROUD OF YOUR AWARD TOO!
THE JUDGES GAVE IT VERY GOOD REVIEWS, SAYING—
"I'VE NEVER SEEN SUCH A DEEP SENSE OF CHAOS" AND, "THIS ART IS MORE THAN A SPRINT—IT'S A RAMPAGE."
ZAWA (CHATTER)
ARE THOSE GOOD?
ZAWA
ZAWA

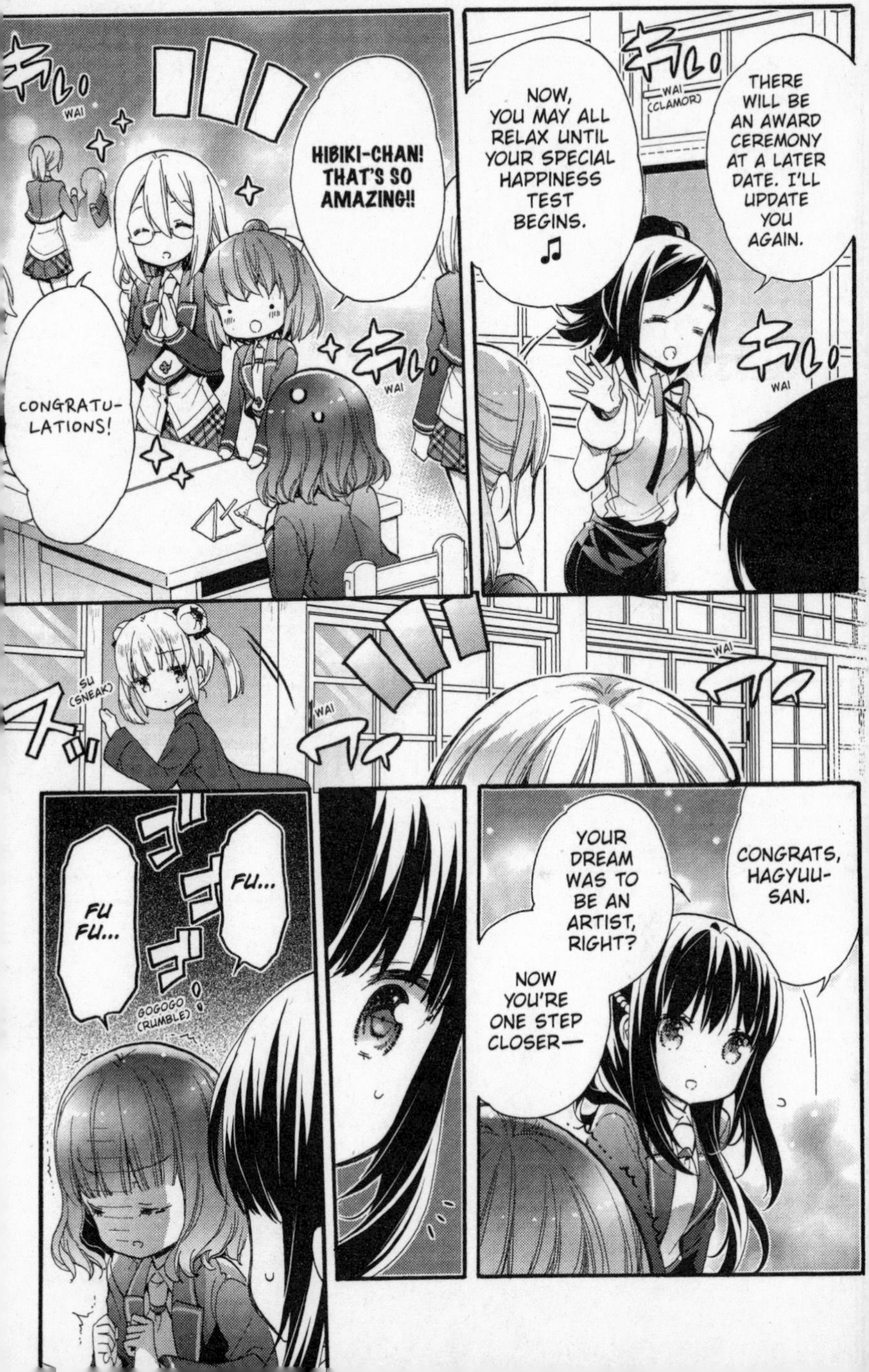
WAI (CLAMOR)
THERE WILL BE AN AWARD CEREMONY AT A LATER DATE. I'LL UPDATE YOU AGAIN.
NOW, YOU MAY ALL RELAX UNTIL YOUR SPECIAL HAPPINESS TEST BEGINS. ♫
WAI
WAI
HIBIKI-CHAN! THAT'S SO AMAZING!!
WAI
CONGRATU-LATIONS!
WAI
SU (SNEAK)
WAI
CONGRATS, HAGYUU-SAN.
YOUR DREAM WAS TO BE AN ARTIST, RIGHT?
NOW YOU'RE ONE STEP CLOSER—
FU...
FU FU...
GOGOGO (RUMBLE)

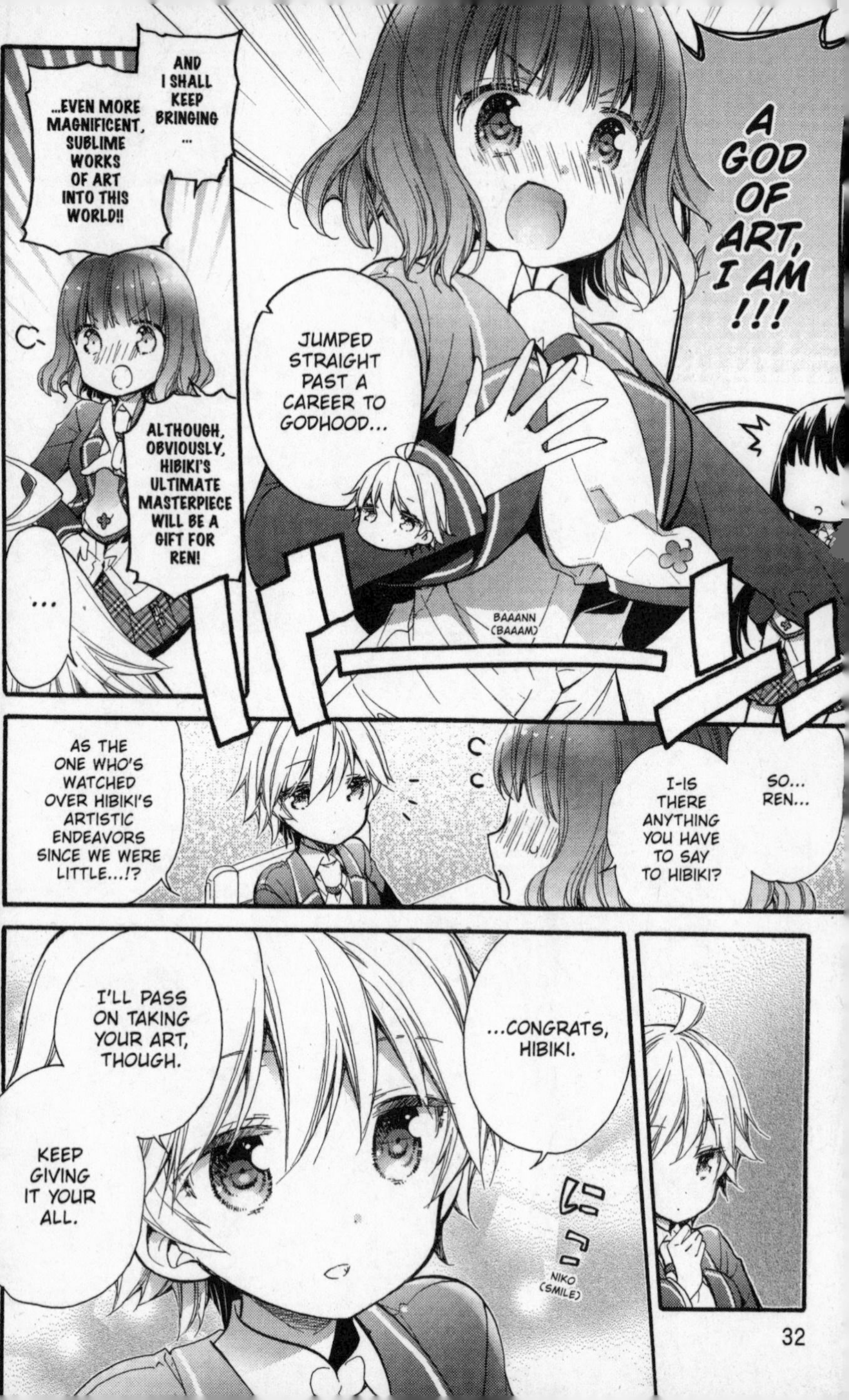
A GOD OF ART, I AM!!!
JUMPED STRAIGHT PAST A CAREER TO GODHOOD...
AND I SHALL KEEP BRINGING...
...EVEN MORE MAGNIFICENT, SUBLIME WORKS OF ART INTO THIS WORLD!!
ALTHOUGH, OBVIOUSLY, HIBIKI'S ULTIMATE MASTERPIECE WILL BE A GIFT FOR REN!
...
BAAANN (BAAAM)
SO... REN...
I-IS THERE ANYTHING YOU HAVE TO SAY TO HIBIKI?
AS THE ONE WHO'S WATCHED OVER HIBIKI'S ARTISTIC ENDEAVORS SINCE WE WERE LITTLE...!?
...CONGRATS, HIBIKI.
NIKO (SMILE)
I'LL PASS ON TAKING YOUR ART, THOUGH.
KEEP GIVING IT YOUR ALL.

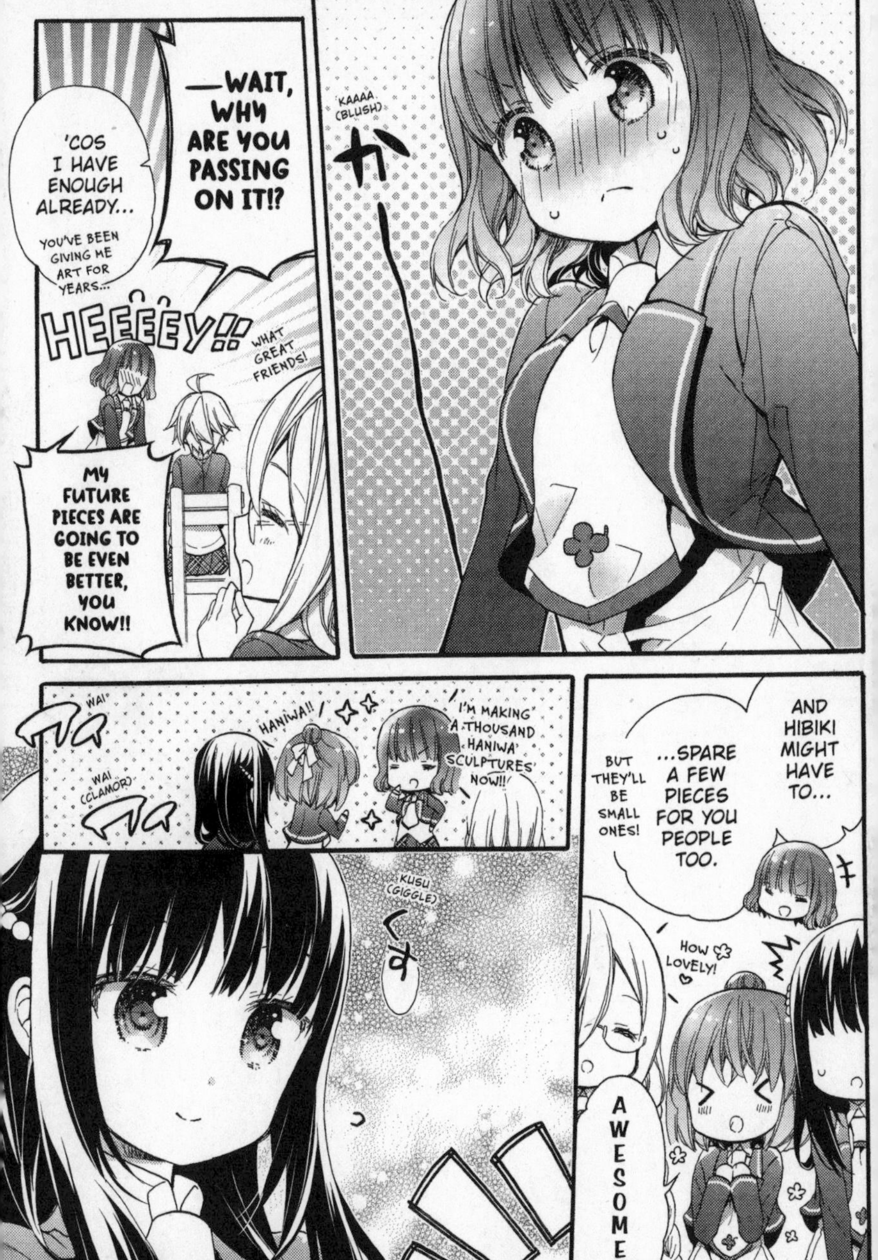
KAAAA (BLUSH)
か
—WAIT, WHY ARE YOU PASSING ON IT!?
'COS I HAVE ENOUGH ALREADY...
YOU'VE BEEN GIVING ME ART FOR YEARS...
HEEEEEY!!
WHAT GREAT FRIENDS!
MY FUTURE PIECES ARE GOING TO BE EVEN BETTER, YOU KNOW!!
AND HIBIKI MIGHT HAVE TO...
...SPARE A FEW PIECES FOR YOU PEOPLE TOO.
BUT THEY'LL BE SMALL ONES!
HOW LOVELY!
AWESOME!
I'M MAKING A THOUSAND HANIWA SCULPTURES NOW!!
HANIWA!!
WAI
WAI (CLAMOR)
KUSU (GIGGLE)
くす

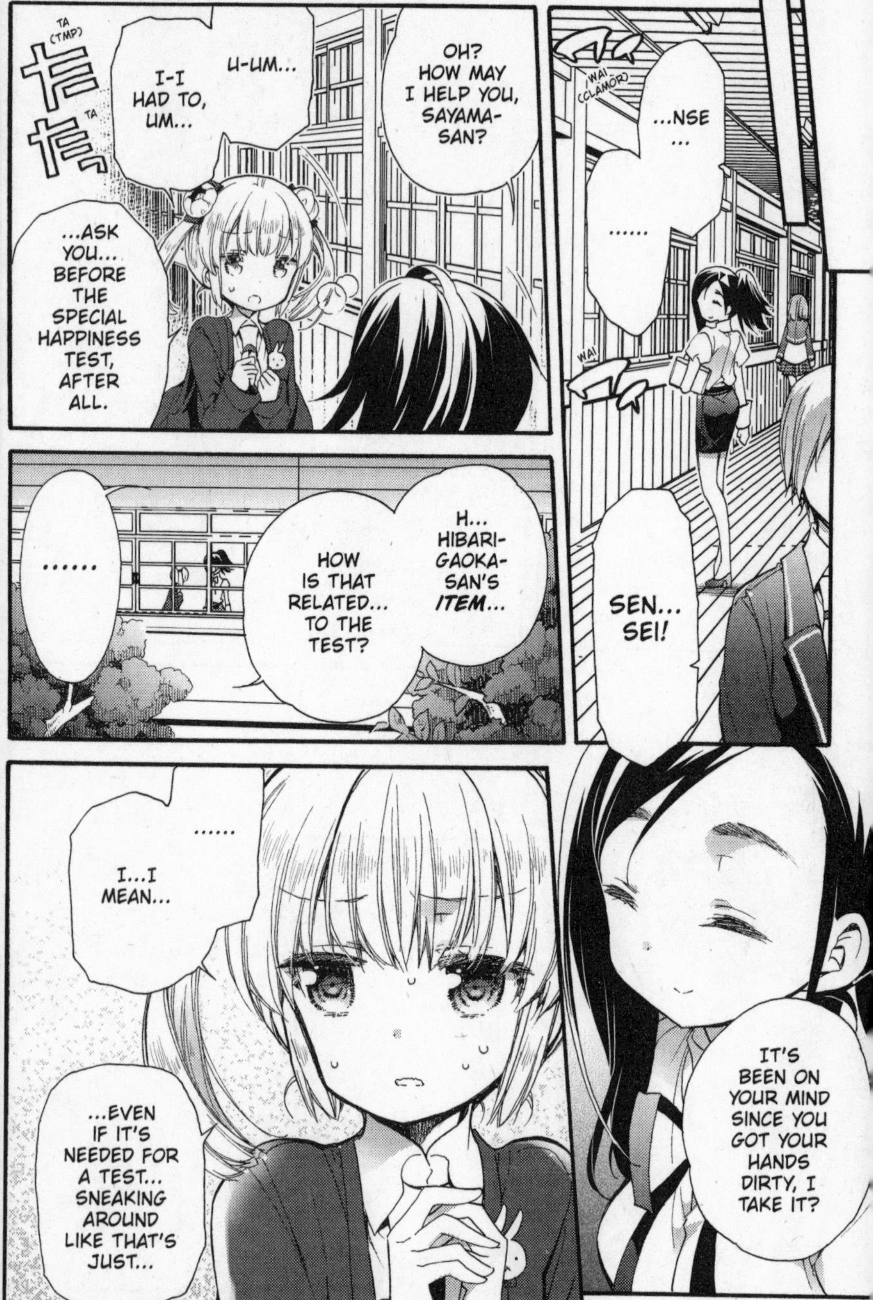

...NSE ...
WAI (CLAMOR)
......
WAI
SEN... SEI!
OH? HOW MAY I HELP YOU, SAYAMA-SAN?
U-UM...
I-I HAD TO, UM...
TA (TMP) TA
...ASK YOU... BEFORE THE SPECIAL HAPPINESS TEST, AFTER ALL.
H... HIBARI-GAOKA-SAN'S *ITEM*...
HOW IS THAT RELATED... TO THE TEST?
......
IT'S BEEN ON YOUR MIND SINCE YOU GOT YOUR HANDS DIRTY, I TAKE IT?
......
I...I MEAN...
...EVEN IF IT'S NEEDED FOR A TEST... SNEAKING AROUND LIKE THAT'S JUST...

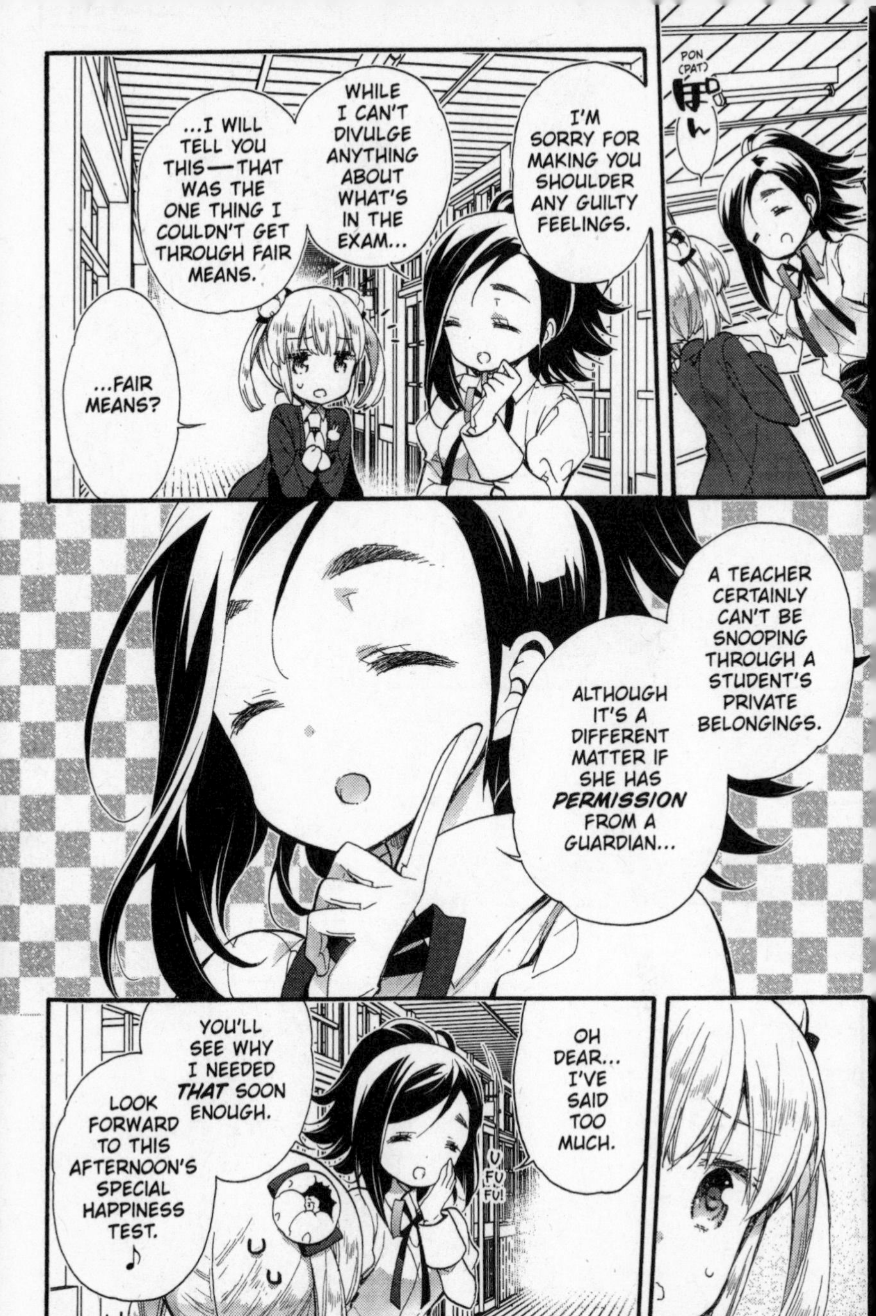
PON (PAT)
I'M SORRY FOR MAKING YOU SHOULDER ANY GUILTY FEELINGS.
WHILE I CAN'T DIVULGE ANYTHING ABOUT WHAT'S IN THE EXAM...
...I WILL TELL YOU THIS—THAT WAS THE ONE THING I COULDN'T GET THROUGH FAIR MEANS.
...FAIR MEANS?
A TEACHER CERTAINLY CAN'T BE SNOOPING THROUGH A STUDENT'S PRIVATE BELONGINGS.
ALTHOUGH IT'S A DIFFERENT MATTER IF SHE HAS *PERMISSION* FROM A GUARDIAN...
OH DEAR... I'VE SAID TOO MUCH.
UFUFU!
YOU'LL SEE WHY I NEEDED *THAT* SOON ENOUGH.
LOOK FORWARD TO THIS AFTERNOON'S SPECIAL HAPPINESS TEST. ♪

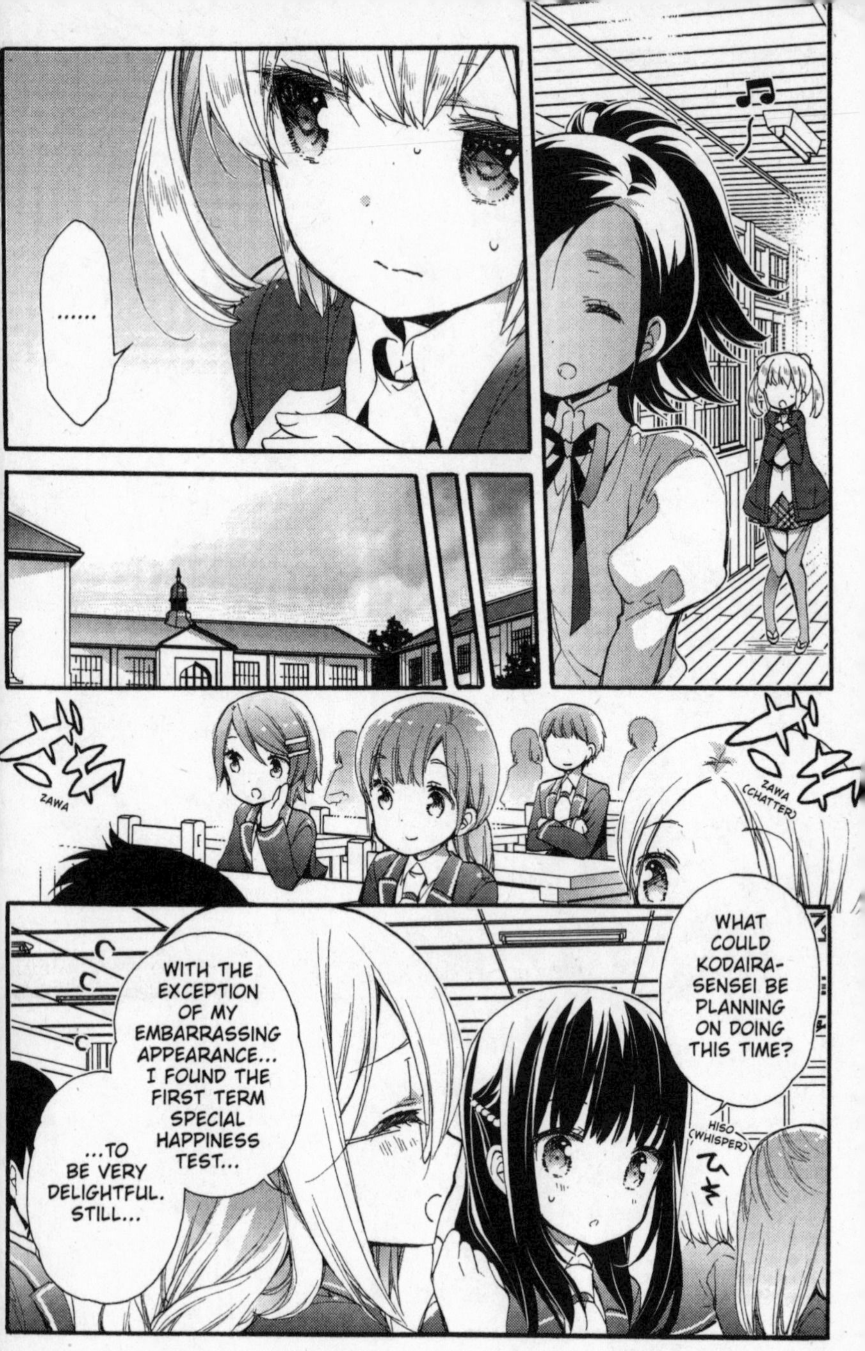
......
ZAWA (CHATTER)
ZAWA
WHAT COULD KODAIRA-SENSEI BE PLANNING ON DOING THIS TIME?
HISO (WHISPER)
WITH THE EXCEPTION OF MY EMBARRASSING APPEARANCE... I FOUND THE FIRST TERM SPECIAL HAPPINESS TEST...
...TO BE VERY DELIGHTFUL. STILL...

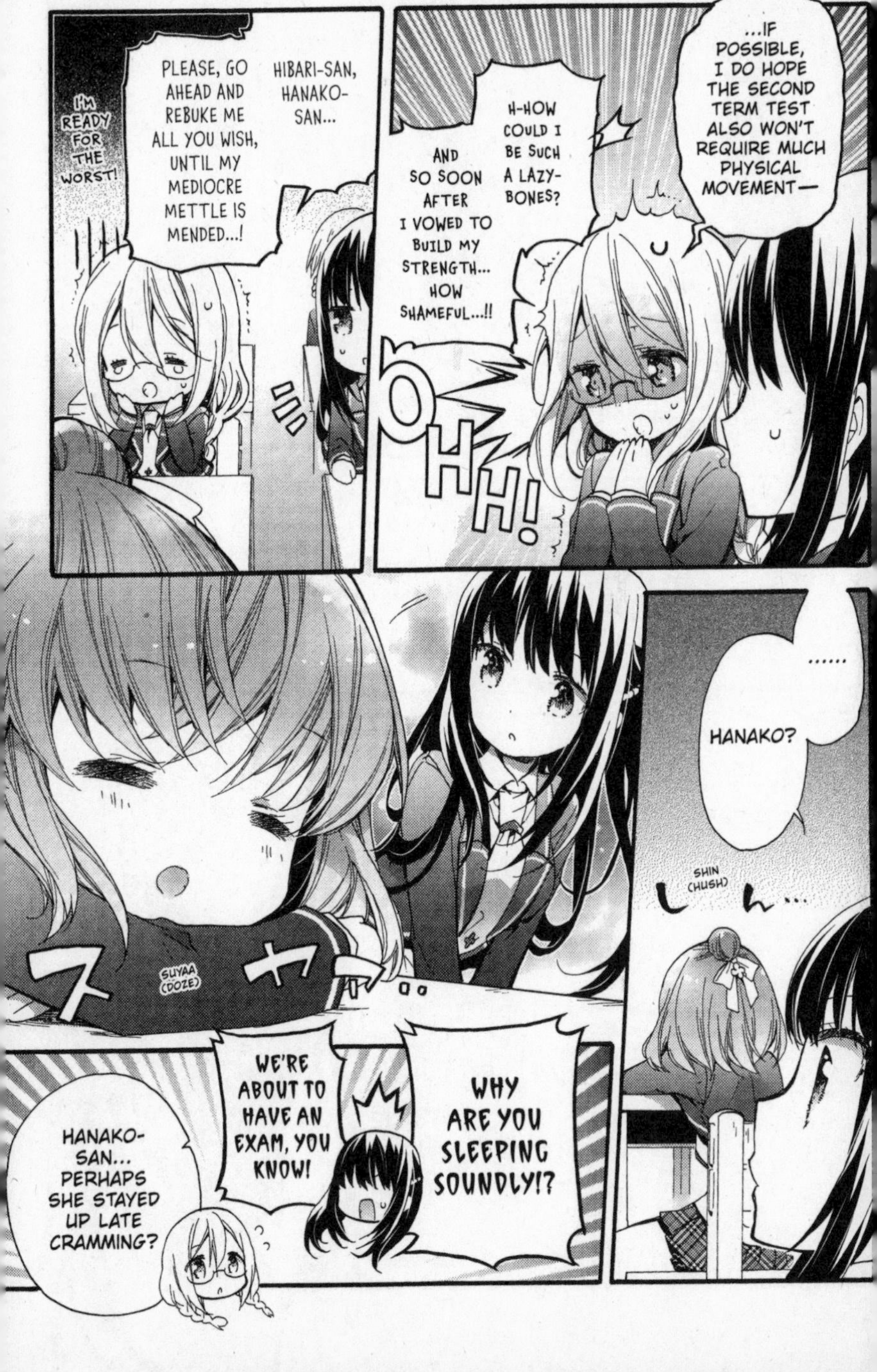
...IF POSSIBLE, I DO HOPE THE SECOND TERM TEST ALSO WON'T REQUIRE MUCH PHYSICAL MOVEMENT—
H-HOW COULD I BE SUCH A LAZY-BONES?
AND SO SOON AFTER I VOWED TO BUILD MY STRENGTH... HOW SHAMEFUL...!!
OHHH!
HIBARI-SAN, HANAKO-SAN...
PLEASE, GO AHEAD AND REBUKE ME ALL YOU WISH, UNTIL MY MEDIOCRE METTLE IS MENDED...!
I'M READY FOR THE WORST!
......
HANAKO?
SHIN (HUSH)
SUYAA (DOZE)
WHY ARE YOU SLEEPING SOUNDLY!?
WE'RE ABOUT TO HAVE AN EXAM, YOU KNOW!
HANAKO-SAN... PERHAPS SHE STAYED UP LATE CRAMMING?

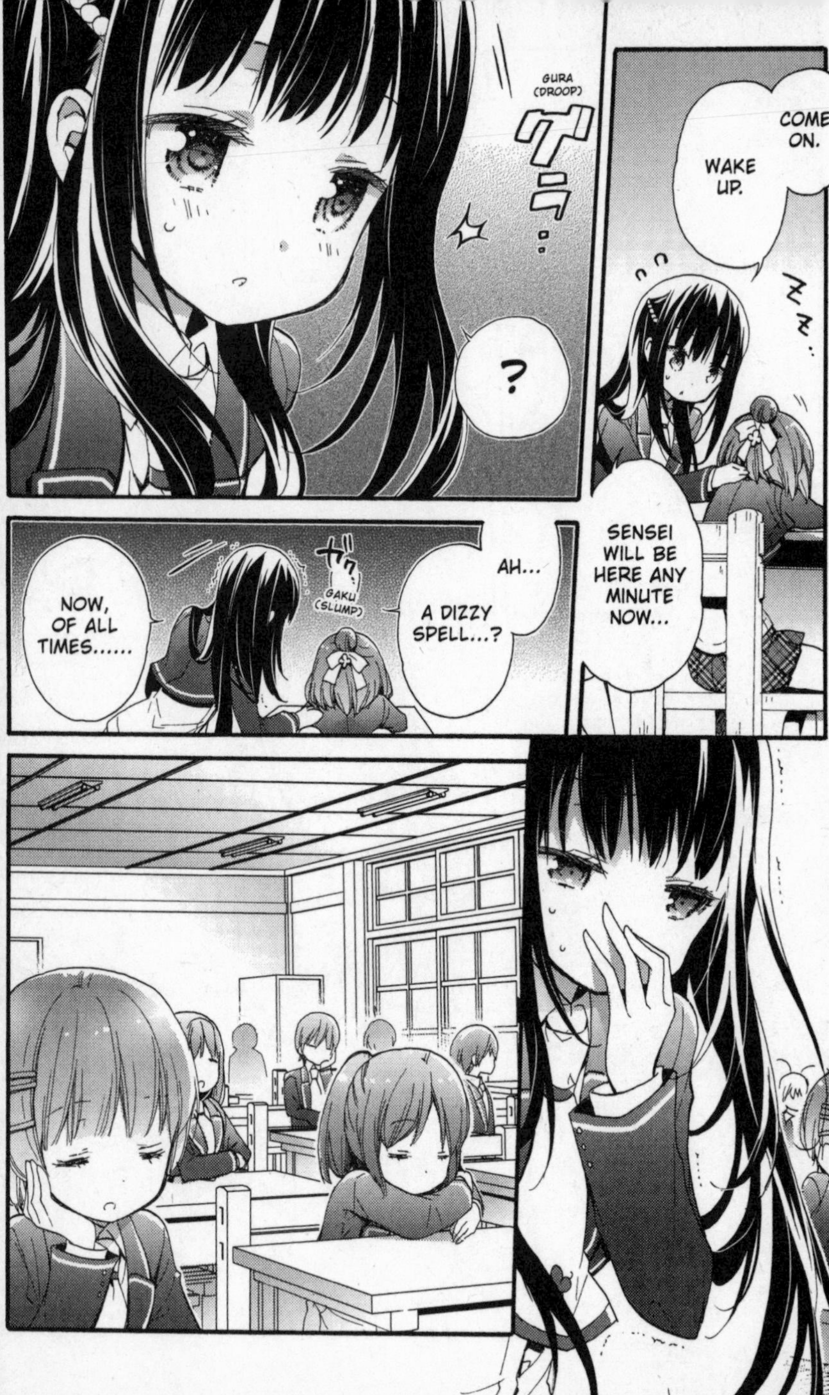
COME ON.
WAKE UP.
Z Z ..
GURA (DROOP)
?
SENSEI WILL BE HERE ANY MINUTE NOW...
AH... A DIZZY SPELL...?
GAKU (SLUMP)
NOW, OF ALL TIMES......

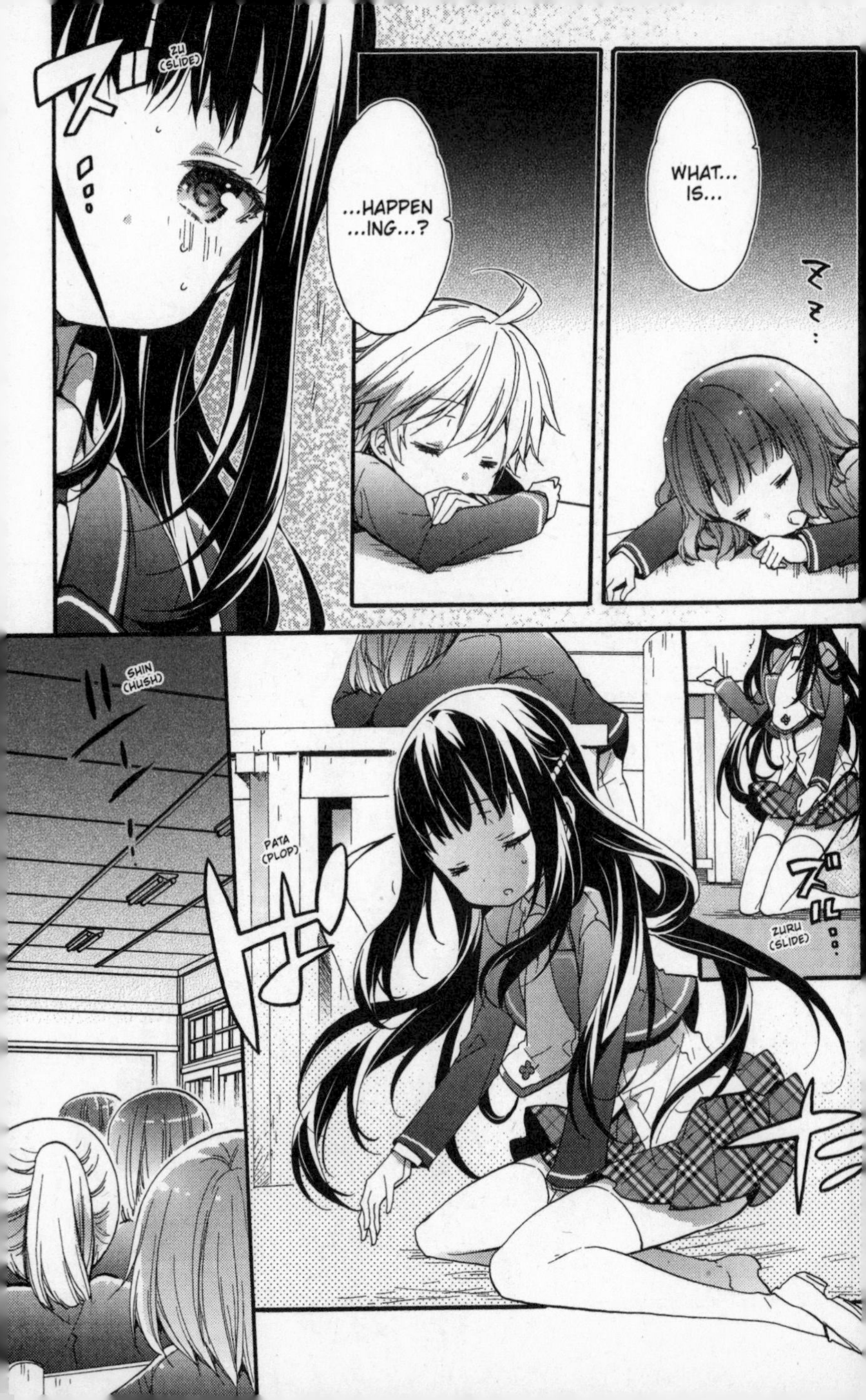
WHAT... IS...
...HAPPEN ...ING...?
ZU (SLIDE)
ZURU (SLIDE)
PATA (PLOP)
SHIN (HUSH)

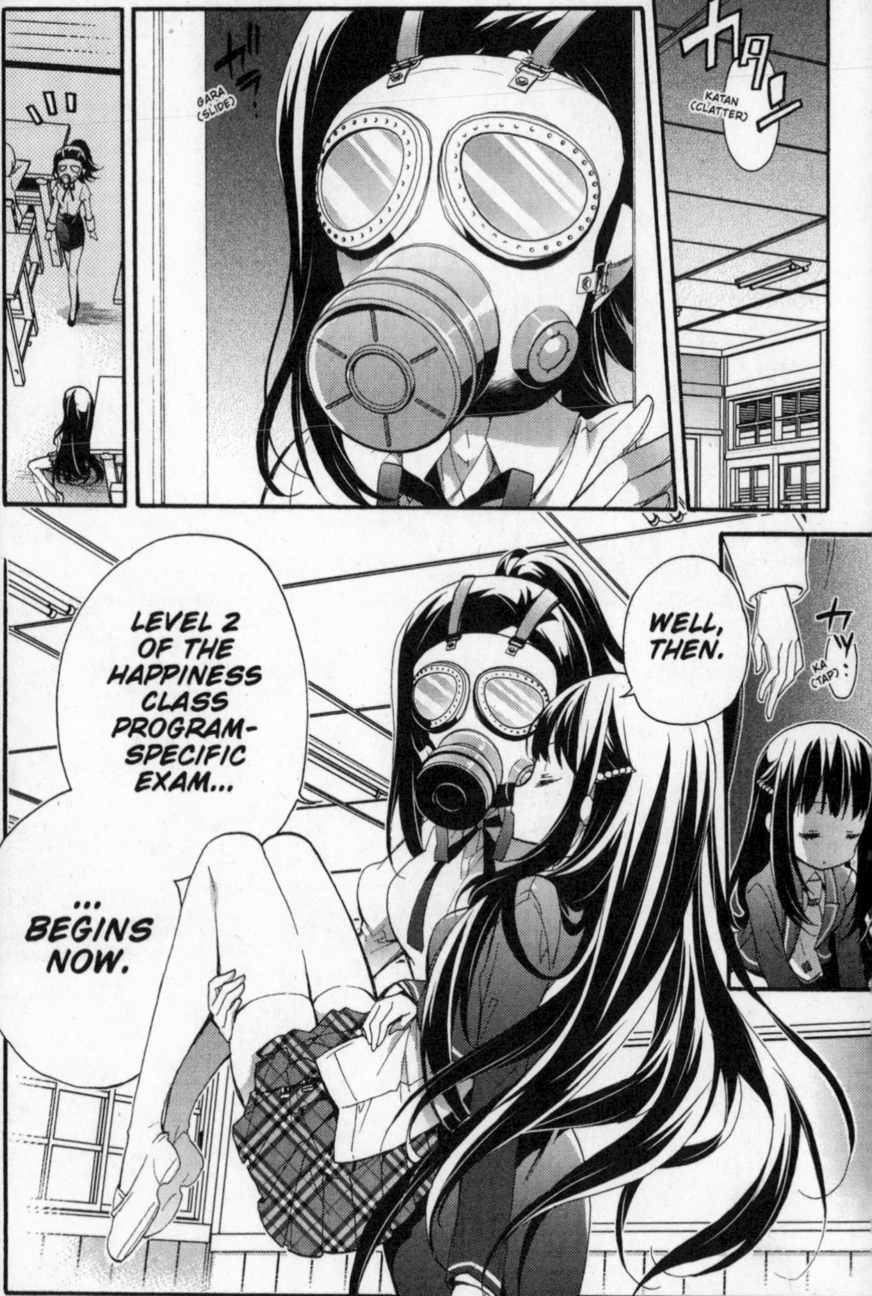
カタン
KATAN (CLATTER)
ガラ
GARA (SLIDE)
カッ
KA (TAP)
WELL, THEN.
LEVEL 2 OF THE HAPPINESS CLASS PROGRAM-SPECIFIC EXAM...
... BEGINS NOW.

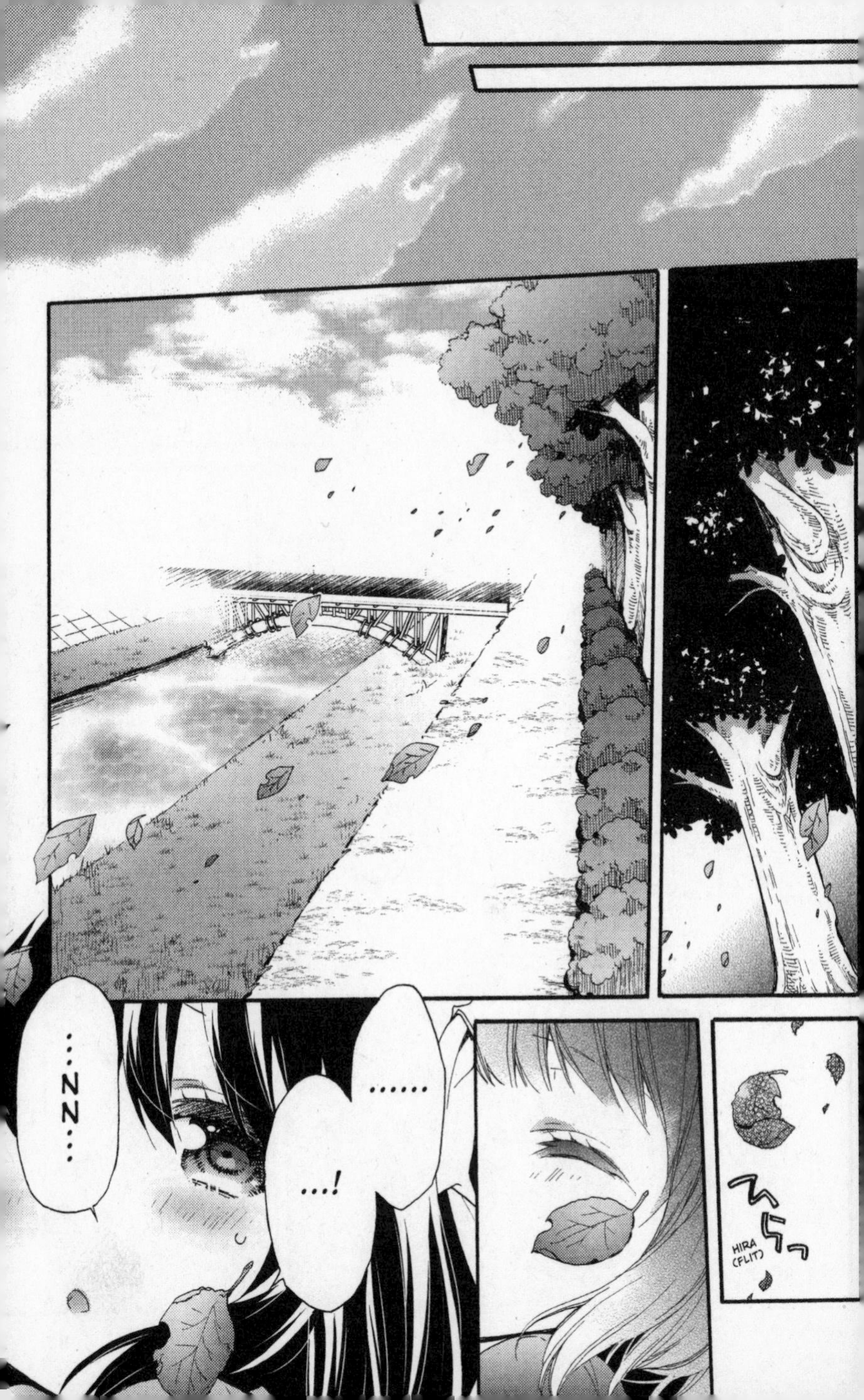
HIRA
(FLIT)
......
...!
...NN...

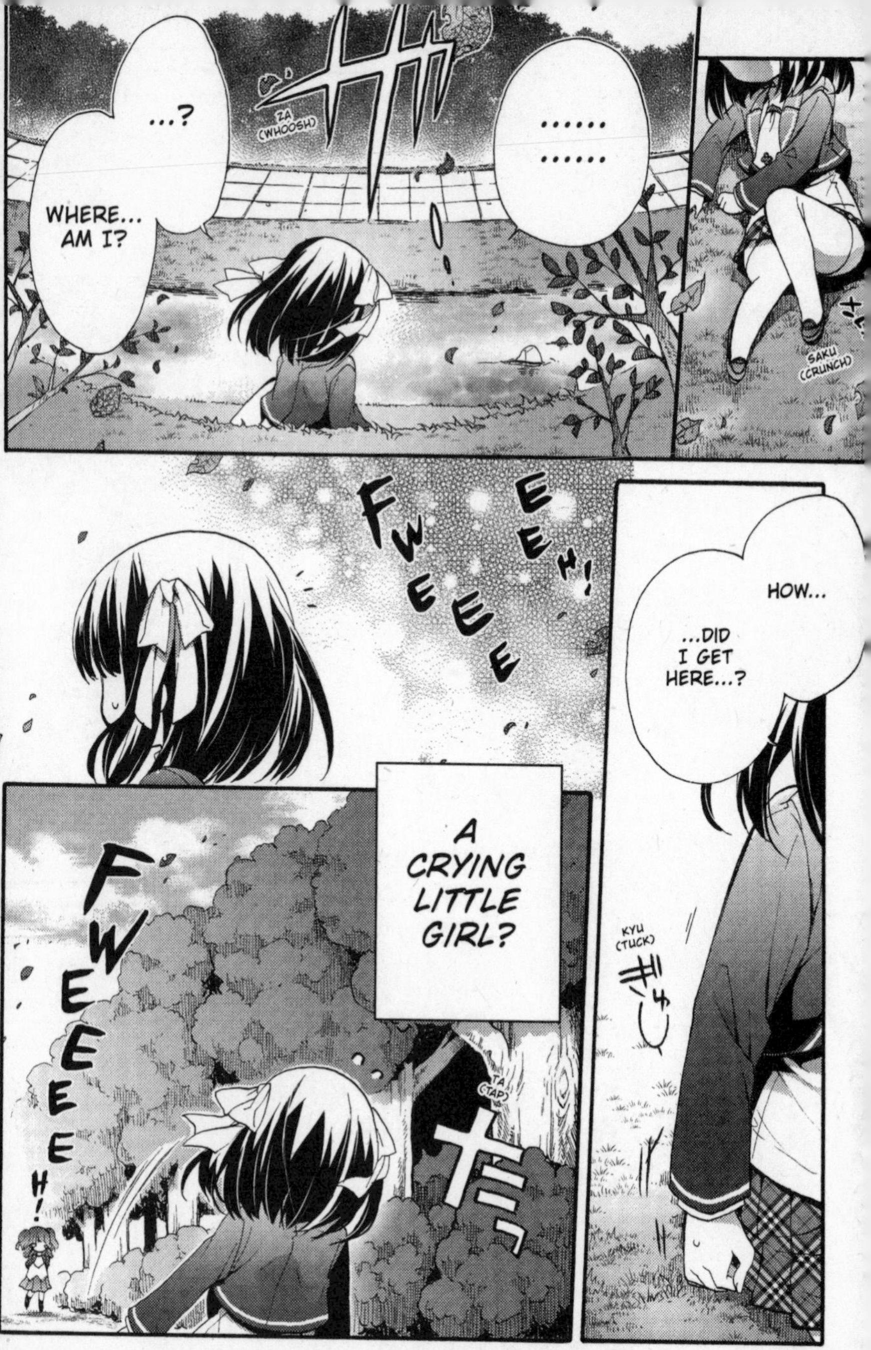
SAKU (CRUNCH)
......
......
ZA (WHOOSH)
...?
WHERE... AM I?
HOW...
...DID I GET HERE...?
KYU (TUCK)
FWEEEEEH!
A CRYING LITTLE GIRL?
TA (TAP)
FWEEEEEH!

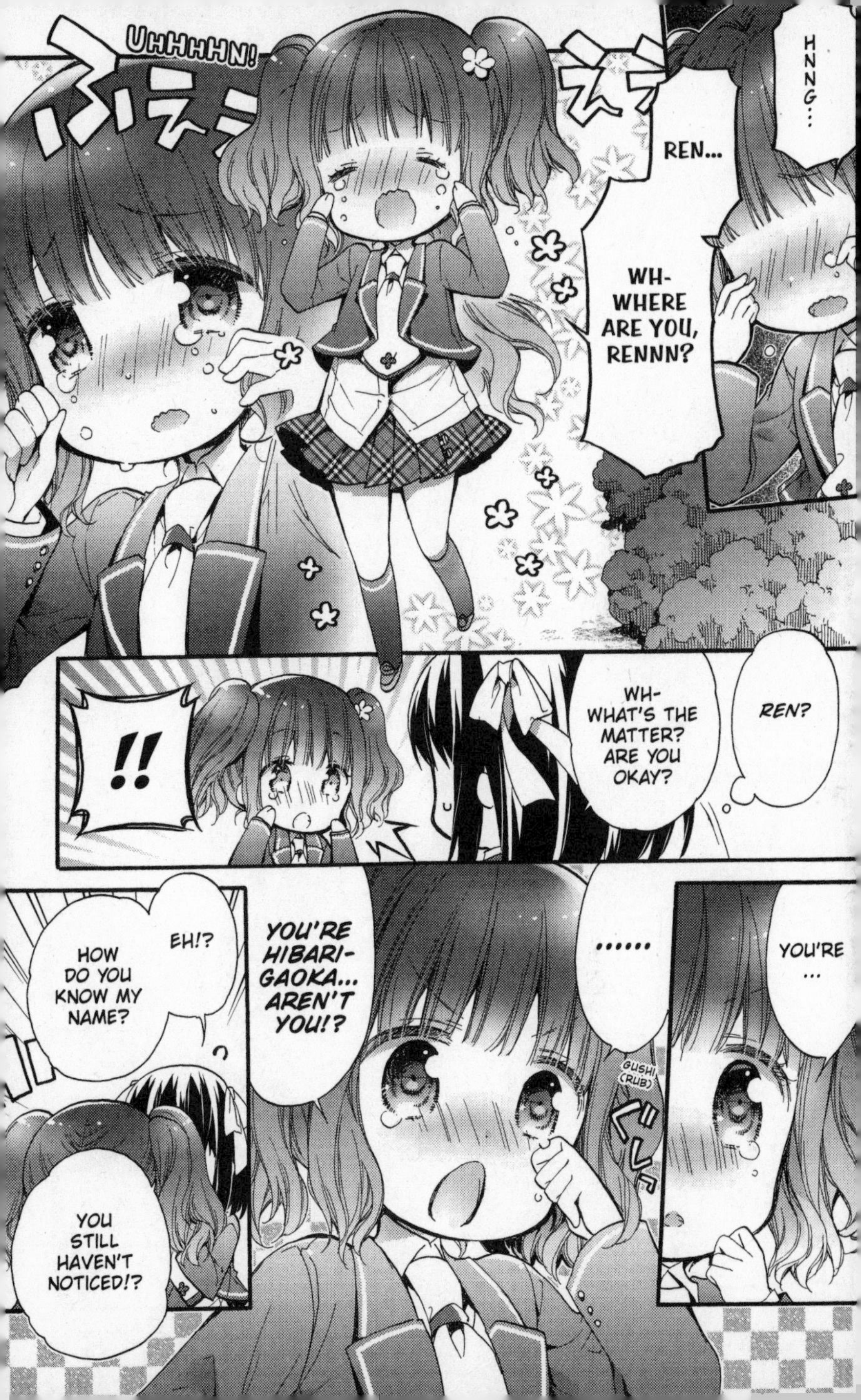
HNNG...
UHHHHN!
REN...
WH- WHERE ARE YOU, RENNN?
REN?
WH- WHAT'S THE MATTER? ARE YOU OKAY?
!!
YOU'RE ...
......
GUSHI (RUB)
YOU'RE HIBARI-GAOKA... AREN'T YOU!?
EH!?
HOW DO YOU KNOW MY NAME?
YOU STILL HAVEN'T NOTICED!?

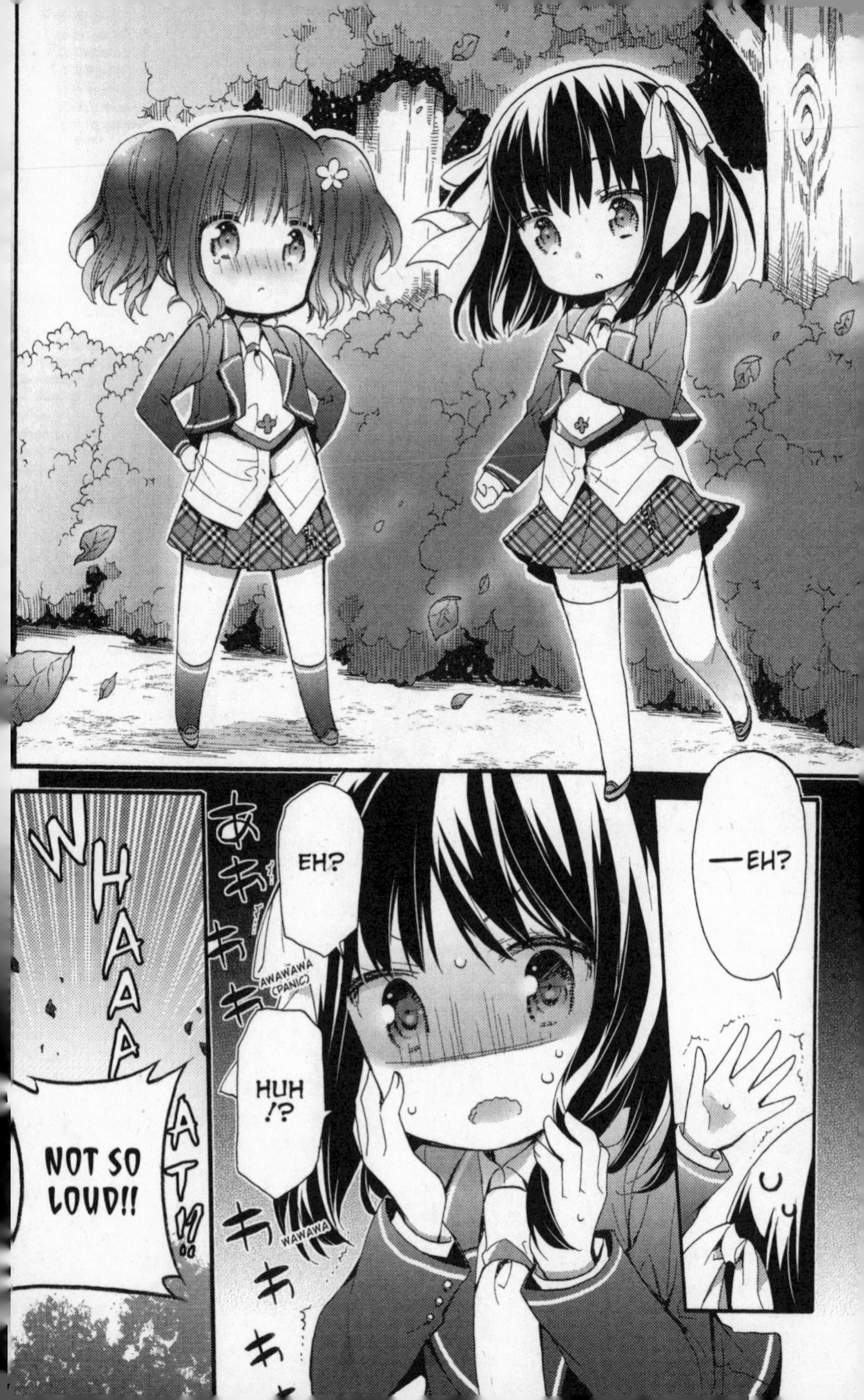
—EH?
EH?
AWAWAWA (PANIC)
HUH!?
WAWAWA
WHAAAAT!!
NOT SO LOUD!!

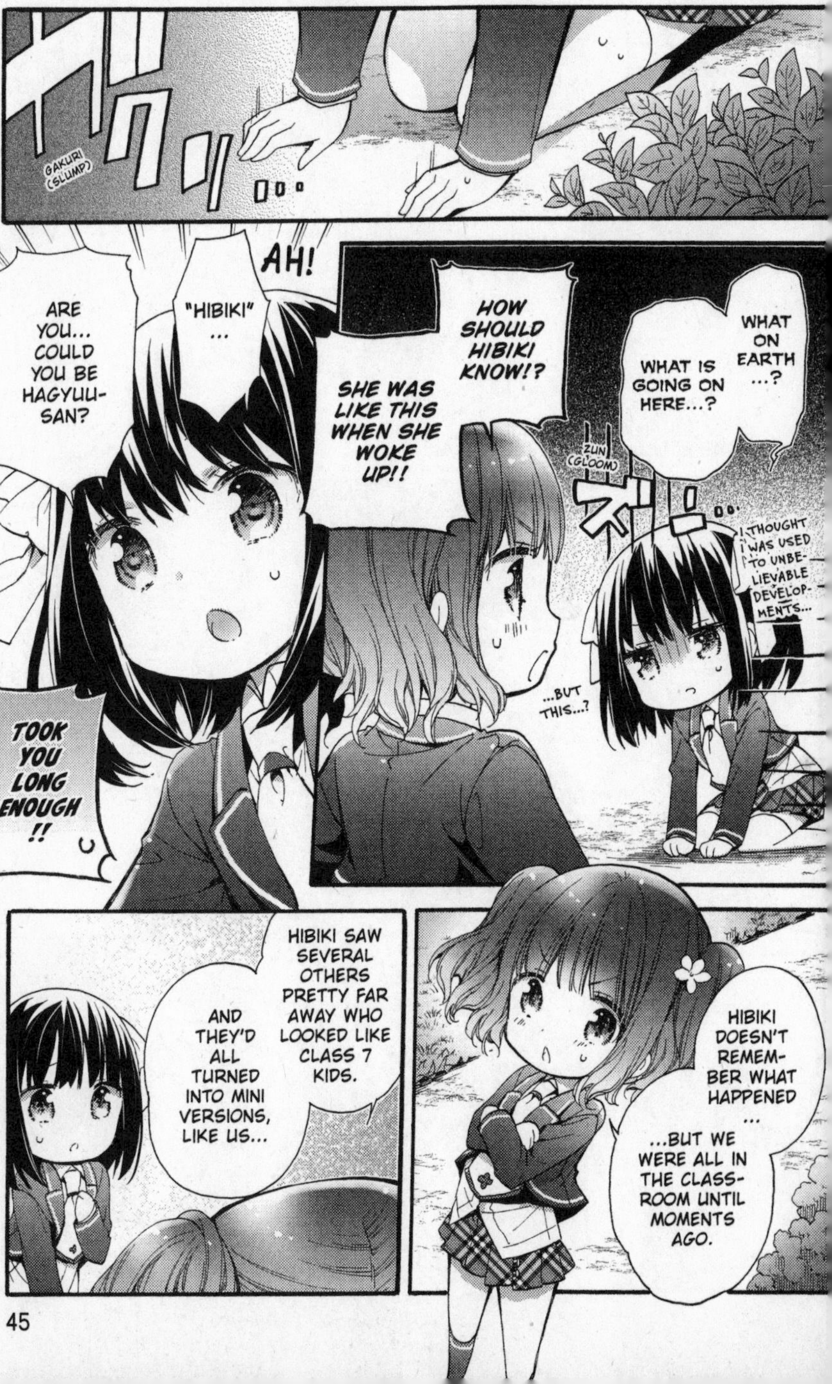
GAKURI (SLUMP)
WHAT ON EARTH ...?
WHAT IS GOING ON HERE...?
ZUN (GLOOM)
I THOUGHT I WAS USED TO UNBELIEVABLE DEVELOPMENTS...
...BUT THIS...?
HOW SHOULD HIBIKI KNOW!?
SHE WAS LIKE THIS WHEN SHE WOKE UP!!
AH!
"HIBIKI" ...
ARE YOU... COULD YOU BE HAGYUU-SAN?
TOOK YOU LONG ENOUGH!!
HIBIKI DOESN'T REMEMBER WHAT HAPPENED ...
...BUT WE WERE ALL IN THE CLASSROOM UNTIL MOMENTS AGO.
HIBIKI SAW SEVERAL OTHERS PRETTY FAR AWAY WHO LOOKED LIKE CLASS 7 KIDS.
AND THEY'D ALL TURNED INTO MINI VERSIONS, LIKE US...

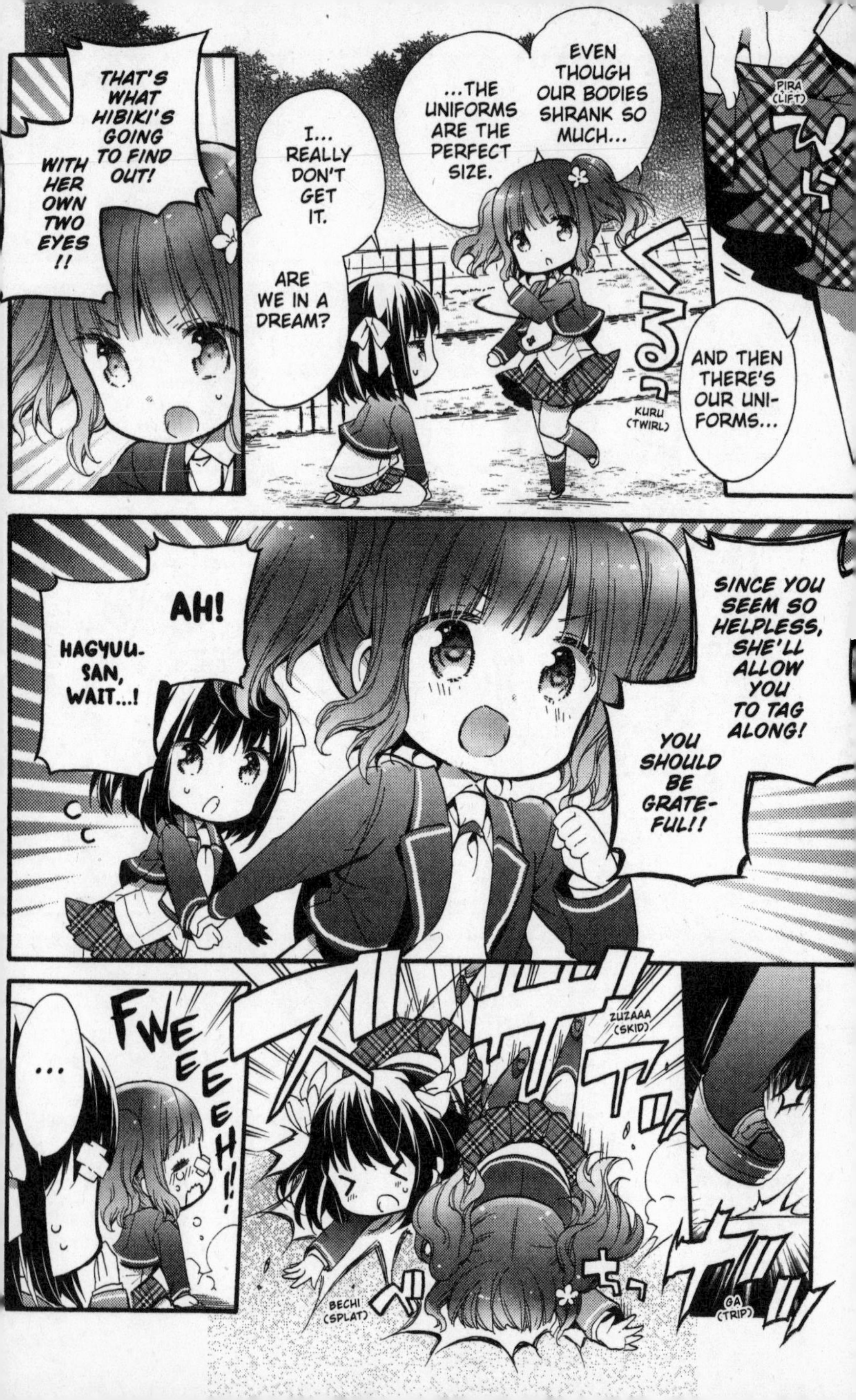
PIRA (LIFT)
AND THEN THERE'S OUR UNI-FORMS...
EVEN THOUGH OUR BODIES SHRANK SO MUCH...
...THE UNIFORMS ARE THE PERFECT SIZE.
KURU (TWIRL)
I... REALLY DON'T GET IT.
ARE WE IN A DREAM?
THAT'S WHAT HIBIKI'S GOING TO FIND OUT!
WITH HER OWN TWO EYES!!
SINCE YOU SEEM SO HELPLESS, SHE'LL ALLOW YOU TO TAG ALONG!
YOU SHOULD BE GRATE-FUL!!
AH!
HAGYUU-SAN, WAIT...!
GA (TRIP)
ZUZAAA (SKID)
BECHI (SPLAT)
FWEEEEEH!!
...

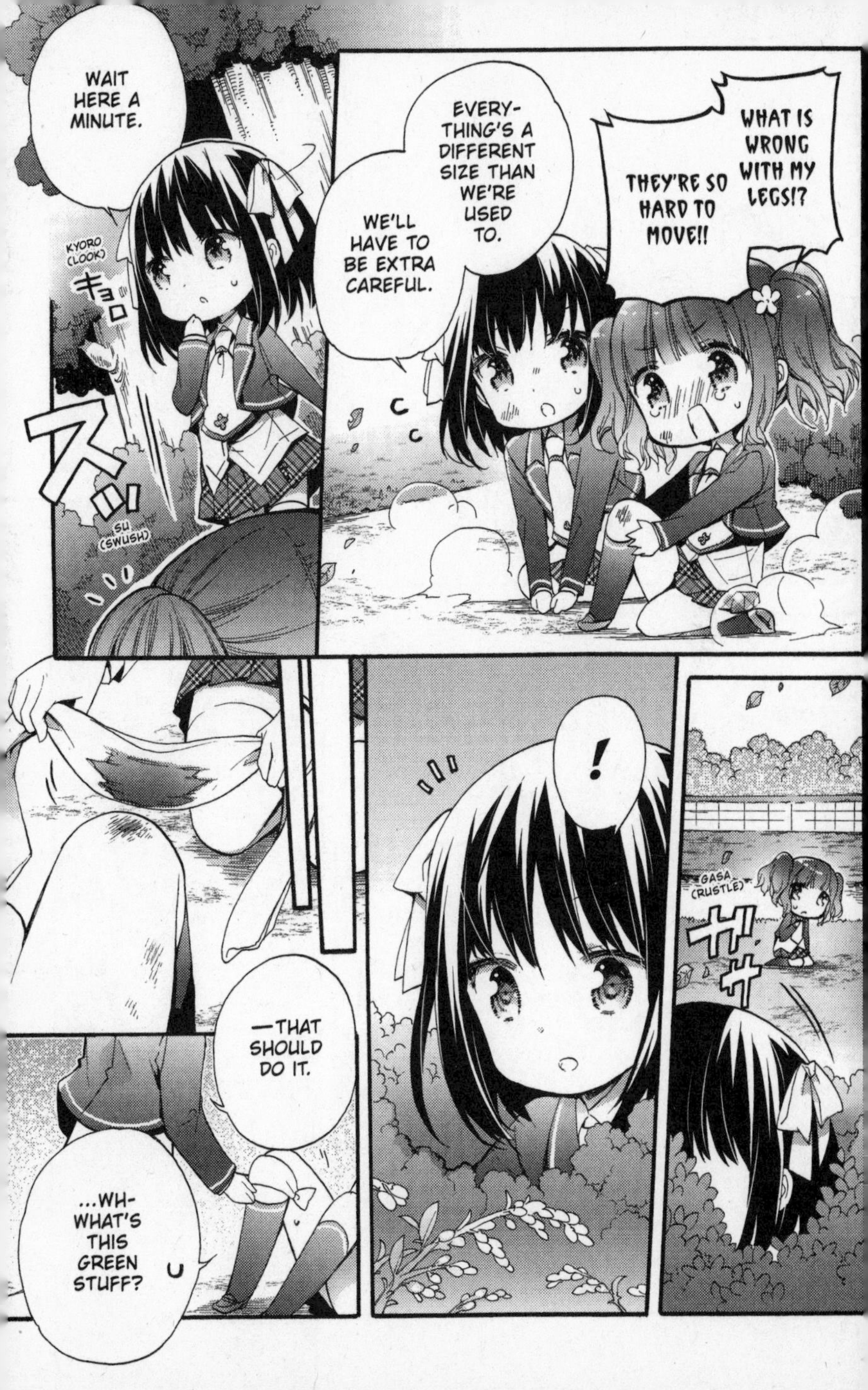
WHAT IS WRONG WITH MY LEGS!?
THEY'RE SO HARD TO MOVE!!
EVERY-THING'S A DIFFERENT SIZE THAN WE'RE USED TO.
WE'LL HAVE TO BE EXTRA CAREFUL.
WAIT HERE A MINUTE.
KYORO (LOOK)
キョロ
スッ
SU (SWUSH)
GASA (RUSTLE)
ガサ
!
—THAT SHOULD DO IT.
...WH-WHAT'S THIS GREEN STUFF?

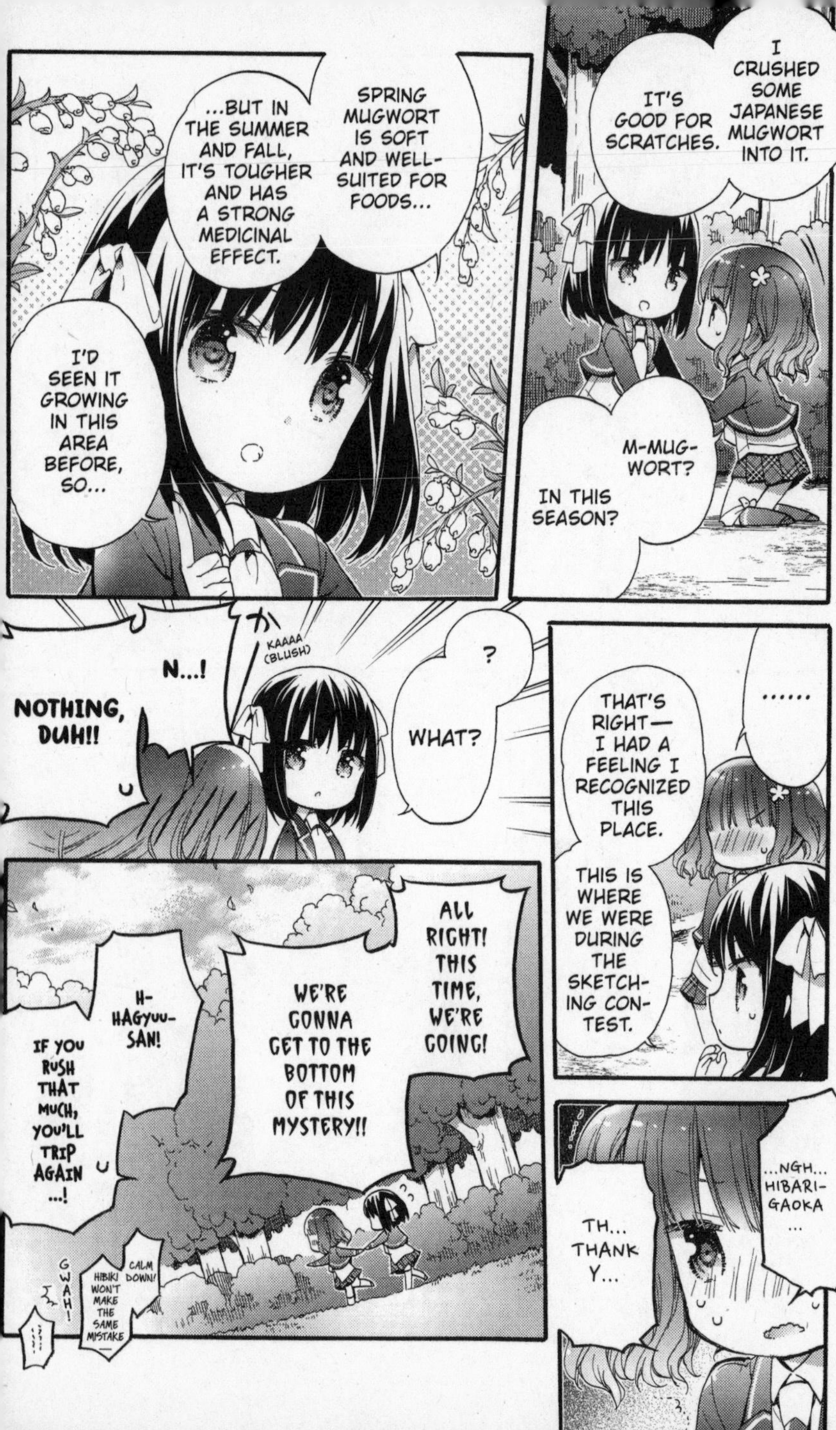
I CRUSHED SOME JAPANESE MUGWORT INTO IT.
IT'S GOOD FOR SCRATCHES.
M-MUG-WORT?
IN THIS SEASON?
SPRING MUGWORT IS SOFT AND WELL-SUITED FOR FOODS...
...BUT IN THE SUMMER AND FALL, IT'S TOUGHER AND HAS A STRONG MEDICINAL EFFECT.
I'D SEEN IT GROWING IN THIS AREA BEFORE, SO...
......
THAT'S RIGHT— I HAD A FEELING I RECOGNIZED THIS PLACE.
THIS IS WHERE WE WERE DURING THE SKETCHING CONTEST.
...NGH... HIBARI-GAOKA...
TH... THANK Y...
?
WHAT?
か
KAAAA (BLUSH)
N...!
NOTHING, DUH!!
ALL RIGHT! THIS TIME, WE'RE GOING!
WE'RE GONNA GET TO THE BOTTOM OF THIS MYSTERY!!
H-HAGYUU-SAN!
IF YOU RUSH THAT MUCH, YOU'LL TRIP AGAIN...!
CALM DOWN!
HIBIKI WON'T MAKE THE SAME MISTAKE—
GWAH!

AnneHappy♪

unhappy
go lucky!

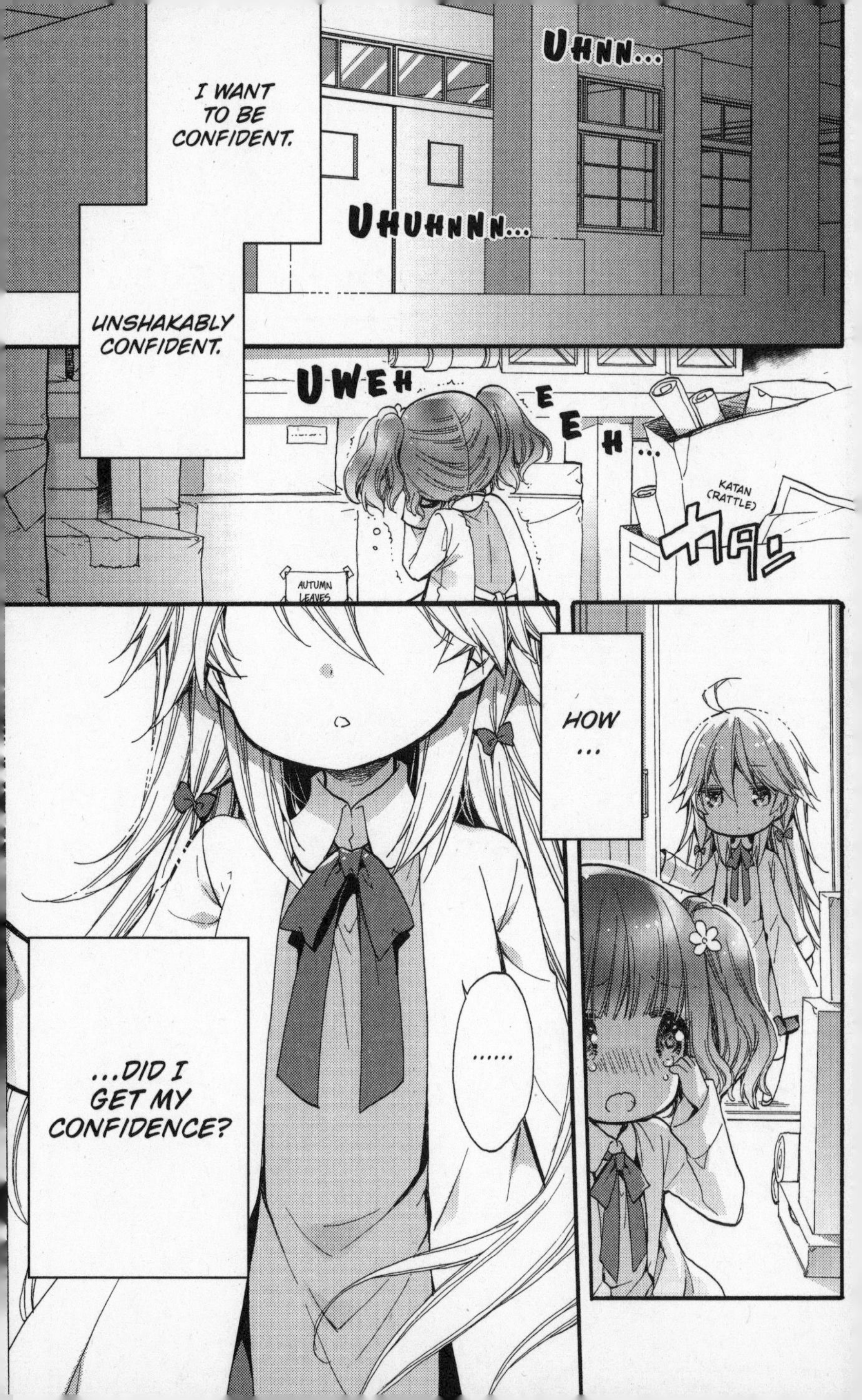
I WANT TO BE CONFIDENT.
UHNN...
UHUHNNN...
UNSHAKABLY CONFIDENT.
KATAN (RATTLE)
UWEH EEH...
AUTUMN LEAVES
HOW...
......
...DID I GET MY CONFIDENCE?

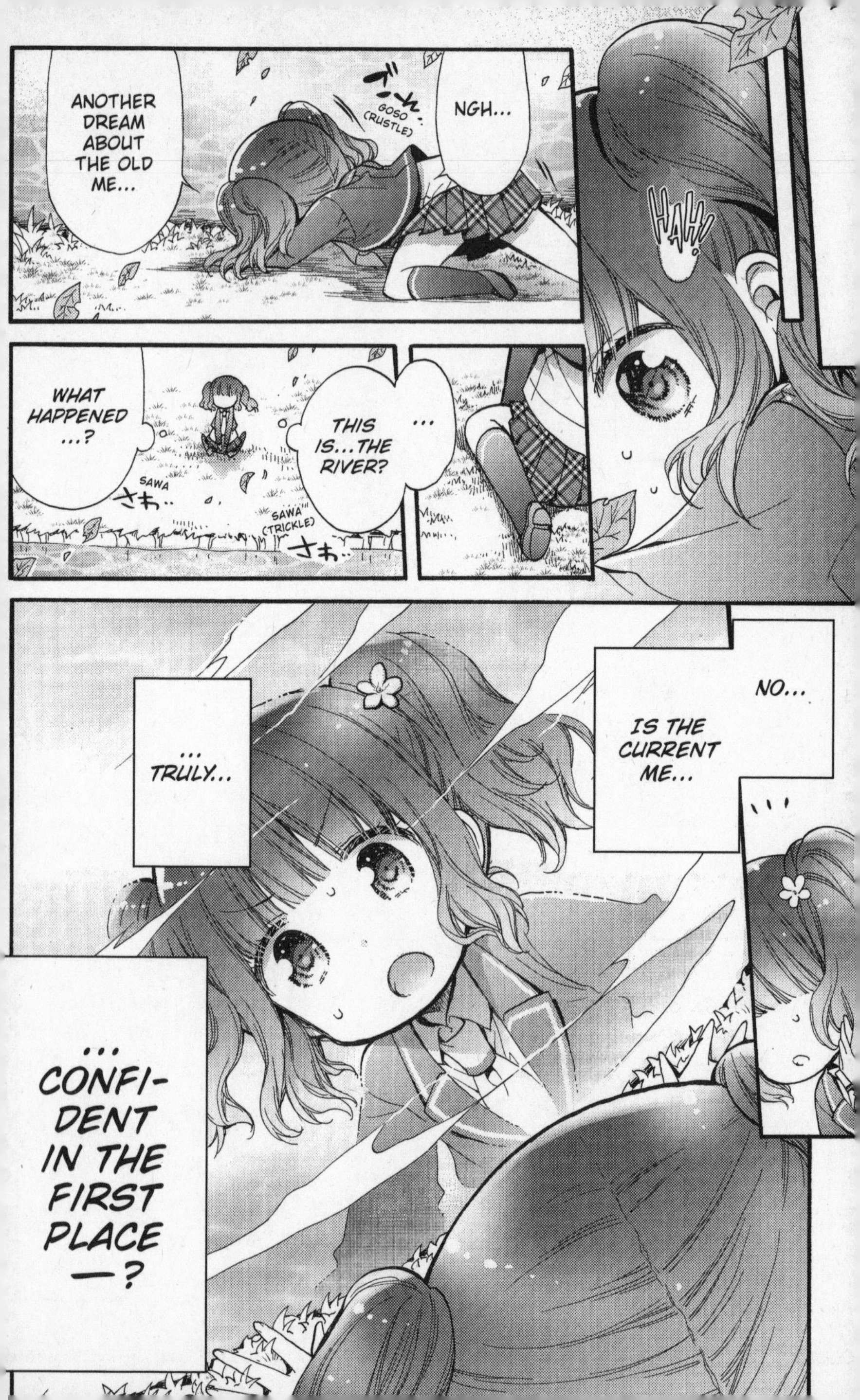
HAH!
NGH...
GOSO (RUSTLE)
ANOTHER DREAM ABOUT THE OLD ME...
...
THIS IS...THE RIVER?
SAWA (TRICKLE)
WHAT HAPPENED ...?
SAWA
NO... IS THE CURRENT ME...
... TRULY...
... CONFI-DENT IN THE FIRST PLACE —?

Lucky. 58

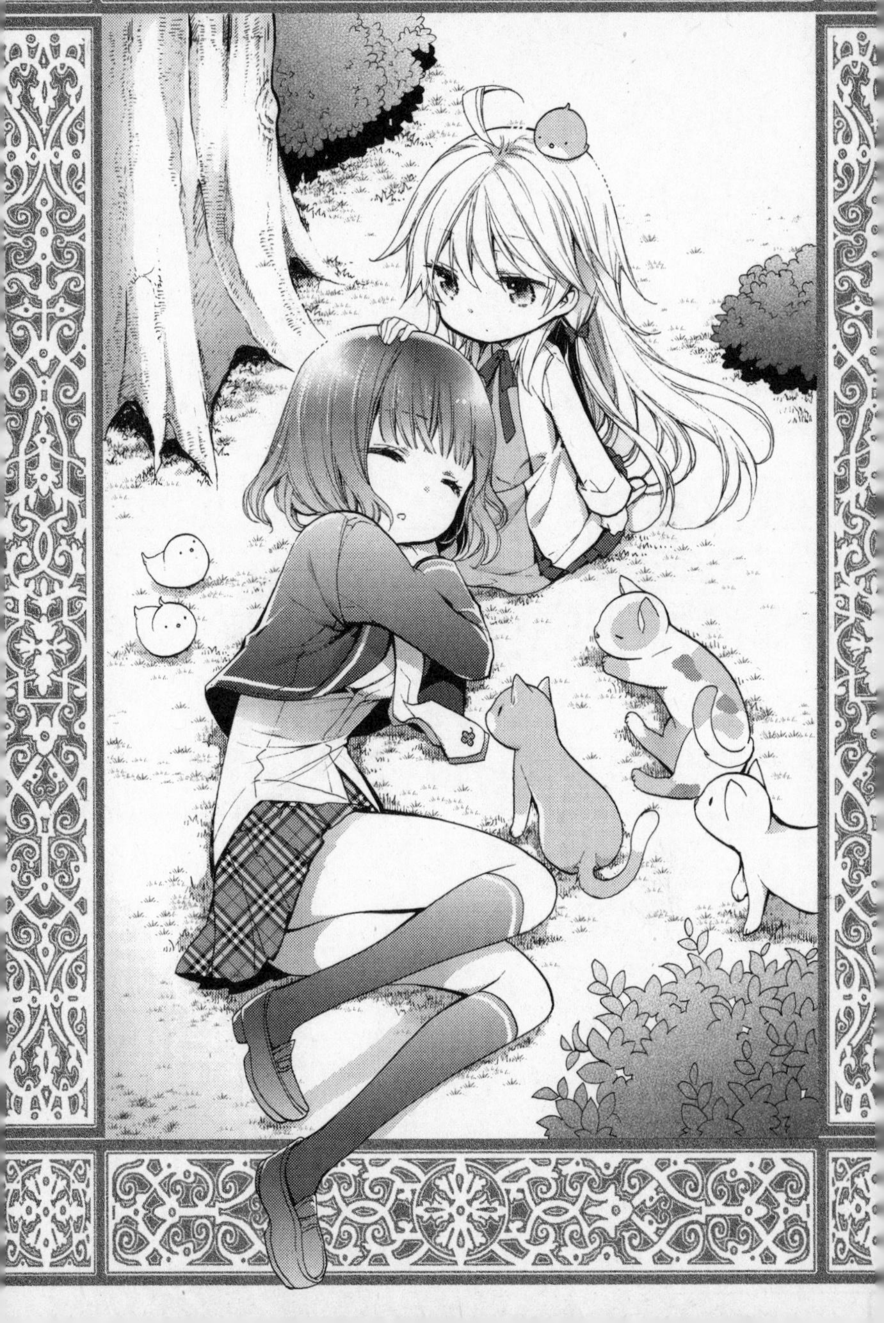

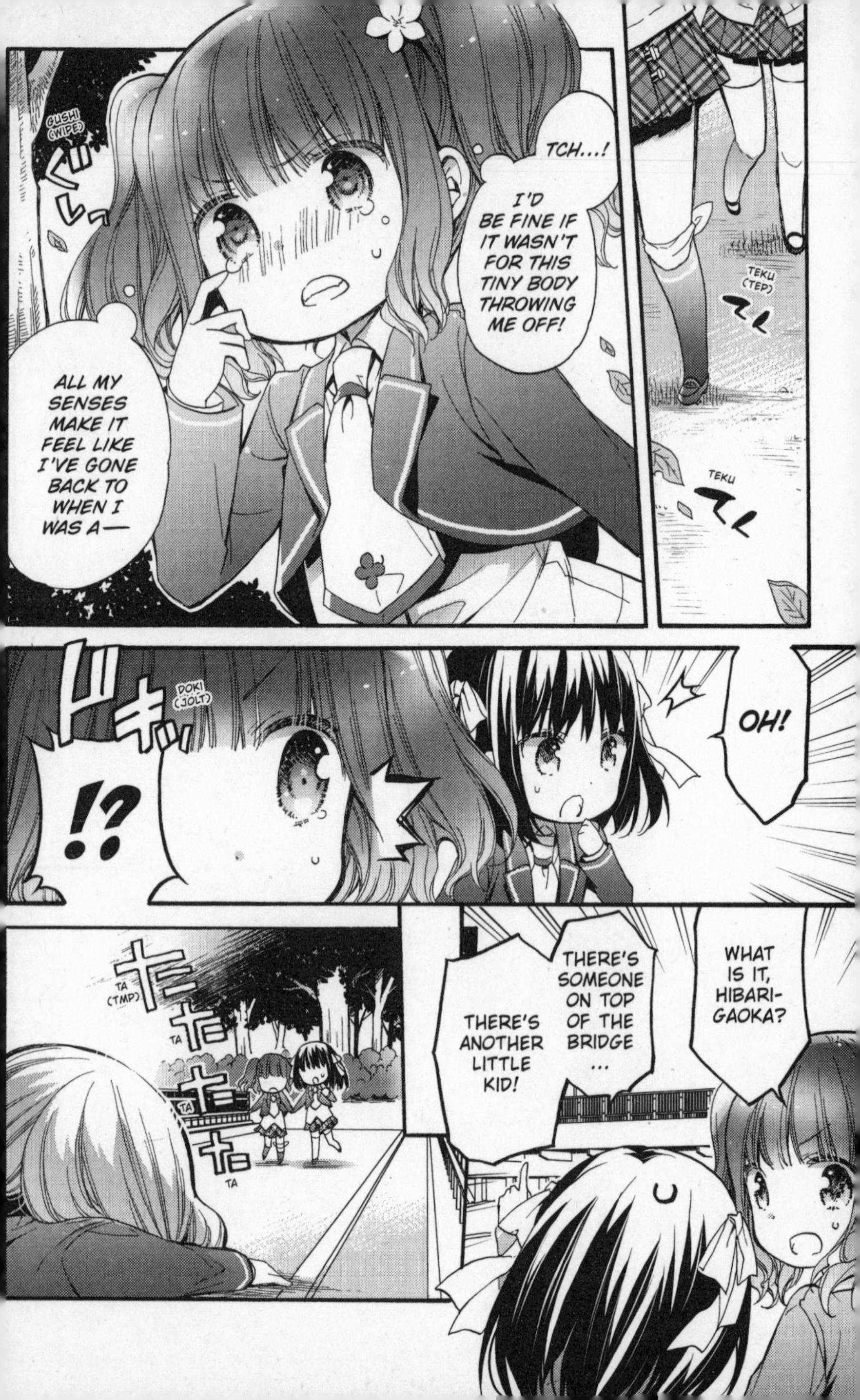
TEKU (TEP)
TEKU
TCH...!
I'D BE FINE IF IT WASN'T FOR THIS TINY BODY THROWING ME OFF!
GUSHI (WIPE)
ALL MY SENSES MAKE IT FEEL LIKE I'VE GONE BACK TO WHEN I WAS A—
OH!
DOKI (JOLT)
!?
WHAT IS IT, HIBARI-GAOKA?
THERE'S SOMEONE ON TOP OF THE BRIDGE...
THERE'S ANOTHER LITTLE KID!
TA (TMP)
TA
TA
TA

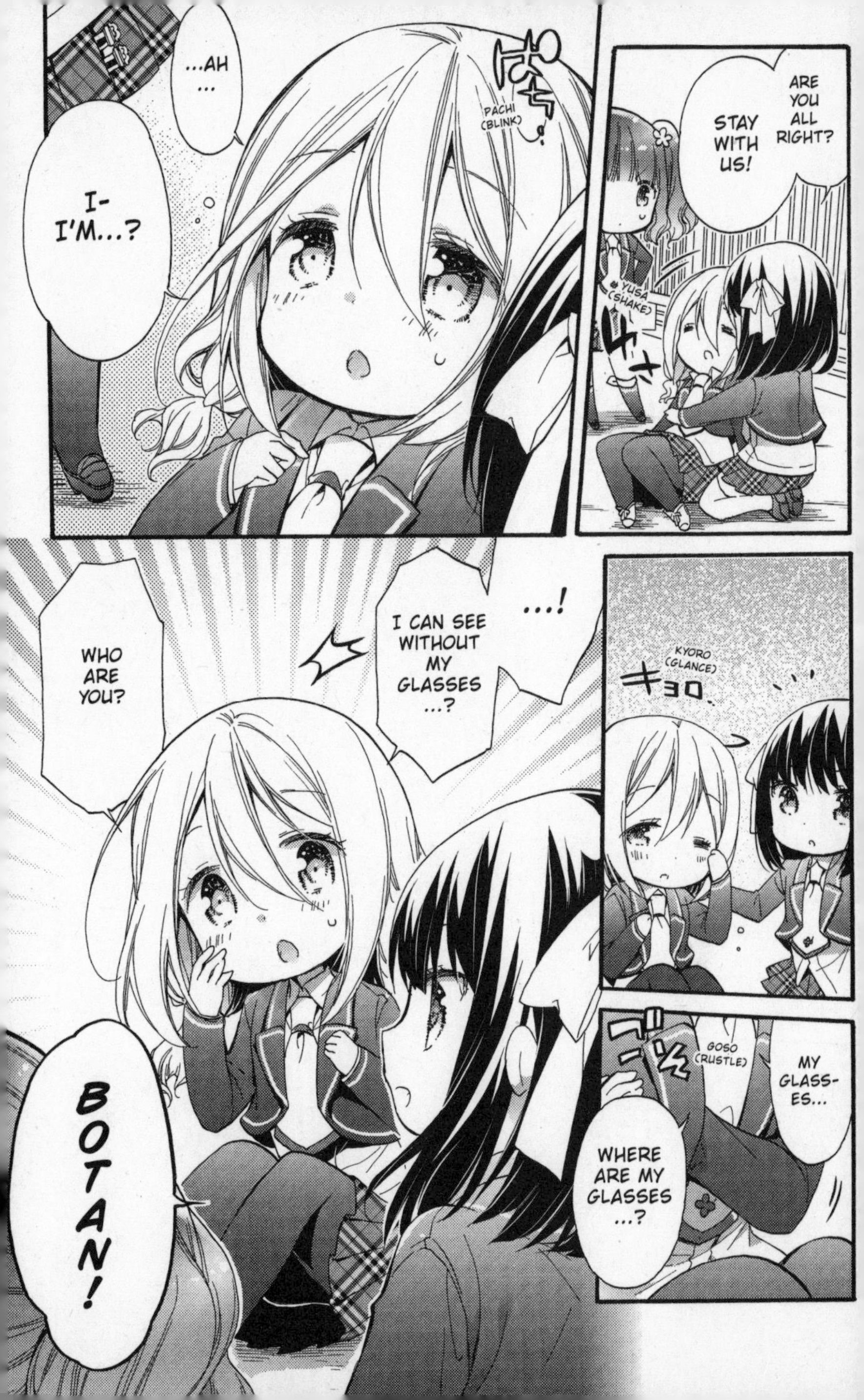
ARE YOU ALL RIGHT?
STAY WITH US!
YUSA (SHAKE)
PACHI (BLINK)
...AH ...
I- I'M...?
KYORO (GLANCE)
MY GLASS-ES...
GOSO (RUSTLE)
WHERE ARE MY GLASSES ...?
...!
I CAN SEE WITHOUT MY GLASSES ...?
WHO ARE YOU?
BOTAN!

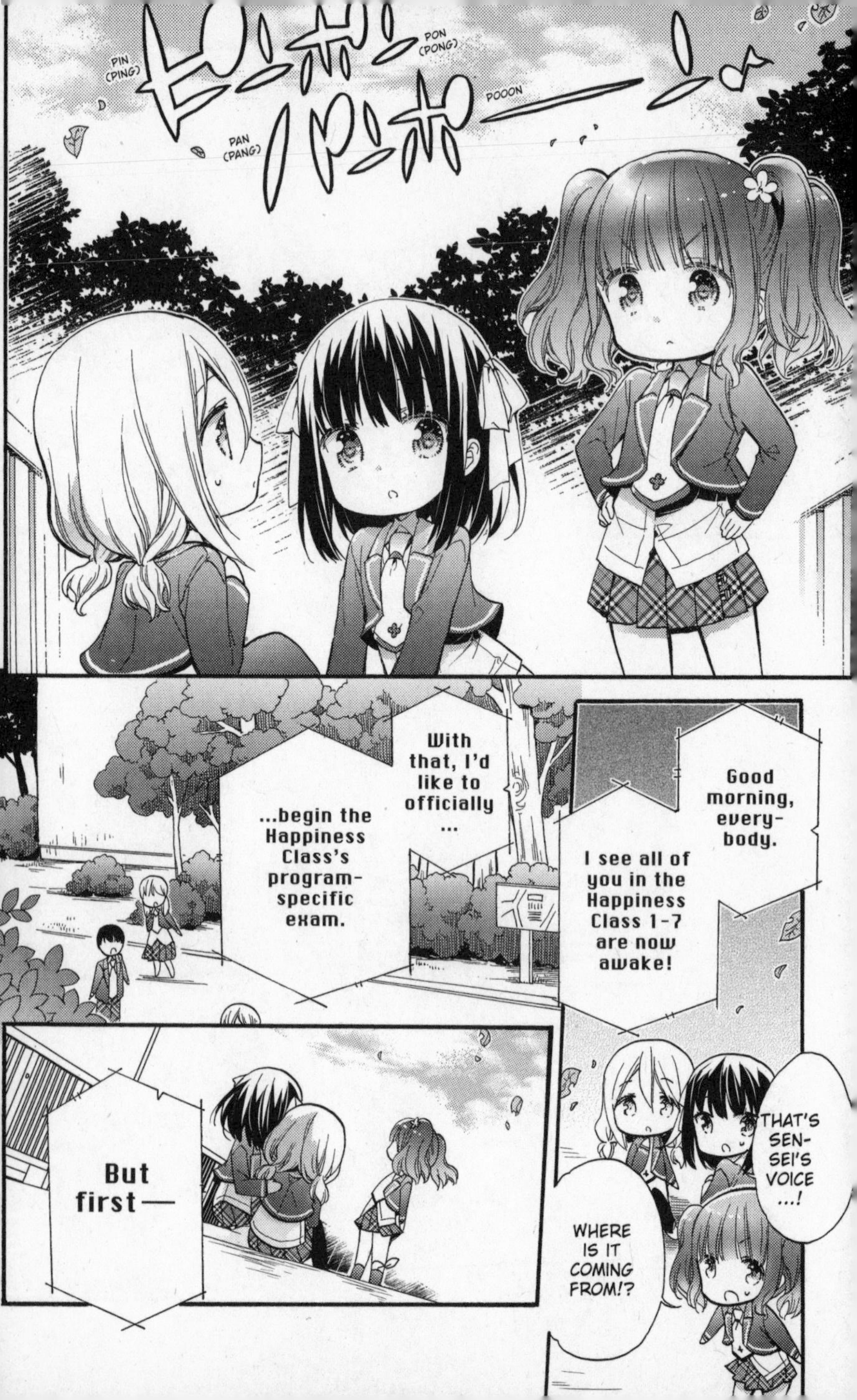

ピンポンパンポーン♪
PIN (PING)
PON (PONG)
PAN (PANG)
POOON
Good morning, every-body.
I see all of you in the Happiness Class 1-7 are now awake!
With that, I'd like to officially...
...begin the Happiness Class's program-specific exam.
THAT'S SEN-SEI'S VOICE...!
WHERE IS IT COMING FROM!?
But first—

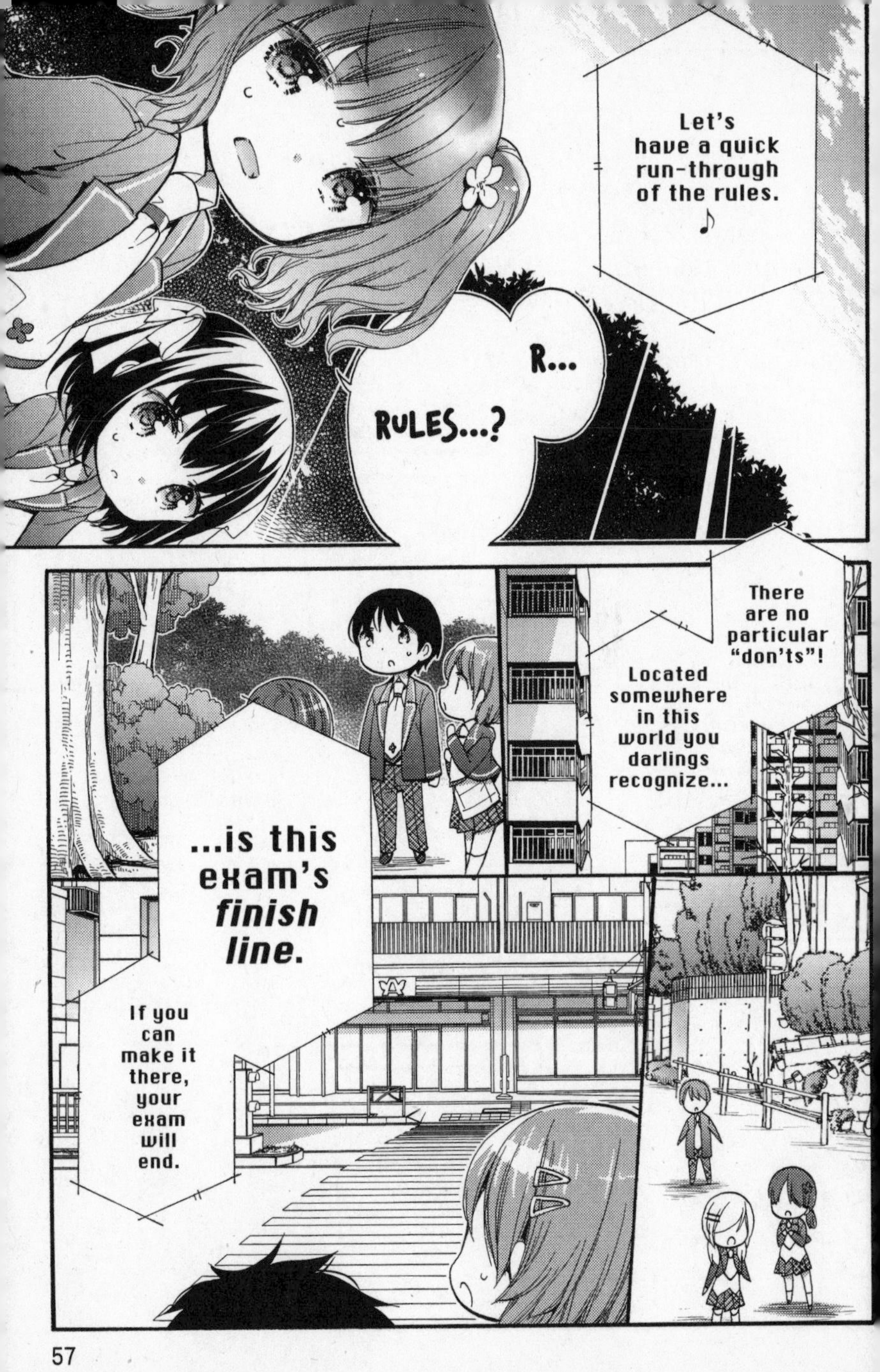
Let's have a quick run-through of the rules. ♪
R... RULES...?
There are no particular "don'ts"!
Located somewhere in this world you darlings recognize...
...is this exam's *finish line*.
If you can make it there, your exam will end.

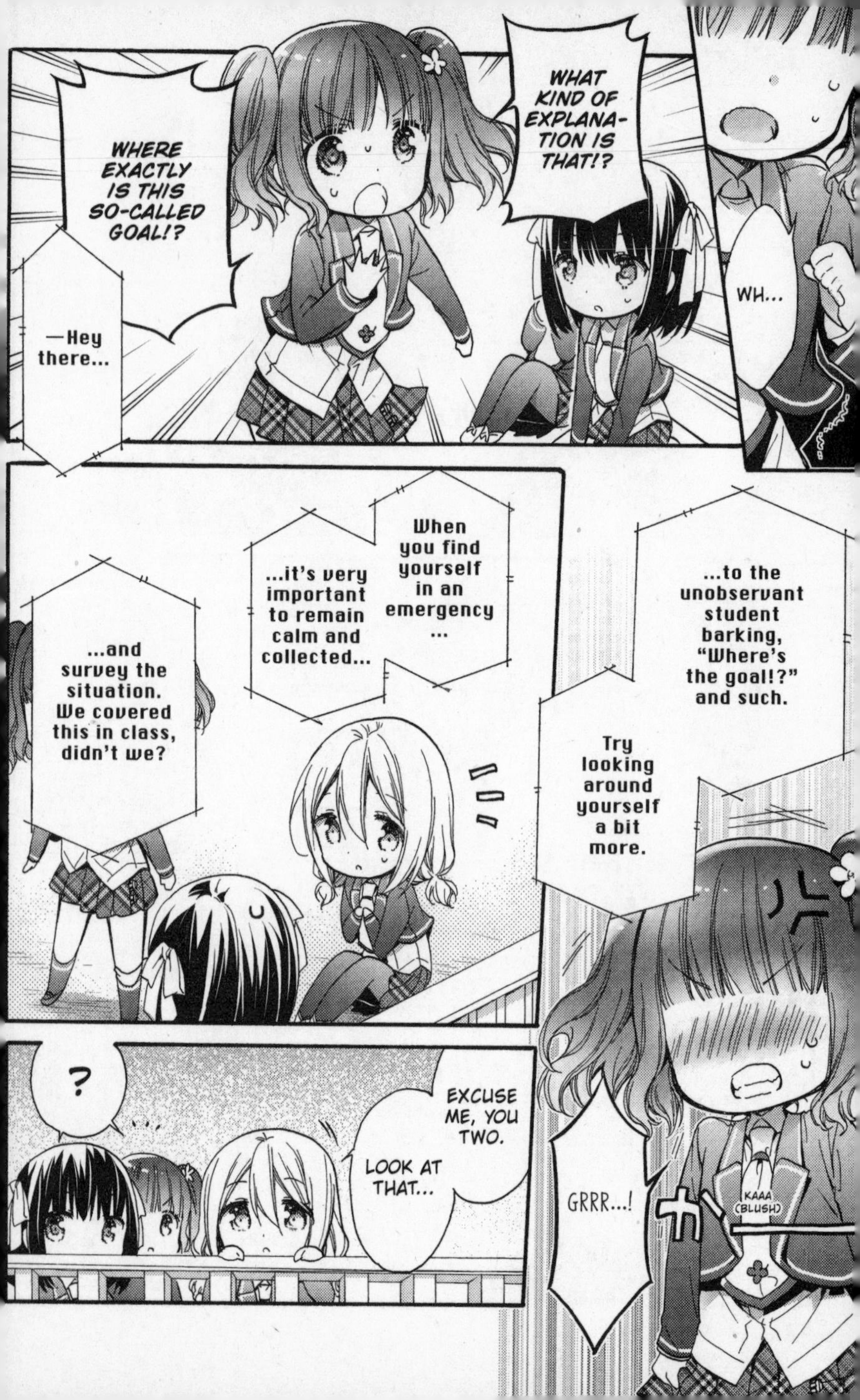
WH...
WHAT KIND OF EXPLANATION IS THAT!?
WHERE EXACTLY IS THIS SO-CALLED GOAL!?
—Hey there...
...to the unobservant student barking, "Where's the goal!?" and such.
Try looking around yourself a bit more.
GRRR...!
KAAA (BLUSH)
When you find yourself in an emergency...
...it's very important to remain calm and collected...
...and survey the situation. We covered this in class, didn't we?
EXCUSE ME, YOU TWO.
LOOK AT THAT...
?

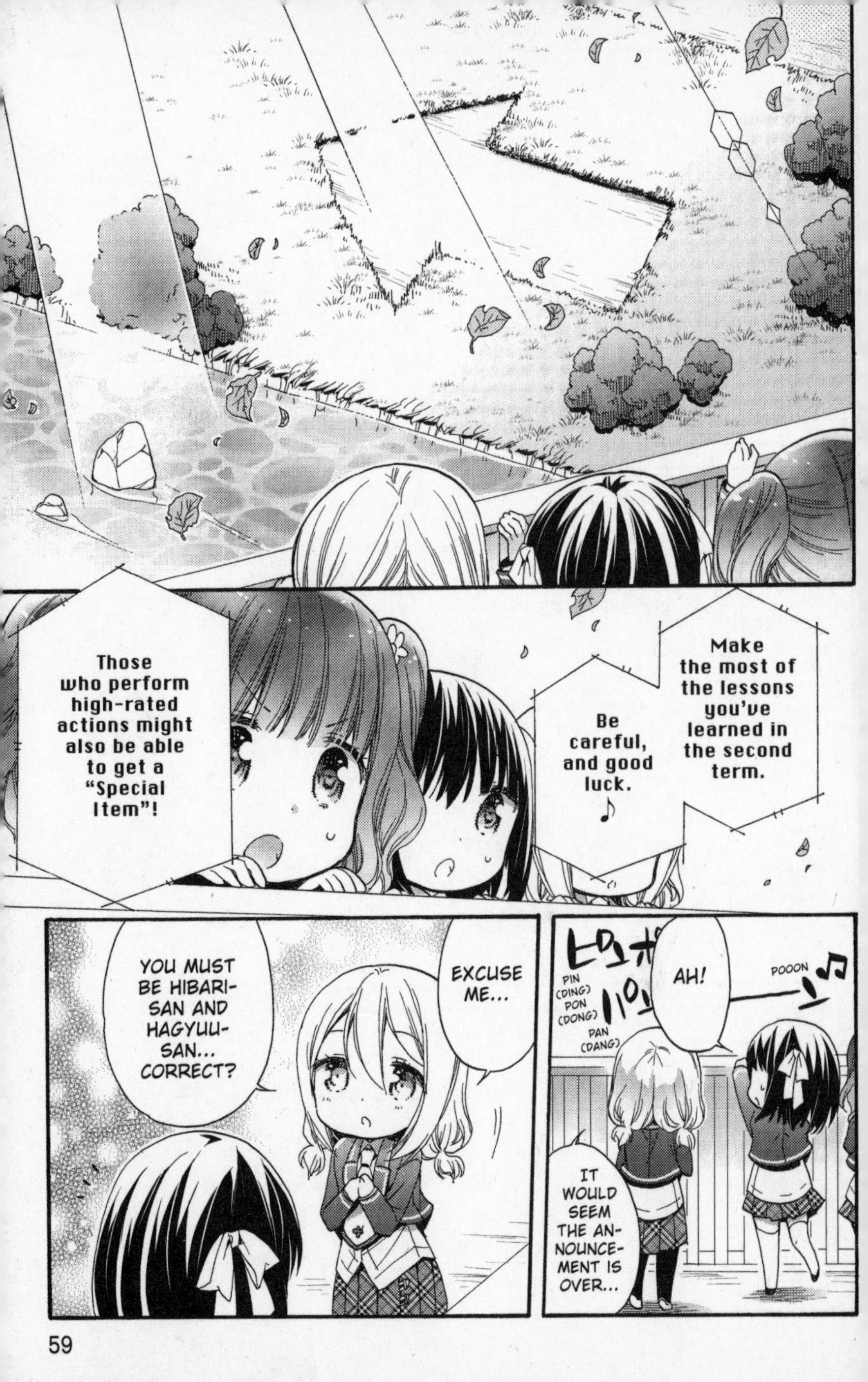
Make the most of the lessons you've learned in the second term.
Be careful, and good luck. ♪
Those who perform high-rated actions might also be able to get a "Special Item"!
POOON ♪
AH!
PIN (DING) PON (DONG) PAN (DANG)
IT WOULD SEEM THE ANNOUNCEMENT IS OVER...
EXCUSE ME...
YOU MUST BE HIBARI-SAN AND HAGYUU-SAN... CORRECT?

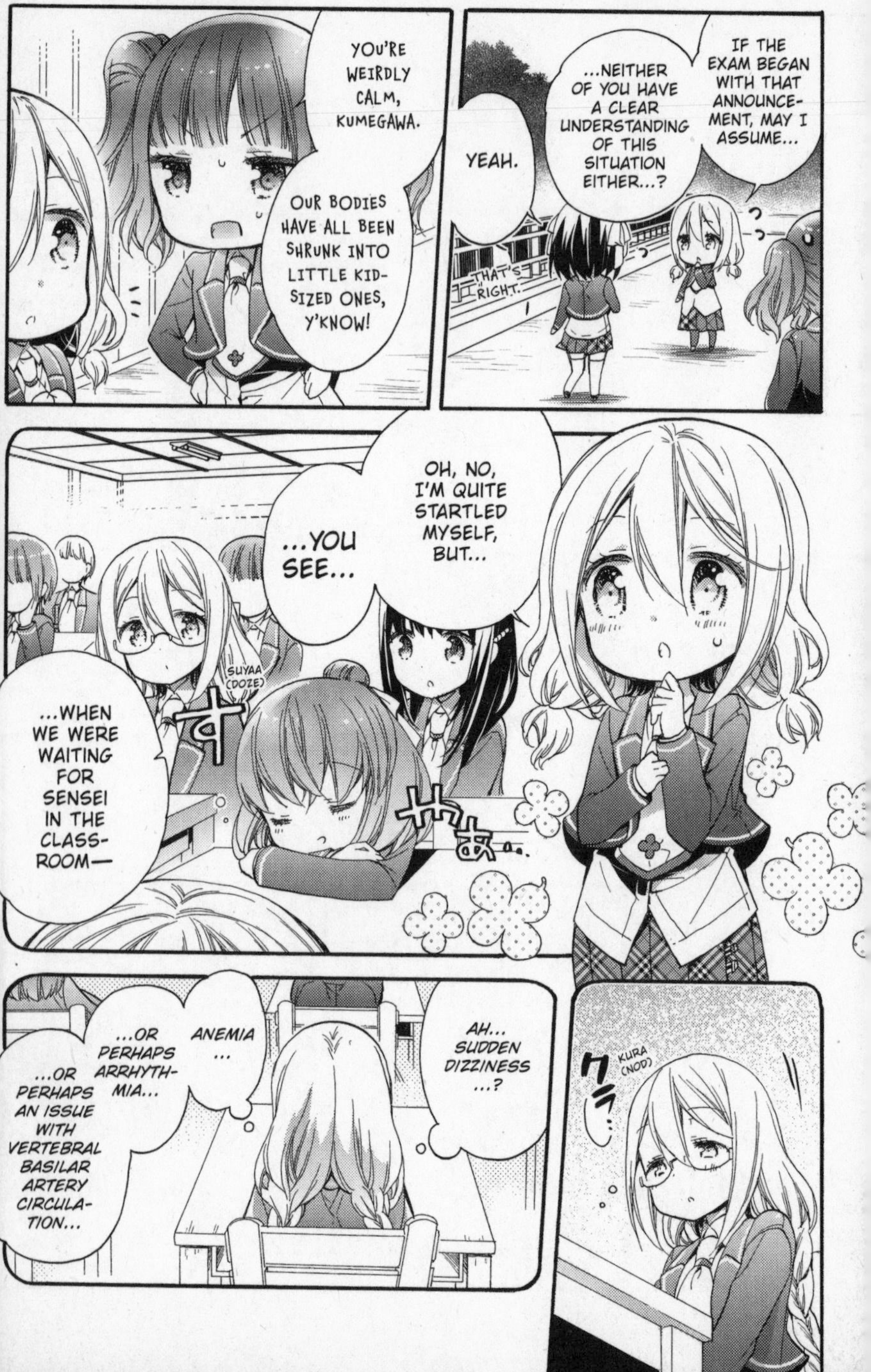
IF THE EXAM BEGAN WITH THAT ANNOUNCEMENT, MAY I ASSUME...
...NEITHER OF YOU HAVE A CLEAR UNDERSTANDING OF THIS SITUATION EITHER...?
YEAH.
THAT'S RIGHT.
YOU'RE WEIRDLY CALM, KUMEGAWA.
OUR BODIES HAVE ALL BEEN SHRUNK INTO LITTLE KID-SIZED ONES, Y'KNOW!
OH, NO, I'M QUITE STARTLED MYSELF, BUT...
...YOU SEE...
SUYAA (DOZE)
...WHEN WE WERE WAITING FOR SENSEI IN THE CLASSROOM—
KURA (NOD)
AH... SUDDEN DIZZINESS...?
ANEMIA...
...OR PERHAPS ARRHYTHMIA...
...OR PERHAPS AN ISSUE WITH VERTEBRAL BASILAR ARTERY CIRCULATION...

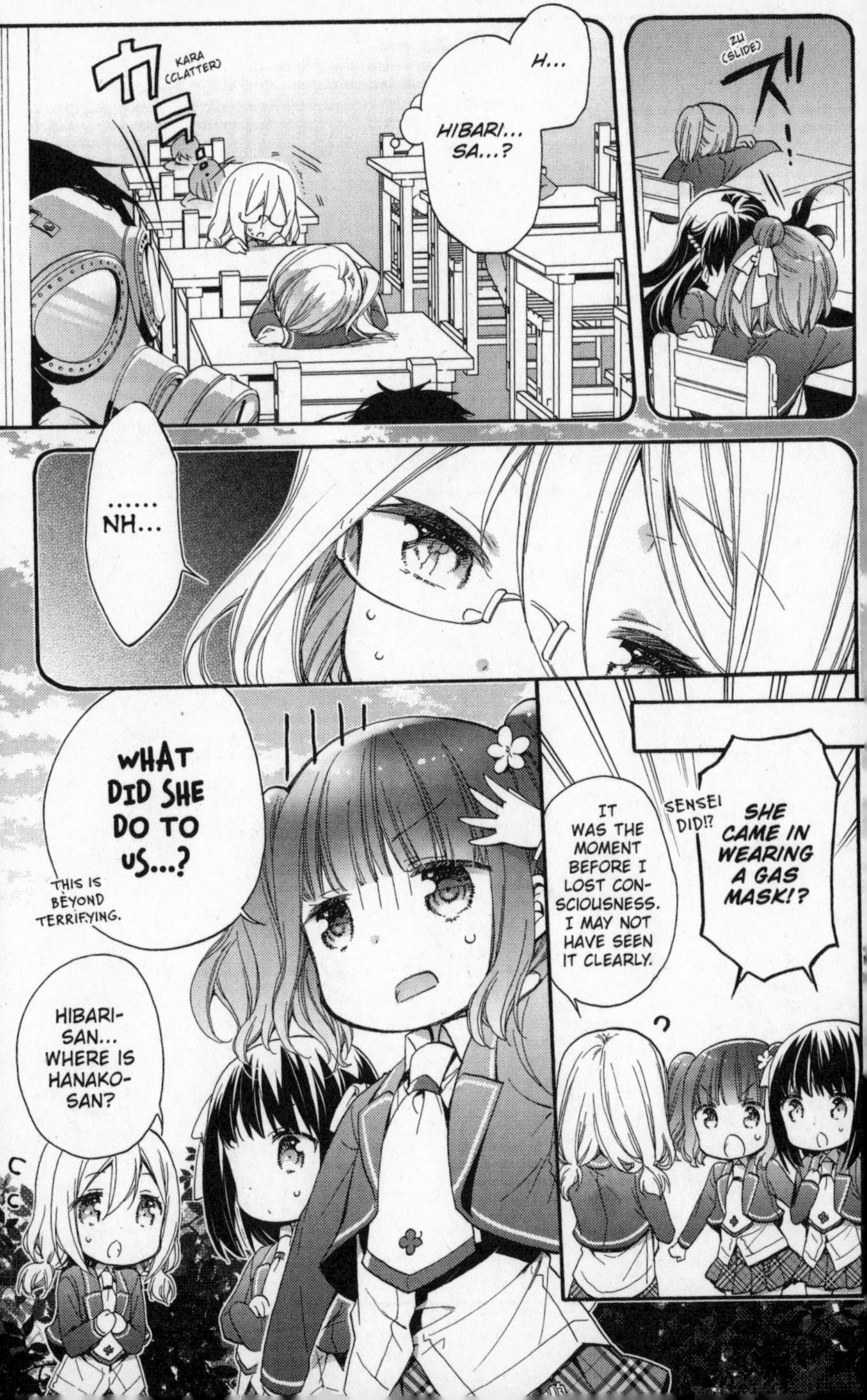
ZU (SLIDE)
H... HIBARI... SA...?
KARA (CLATTER)
...... NH...
SHE CAME IN WEARING A GAS MASK!?
SENSEI DID!?
IT WAS THE MOMENT BEFORE I LOST CONSCIOUSNESS. I MAY NOT HAVE SEEN IT CLEARLY.
WHAT DID SHE DO TO US...?
THIS IS BEYOND TERRIFYING.
HIBARI-SAN... WHERE IS HANAKO-SAN?

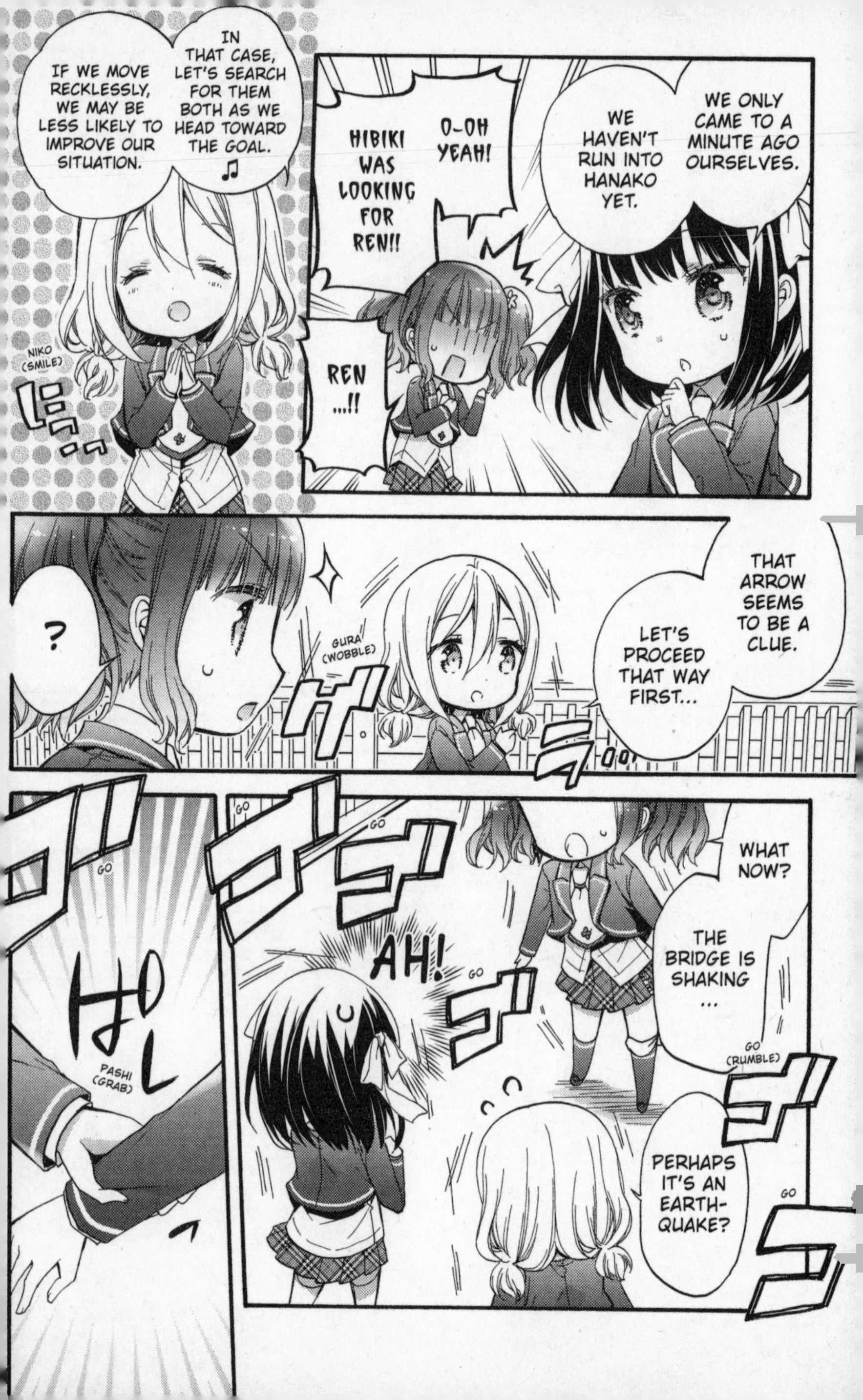
WE ONLY CAME TO A MINUTE AGO OURSELVES.
WE HAVEN'T RUN INTO HANAKO YET.
O-OH YEAH!
HIBIKI WAS LOOKING FOR REN!!
REN ...!!
IN THAT CASE, LET'S SEARCH FOR THEM BOTH AS WE HEAD TOWARD THE GOAL. ♫
IF WE MOVE RECKLESSLY, WE MAY BE LESS LIKELY TO IMPROVE OUR SITUATION.
NIKO (SMILE)
THAT ARROW SEEMS TO BE A CLUE.
LET'S PROCEED THAT WAY FIRST...
GURA (WOBBLE)
?
WHAT NOW?
THE BRIDGE IS SHAKING ...
GO
GO
AH!
GO
GO (RUMBLE)
PERHAPS IT'S AN EARTHQUAKE?
GO
GO
PASHI (GRAB)

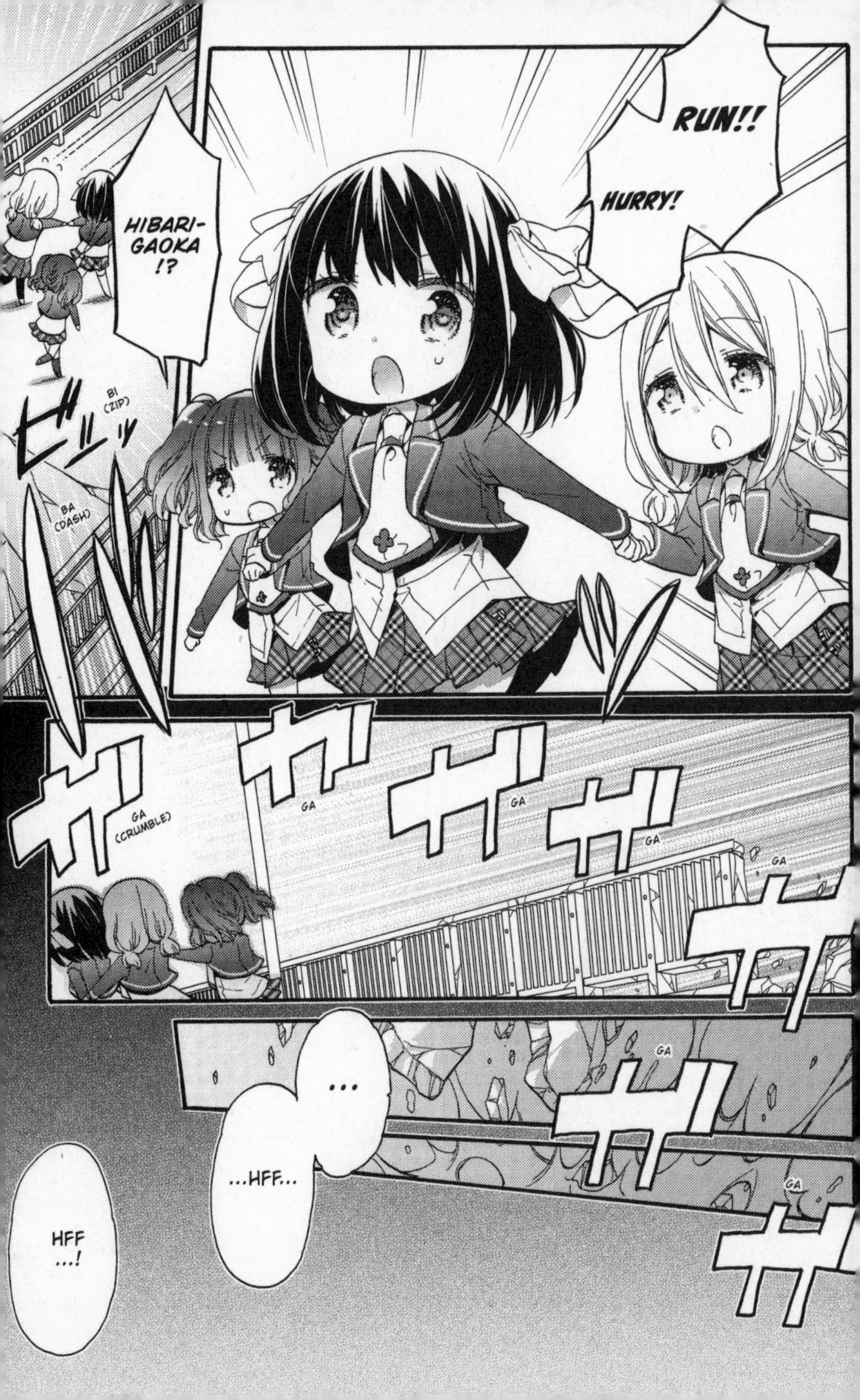
RUN!!
HURRY!
HIBARI-GAOKA!?
BI (ZIP)
BA (DASH)
GA
GA
GA
GA
GA (CRUMBLE)
GA
GA
...
...HFF...
HFF ...!

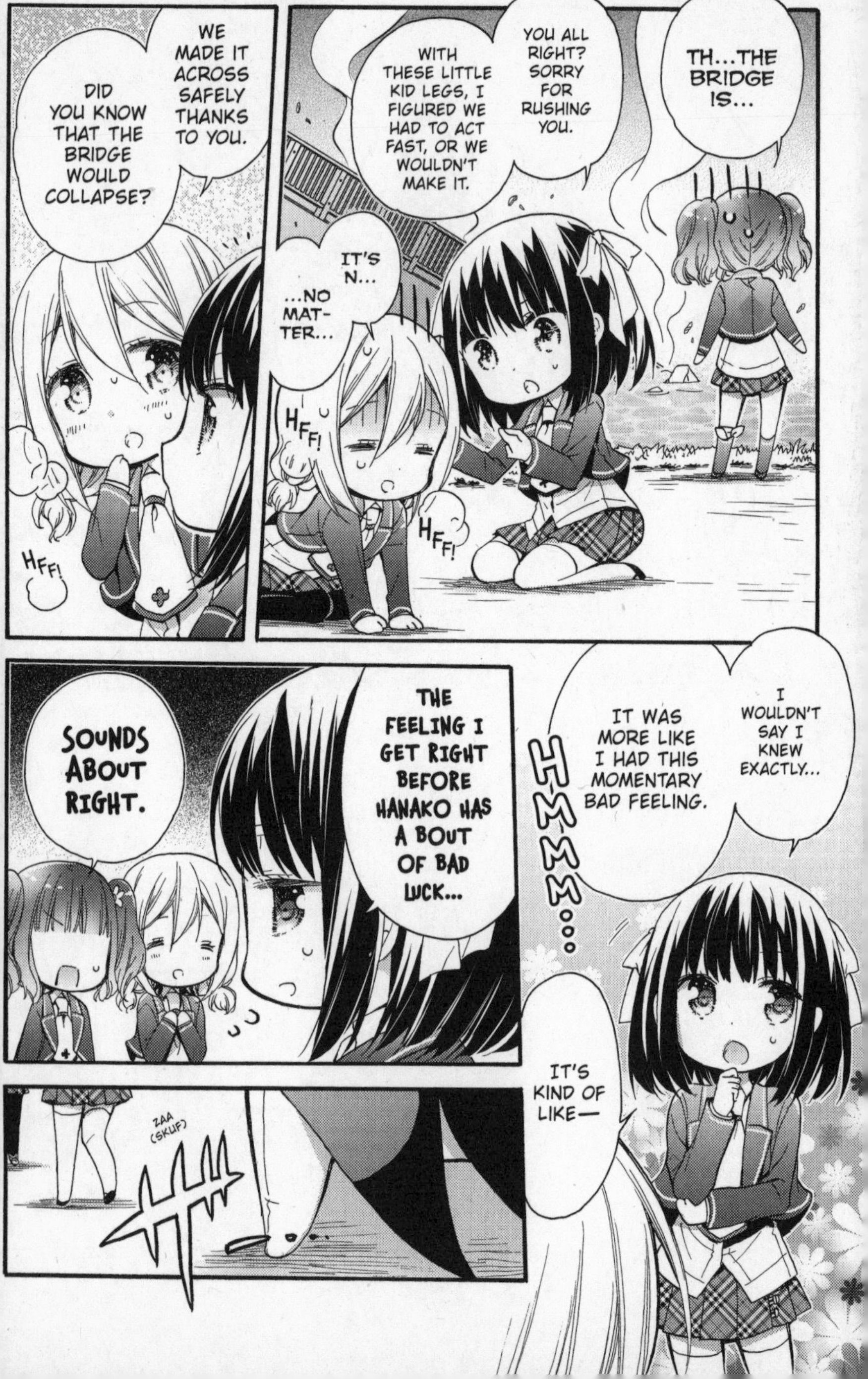
TH...THE BRIDGE IS...
YOU ALL RIGHT? SORRY FOR RUSHING YOU.
WITH THESE LITTLE KID LEGS, I FIGURED WE HAD TO ACT FAST, OR WE WOULDN'T MAKE IT.
IT'S N...
...NO MAT-TER...
HFF!
HFF!
WE MADE IT ACROSS SAFELY THANKS TO YOU.
DID YOU KNOW THAT THE BRIDGE WOULD COLLAPSE?
HFF!
I WOULDN'T SAY I KNEW EXACTLY...
IT WAS MORE LIKE I HAD THIS MOMENTARY BAD FEELING.
HMMM...
IT'S KIND OF LIKE—
THE FEELING I GET RIGHT BEFORE HANAKO HAS A BOUT OF BAD LUCK...
SOUNDS ABOUT RIGHT.
ZAA (SKUF)

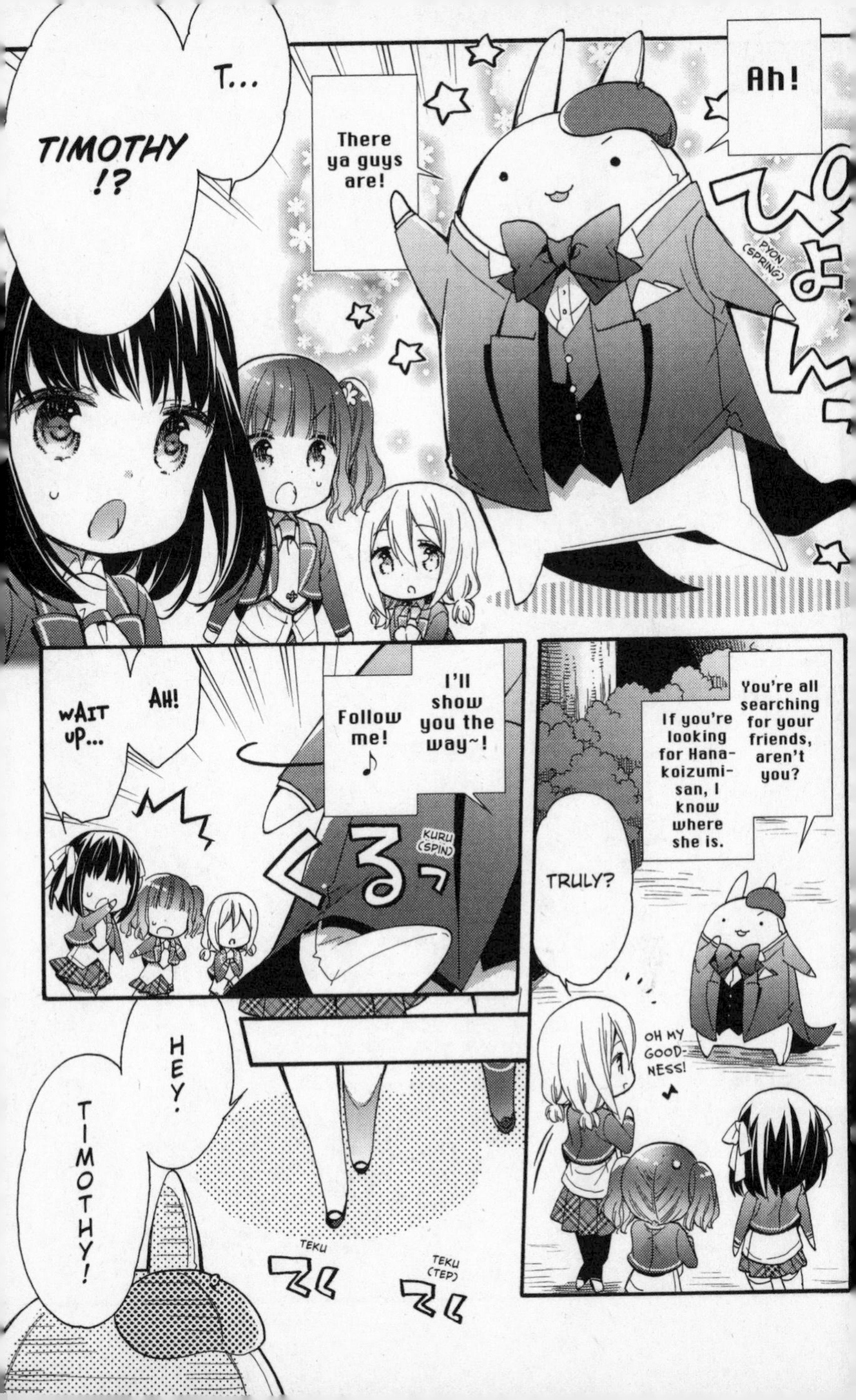
Ah!
ぴょんっ
PYON (SPRING)
There ya guys are!
T...
TIMOTHY !?
You're all searching for your friends, aren't you?
If you're looking for Hana-koizumi-san, I know where she is.
TRULY?
OH MY GOOD-NESS!
I'll show you the way~!
Follow me! ♪
くるっ
KURU (SPIN)
AH!
WAIT UP...
HEY!
TIMOTHY!
てく
TEKU (TEP)
てく
TEKU

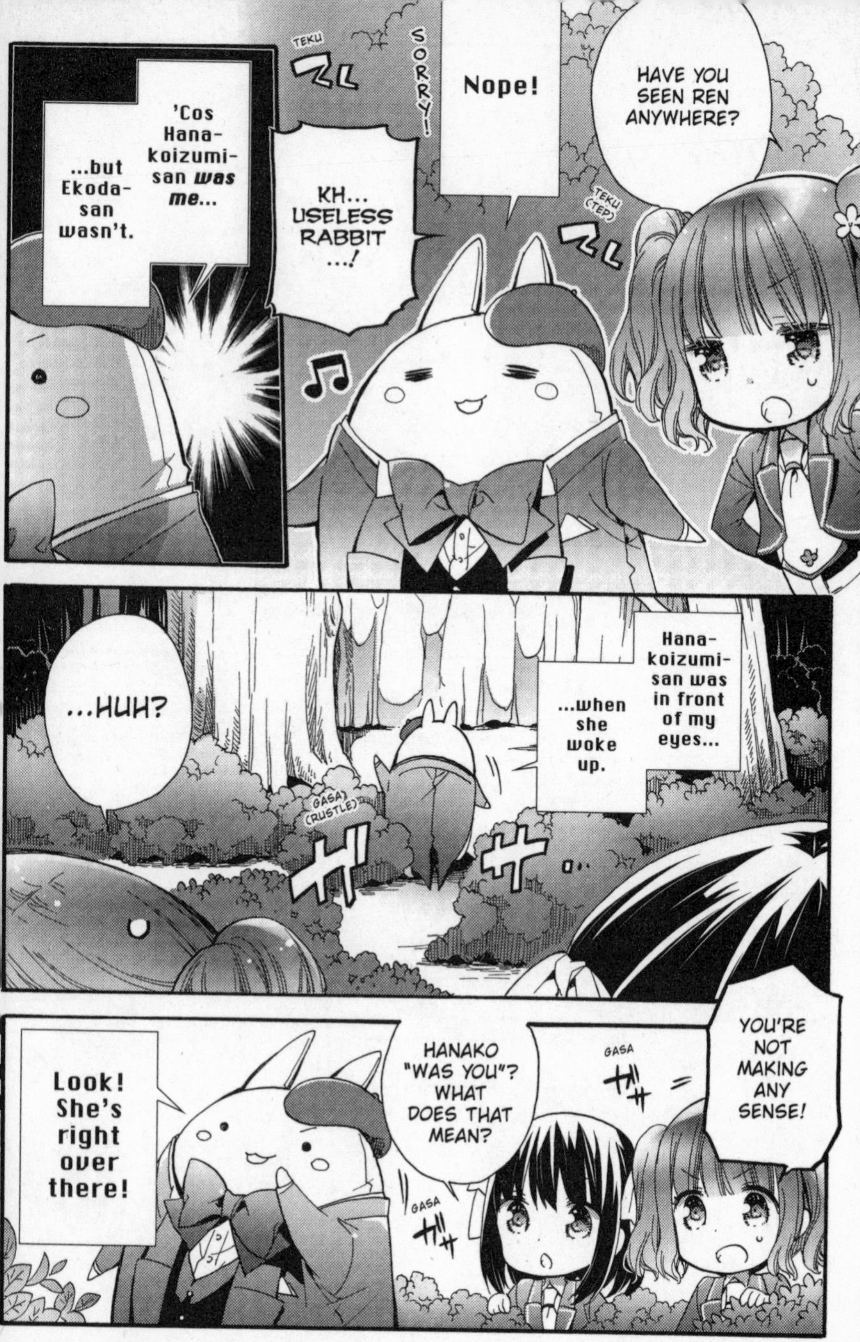
HAVE YOU SEEN REN ANYWHERE?
TEKU (TEP)
Nope!
SORRY!
TEKU
KH... USELESS RABBIT...!
'Cos Hana-koizumi-san *was* me...
...but Ekoda-san wasn't.
Hana-koizumi-san was in front of my eyes...
...when she woke up.
GASA (RUSTLE)
...HUH?
YOU'RE NOT MAKING ANY SENSE!
GASA
HANAKO "WAS YOU"? WHAT DOES THAT MEAN?
GASA
Look! She's right over there!

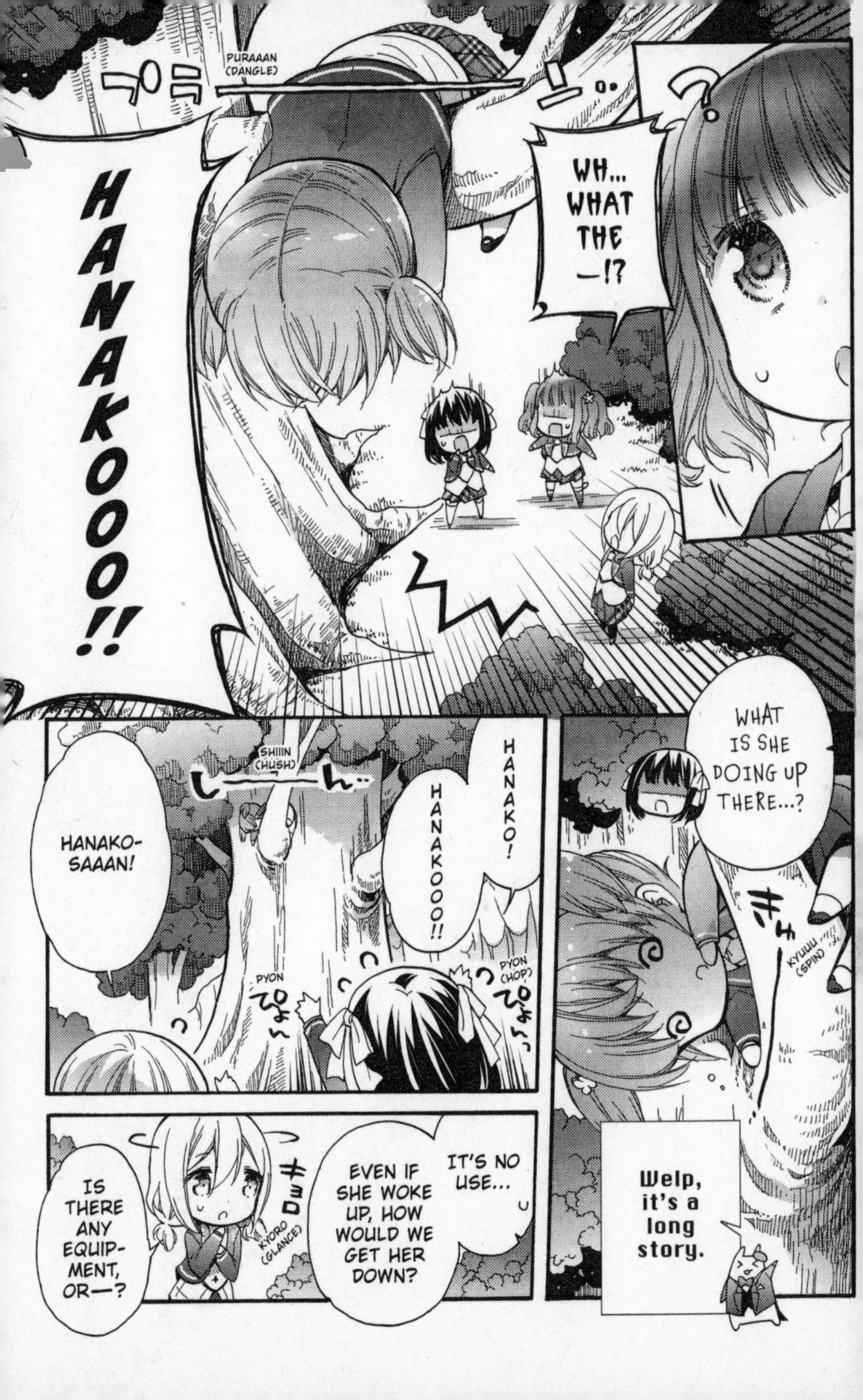
WH... WHAT THE—!?
PURAAAN (DANGLE)
HANAKOOOO!!
WHAT IS SHE DOING UP THERE...?
KYUUU (SPIN)
HANAKO! HANAKOOOO!!
SHIIIN (HUSH)
HANAKO-SAAAN!
PYON (HOP)
PYON
IT'S NO USE...
EVEN IF SHE WOKE UP, HOW WOULD WE GET HER DOWN?
KYORO (GLANCE)
IS THERE ANY EQUIPMENT, OR—?
Welp, it's a long story.

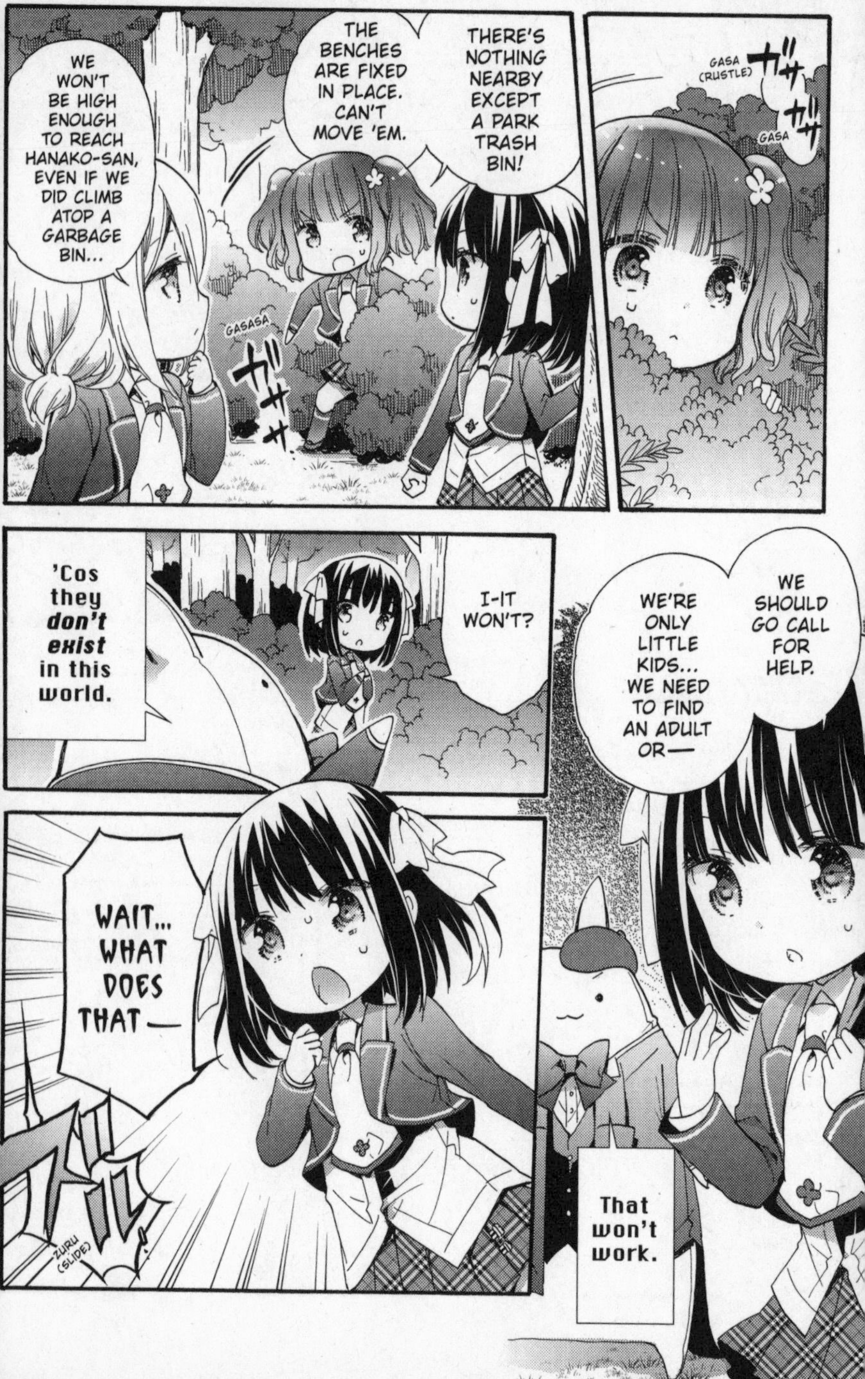
GASA (RUSTLE)
GASA
THERE'S NOTHING NEARBY EXCEPT A PARK TRASH BIN!
THE BENCHES ARE FIXED IN PLACE. CAN'T MOVE 'EM.
WE WON'T BE HIGH ENOUGH TO REACH HANAKO-SAN, EVEN IF WE DID CLIMB ATOP A GARBAGE BIN...
GASASA
WE SHOULD GO CALL FOR HELP.
WE'RE ONLY LITTLE KIDS... WE NEED TO FIND AN ADULT OR—
That won't work.
I-IT WON'T?
'Cos they *don't exist* in this world.
WAIT... WHAT DOES THAT—
ZURU (SLIDE)

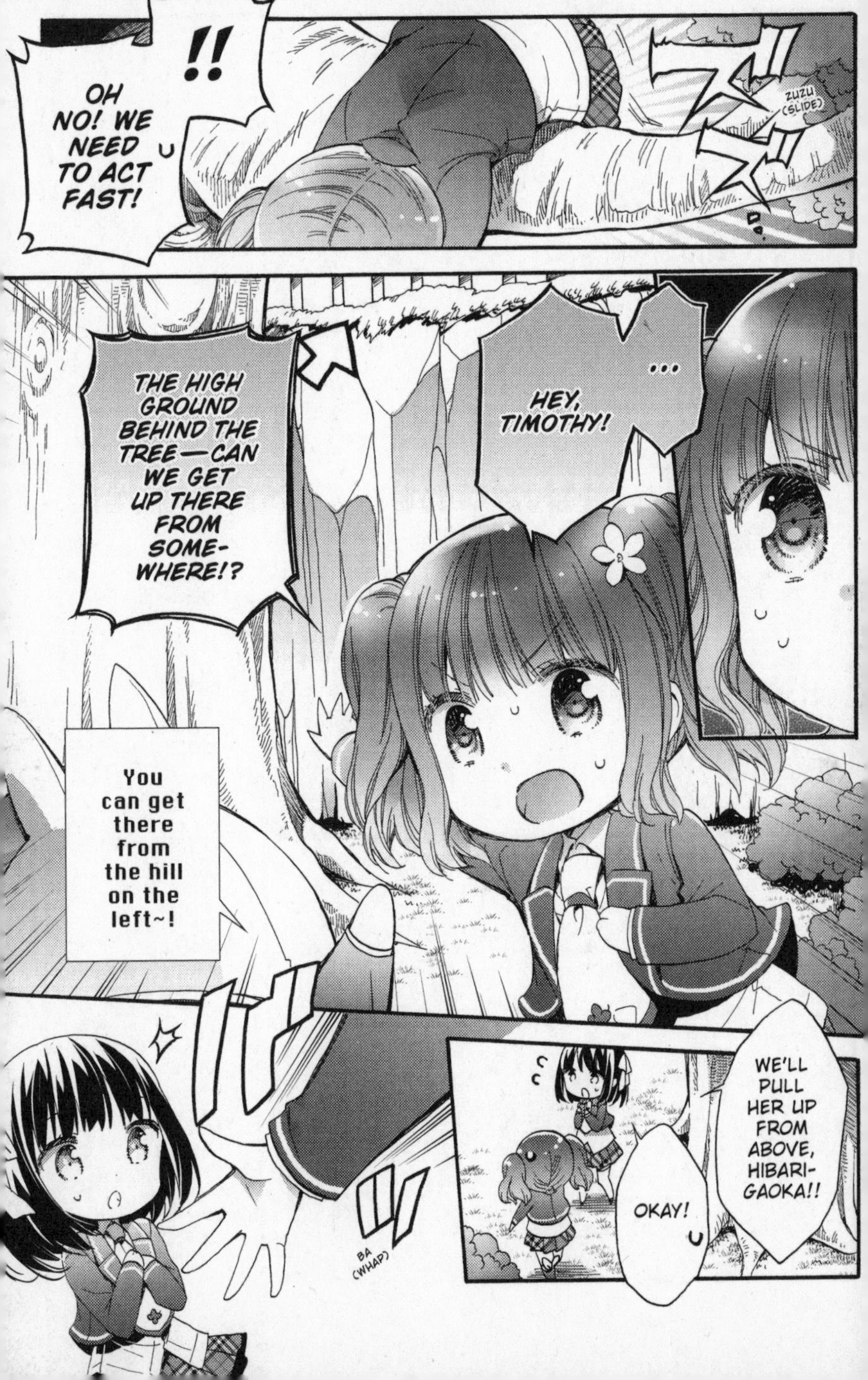
ZUZU (SLIDE)
!!
OH NO! WE NEED TO ACT FAST!
...
HEY, TIMOTHY!
THE HIGH GROUND BEHIND THE TREE—CAN WE GET UP THERE FROM SOME-WHERE!?
You can get there from the hill on the left~!
WE'LL PULL HER UP FROM ABOVE, HIBARI-GAOKA!!
OKAY!
BA (WHAP)

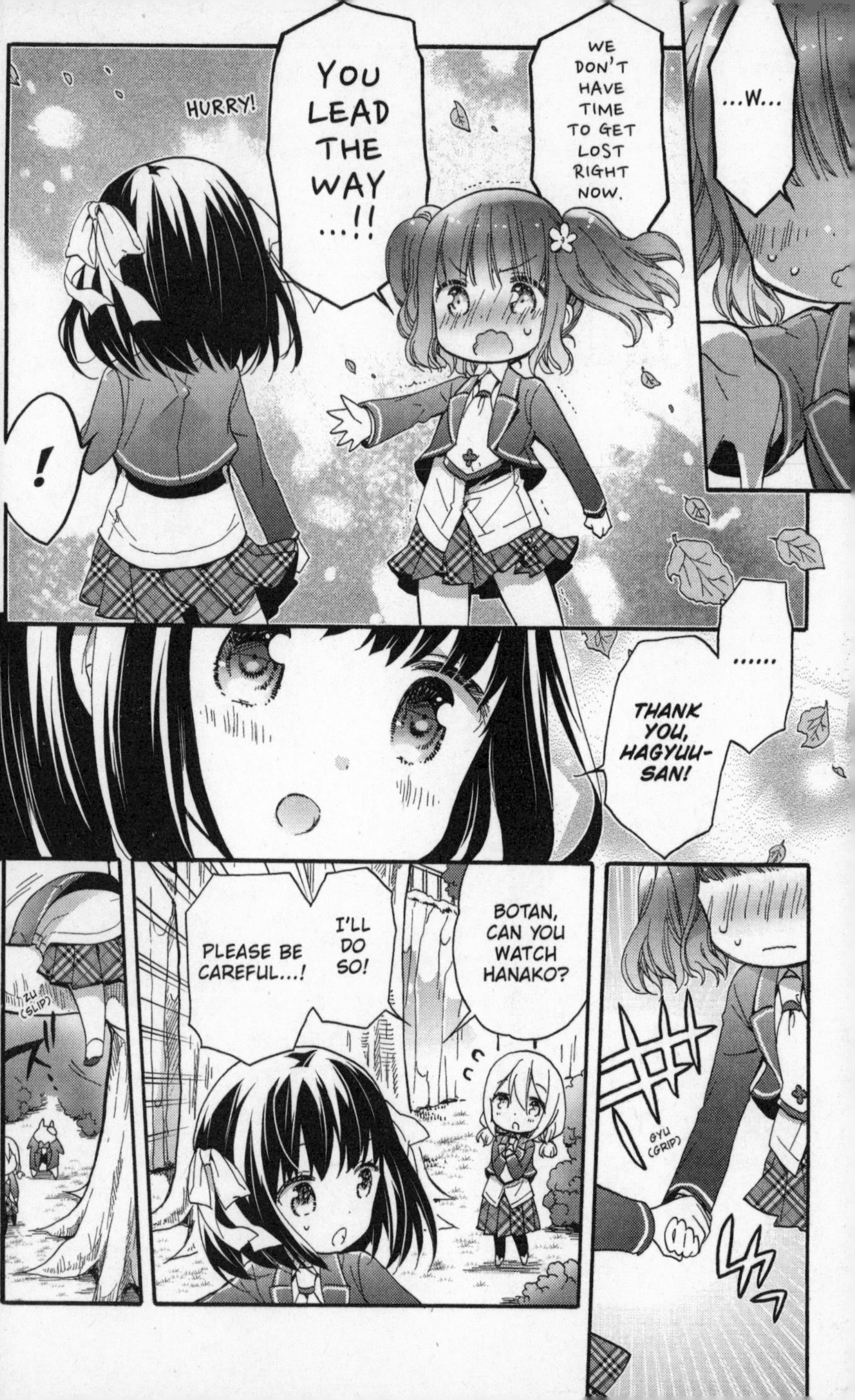
...W...
WE DON'T HAVE TIME TO GET LOST RIGHT NOW.
YOU LEAD THE WAY ...!!
HURRY!
!
......
THANK YOU, HAGYUU-SAN!
GYU (GRIP)
BOTAN, CAN YOU WATCH HANAKO?
I'LL DO SO!
PLEASE BE CAREFUL...!
ZU (SLIP)

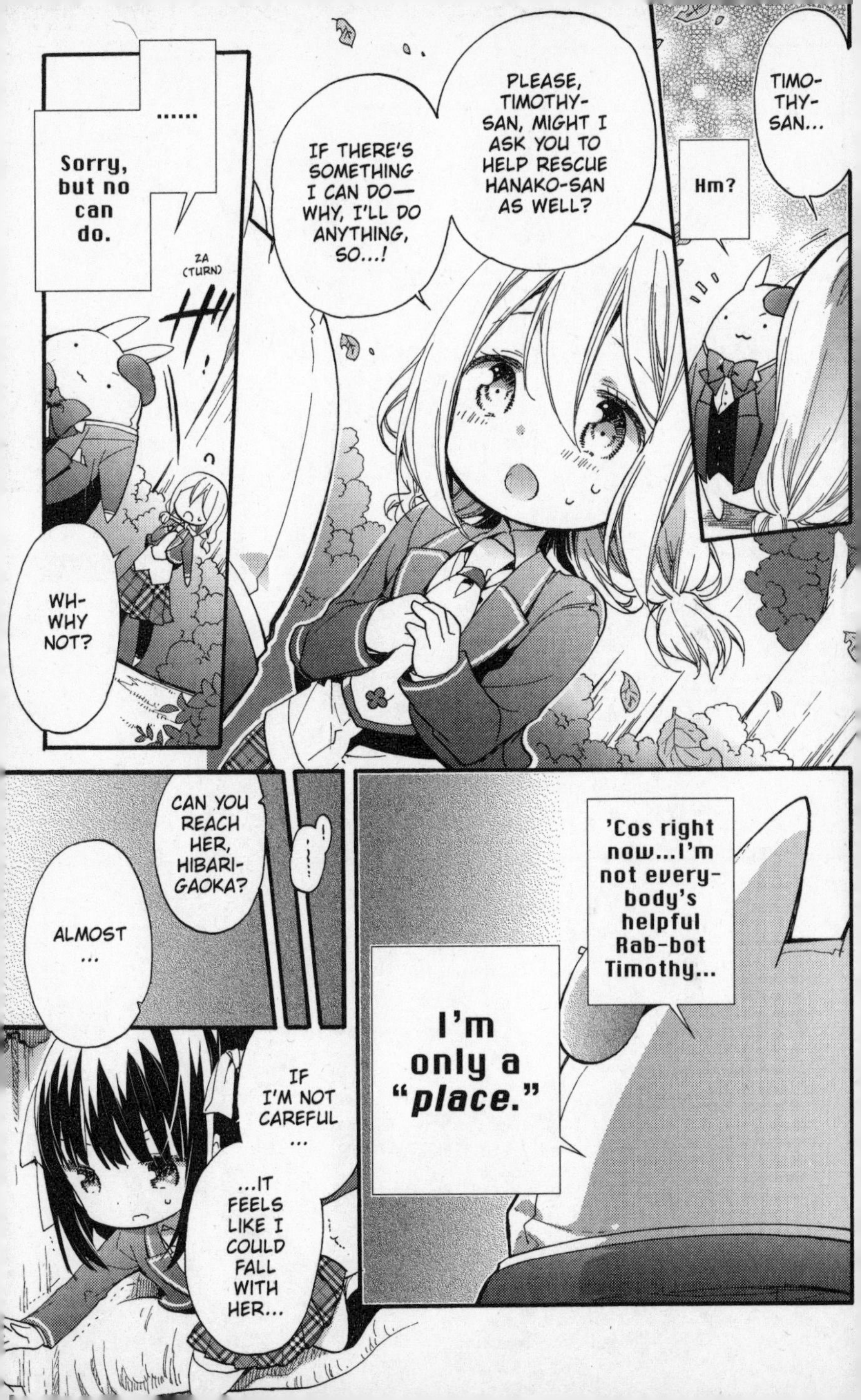
TIMO-THY-SAN...
Hm?
PLEASE, TIMOTHY-SAN, MIGHT I ASK YOU TO HELP RESCUE HANAKO-SAN AS WELL?
IF THERE'S SOMETHING I CAN DO—WHY, I'LL DO ANYTHING, SO...!
......
Sorry, but no can do.
ZA (TURN)
WH-WHY NOT?
'Cos right now...I'm not every-body's helpful Rab-bot Timothy...
I'm only a "*place*."
CAN YOU REACH HER, HIBARI-GAOKA?
!
ALMOST ...
IF I'M NOT CAREFUL ...
...IT FEELS LIKE I COULD FALL WITH HER...

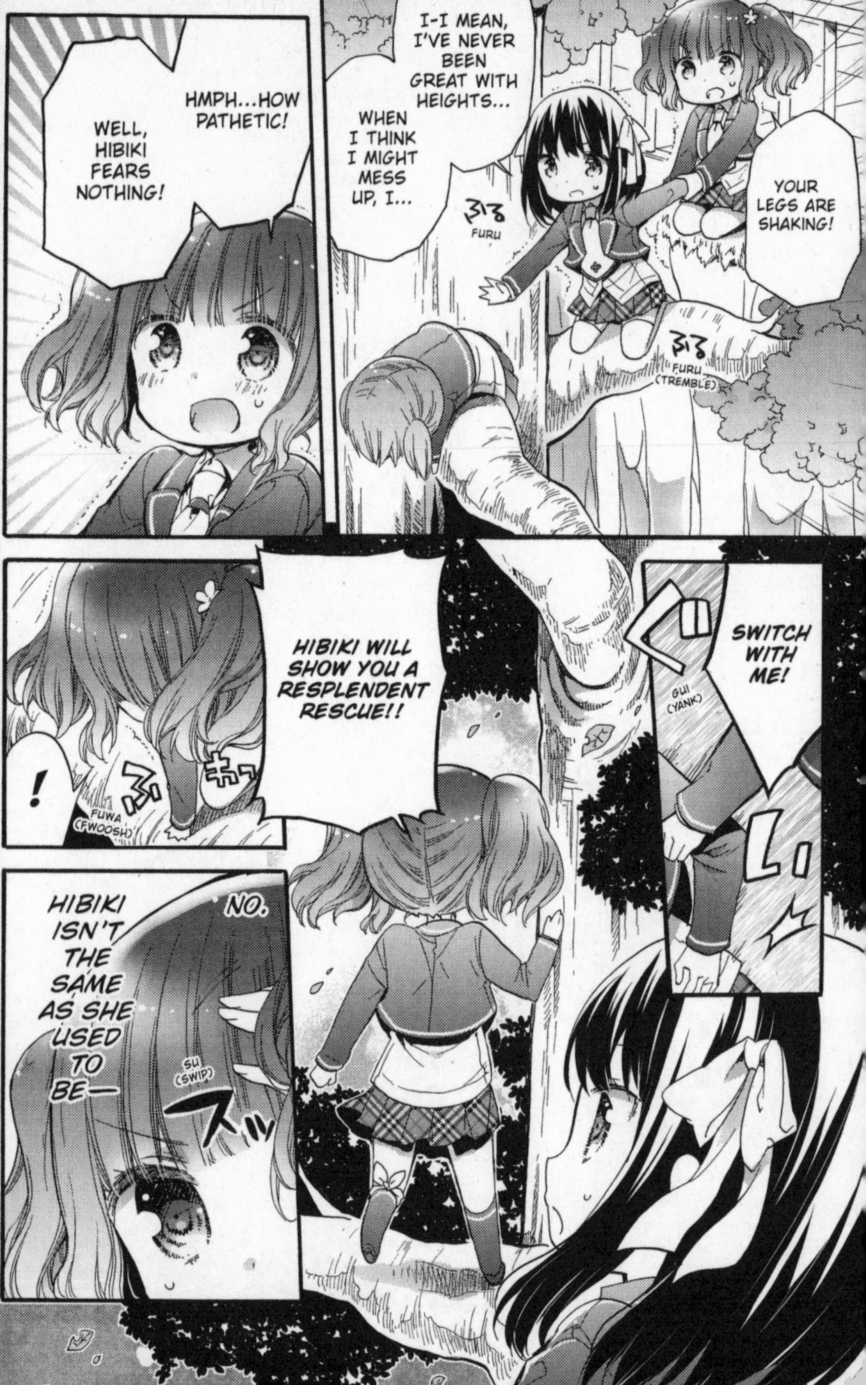
YOUR LEGS ARE SHAKING!
I-I MEAN, I'VE NEVER BEEN GREAT WITH HEIGHTS...
WHEN I THINK I MIGHT MESS UP, I...
ふる
FURU
ふる
FURU (TREMBLE)
HMPH...HOW PATHETIC!
WELL, HIBIKI FEARS NOTHING!
SWITCH WITH ME!
ぐい
GUI (YANK)
HIBIKI WILL SHOW YOU A RESPLENDENT RESCUE!!
!
ふわっ
FUWA (FWOOSH)
NO.
HIBIKI ISN'T THE SAME AS SHE USED TO BE—
スッ
SU (SWIP)

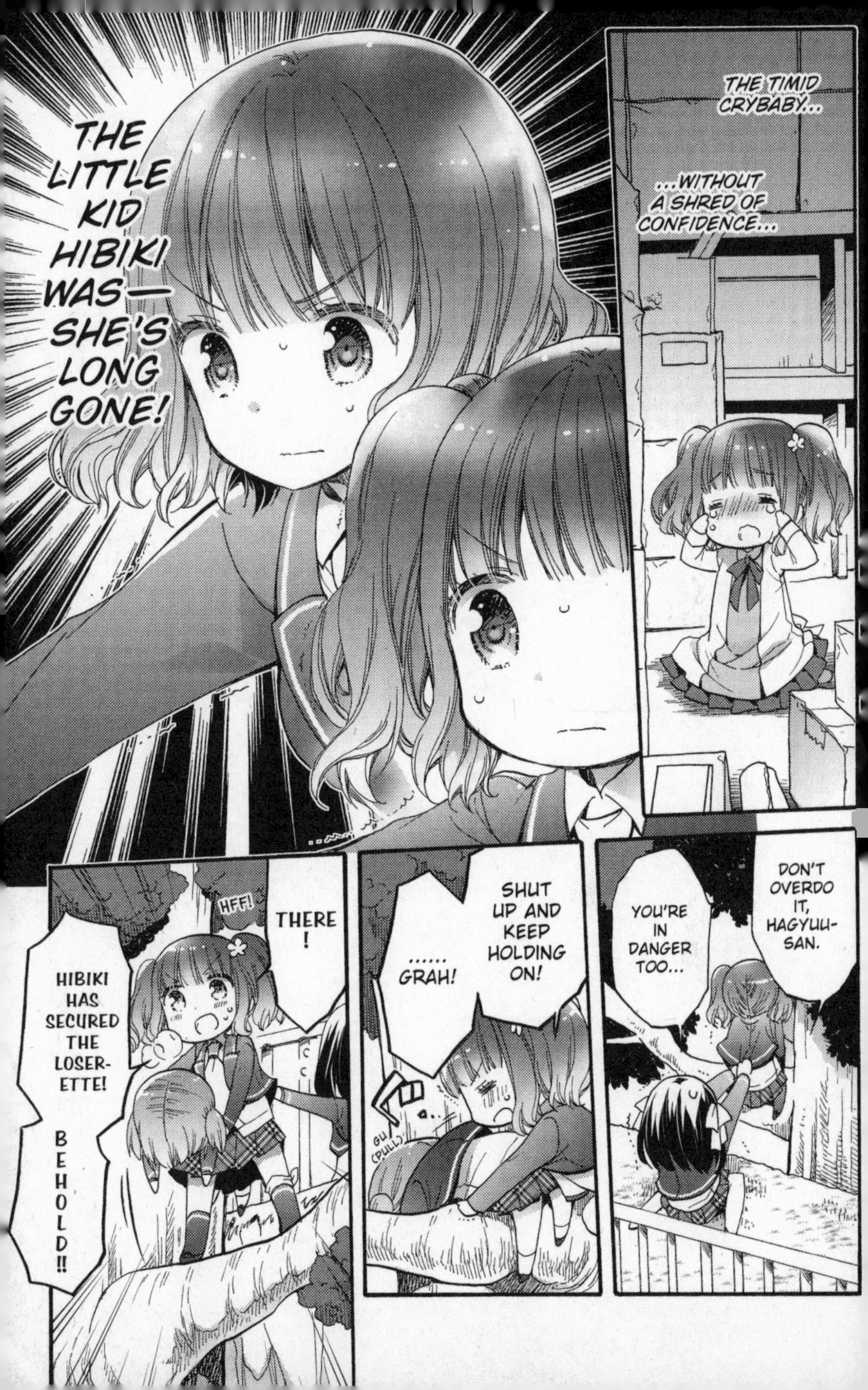
THE TIMID CRYBABY...
...WITHOUT A SHRED OF CONFIDENCE...
THE LITTLE KID HIBIKI WAS—SHE'S LONG GONE!
DON'T OVERDO IT, HAGYUU-SAN.
YOU'RE IN DANGER TOO...
SHUT UP AND KEEP HOLDING ON!
......GRAH!
GU (PULL)
THERE!
HFF!
HIBIKI HAS SECURED THE LOSER-ETTE!
BEHOLD!!

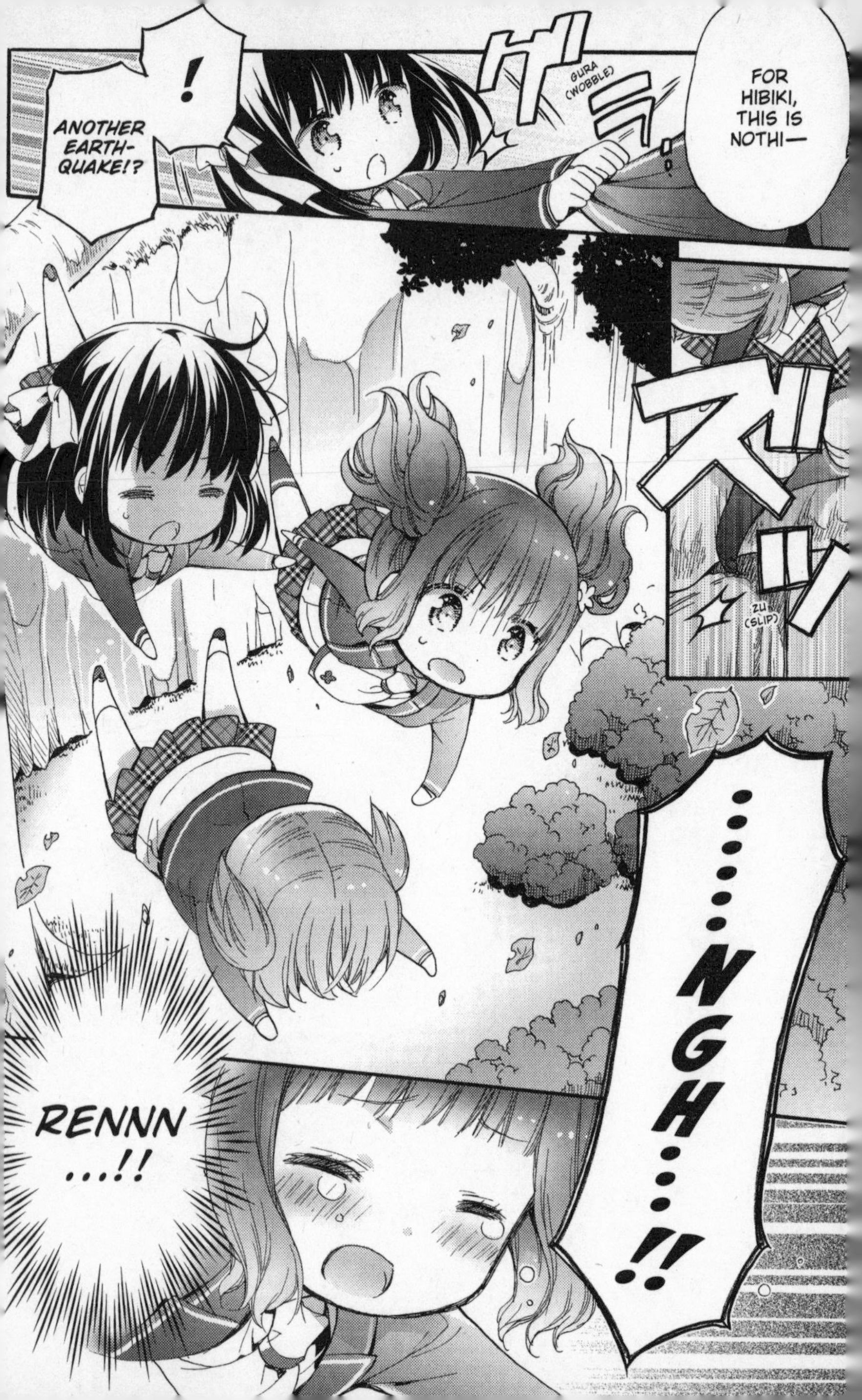
FOR HIBIKI, THIS IS NOTHI—
GURA (WOBBLE)
!
ANOTHER EARTH-QUAKE!?
ZU (SLIP)
......NGH...!!
RENNN ...!!

AnneHappy
unhappy go lucky!

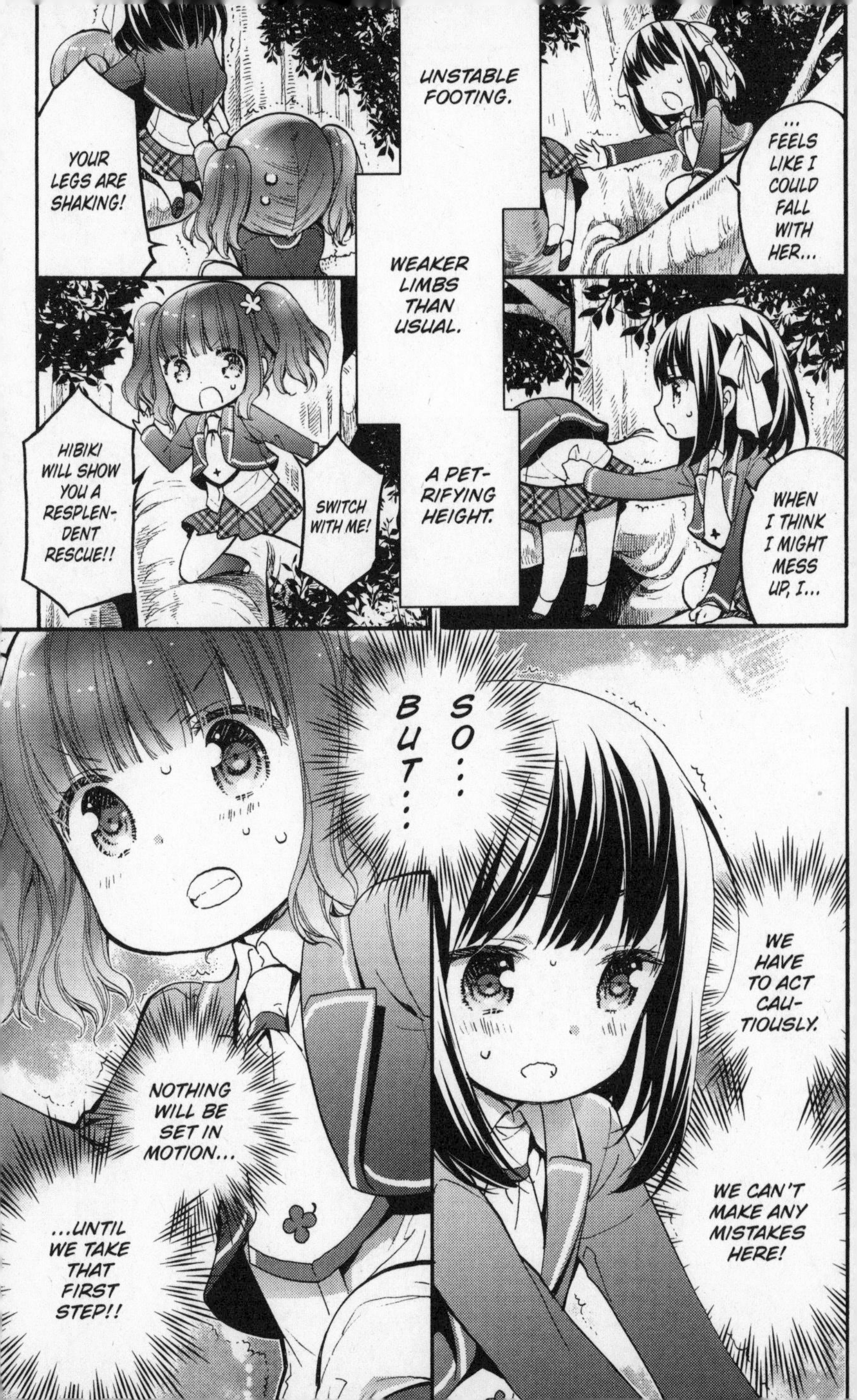
... FEELS LIKE I COULD FALL WITH HER...
WHEN I THINK I MIGHT MESS UP, I...
UNSTABLE FOOTING.
WEAKER LIMBS THAN USUAL.
A PET-RIFYING HEIGHT.
YOUR LEGS ARE SHAKING!
SWITCH WITH ME!
HIBIKI WILL SHOW YOU A RESPLEN-DENT RESCUE!!
WE HAVE TO ACT CAU-TIOUSLY.
SO...
WE CAN'T MAKE ANY MISTAKES HERE!
BUT...
NOTHING WILL BE SET IN MOTION...
...UNTIL WE TAKE THAT FIRST STEP!!

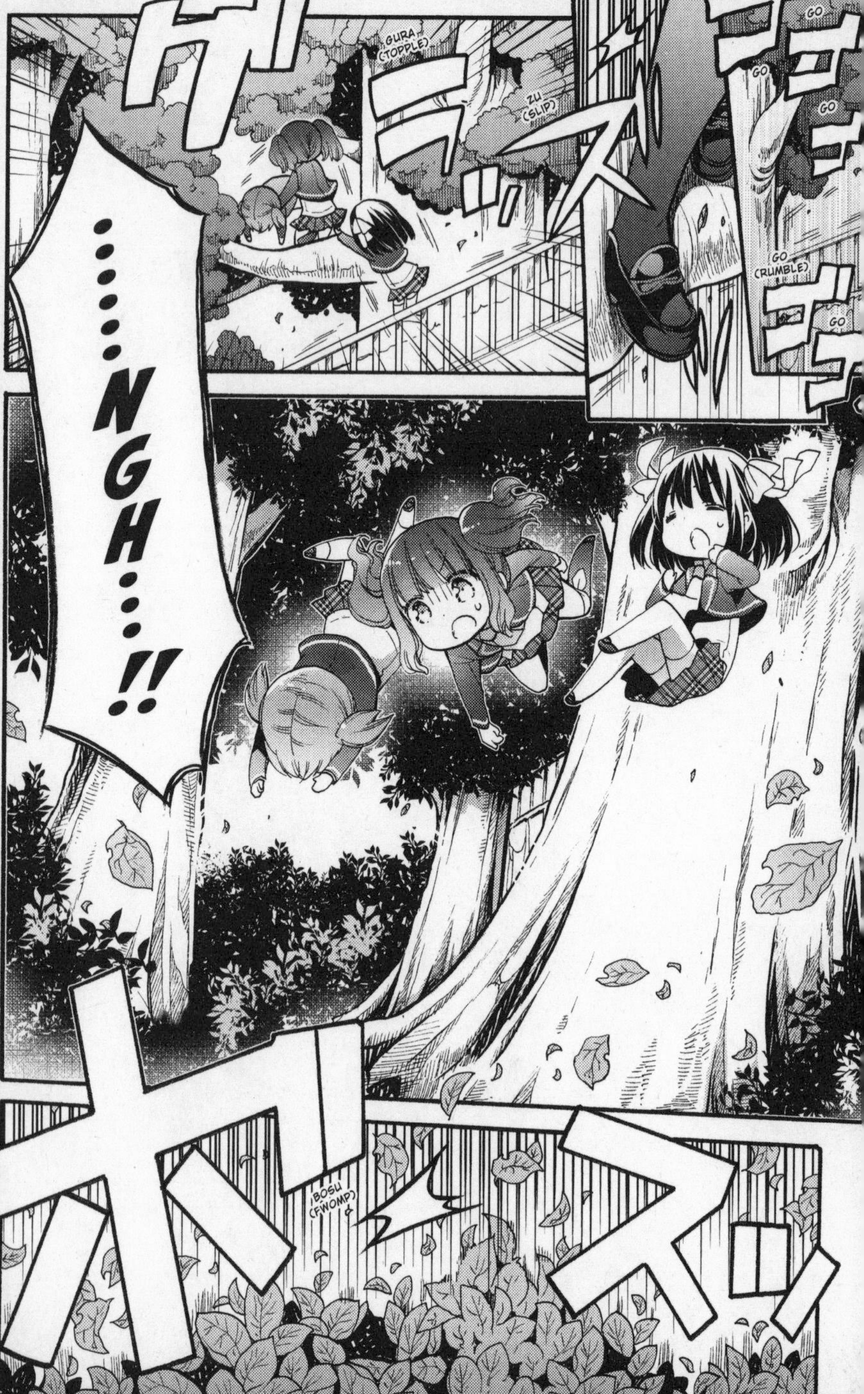
GO
GO
GO
GO
(RUMBLE)
GO
GURA
(TOPPLE)
ZU
(SLIP)
......NGH...!!
BOSU
(FWOMP)

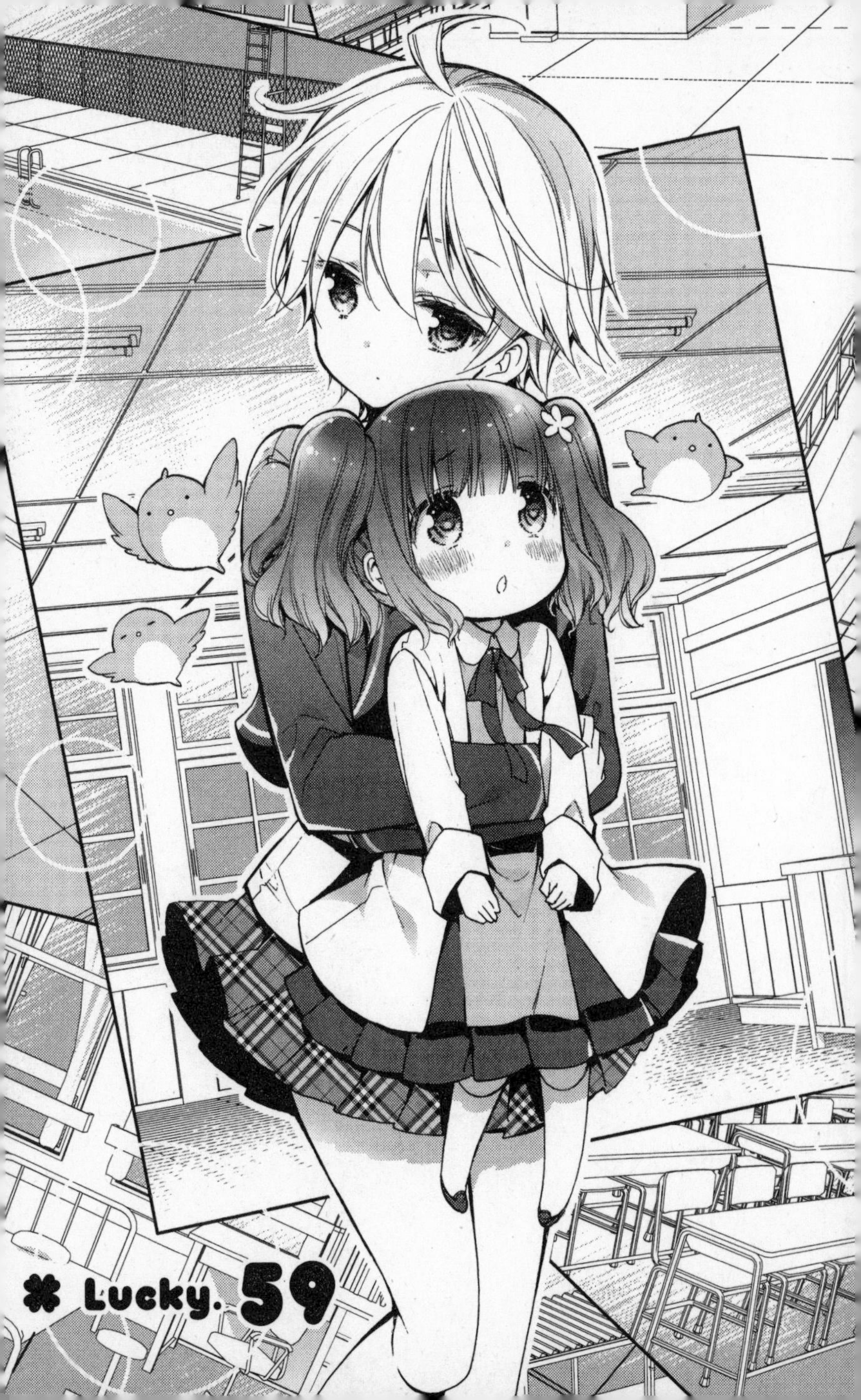
Lucky. 59

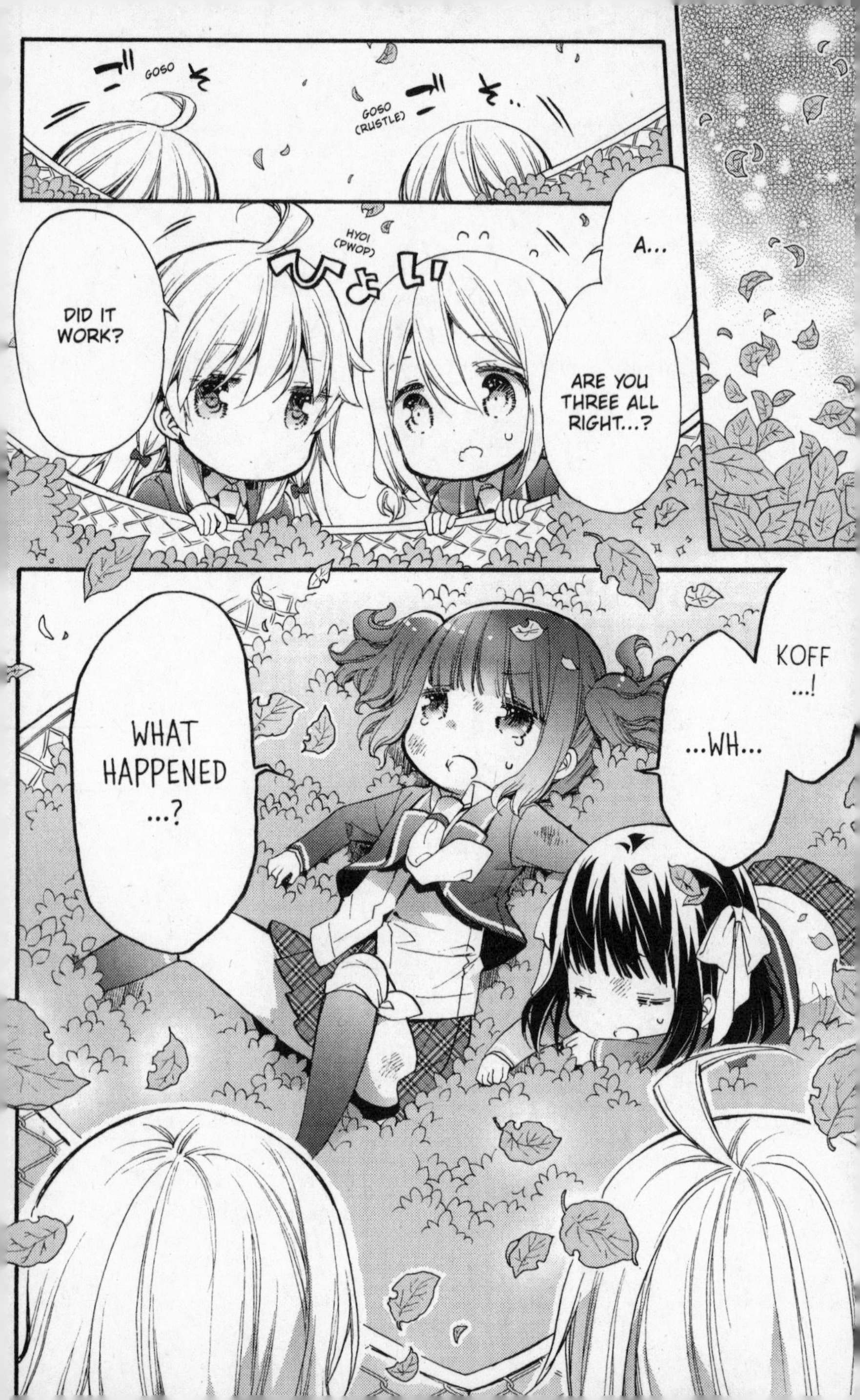
GOSO (RUSTLE)
GOSO
A...
ARE YOU THREE ALL RIGHT...?
HYOI (PWOP)
DID IT WORK?
KOFF ...!
...WH...
WHAT HAPPENED ...?

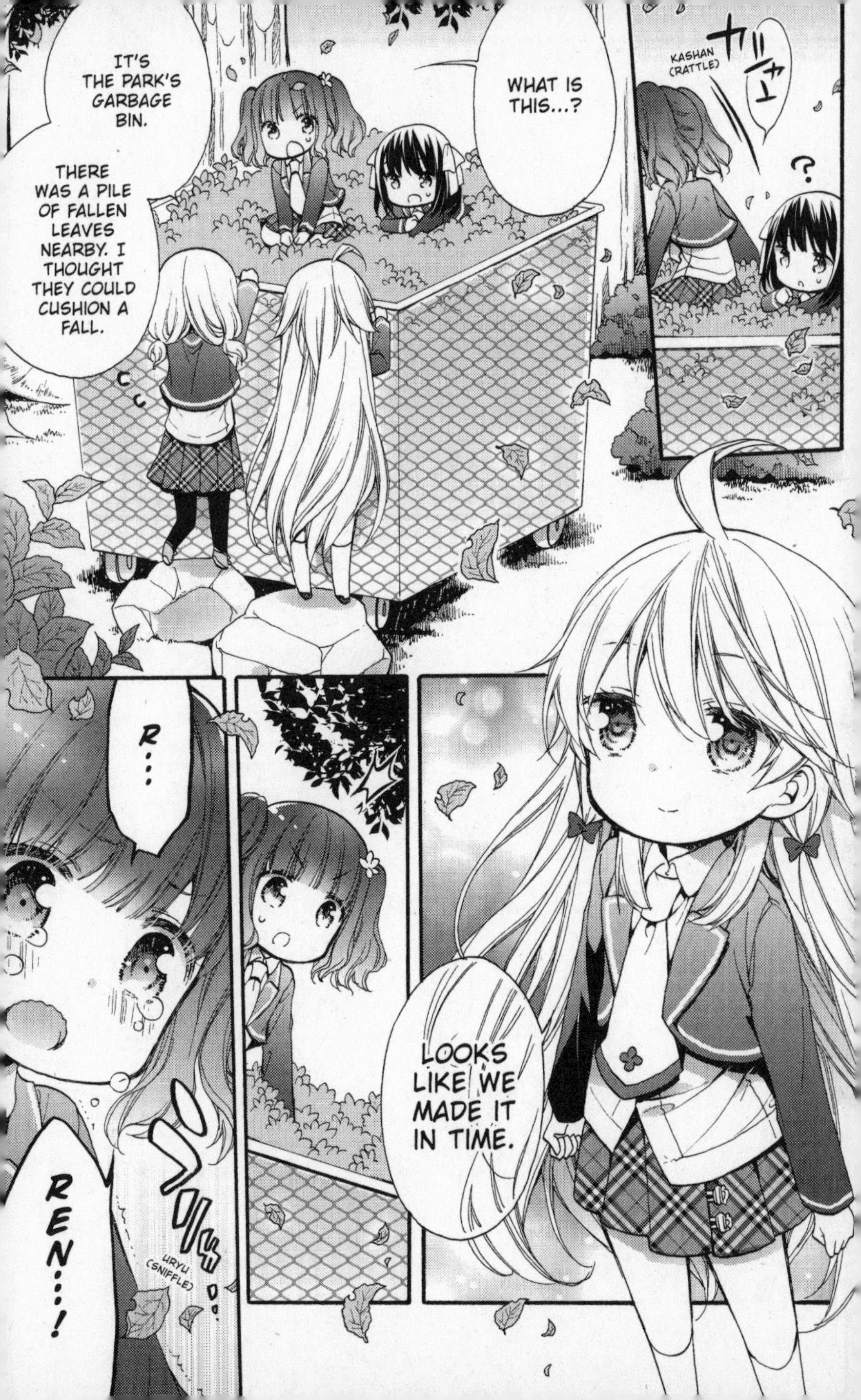
KASHAN (RATTLE)
?
WHAT IS THIS...?
IT'S THE PARK'S GARBAGE BIN.
THERE WAS A PILE OF FALLEN LEAVES NEARBY. I THOUGHT THEY COULD CUSHION A FALL.
LOOKS LIKE WE MADE IT IN TIME.
R...
URYU (SNIFFLE)
REN...!

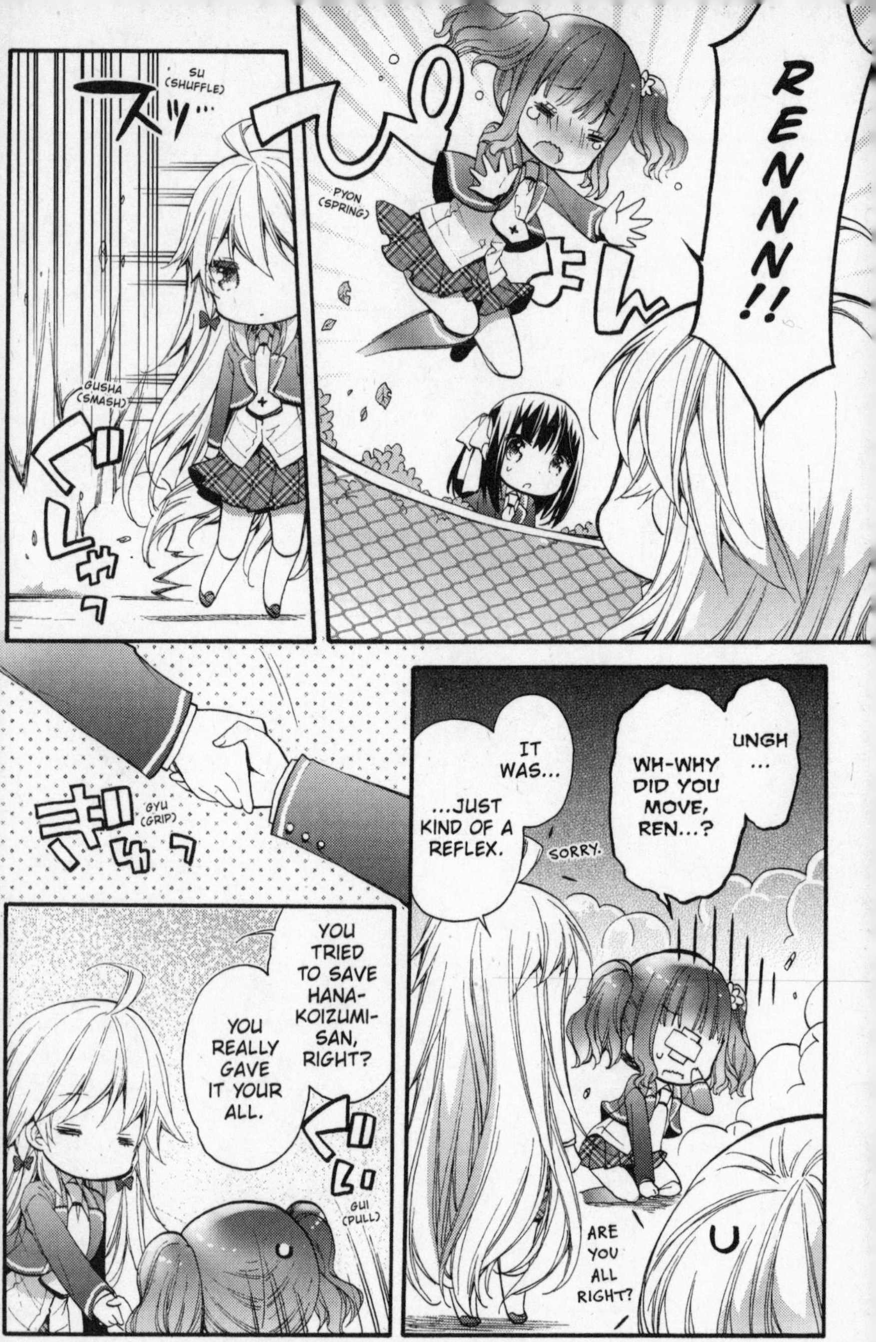
RENNNN!!
PYON (SPRING)
SU (SHUFFLE)
GUSHA (SMASH)
UNGH ...
WH-WHY DID YOU MOVE, REN...?
IT WAS...
...JUST KIND OF A REFLEX.
SORRY.
ARE YOU ALL RIGHT?
GYU (GRIP)
YOU TRIED TO SAVE HANA-KOIZUMI-SAN, RIGHT?
YOU REALLY GAVE IT YOUR ALL.
GUI (PULL)

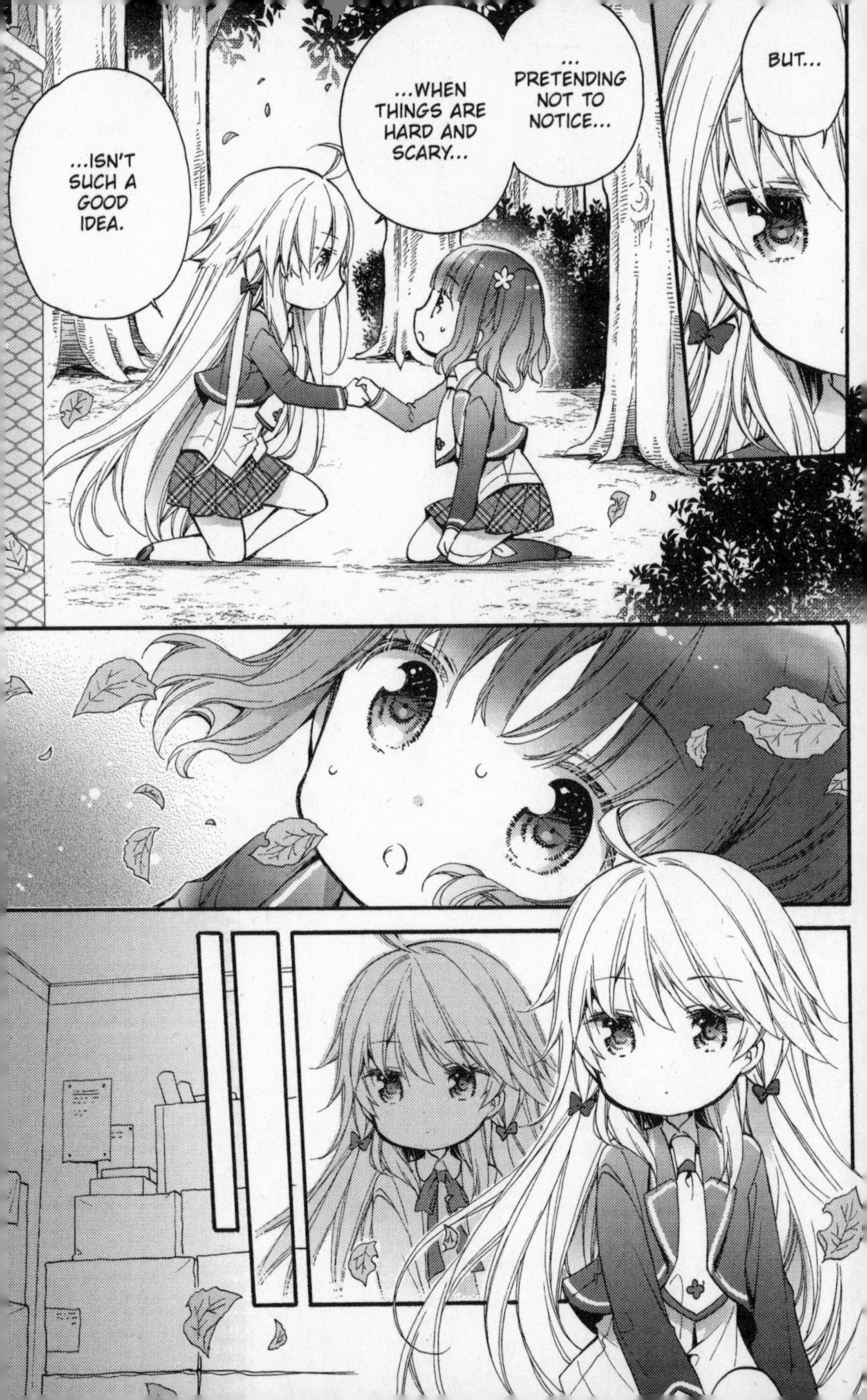
BUT...
...PRETENDING NOT TO NOTICE...
...WHEN THINGS ARE HARD AND SCARY...
...ISN'T SUCH A GOOD IDEA.

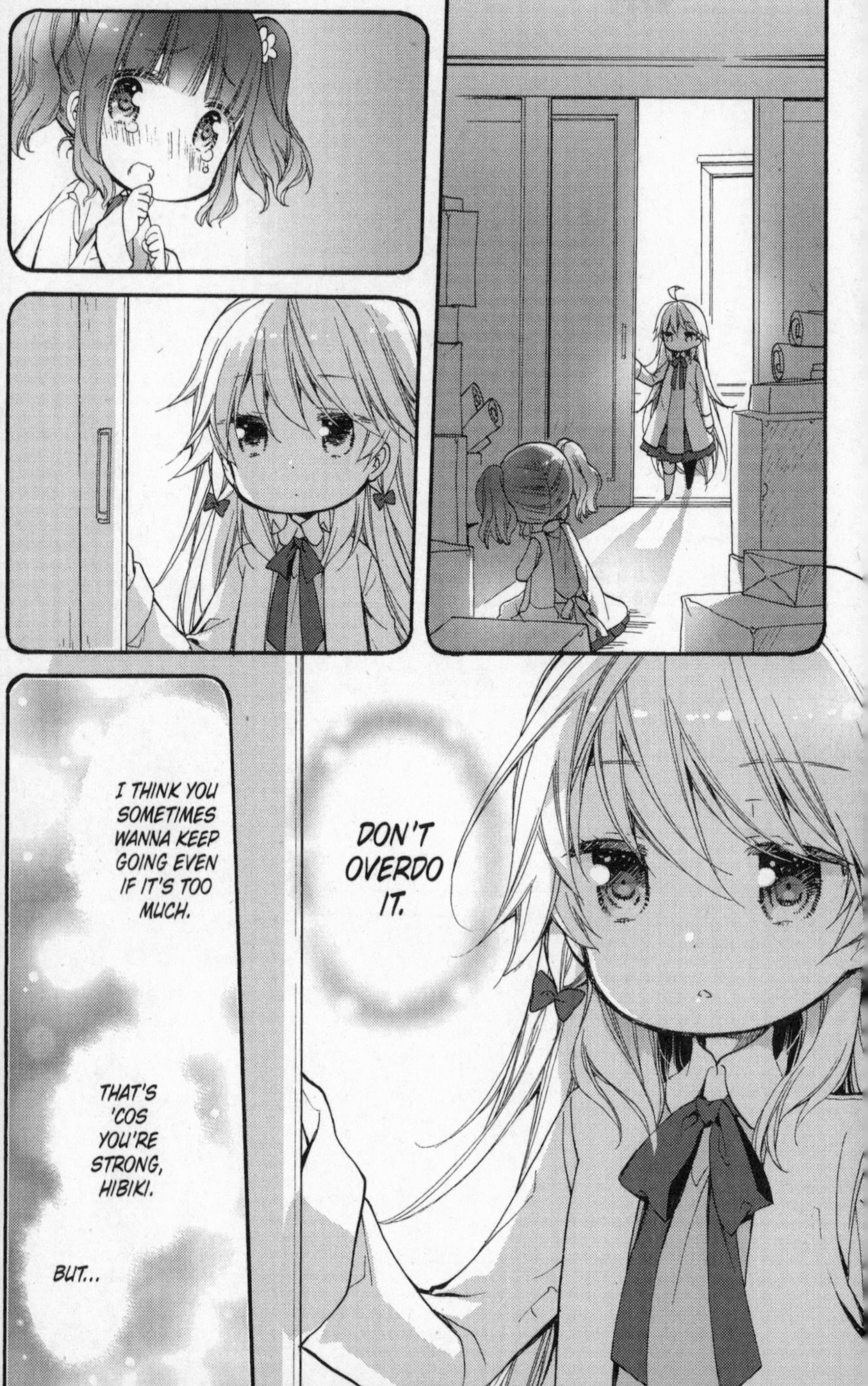
DON'T OVERDO IT.
I THINK YOU SOMETIMES WANNA KEEP GOING EVEN IF IT'S TOO MUCH.
THAT'S 'COS YOU'RE STRONG, HIBIKI.
BUT...

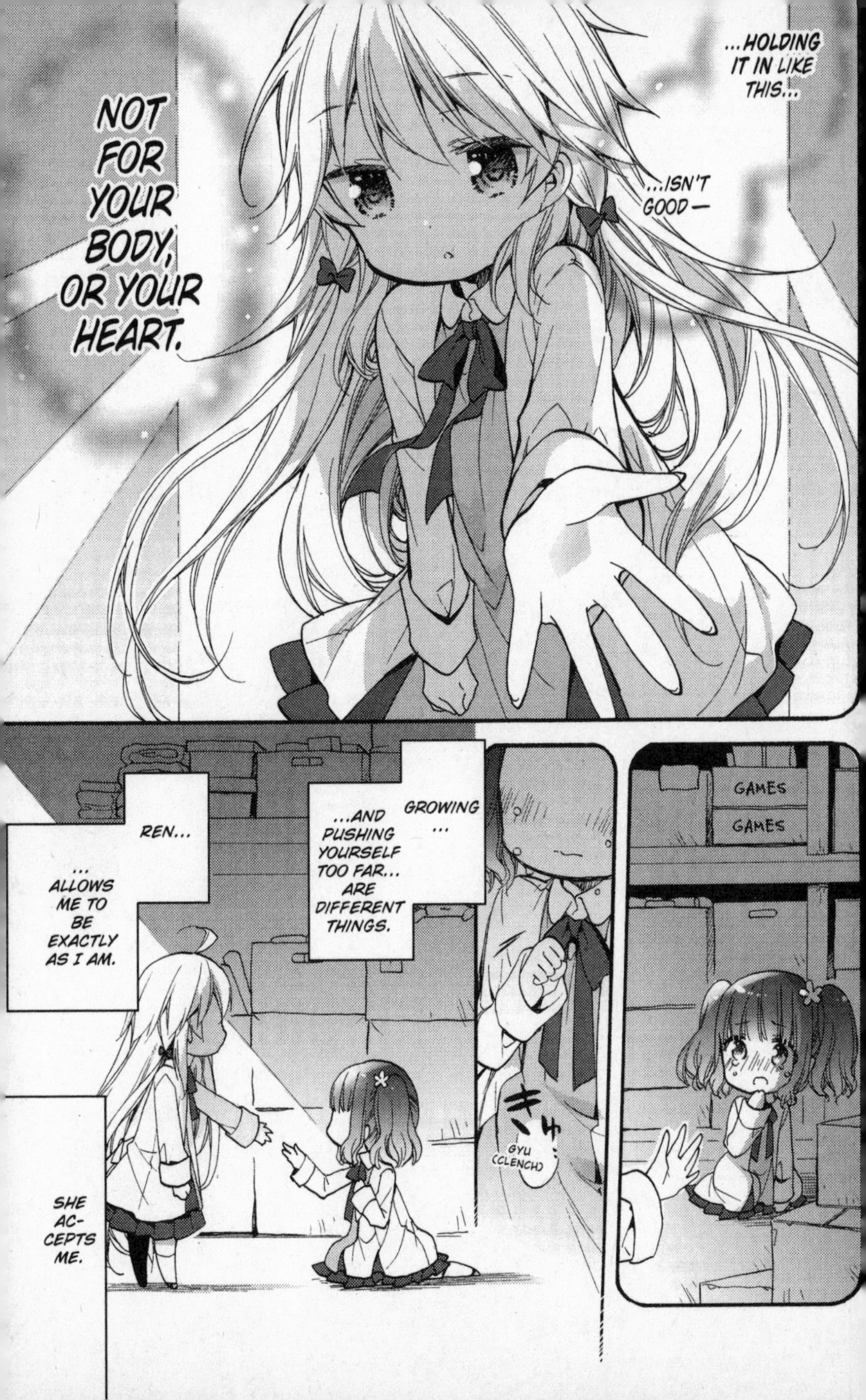
...HOLDING IT IN LIKE THIS...
...ISN'T GOOD—
NOT FOR YOUR BODY, OR YOUR HEART.
GAMES
GAMES
GYU (CLENCH)
GROWING...
...AND PUSHING YOURSELF TOO FAR... ARE DIFFERENT THINGS.
REN...
...ALLOWS ME TO BE EXACTLY AS I AM.
SHE ACCEPTS ME.

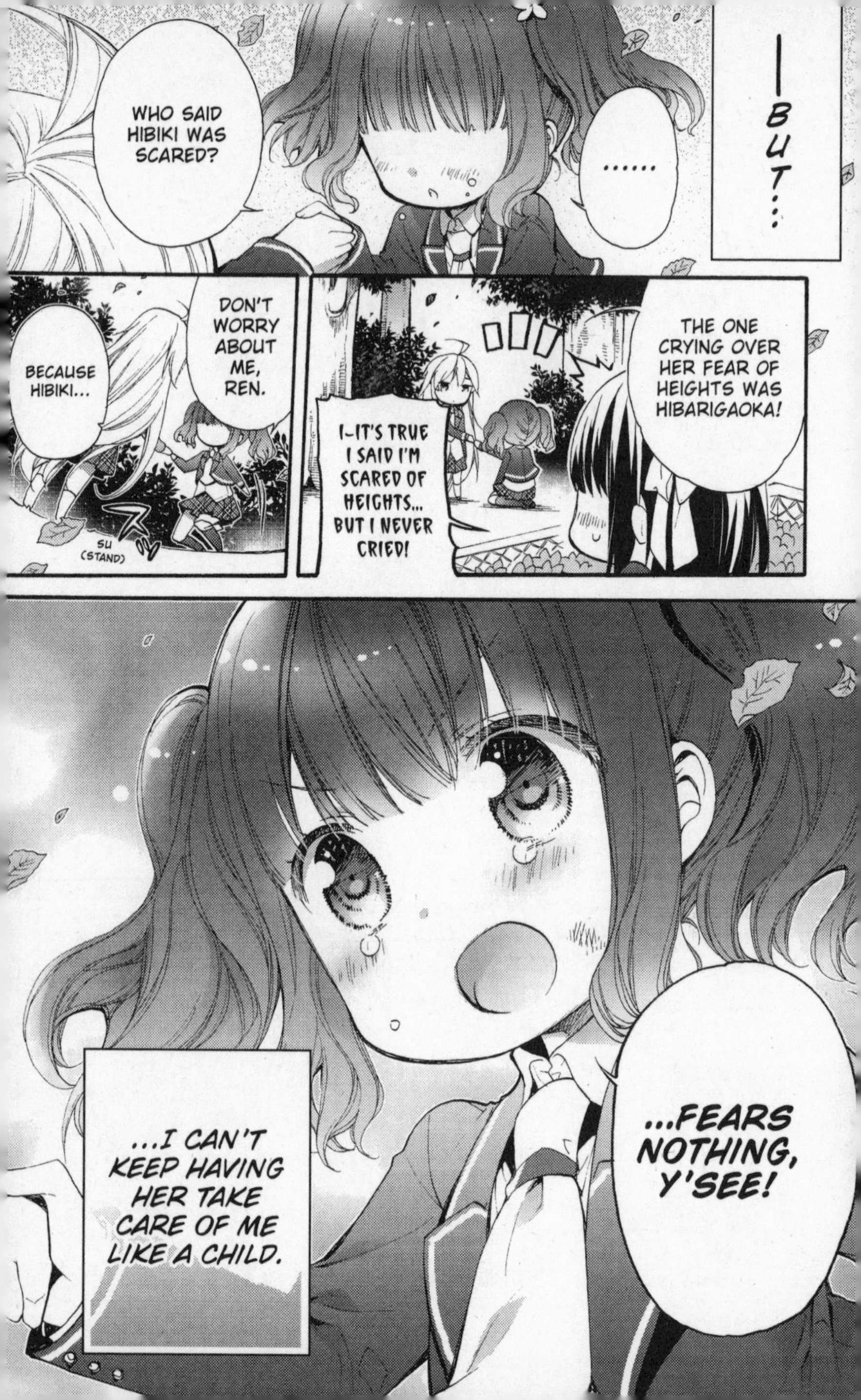
—BUT...
......
WHO SAID HIBIKI WAS SCARED?
THE ONE CRYING OVER HER FEAR OF HEIGHTS WAS HIBARIGAOKA!
I-IT'S TRUE I SAID I'M SCARED OF HEIGHTS... BUT I NEVER CRIED!
DON'T WORRY ABOUT ME, REN.
BECAUSE HIBIKI...
SU (STAND)
...FEARS NOTHING, Y'SEE!
...I CAN'T KEEP HAVING HER TAKE CARE OF ME LIKE A CHILD.

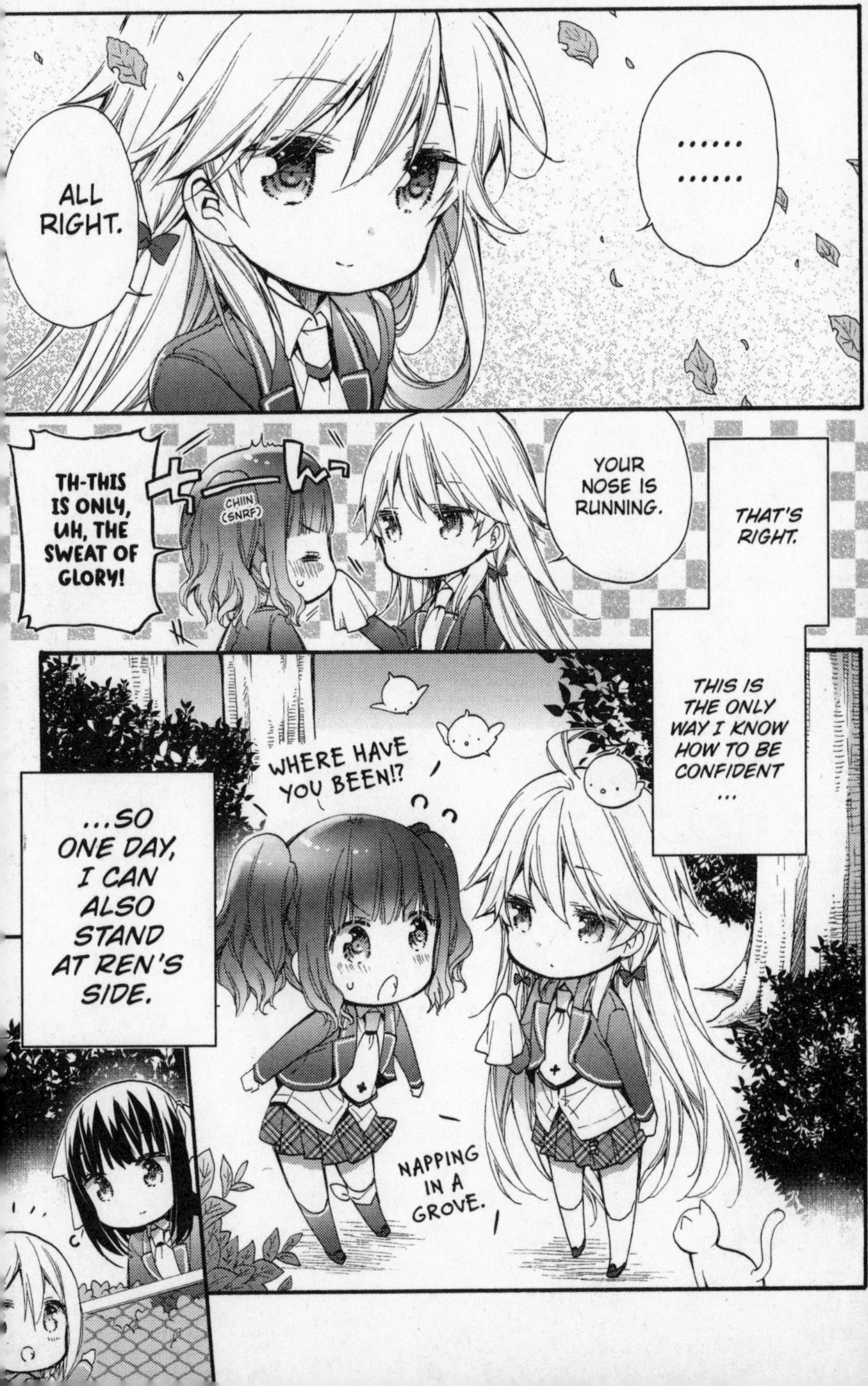
……
……
ALL RIGHT.
THAT'S RIGHT.
YOUR NOSE IS RUNNING.
CHIIN (SNRF)
TH-THIS IS ONLY, UH, THE SWEAT OF GLORY!
THIS IS THE ONLY WAY I KNOW HOW TO BE CONFIDENT ...
WHERE HAVE YOU BEEN!?
...SO ONE DAY, I CAN ALSO STAND AT REN'S SIDE.
NAPPING IN A GROVE.

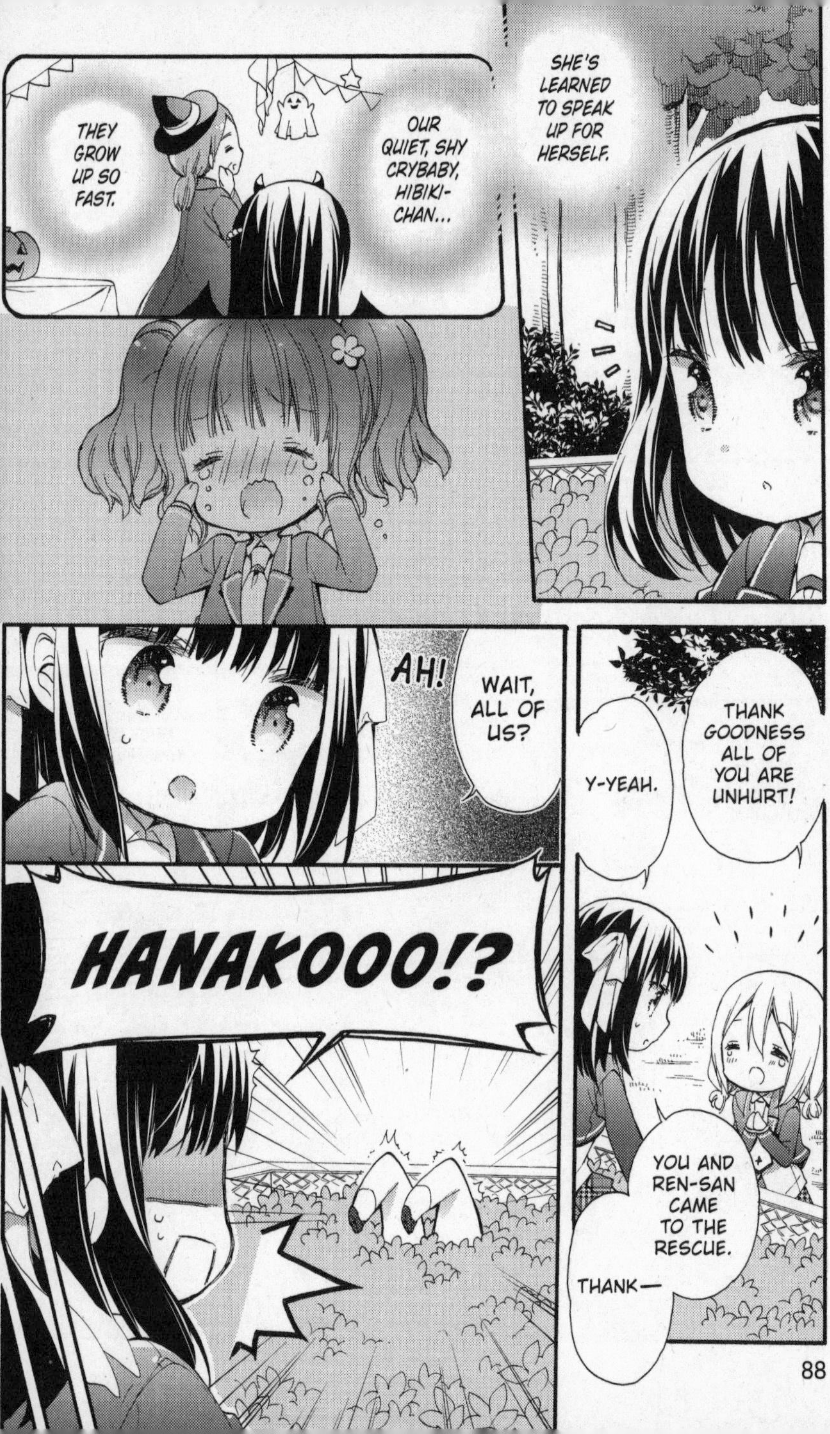

SHE'S LEARNED TO SPEAK UP FOR HERSELF.
OUR QUIET, SHY CRYBABY, HIBIKI-CHAN...
THEY GROW UP SO FAST.
THANK GOODNESS ALL OF YOU ARE UNHURT!
Y-YEAH.
YOU AND REN-SAN CAME TO THE RESCUE.
THANK—
WAIT, ALL OF US?
AH!
HANAKOOO!?

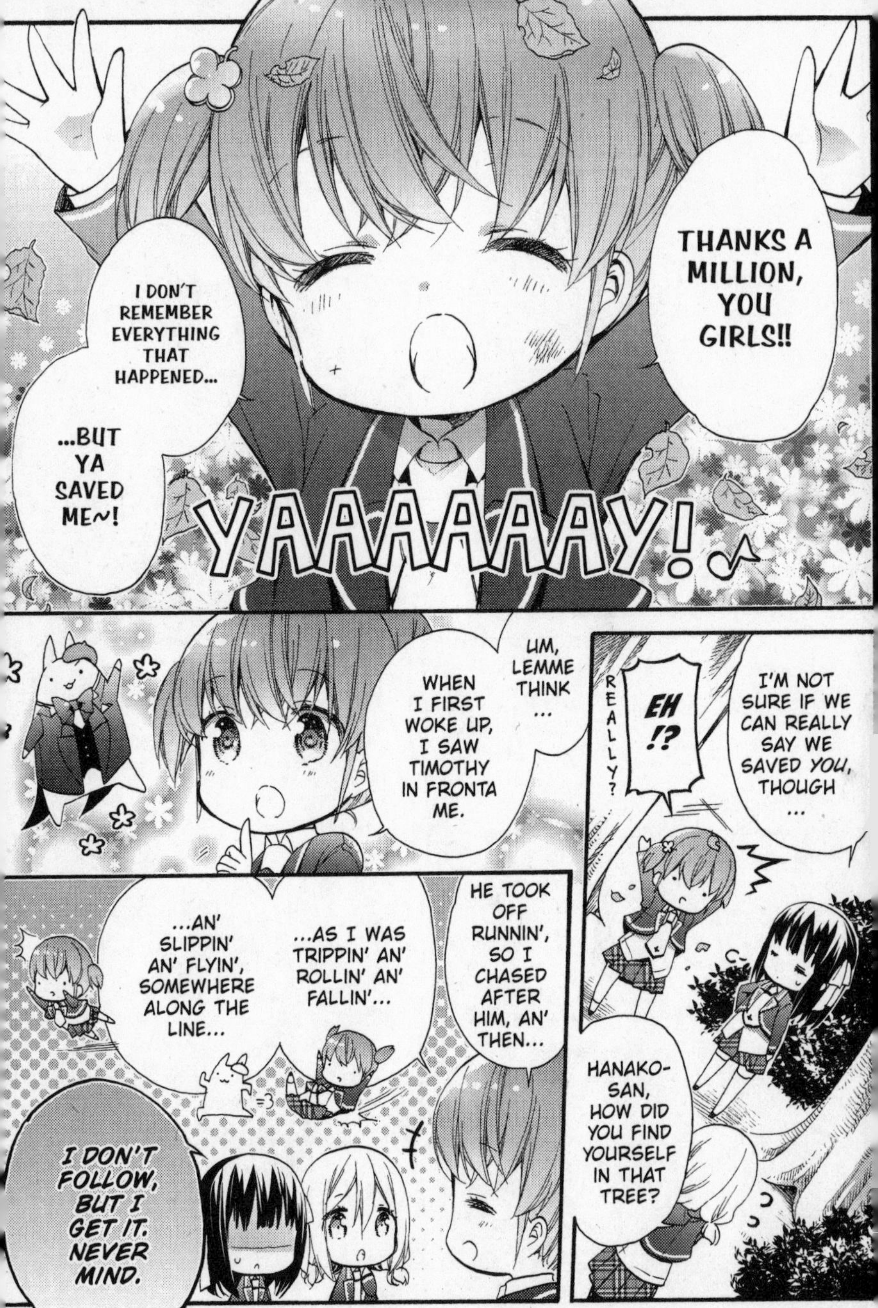
THANKS A MILLION, YOU GIRLS!!
I DON'T REMEMBER EVERYTHING THAT HAPPENED...
...BUT YA SAVED ME~!
YAAAAAAY!♪
I'M NOT SURE IF WE CAN REALLY SAY WE SAVED *YOU*, THOUGH...
EH!?
REALLY?
HANAKO-SAN, HOW DID YOU FIND YOURSELF IN THAT TREE?
UM, LEMME THINK...
WHEN I FIRST WOKE UP, I SAW TIMOTHY IN FRONTA ME.
HE TOOK OFF RUNNIN', SO I CHASED AFTER HIM, AN' THEN...
...AS I WAS TRIPPIN' AN' ROLLIN' AN' FALLIN'...
...AN' SLIPPIN' AN' FLYIN', SOMEWHERE ALONG THE LINE...
I DON'T FOLLOW, BUT I GET IT. NEVER MIND.

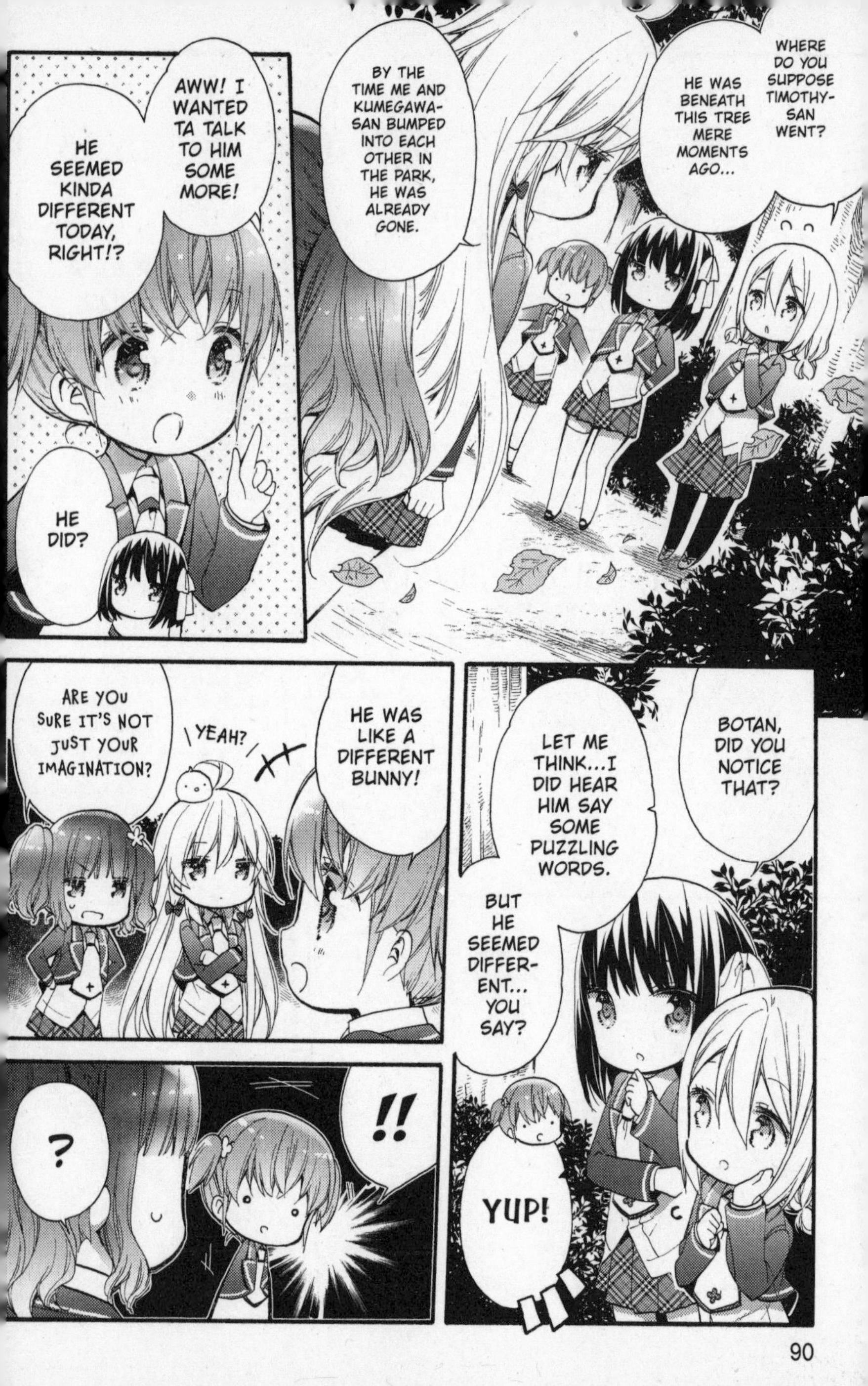
WHERE DO YOU SUPPOSE TIMOTHY-SAN WENT?
HE WAS BENEATH THIS TREE MERE MOMENTS AGO...
BY THE TIME ME AND KUMEGAWA-SAN BUMPED INTO EACH OTHER IN THE PARK, HE WAS ALREADY GONE.
AWW! I WANTED TA TALK TO HIM SOME MORE!
HE SEEMED KINDA DIFFERENT TODAY, RIGHT!?
HE DID?
BOTAN, DID YOU NOTICE THAT?
LET ME THINK...I DID HEAR HIM SAY SOME PUZZLING WORDS.
BUT HE SEEMED DIFFERENT... YOU SAY?
YUP!
HE WAS LIKE A DIFFERENT BUNNY!
YEAH?
ARE YOU SURE IT'S NOT JUST YOUR IMAGINATION?
!!
?

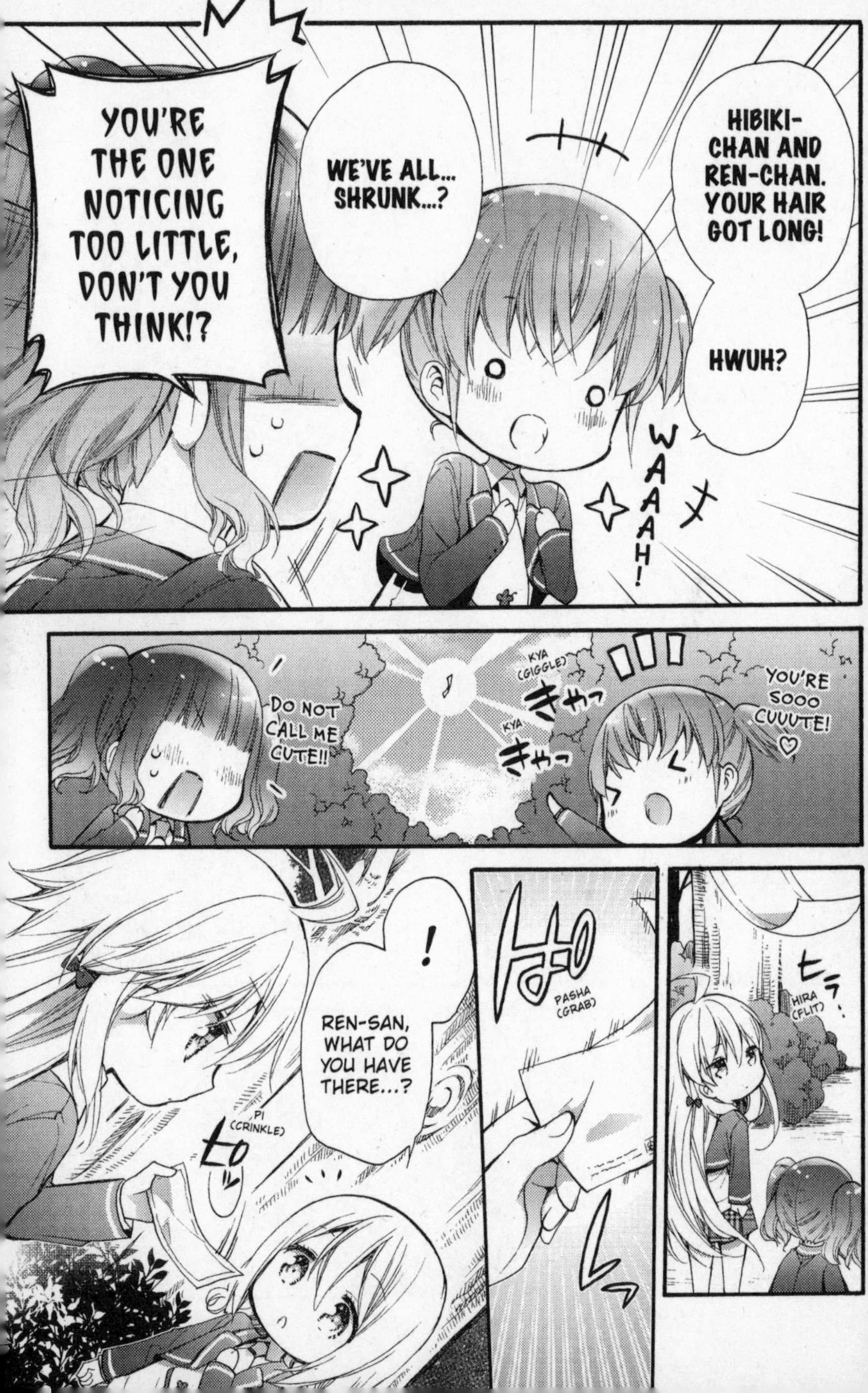
HIBIKI-CHAN AND REN-CHAN. YOUR HAIR GOT LONG!
HWUH?
WAAAAH!
WE'VE ALL... SHRUNK...?
YOU'RE THE ONE NOTICING TOO LITTLE, DON'T YOU THINK!?
YOU'RE SOOO CUUUTE! ♡
KYA (GIGGLE)
きゃっ
KYA
きゃっ
DO NOT CALL ME CUTE!!
ヒラ
HIRA (FLIT)
はっ
PASHA (GRAB)
!
REN-SAN, WHAT DO YOU HAVE THERE...?
PI (CRINKLE)
ピッ

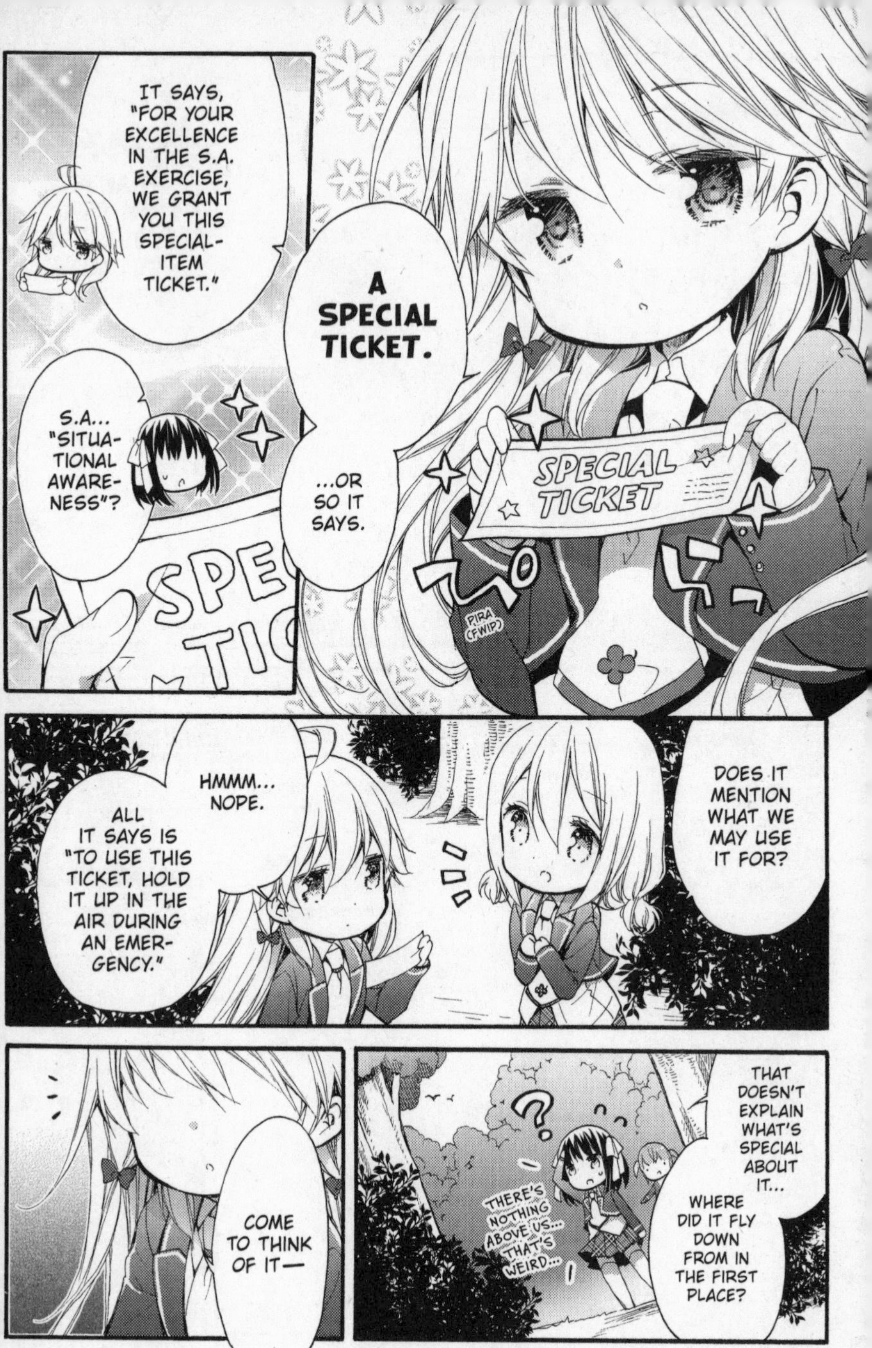
A SPECIAL TICKET.
...OR SO IT SAYS.
SPECIAL TICKET
PIRA (FWIP)
IT SAYS, "FOR YOUR EXCELLENCE IN THE S.A. EXERCISE, WE GRANT YOU THIS SPECIAL-ITEM TICKET."
S.A... "SITUATIONAL AWARENESS"?
SPEC TIC
DOES IT MENTION WHAT WE MAY USE IT FOR?
HMMM... NOPE.
ALL IT SAYS IS "TO USE THIS TICKET, HOLD IT UP IN THE AIR DURING AN EMERGENCY."
THAT DOESN'T EXPLAIN WHAT'S SPECIAL ABOUT IT...
WHERE DID IT FLY DOWN FROM IN THE FIRST PLACE?
THERE'S NOTHING ABOVE US... THAT'S WEIRD...
COME TO THINK OF IT—

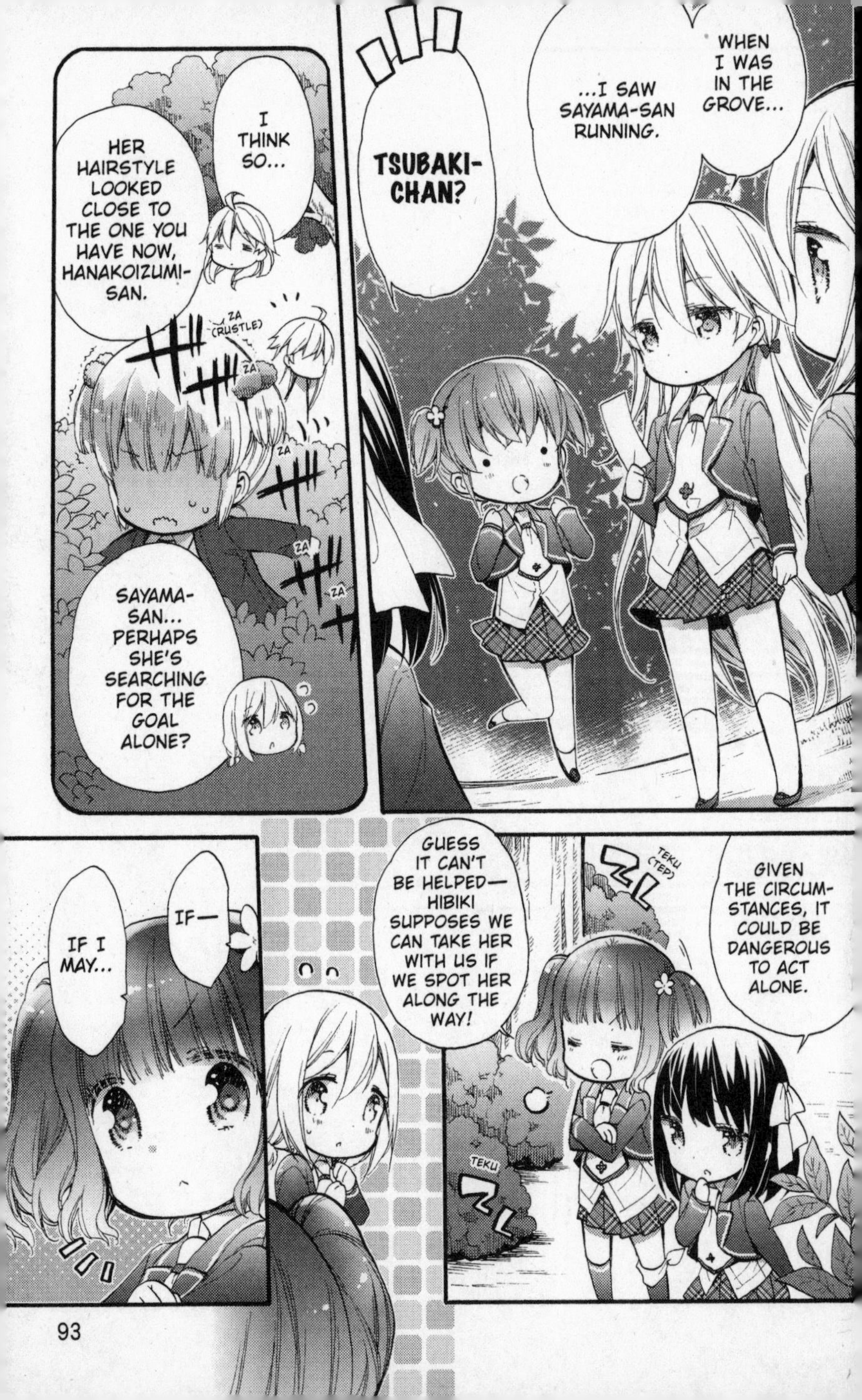
WHEN I WAS IN THE GROVE...
...I SAW SAYAMA-SAN RUNNING.
TSUBAKI-CHAN?
I THINK SO...
HER HAIRSTYLE LOOKED CLOSE TO THE ONE YOU HAVE NOW, HANAKOIZUMI-SAN.
ZA (RUSTLE)
ZA
ZA
ZA
ZA
SAYAMA-SAN... PERHAPS SHE'S SEARCHING FOR THE GOAL ALONE?
GIVEN THE CIRCUMSTANCES, IT COULD BE DANGEROUS TO ACT ALONE.
TEKU (TEP)
TEKU
GUESS IT CAN'T BE HELPED—HIBIKI SUPPOSES WE CAN TAKE HER WITH US IF WE SPOT HER ALONG THE WAY!
IF—
IF I MAY...

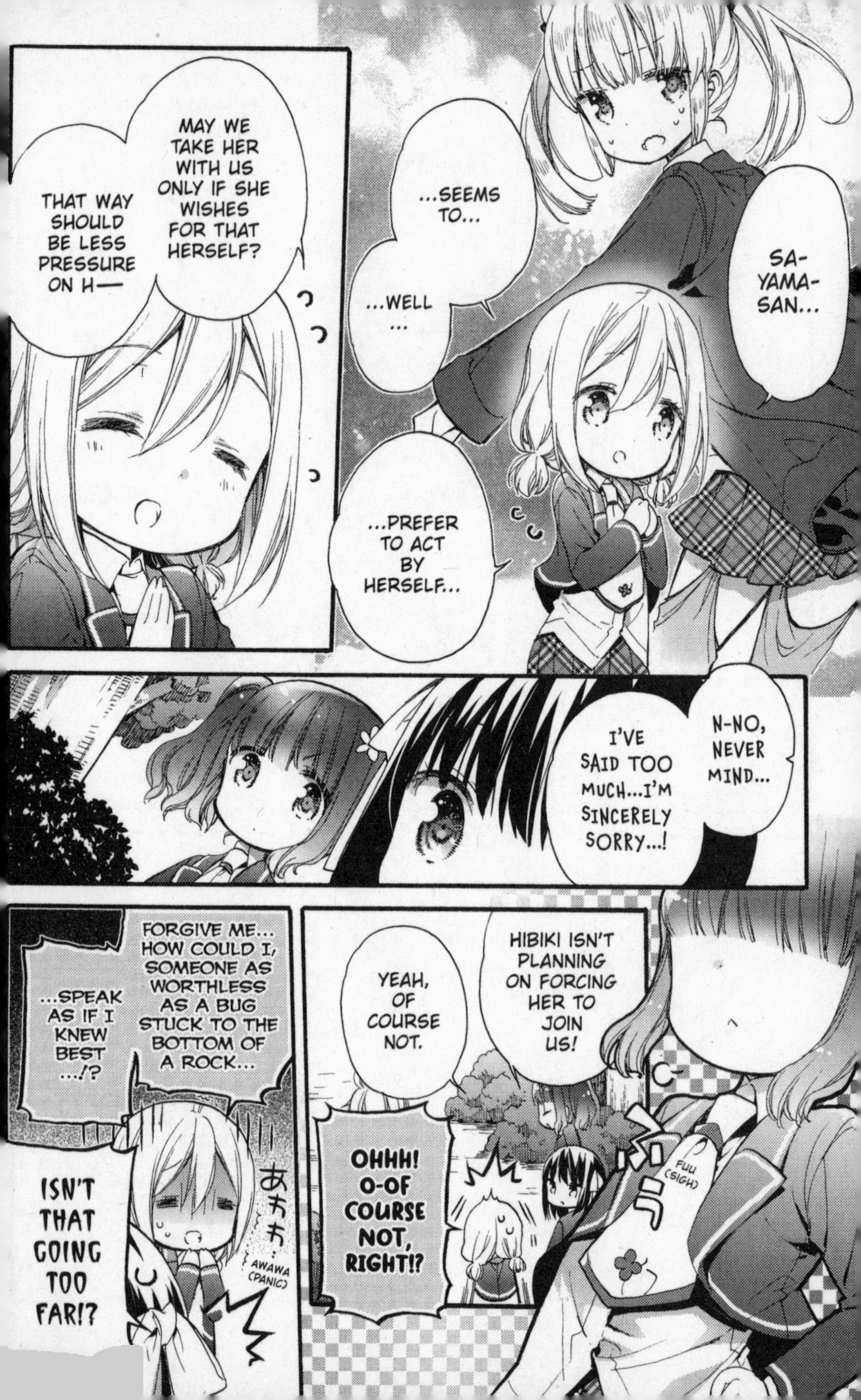
SA-YAMA-SAN...
...SEEMS TO...
...WELL...
...PREFER TO ACT BY HERSELF...
MAY WE TAKE HER WITH US ONLY IF SHE WISHES FOR THAT HERSELF?
THAT WAY SHOULD BE LESS PRESSURE ON H—
N-NO, NEVER MIND...
I'VE SAID TOO MUCH...I'M SINCERELY SORRY...!
HIBIKI ISN'T PLANNING ON FORCING HER TO JOIN US!
YEAH, OF COURSE NOT.
FUU (SIGH)
OHHH! O-OF COURSE NOT, RIGHT!?
FORGIVE ME... HOW COULD I, SOMEONE AS WORTHLESS AS A BUG STUCK TO THE BOTTOM OF A ROCK...
...SPEAK AS IF I KNEW BEST ...!?
あわわ
AWAWA (PANIC)
ISN'T THAT GOING TOO FAR!?

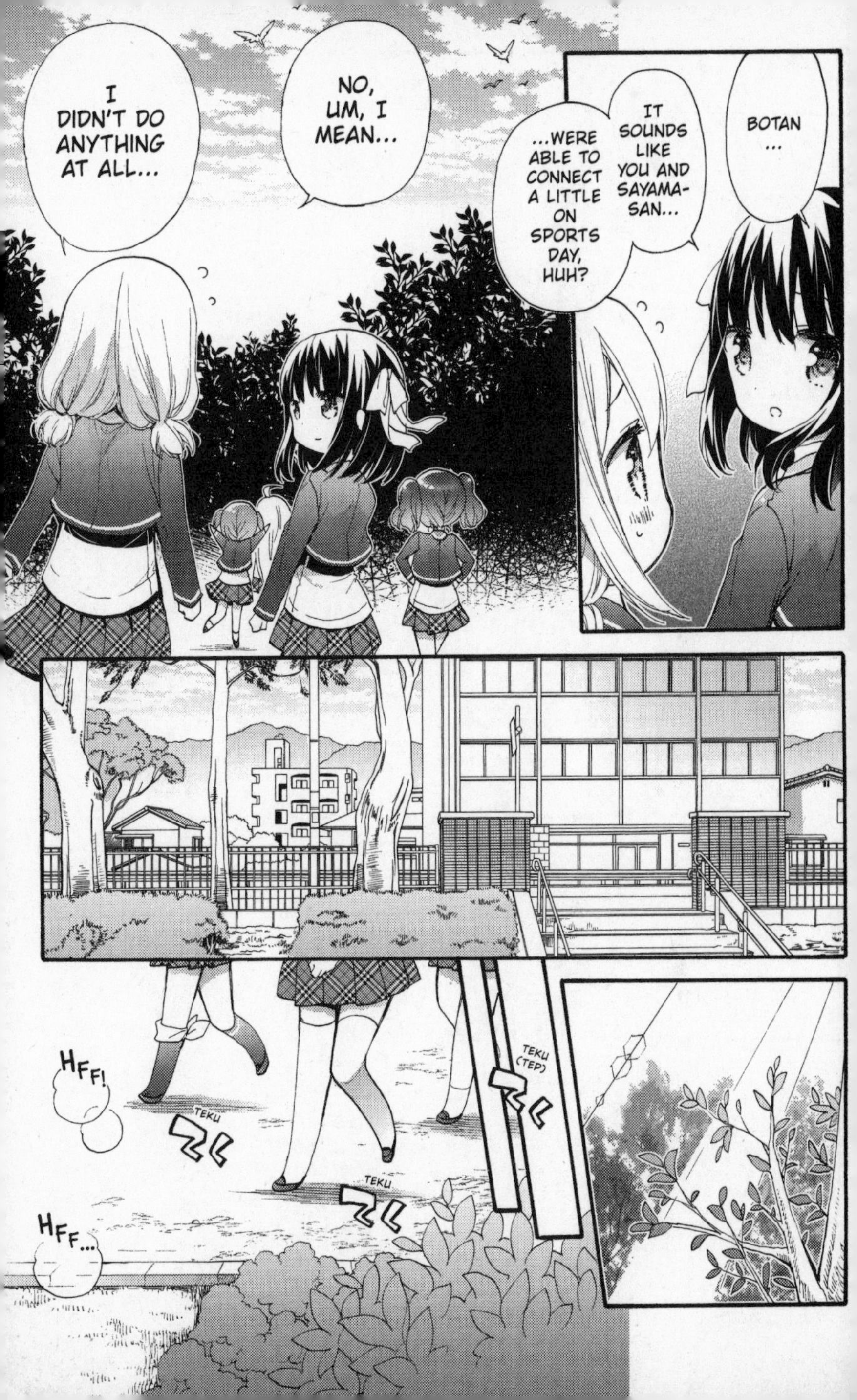
BOTAN ...
IT SOUNDS LIKE YOU AND SAYAMA-SAN...
...WERE ABLE TO CONNECT A LITTLE ON SPORTS DAY, HUH?
NO, UM, I MEAN...
I DIDN'T DO ANYTHING AT ALL...
TEKU (TEP)
TEKU
HFF!
TEKU
HFF...

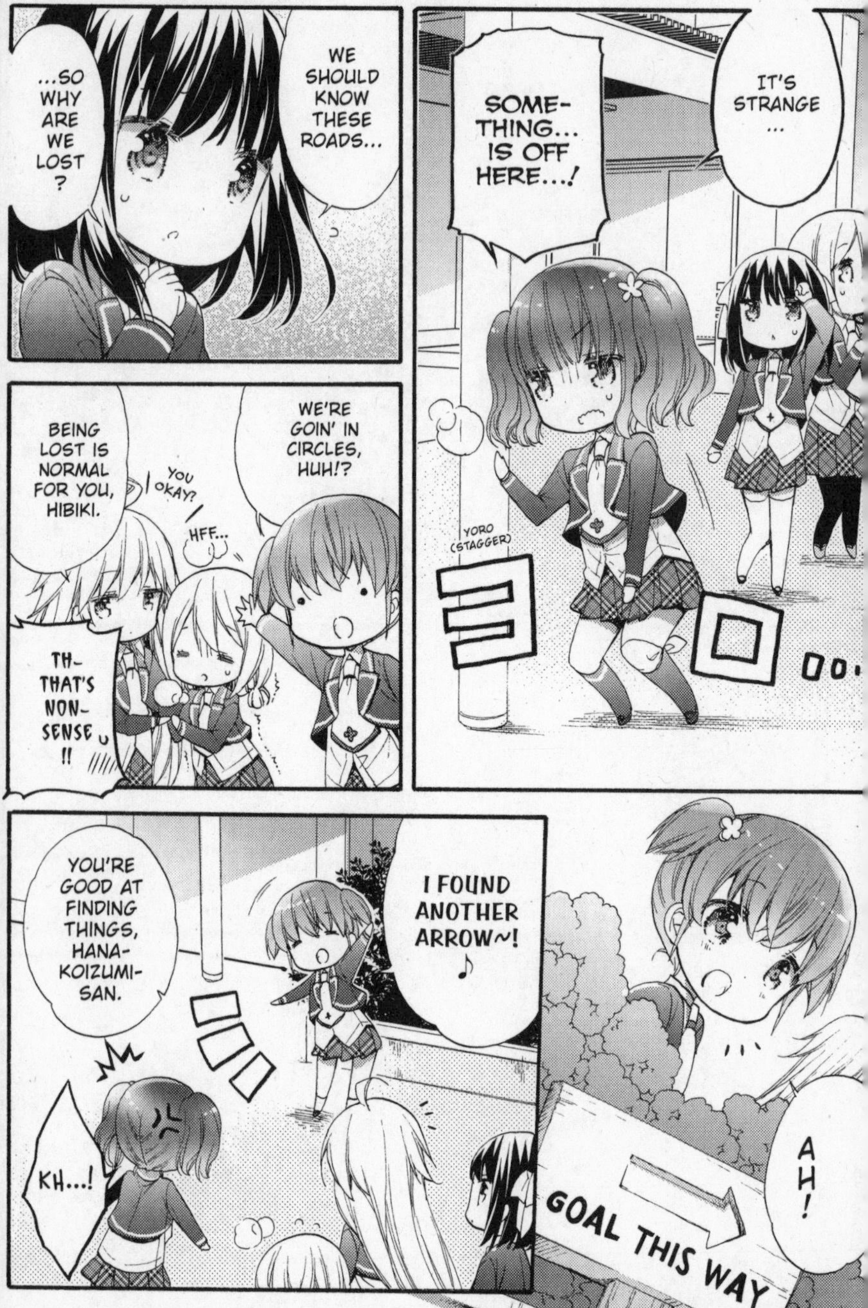
IT'S STRANGE...
SOMETHING... IS OFF HERE...!
YORO (STAGGER)
WE SHOULD KNOW THESE ROADS...
...SO WHY ARE WE LOST?
WE'RE GOIN' IN CIRCLES, HUH!?
YOU OKAY?
HFF...
BEING LOST IS NORMAL FOR YOU, HIBIKI.
TH-THAT'S NONSENSE!!
AH!
GOAL THIS WAY
I FOUND ANOTHER ARROW~! ♪
YOU'RE GOOD AT FINDING THINGS, HANAKOIZUMI-SAN.
KH...!

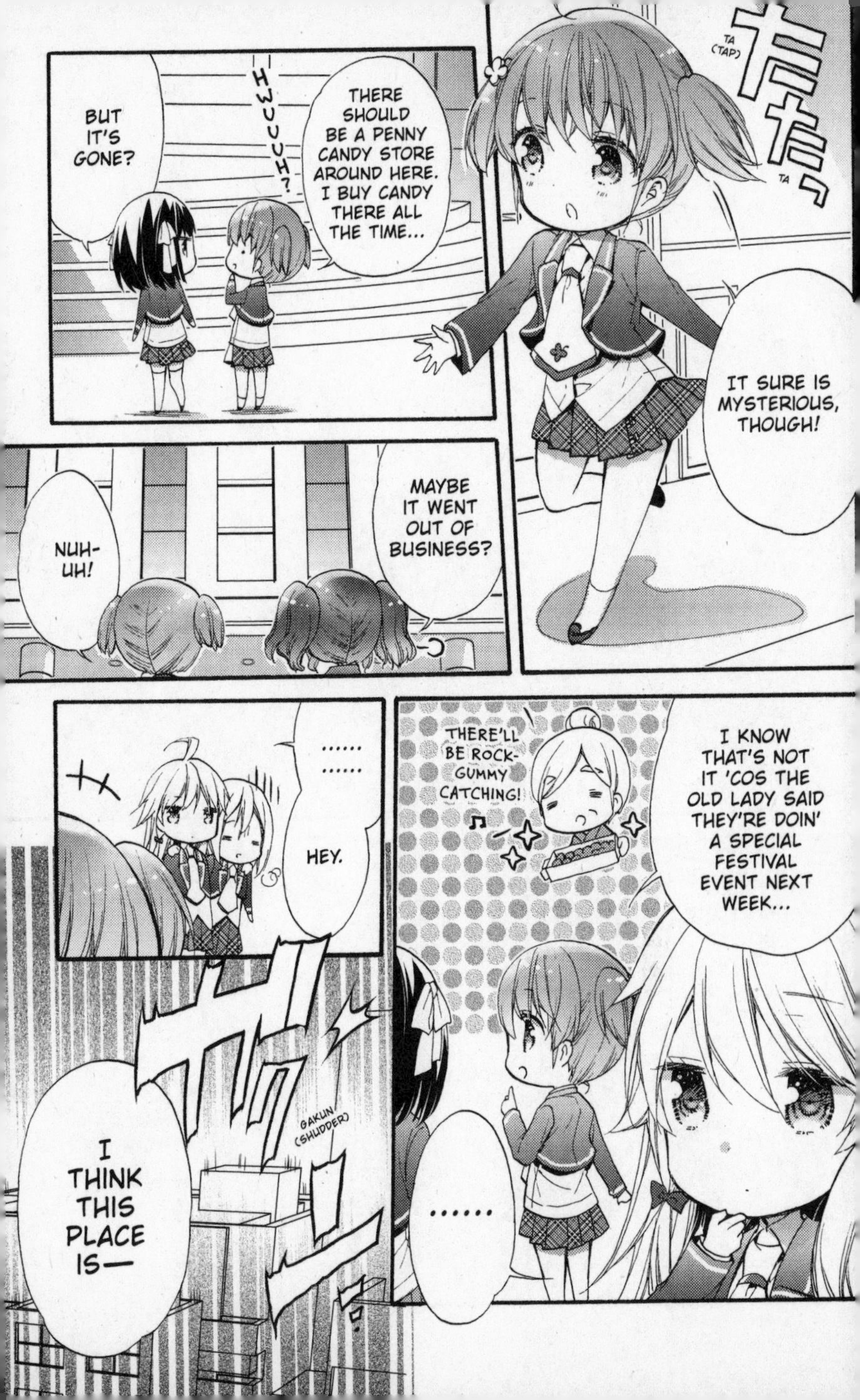
TA (TAP)
TA
IT SURE IS MYSTERIOUS, THOUGH!
THERE SHOULD BE A PENNY CANDY STORE AROUND HERE. I BUY CANDY THERE ALL THE TIME...
HWUUUH?
BUT IT'S GONE?
MAYBE IT WENT OUT OF BUSINESS?
NUH-UH!
I KNOW THAT'S NOT IT 'COS THE OLD LADY SAID THEY'RE DOIN' A SPECIAL FESTIVAL EVENT NEXT WEEK...
THERE'LL BE ROCK-GUMMY CATCHING! ♫
......
....
HEY.
GAKUN (SHUDDER)
I THINK THIS PLACE IS—

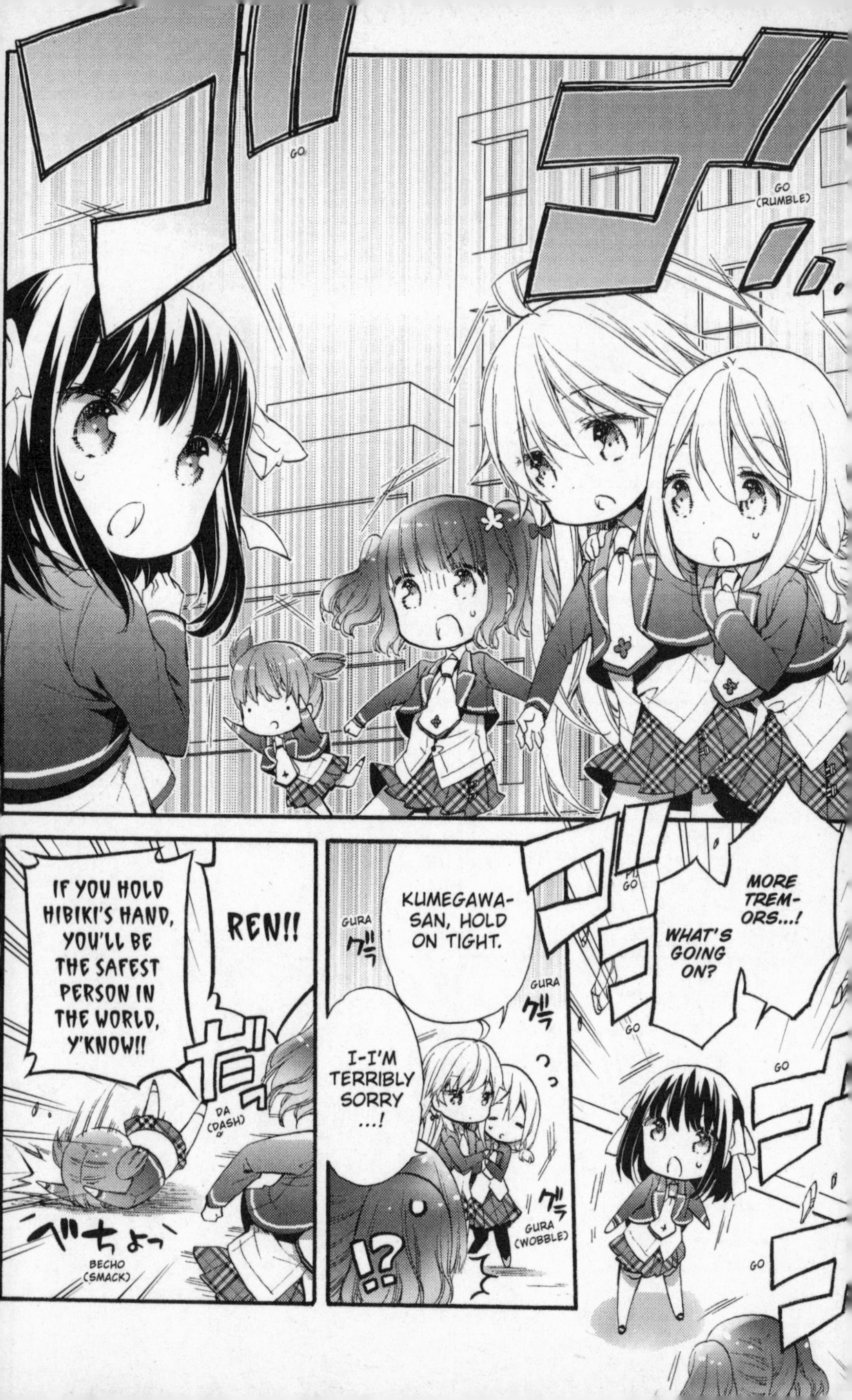
GO
(RUMBLE)
GO
GO
MORE TREM-ORS...!
WHAT'S GOING ON?
GO
GO
GO
KUMEGAWA-SAN, HOLD ON TIGHT.
GURA
GURA
I-I'M TERRIBLY SORRY ...!
GURA
(WOBBLE)
!?
REN!!
IF YOU HOLD HIBIKI'S HAND, YOU'LL BE THE SAFEST PERSON IN THE WORLD, Y'KNOW!!
DA
(DASH)
BECHO
(SMACK)

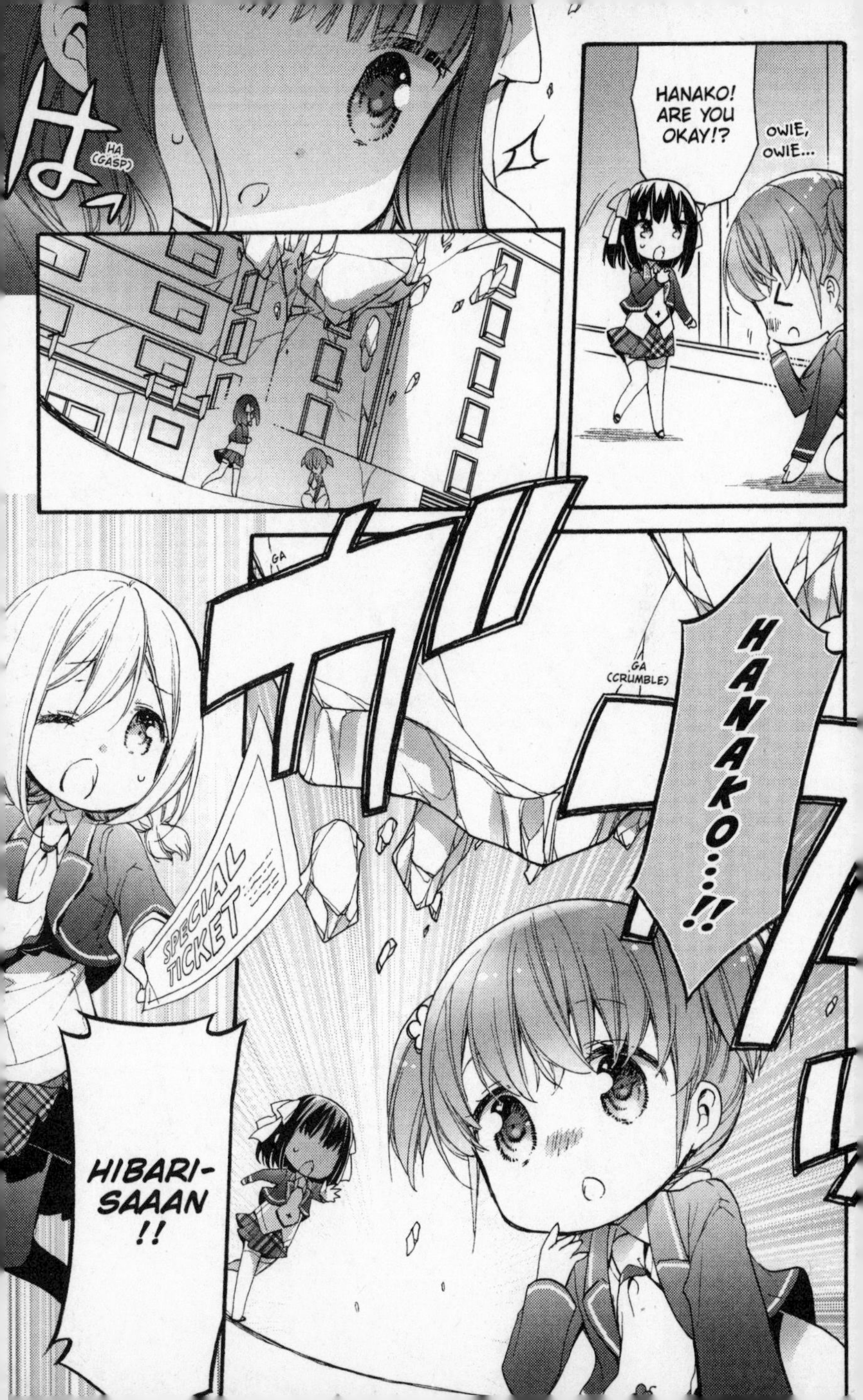
HA (GASP)
HANAKO! ARE YOU OKAY!?
OWIE, OWIE...
GA (CRUMBLE)
GA
HANAKO...!!
SPECIAL TICKET
HIBARI-SAAAN!!

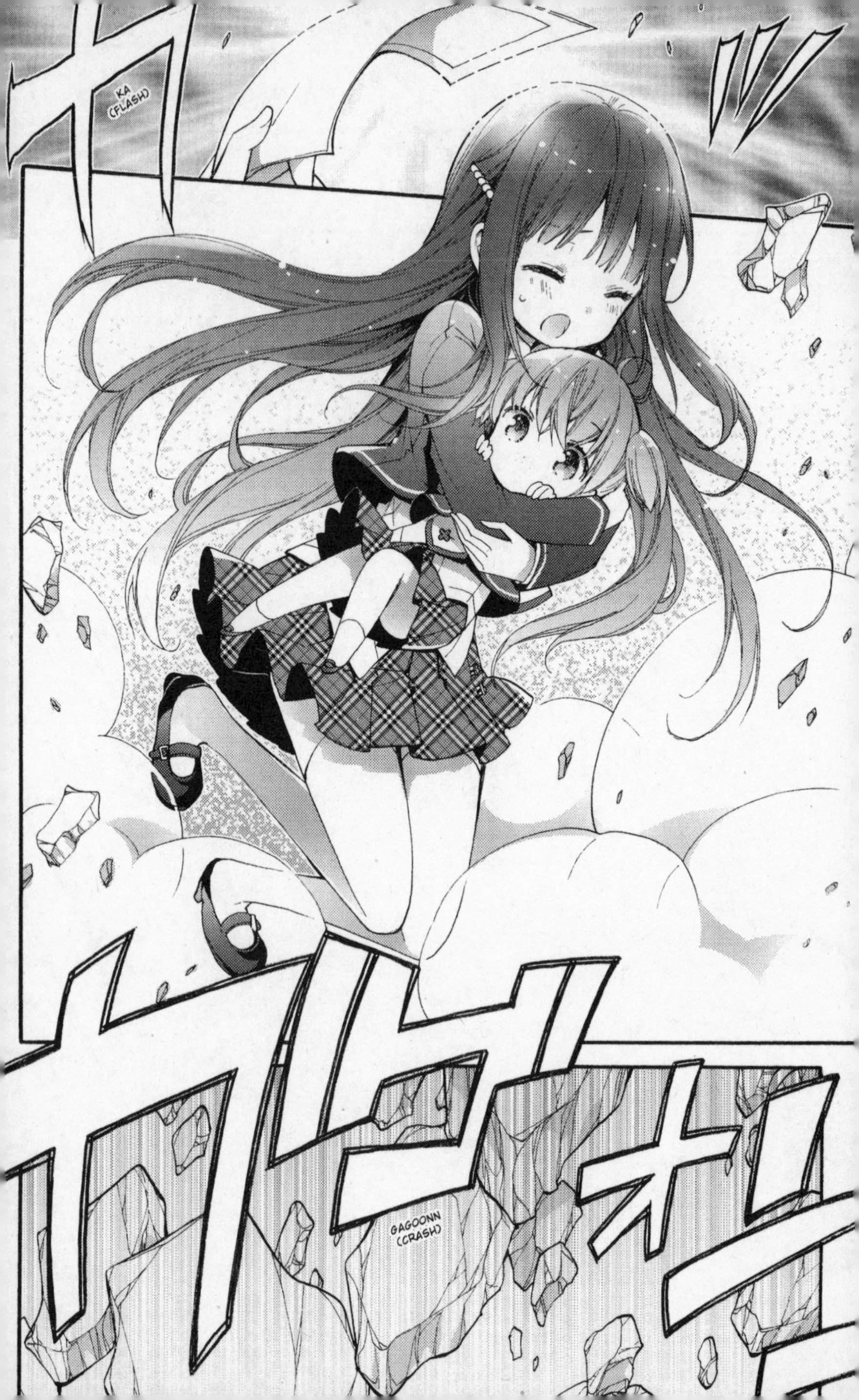
KA
(FLASH)
GAGOONN
(CRASH)

Anne Happy

unhappy go lucky!

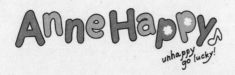

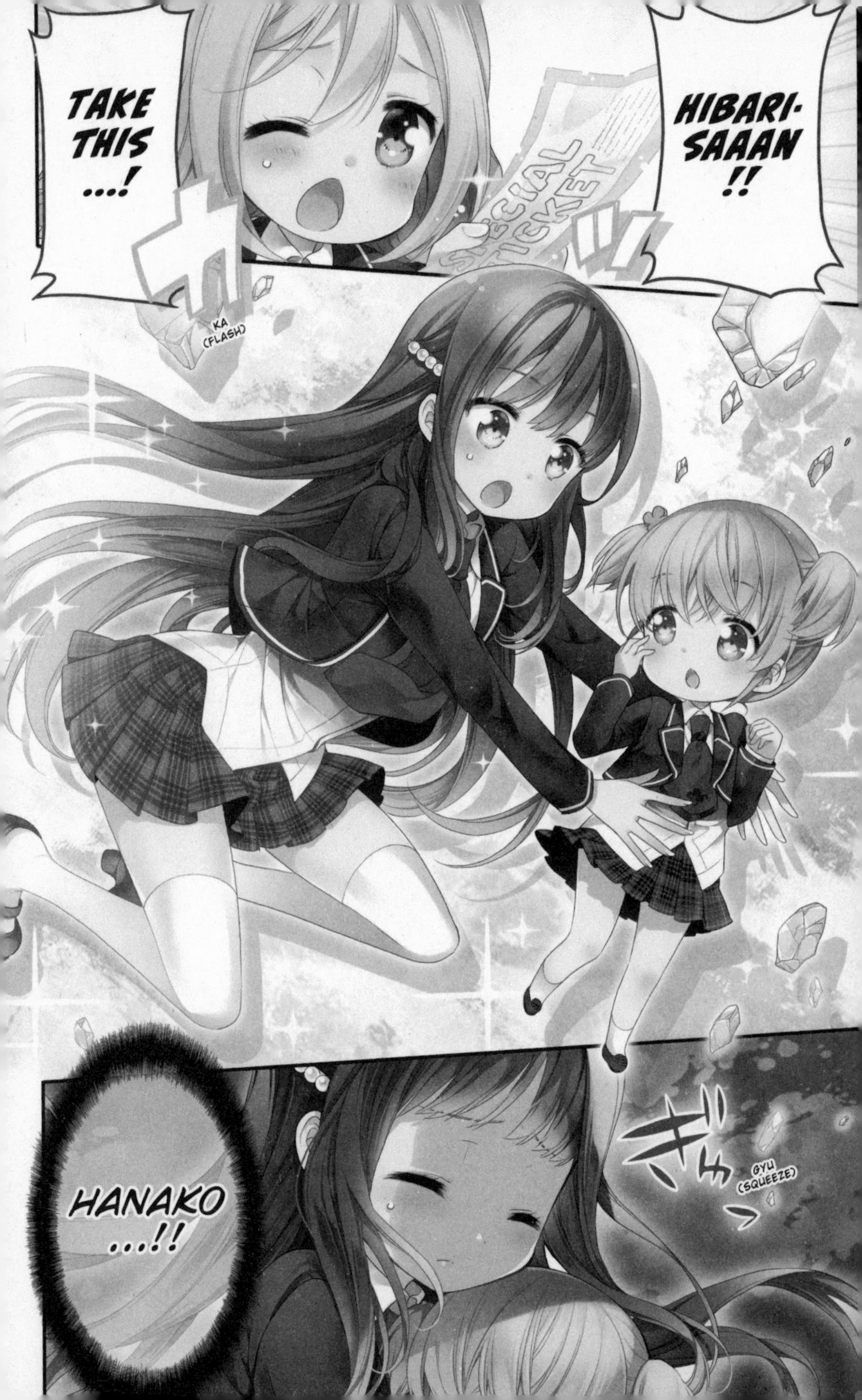
HIBARI-SAAAN!!
TAKE THIS...!
KA (FLASH)
GYU (SQUEEZE)
HANAKO...!!

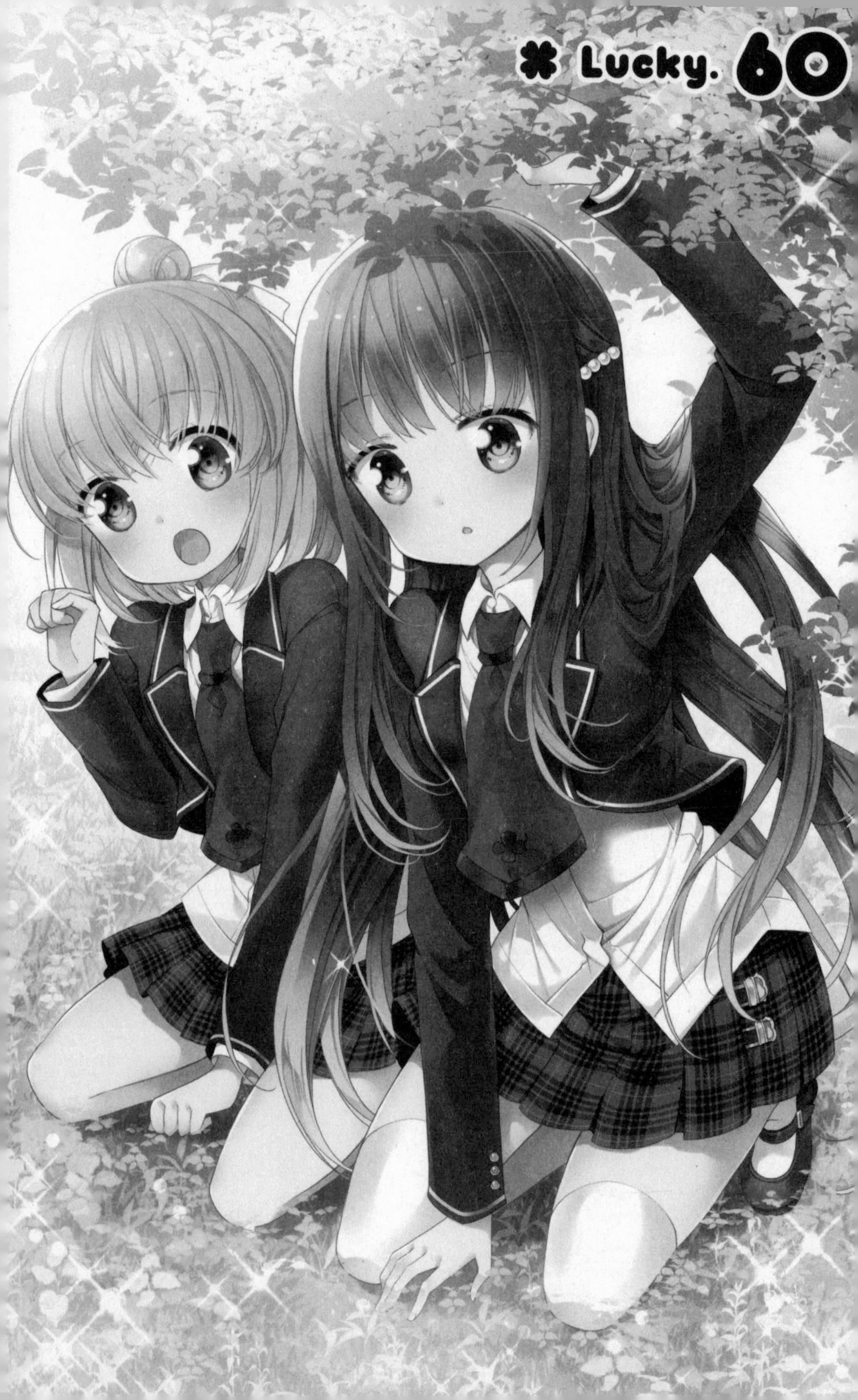
Lucky. 60

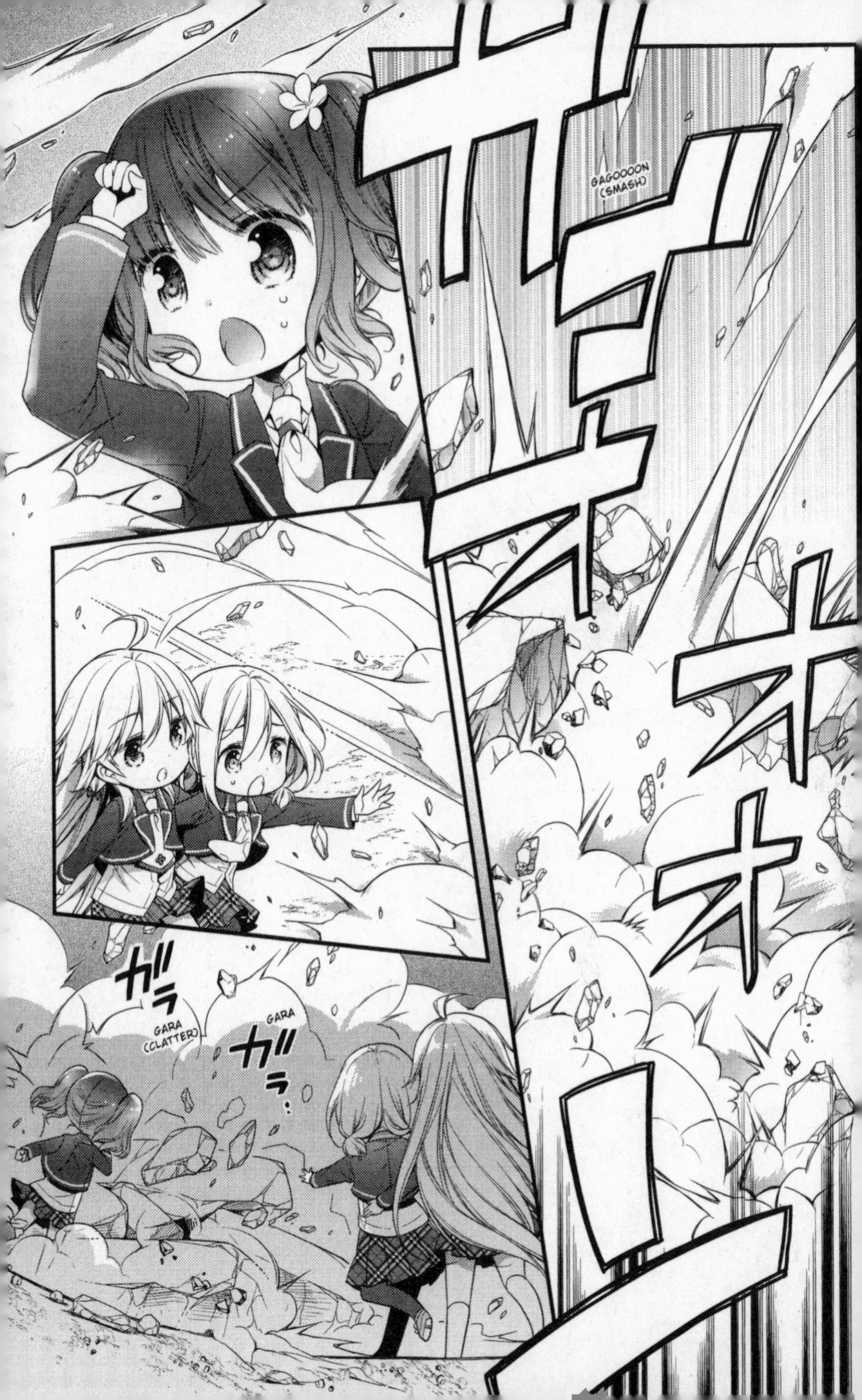
GAGOOOON (SMASH)
ガラ
GARA (CLATTER)
ガラ
GARA

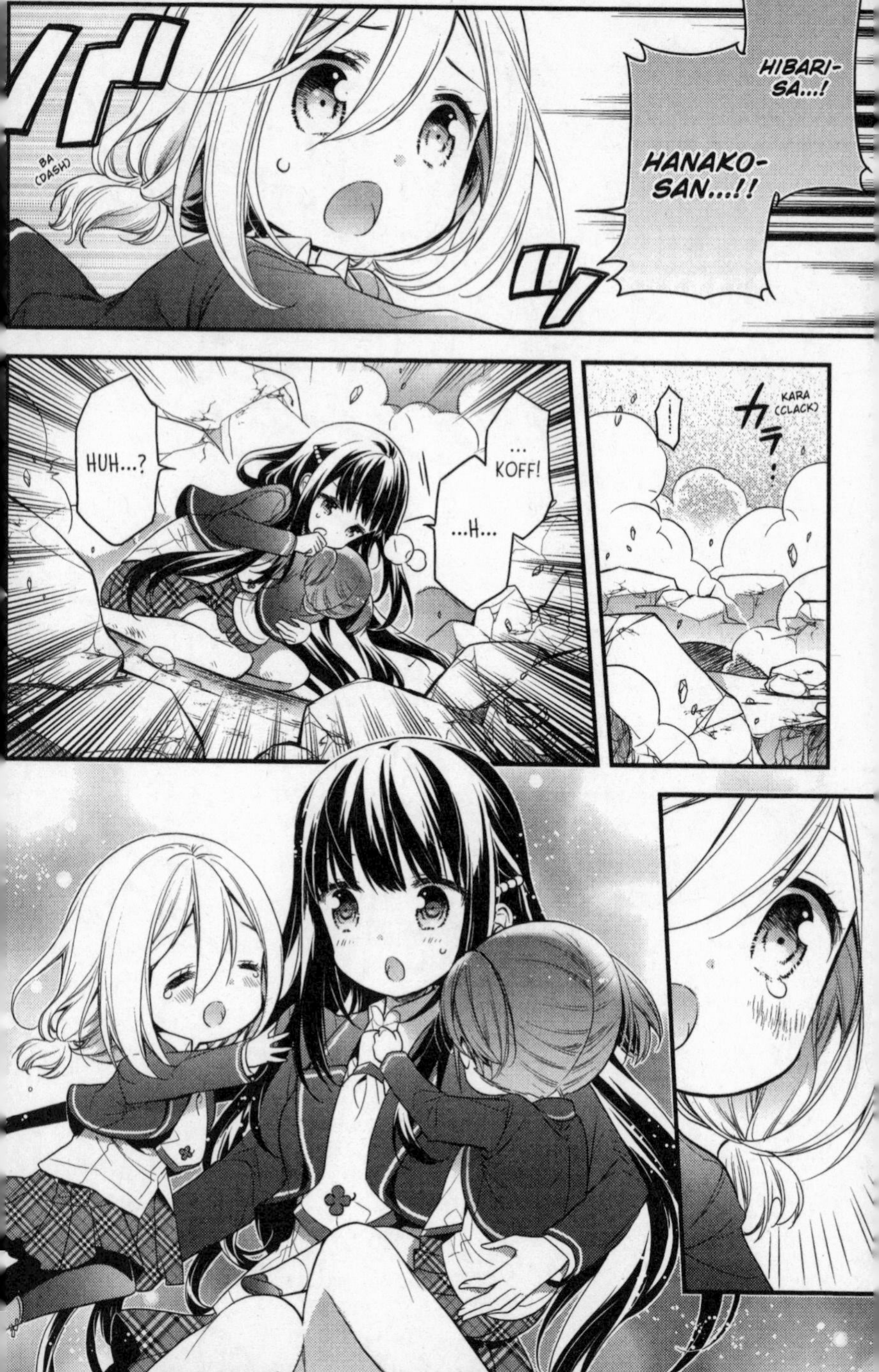
HIBARI-SA...!
HANAKO-SAN...!!
BA (DASH)
KARA (CLACK)
... KOFF!
...H...
HUH...?

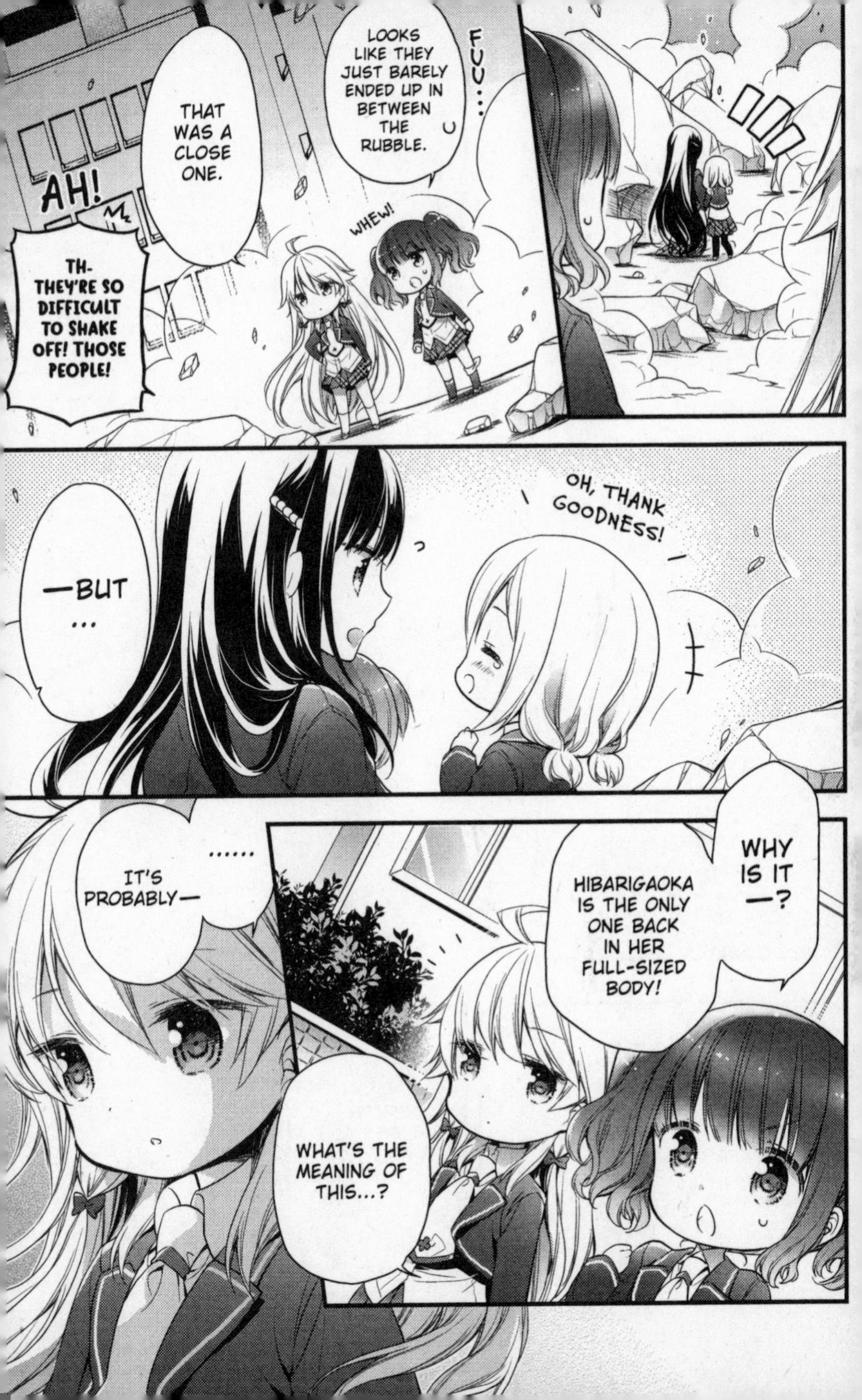
FUU...
LOOKS LIKE THEY JUST BARELY ENDED UP IN BETWEEN THE RUBBLE.
WHEW!
THAT WAS A CLOSE ONE.
AH!
TH-THEY'RE SO DIFFICULT TO SHAKE OFF! THOSE PEOPLE!
OH, THANK GOODNESS!
—BUT ...
WHY IS IT —?
HIBARIGAOKA IS THE ONLY ONE BACK IN HER FULL-SIZED BODY!
WHAT'S THE MEANING OF THIS...?
......
IT'S PROBABLY—

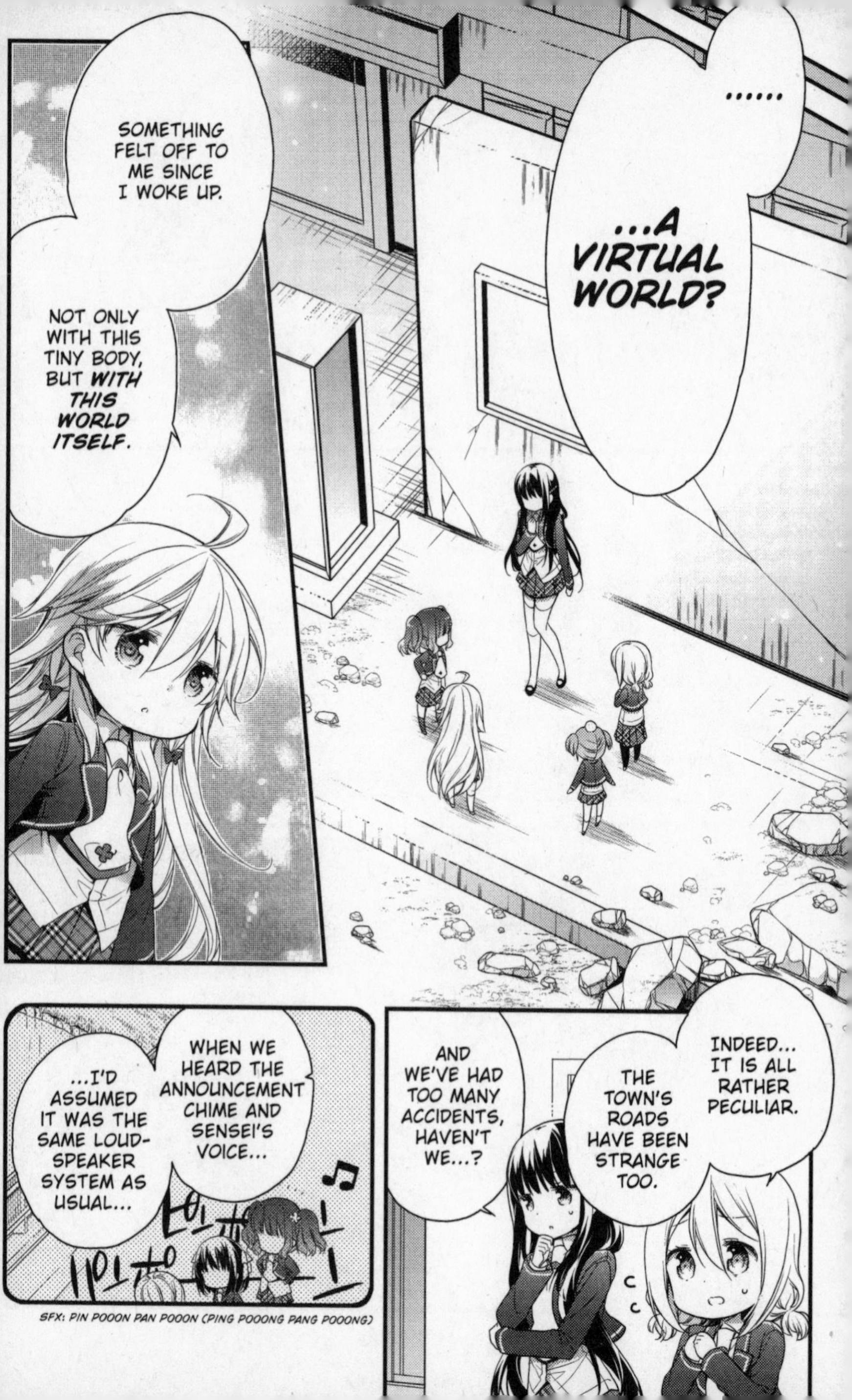
......
...A VIRTUAL WORLD?
SOMETHING FELT OFF TO ME SINCE I WOKE UP.
NOT ONLY WITH THIS TINY BODY, BUT *WITH THIS WORLD ITSELF*.
INDEED... IT IS ALL RATHER PECULIAR.
THE TOWN'S ROADS HAVE BEEN STRANGE TOO.
AND WE'VE HAD TOO MANY ACCIDENTS, HAVEN'T WE...?
WHEN WE HEARD THE ANNOUNCEMENT CHIME AND SENSEI'S VOICE...
...I'D ASSUMED IT WAS THE SAME LOUD-SPEAKER SYSTEM AS USUAL...
SFX: PIN POOON PAN POOON (PING POOONG PANG POOONG)

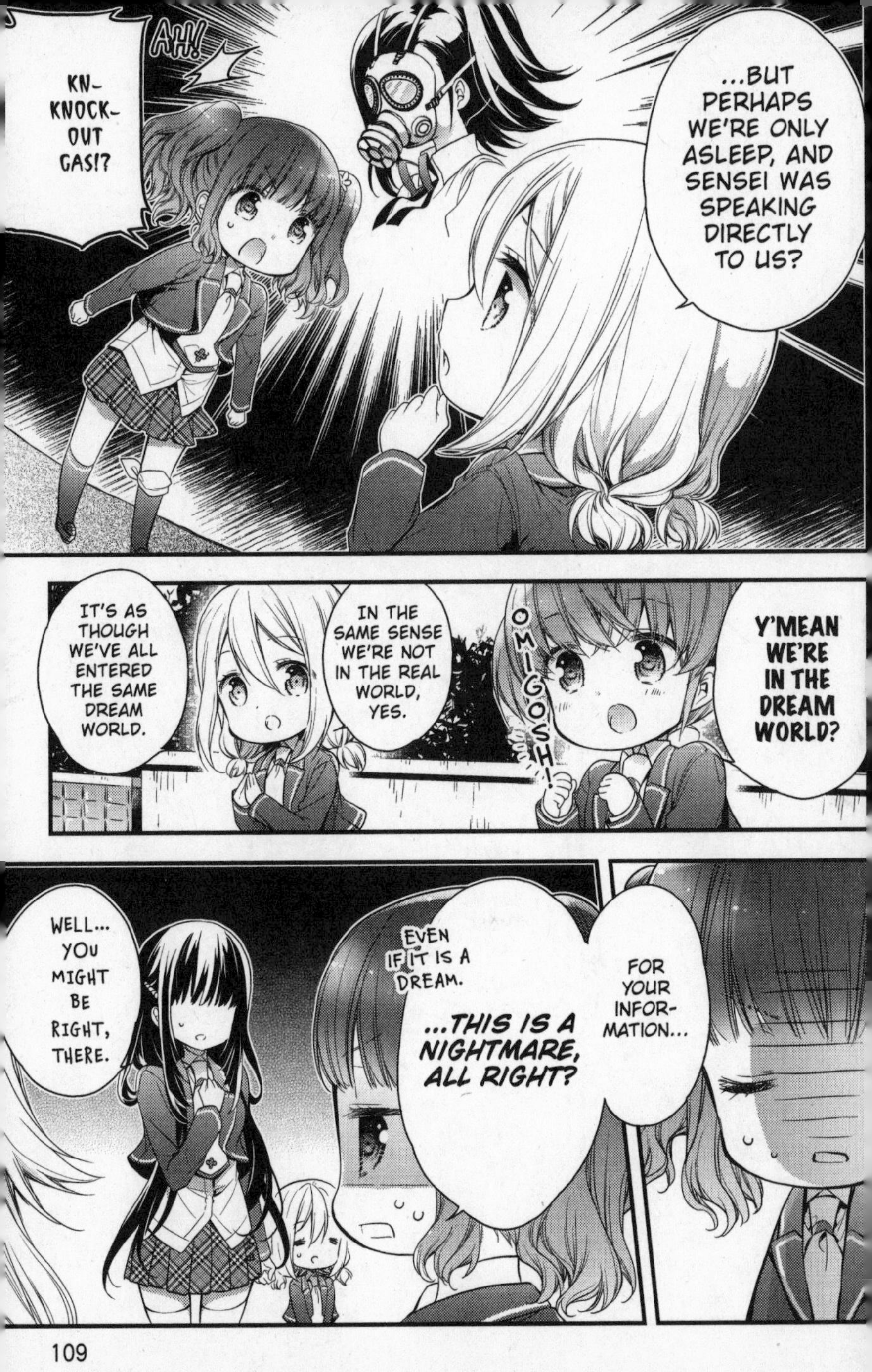
...BUT PERHAPS WE'RE ONLY ASLEEP, AND SENSEI WAS SPEAKING DIRECTLY TO US?
AH!
KN-KNOCK-OUT GAS!?
Y'MEAN WE'RE IN THE DREAM WORLD?
OMIGOSH!
IN THE SAME SENSE WE'RE NOT IN THE REAL WORLD, YES.
IT'S AS THOUGH WE'VE ALL ENTERED THE SAME DREAM WORLD.
FOR YOUR INFORMATION...
...THIS IS A NIGHTMARE, ALL RIGHT?
EVEN IF IT IS A DREAM.
WELL... YOU MIGHT BE RIGHT, THERE.

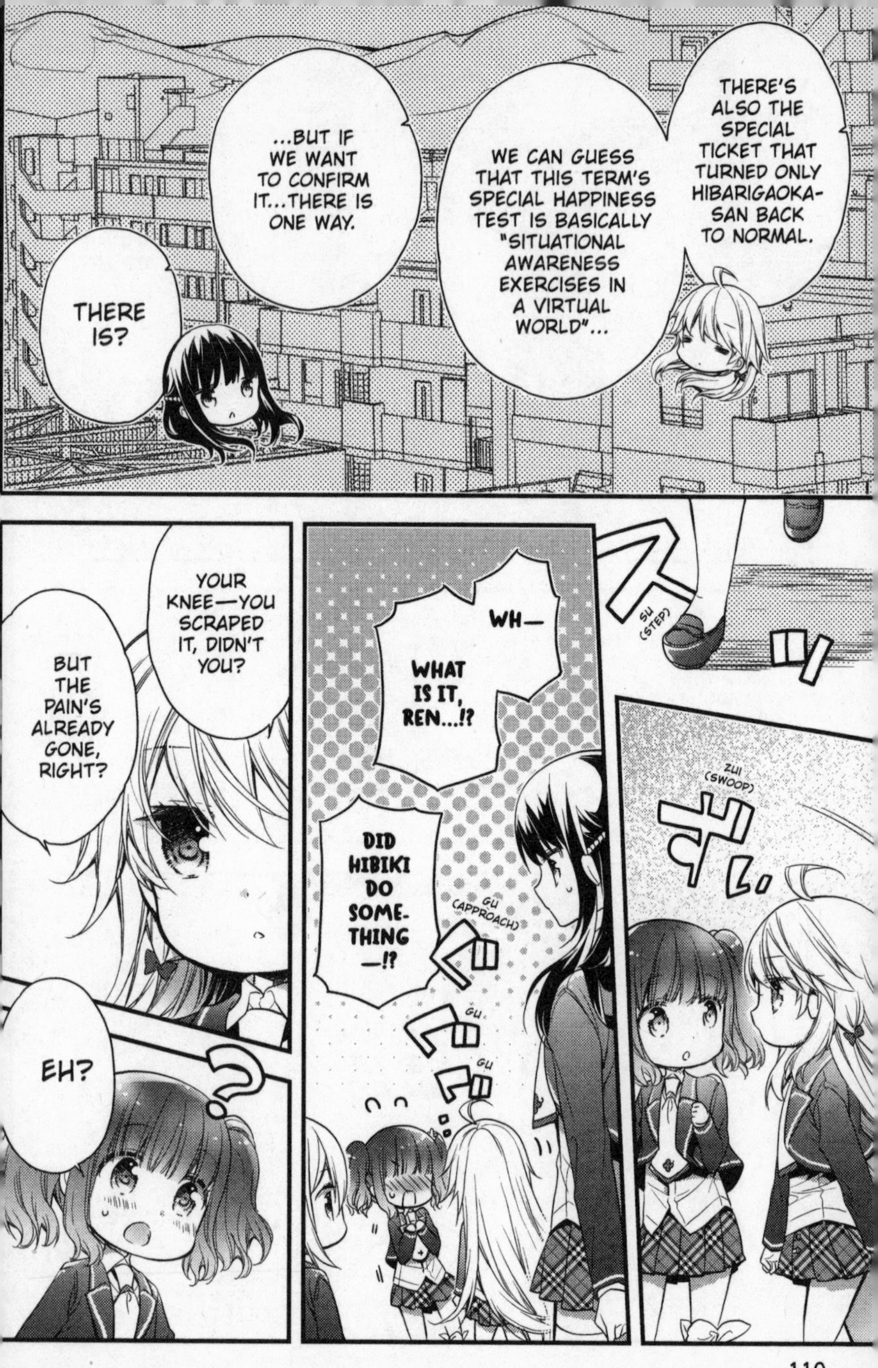
THERE'S ALSO THE SPECIAL TICKET THAT TURNED ONLY HIBARIGAOKA-SAN BACK TO NORMAL.
WE CAN GUESS THAT THIS TERM'S SPECIAL HAPPINESS TEST IS BASICALLY "SITUATIONAL AWARENESS EXERCISES IN A VIRTUAL WORLD"...
...BUT IF WE WANT TO CONFIRM IT...THERE IS ONE WAY.
THERE IS?
SU (STEP)
ZUI (SWOOP)
WH—
WHAT IS IT, REN...!?
DID HIBIKI DO SOME-THING—!?
GU (APPROACH)
GU
GU
YOUR KNEE—YOU SCRAPED IT, DIDN'T YOU?
BUT THE PAIN'S ALREADY GONE, RIGHT?
EH?

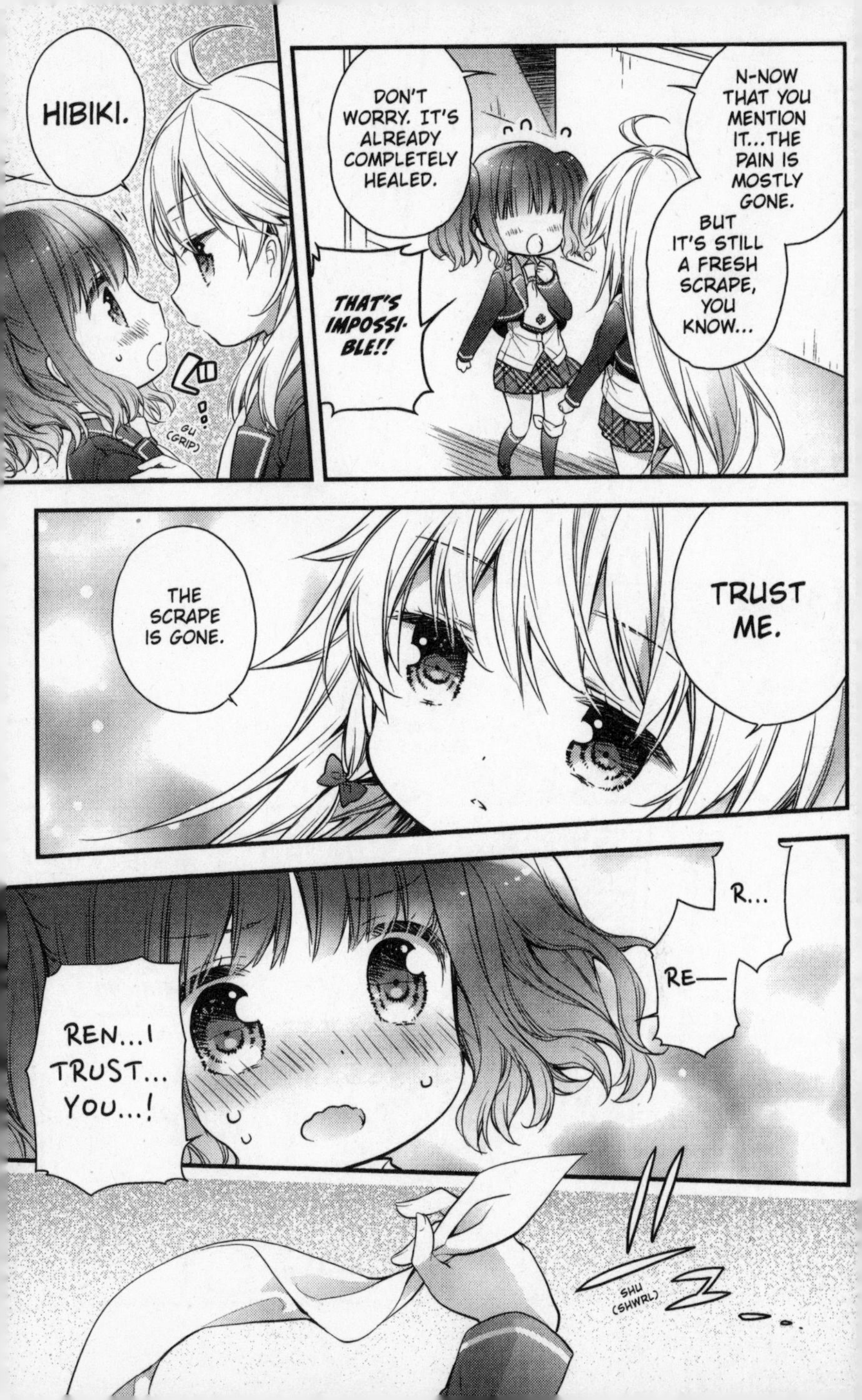
N-NOW THAT YOU MENTION IT...THE PAIN IS MOSTLY GONE.
BUT IT'S STILL A FRESH SCRAPE, YOU KNOW...
DON'T WORRY. IT'S ALREADY COMPLETELY HEALED.
THAT'S IMPOSSIBLE!!
HIBIKI.
GU (GRIP)
TRUST ME.
THE SCRAPE IS GONE.
R...
RE—
REN...I TRUST... YOU...!
SHU (SHWRL)

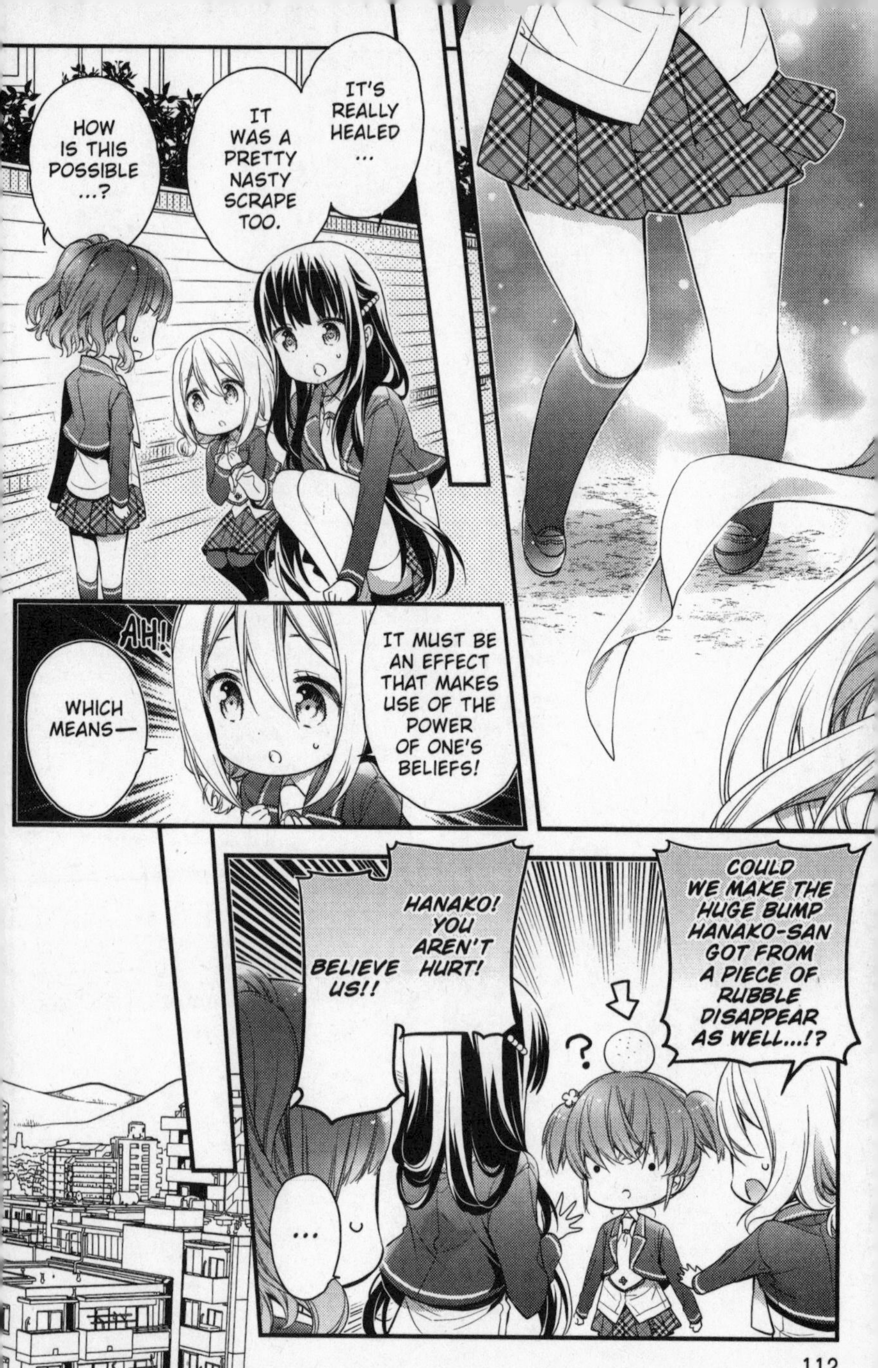
IT'S REALLY HEALED...
IT WAS A PRETTY NASTY SCRAPE TOO.
HOW IS THIS POSSIBLE...?
IT MUST BE AN EFFECT THAT MAKES USE OF THE POWER OF ONE'S BELIEFS!
AH!
WHICH MEANS—
COULD WE MAKE THE HUGE BUMP HANAKO-SAN GOT FROM A PIECE OF RUBBLE DISAPPEAR AS WELL...!?
HANAKO! YOU AREN'T HURT!
BELIEVE US!!
?
...

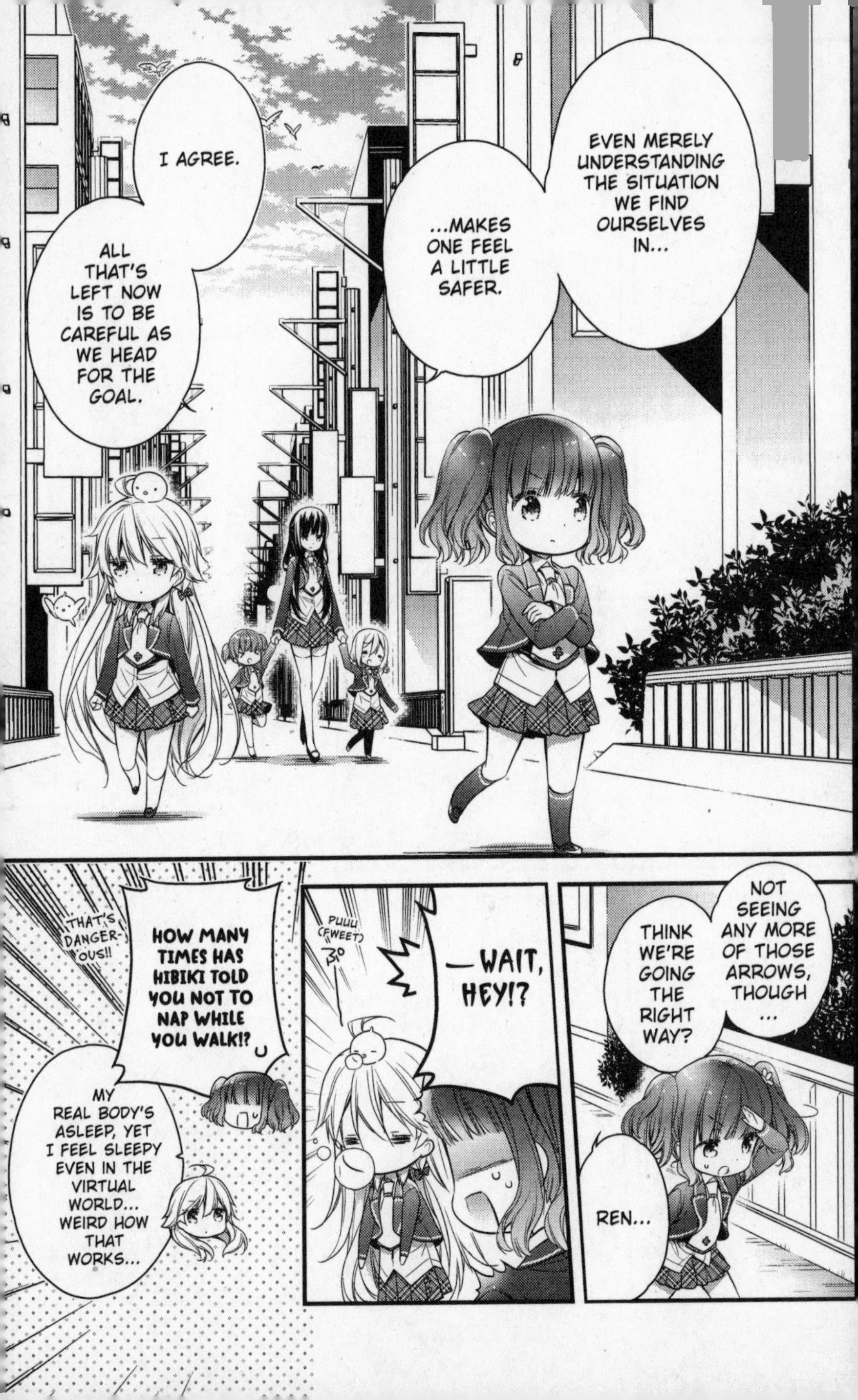
EVEN MERELY UNDERSTANDING THE SITUATION WE FIND OURSELVES IN...
...MAKES ONE FEEL A LITTLE SAFER.
I AGREE.
ALL THAT'S LEFT NOW IS TO BE CAREFUL AS WE HEAD FOR THE GOAL.
NOT SEEING ANY MORE OF THOSE ARROWS, THOUGH...
THINK WE'RE GOING THE RIGHT WAY?
REN...
—WAIT, HEY!?
PUUU (FWEET)
HOW MANY TIMES HAS HIBIKI TOLD YOU NOT TO NAP WHILE YOU WALK!?
THAT'S DANGER-OUS!!
MY REAL BODY'S ASLEEP, YET I FEEL SLEEPY EVEN IN THE VIRTUAL WORLD... WEIRD HOW THAT WORKS...

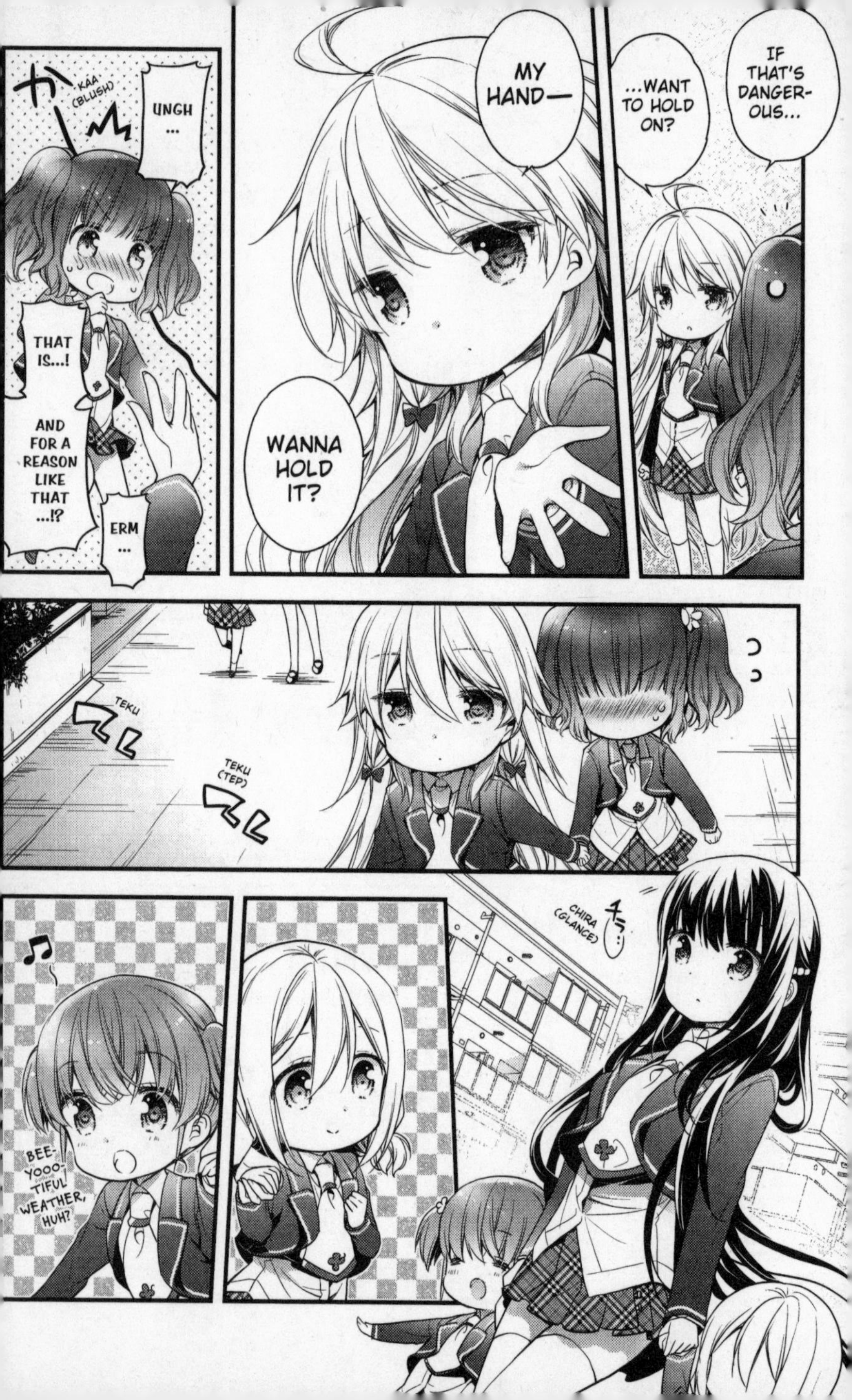
IF THAT'S DANGER-OUS...
...WANT TO HOLD ON?
MY HAND—
WANNA HOLD IT?
KAA (BLUSH)
UNGH...
THAT IS...!
AND FOR A REASON LIKE THAT...!?
ERM...
TEKU
TEKU (TEP)
CHIRA (GLANCE)
BEE-YOOO-TIFUL WEATHER, HUH?

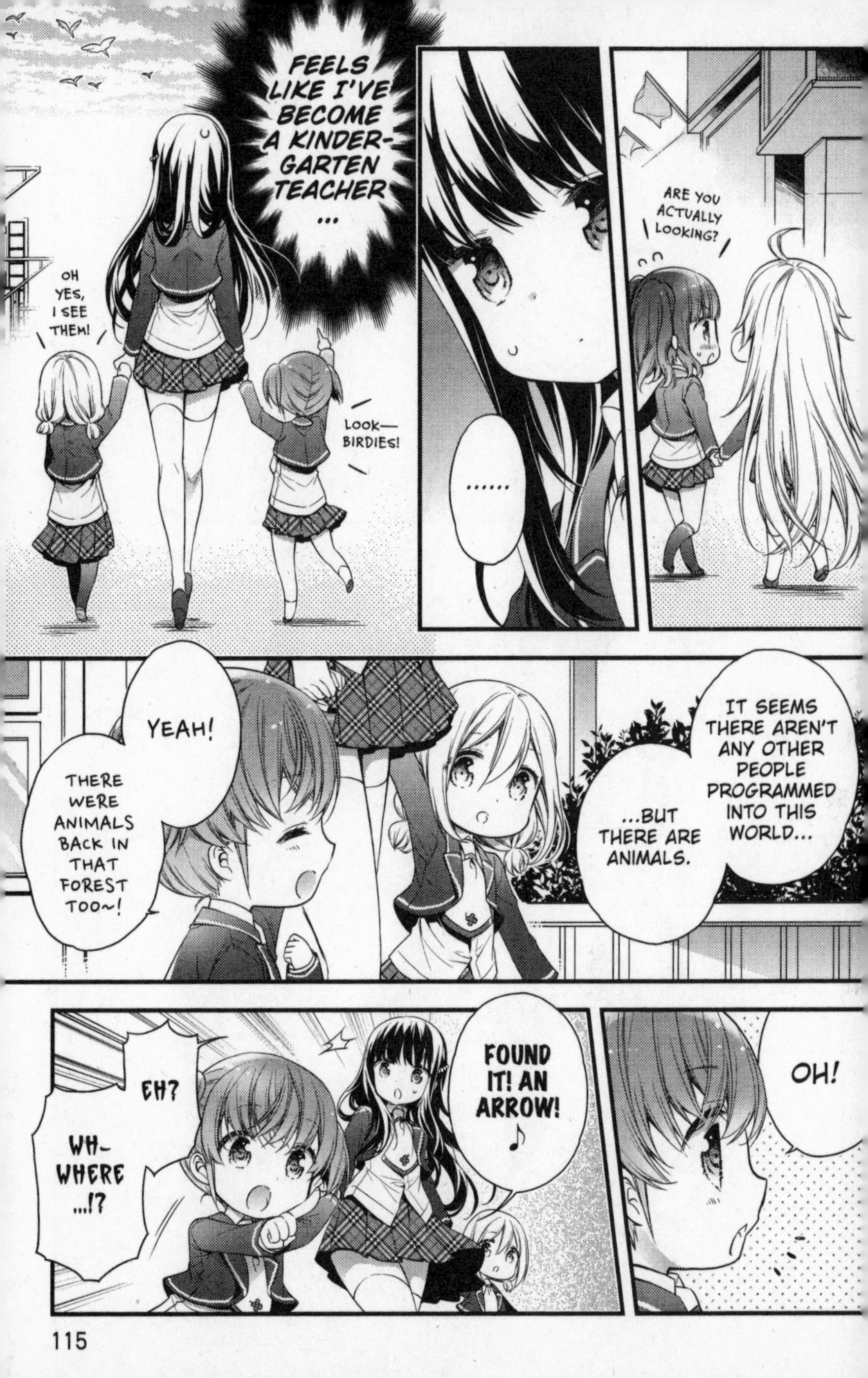
ARE YOU ACTUALLY LOOKING?
......
FEELS LIKE I'VE BECOME A KINDER-GARTEN TEACHER...
LOOK— BIRDIES!
OH YES, I SEE THEM!
IT SEEMS THERE AREN'T ANY OTHER PEOPLE PROGRAMMED INTO THIS WORLD...
...BUT THERE ARE ANIMALS.
YEAH!
THERE WERE ANIMALS BACK IN THAT FOREST TOO~!
OH!
FOUND IT! AN ARROW! ♪
EH?
WH-WHERE ...!?

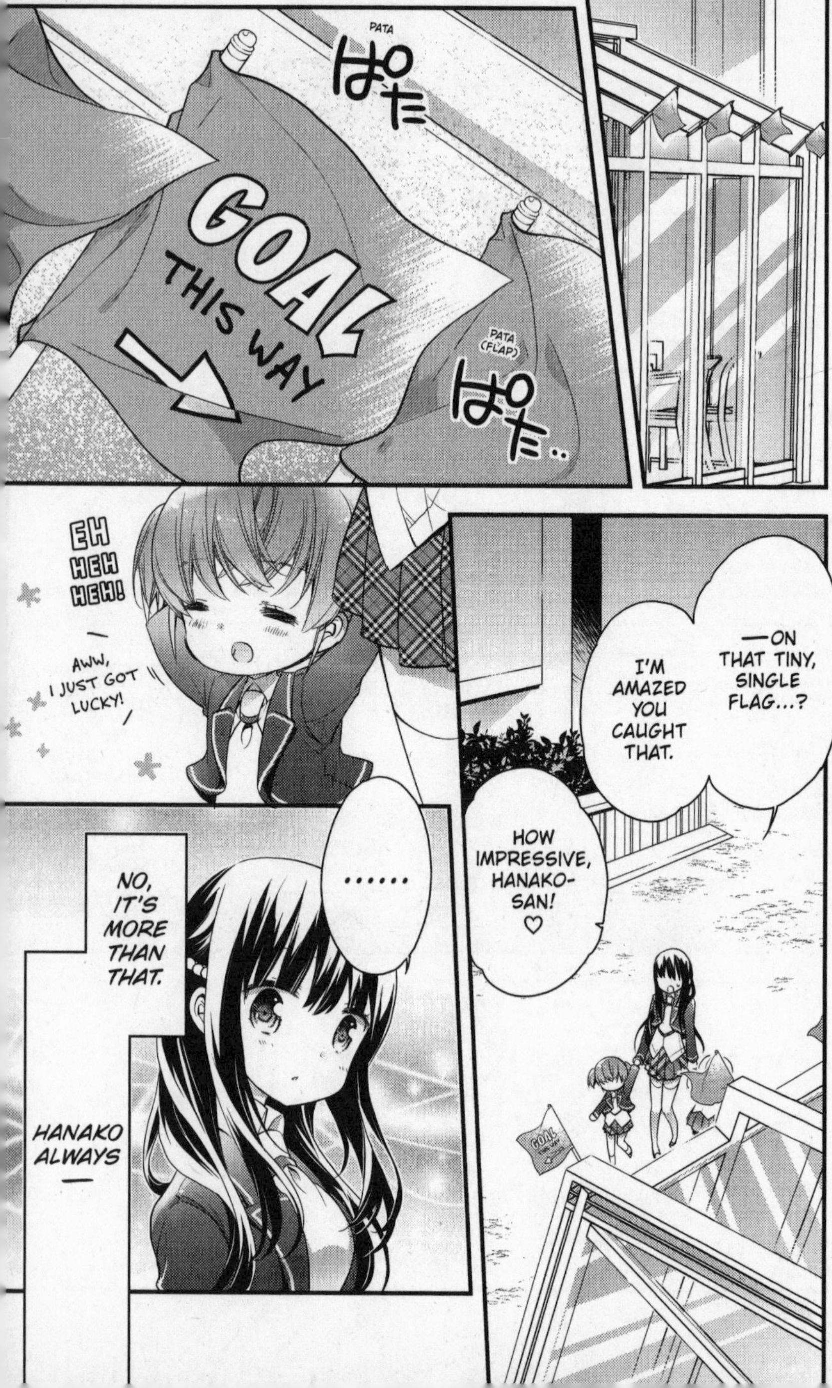
PATA
ぱた
GOAL
THIS WAY
PATA (FLAP)
ぱた..
—ON THAT TINY, SINGLE FLAG...?
I'M AMAZED YOU CAUGHT THAT.
HOW IMPRESSIVE, HANAKO-SAN! ♡
EH HEH HEH!
AWW, I JUST GOT LUCKY!
......
NO, IT'S MORE THAN THAT.
HANAKO ALWAYS —

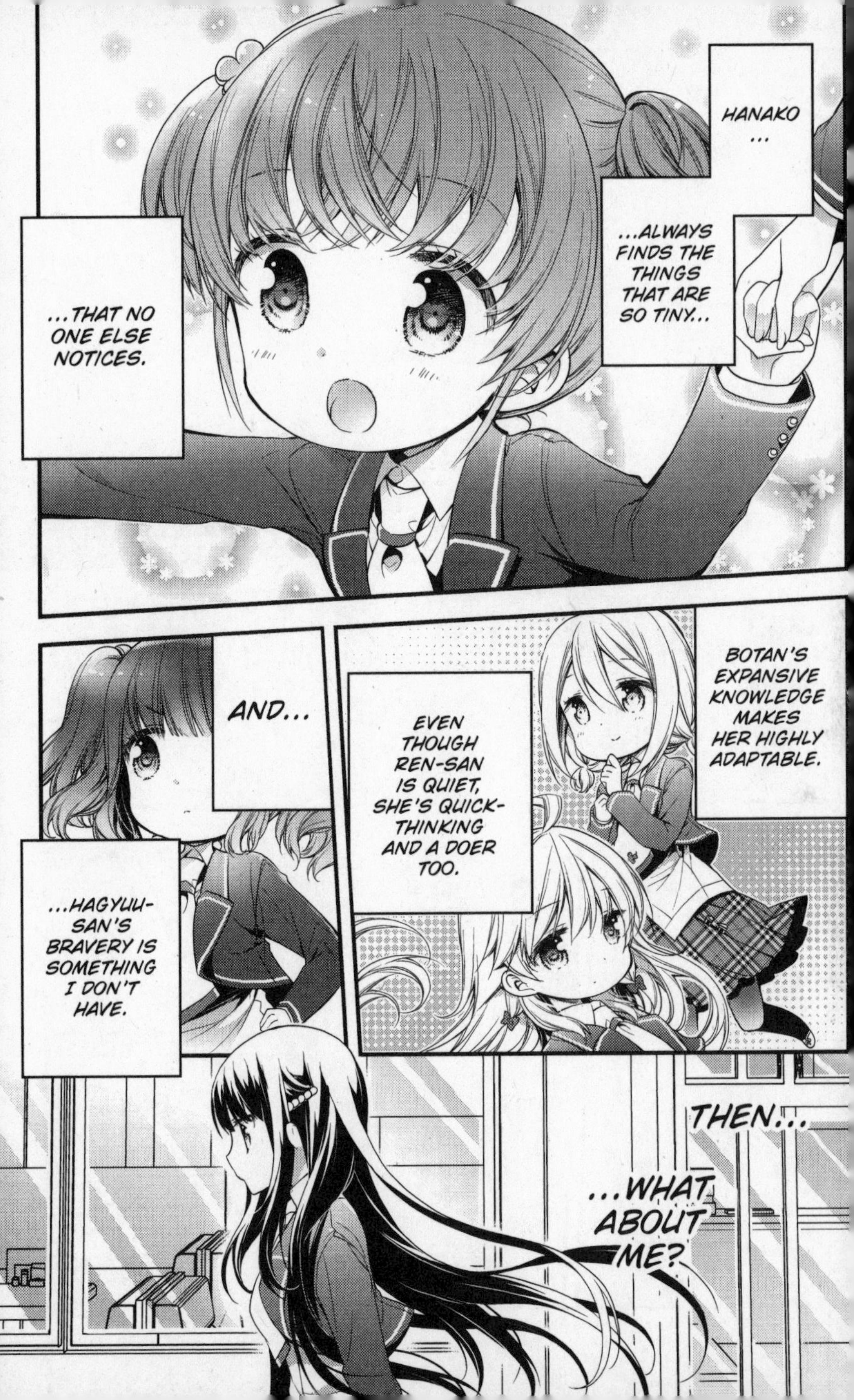
HANAKO ...
...ALWAYS FINDS THE THINGS THAT ARE SO TINY...
...THAT NO ONE ELSE NOTICES.
BOTAN'S EXPANSIVE KNOWLEDGE MAKES HER HIGHLY ADAPTABLE.
EVEN THOUGH REN-SAN IS QUIET, SHE'S QUICK-THINKING AND A DOER TOO.
AND...
...HAGYUU-SAN'S BRAVERY IS SOMETHING I DON'T HAVE.
THEN...
...WHAT ABOUT ME?

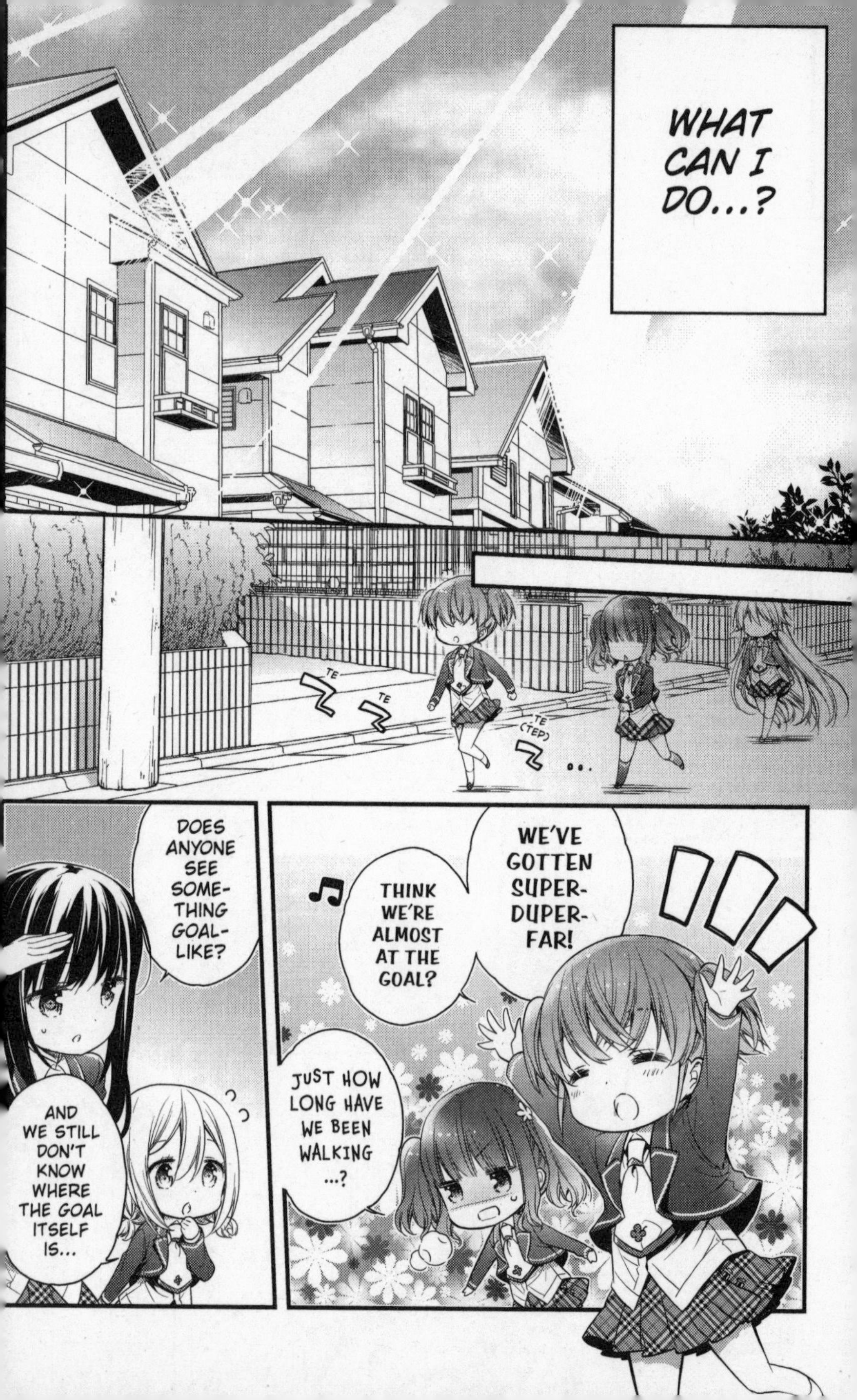
WHAT CAN I DO...?
TE
TE
TE (TEP)
...
WE'VE GOTTEN SUPER-DUPER-FAR!
THINK WE'RE ALMOST AT THE GOAL?
JUST HOW LONG HAVE WE BEEN WALKING ...?
DOES ANYONE SEE SOME-THING GOAL-LIKE?
AND WE STILL DON'T KNOW WHERE THE GOAL ITSELF IS...

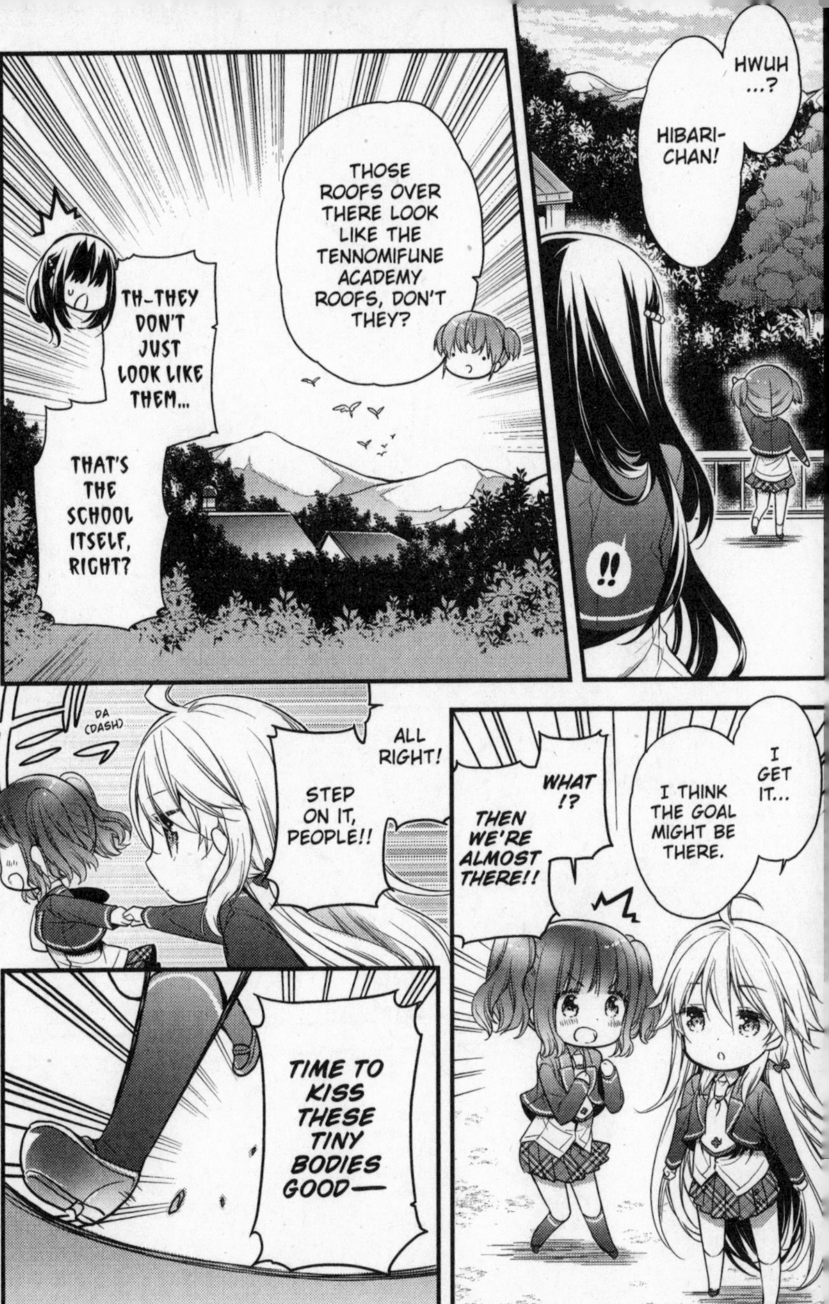
HWUH ...?
HIBARI-CHAN!
!!
THOSE ROOFS OVER THERE LOOK LIKE THE TENNOMIFUNE ACADEMY ROOFS, DON'T THEY?
TH-THEY DON'T JUST LOOK LIKE THEM...
THAT'S THE SCHOOL ITSELF, RIGHT?
I GET IT...
I THINK THE GOAL MIGHT BE THERE.
WHAT!?
THEN WE'RE ALMOST THERE!!
ALL RIGHT!
STEP ON IT, PEOPLE!!
DA (DASH)
TIME TO KISS THESE TINY BODIES GOOD—

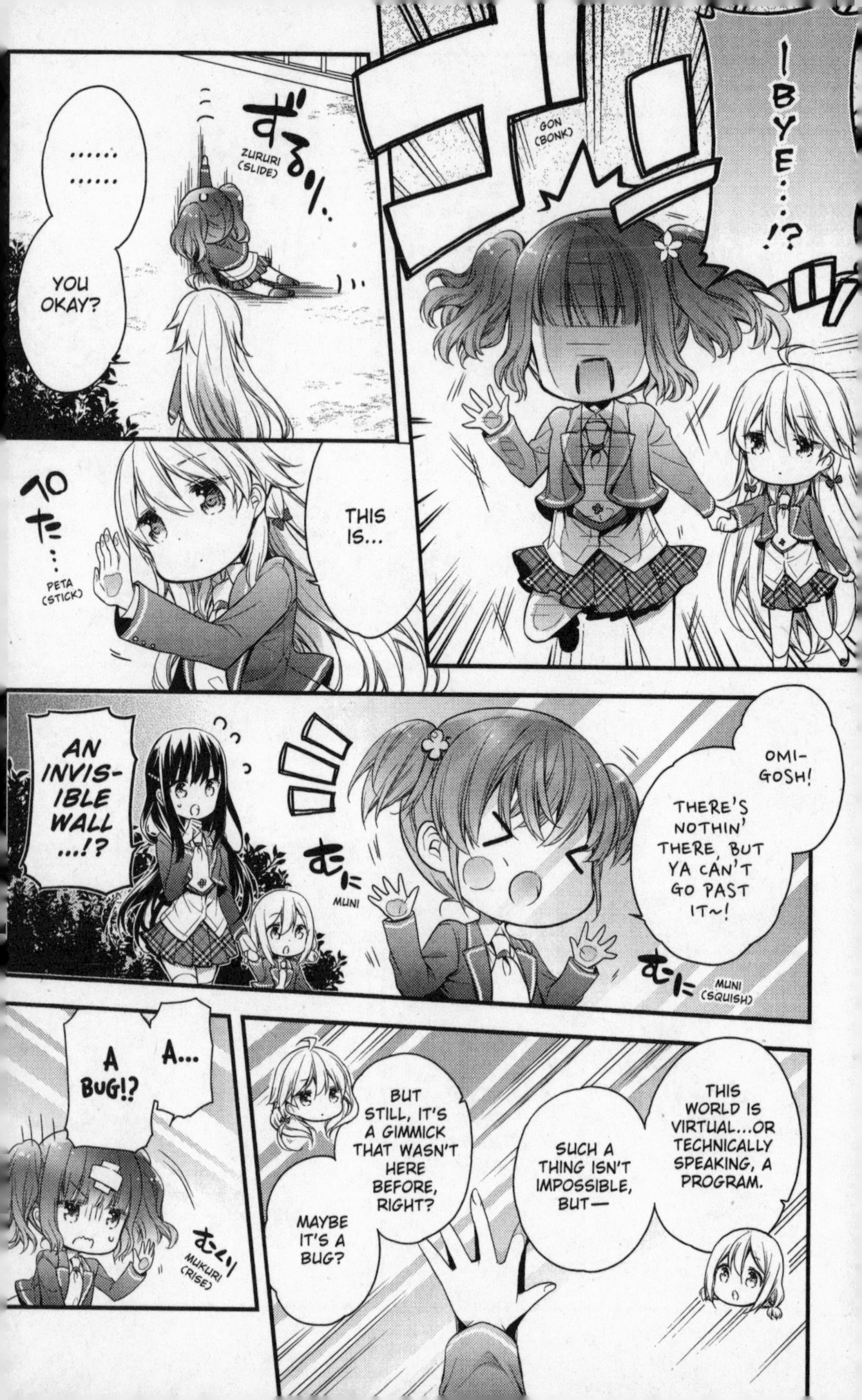

BYE...!?
GON (BONK)
ずるり
ZURURI (SLIDE)
....
YOU OKAY?
THIS IS...
ぺた...
PETA (STICK)
OMI-GOSH!
THERE'S NOTHIN' THERE, BUT YA CAN'T GO PAST IT~!
むに
MUNI (SQUISH)
むに
MUNI
AN INVISIBLE WALL...!?
THIS WORLD IS VIRTUAL...OR TECHNICALLY SPEAKING, A PROGRAM.
SUCH A THING ISN'T IMPOSSIBLE, BUT—
BUT STILL, IT'S A GIMMICK THAT WASN'T HERE BEFORE, RIGHT?
MAYBE IT'S A BUG?
A...
A BUG!?
むくり
MUKURI (RISE)

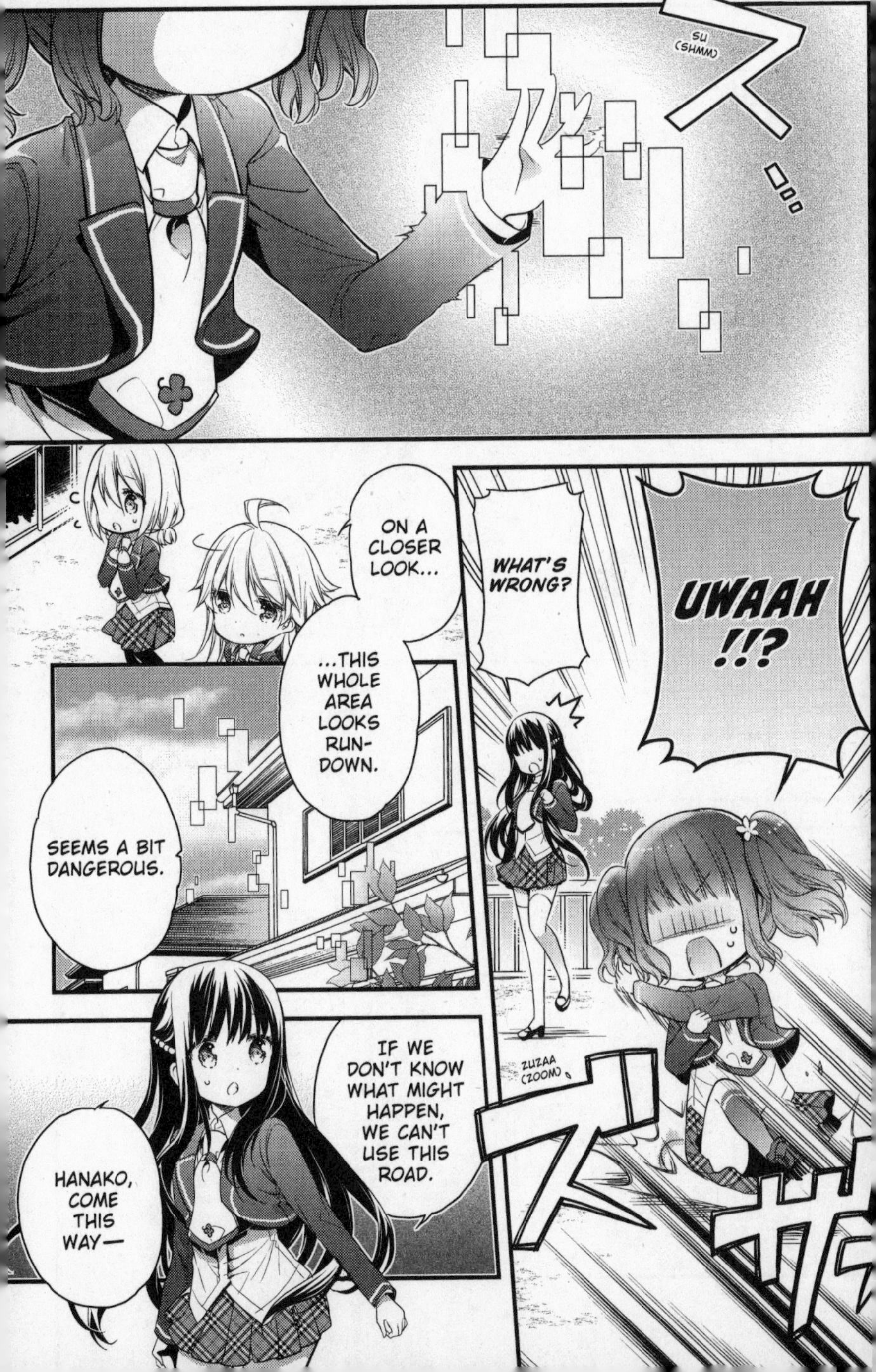
SU (SHMM)
UWAAH !!?
WHAT'S WRONG?
ZUZAA (ZOOM)
ON A CLOSER LOOK...
...THIS WHOLE AREA LOOKS RUN-DOWN.
SEEMS A BIT DANGEROUS.
IF WE DON'T KNOW WHAT MIGHT HAPPEN, WE CAN'T USE THIS ROAD.
HANAKO, COME THIS WAY—

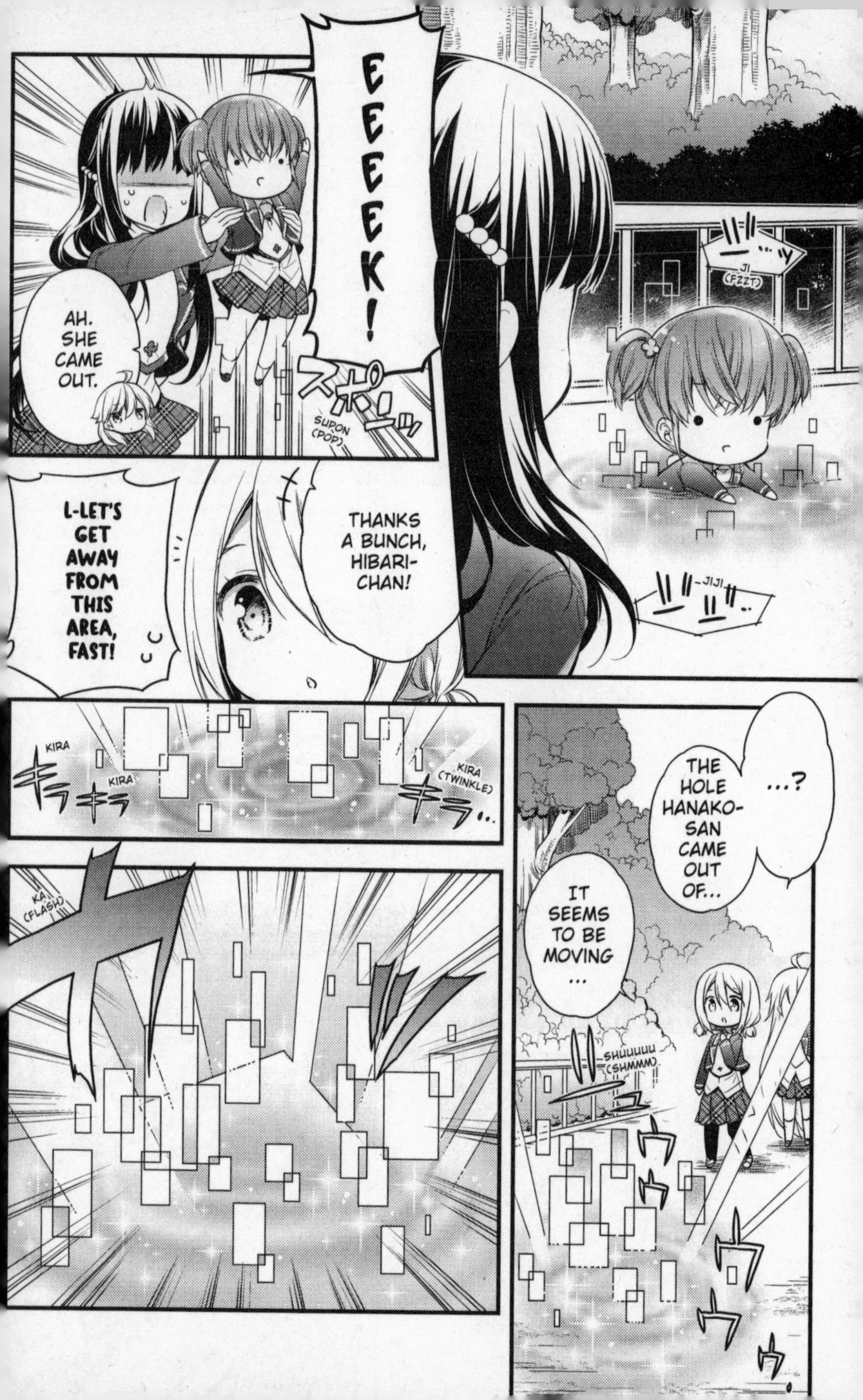
JI
(FZZT)
JIJI
EEEEK!
スポンッ
SUPON
(POP)
AH. SHE CAME OUT.
THANKS A BUNCH, HIBARI-CHAN!
L-LET'S GET AWAY FROM THIS AREA, FAST!
THE HOLE HANAKO-SAN CAME OUT OF...
...?
IT SEEMS TO BE MOVING...
SHUUUUU
(SHMMM)
KIRA
(TWINKLE)
キラ
KIRA
キラ
KIRA
キラ
KA
(FLASH)

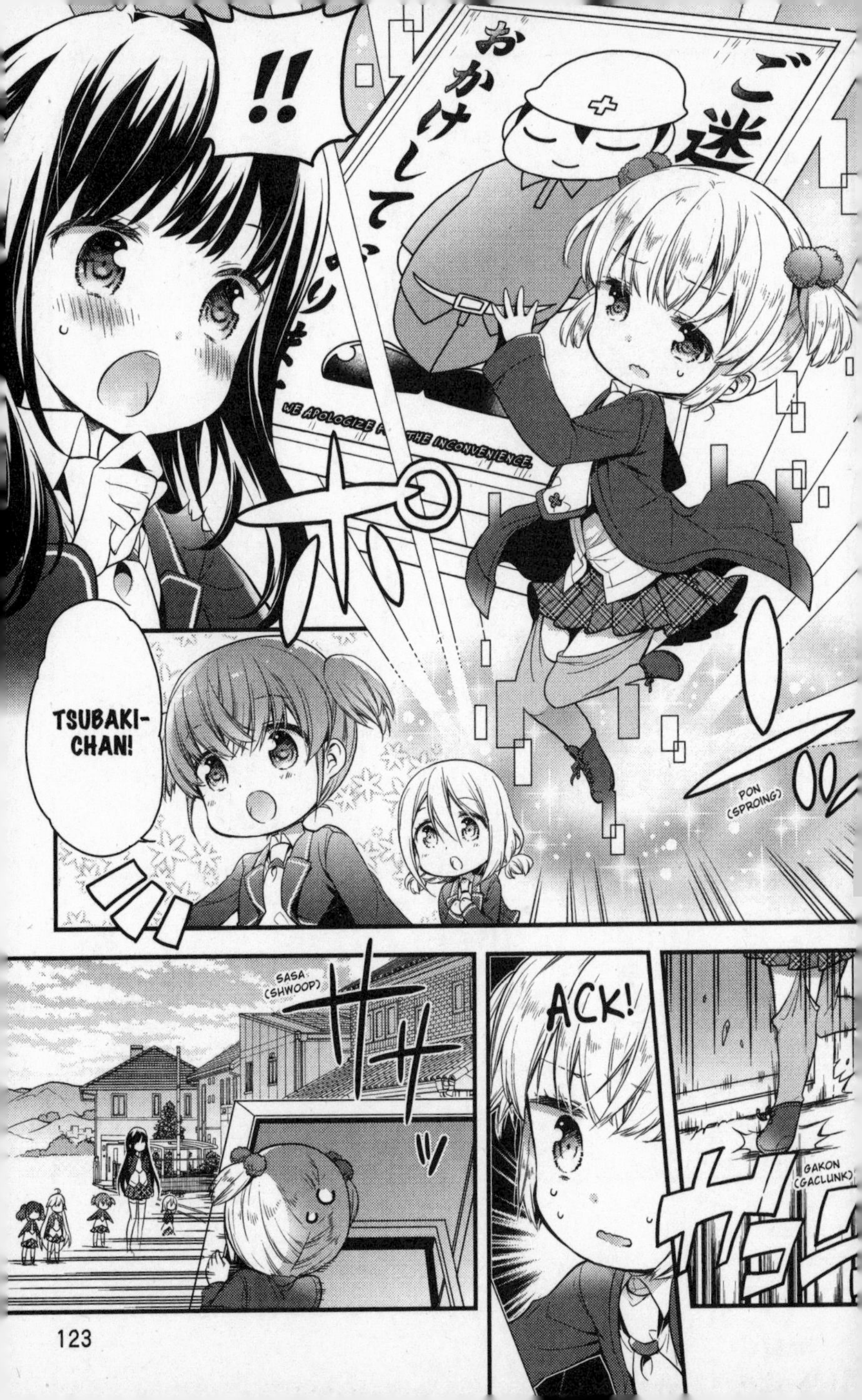
ご迷
おかけして
WE APOLOGIZE F THE INCONVENIENCE.
!!
PON (SPROING)
TSUBAKI-CHAN!
GAKON (GACLUNK)
ACK!
SASA (SHWOOP)

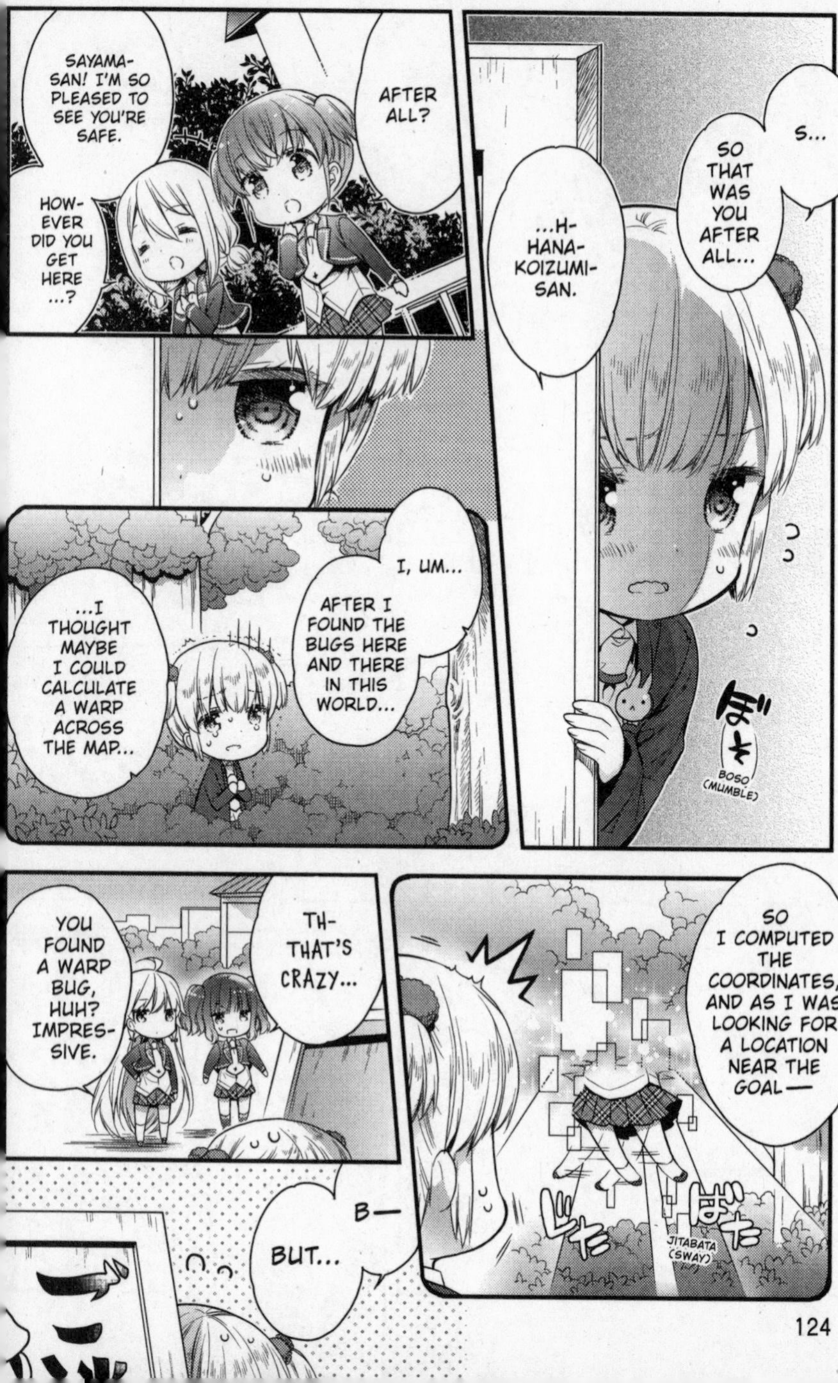
S...
SO THAT WAS YOU AFTER ALL...
...H-HANA-KOIZUMI-SAN.
BOSO (MUMBLE)
AFTER ALL?
SAYAMA-SAN! I'M SO PLEASED TO SEE YOU'RE SAFE.
HOW-EVER DID YOU GET HERE ...?
I, UM...
AFTER I FOUND THE BUGS HERE AND THERE IN THIS WORLD...
...I THOUGHT MAYBE I COULD CALCULATE A WARP ACROSS THE MAP...
SO I COMPUTED THE COORDINATES, AND AS I WAS LOOKING FOR A LOCATION NEAR THE GOAL—
JITABATA (SWAY)
TH-THAT'S CRAZY...
YOU FOUND A WARP BUG, HUH? IMPRES-SIVE.
B—
BUT...

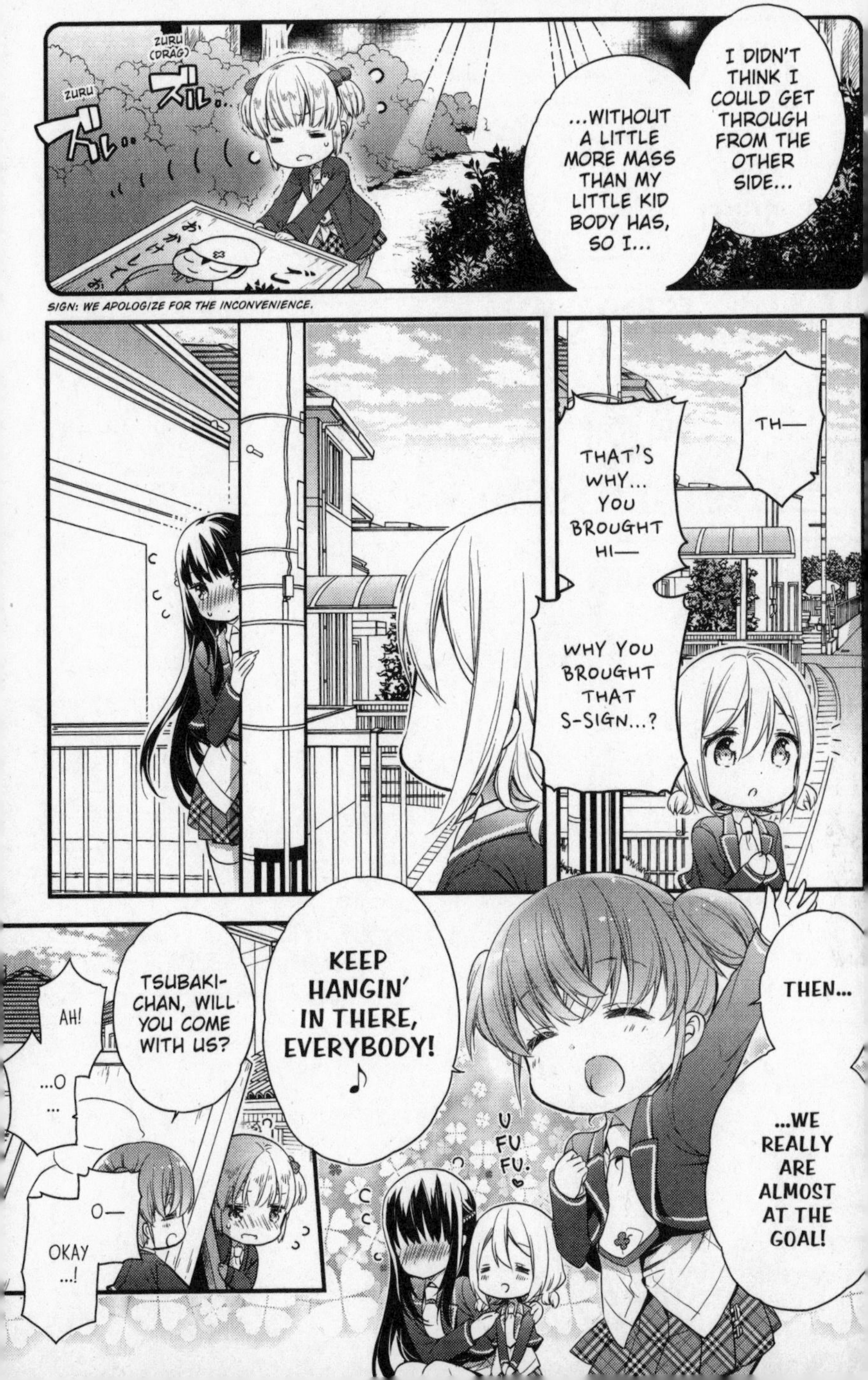
I DIDN'T THINK I COULD GET THROUGH FROM THE OTHER SIDE...
...WITHOUT A LITTLE MORE MASS THAN MY LITTLE KID BODY HAS, SO I...
ZURU (DRAG)
ZURU
SIGN: WE APOLOGIZE FOR THE INCONVENIENCE.
TH—
THAT'S WHY... YOU BROUGHT HI—
WHY YOU BROUGHT THAT S-SIGN...?
THEN...
...WE REALLY ARE ALMOST AT THE GOAL!
KEEP HANGIN' IN THERE, EVERYBODY! ♪
UFUFU.
TSUBAKI-CHAN, WILL YOU COME WITH US?
AH!
...O...
O—
OKAY...!

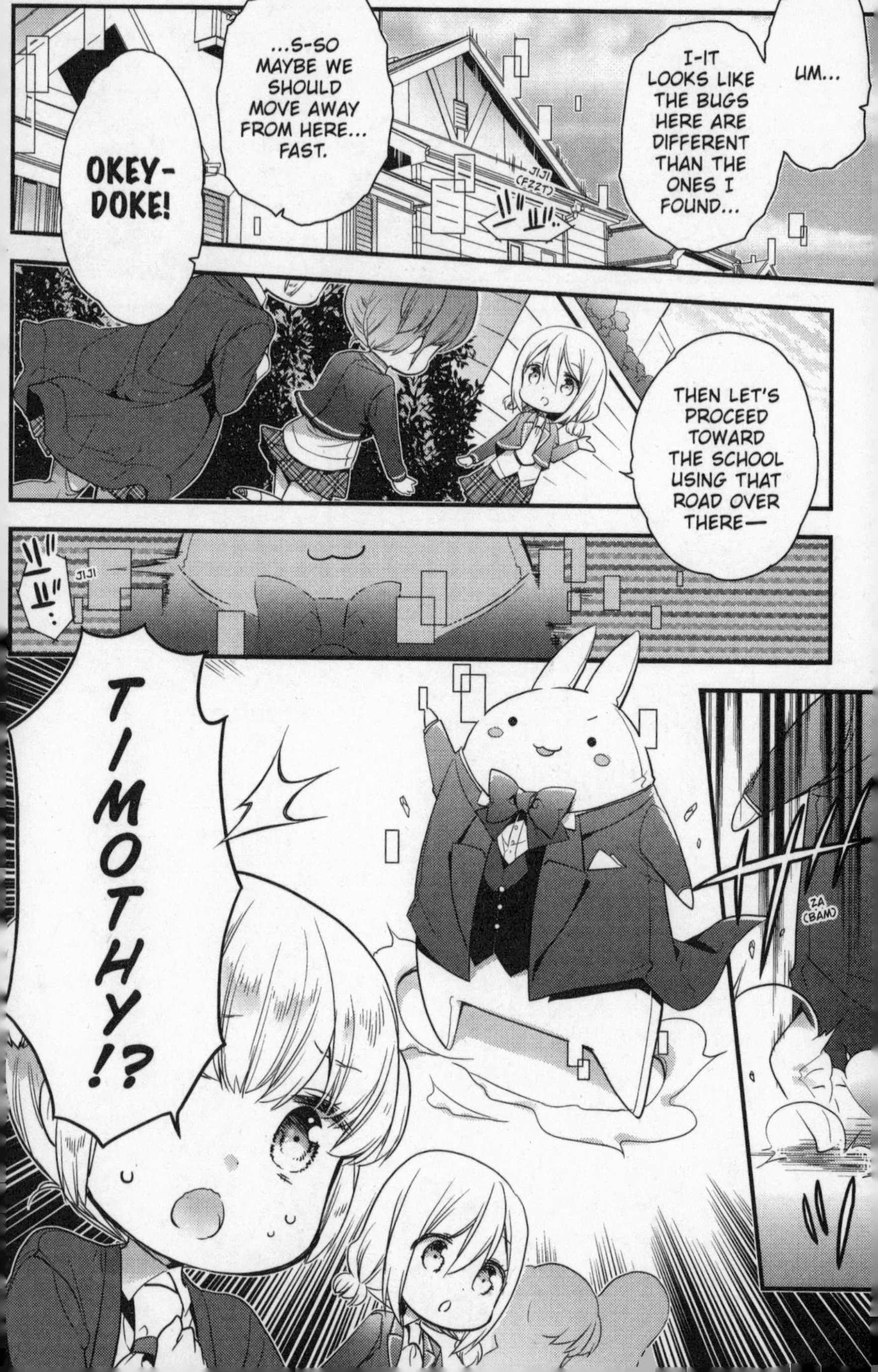
UM...
I-IT LOOKS LIKE THE BUGS HERE ARE DIFFERENT THAN THE ONES I FOUND...
JIJI (FZZT)
...S-SO MAYBE WE SHOULD MOVE AWAY FROM HERE... FAST.
OKEY-DOKE!
THEN LET'S PROCEED TOWARD THE SCHOOL USING THAT ROAD OVER THERE—
JIJI
ZA (BAM)
TIMOTHY!?

Anne Happy
unhappy go lucky!

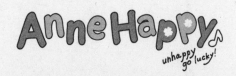

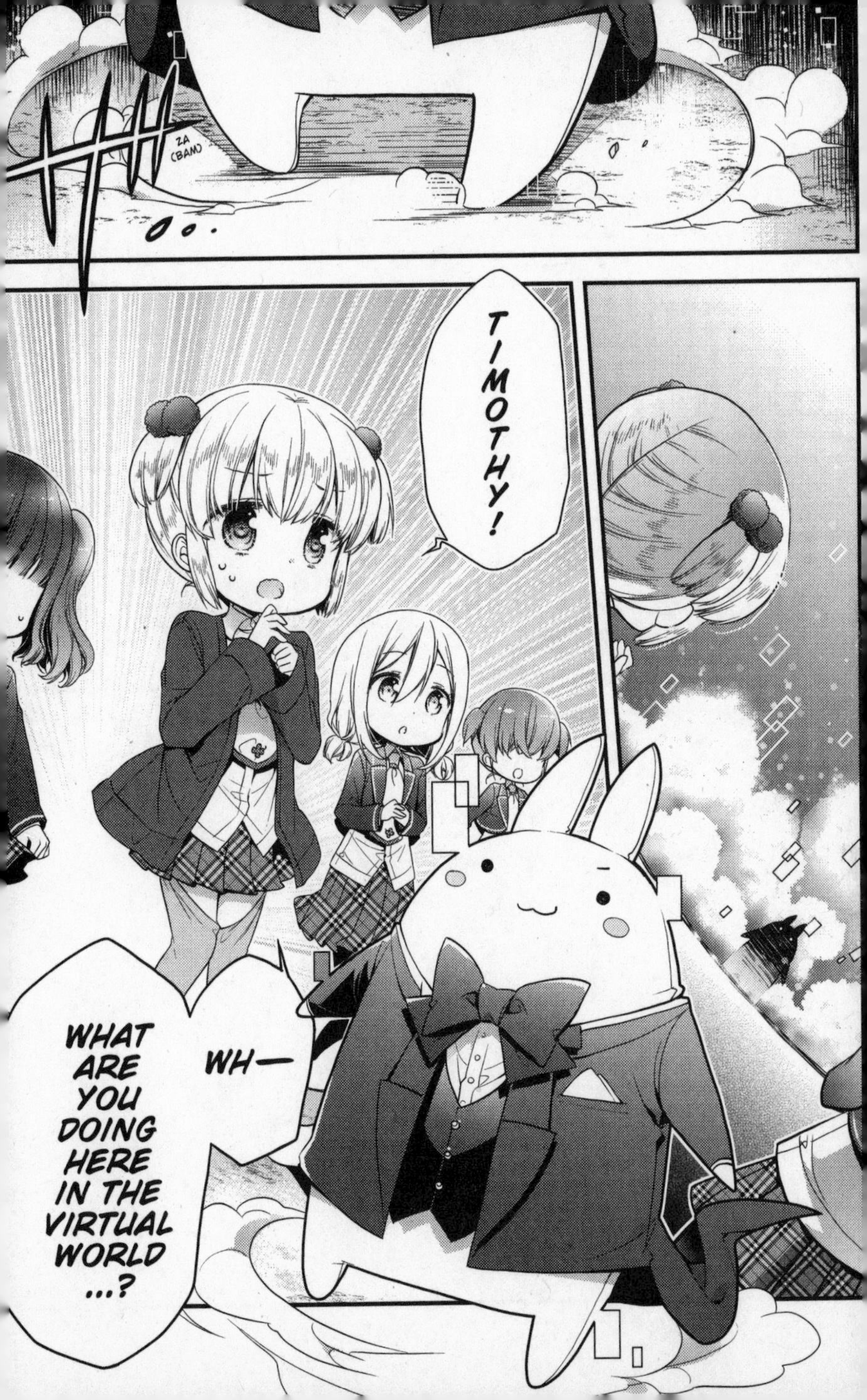
ZA (BAM)
TIMOTHY!
WH—
WHAT ARE YOU DOING HERE IN THE VIRTUAL WORLD ...?

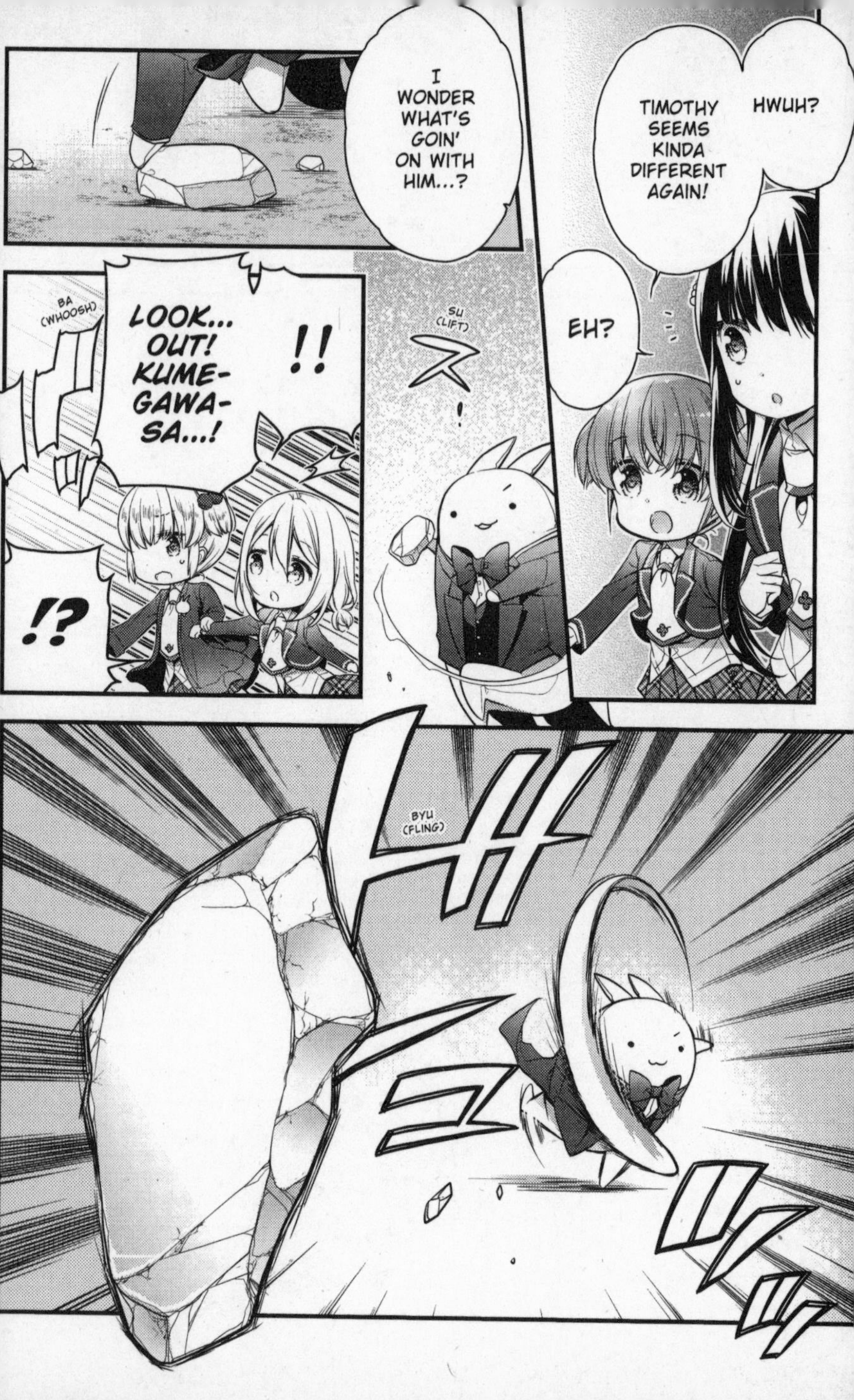
HWUH?
TIMOTHY SEEMS KINDA DIFFERENT AGAIN!
EH?
I WONDER WHAT'S GOIN' ON WITH HIM...?
SU (LIFT)
!
!!
LOOK... OUT! KUME-GAWA-SA...!
BA (WHOOSH)
!?
BYU (FLING)

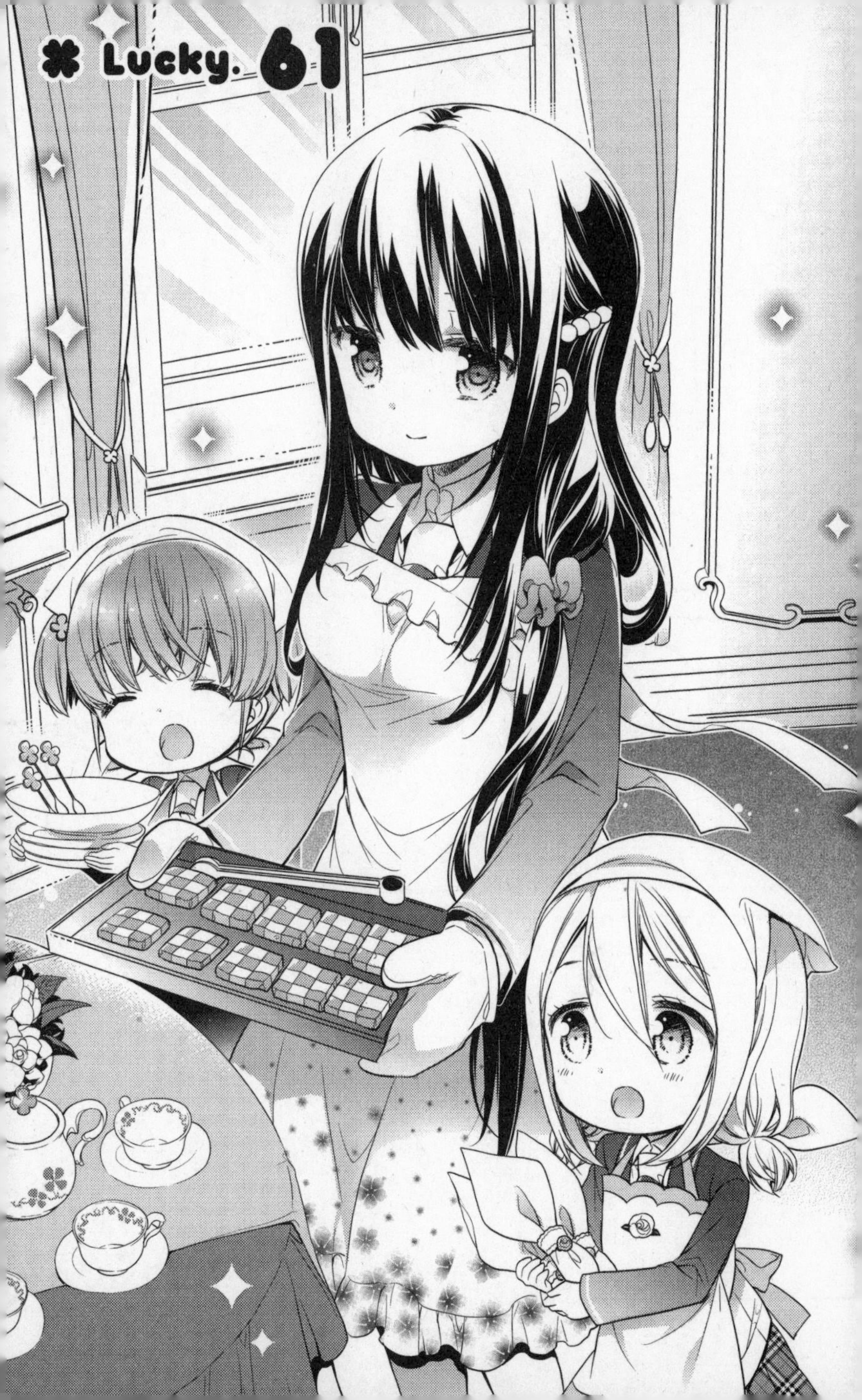
Lucky. 61

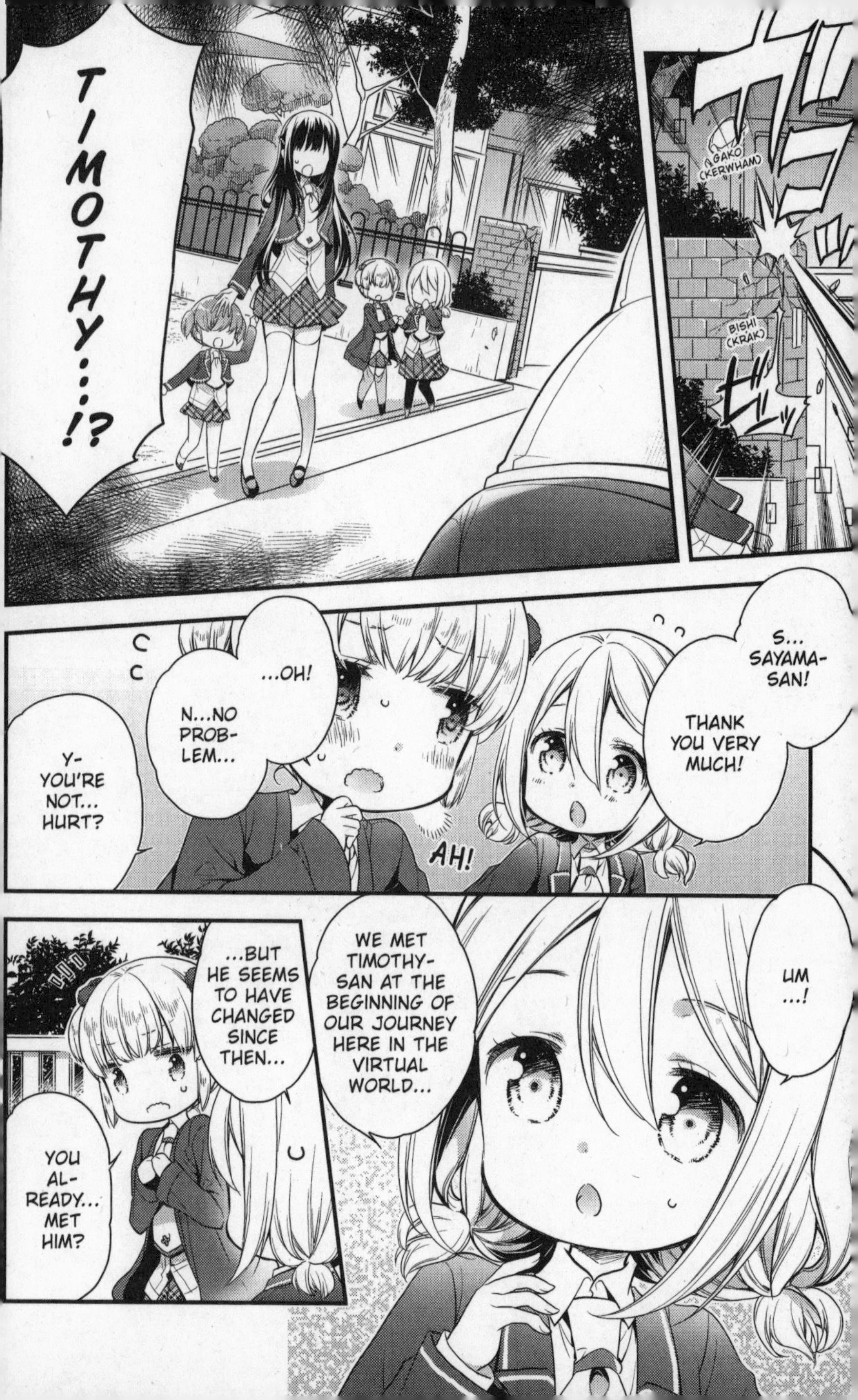
GAKO (KERWHAM)
BISHI (KRAK)
TIMOTHY...!?
S... SAYAMA-SAN!
THANK YOU VERY MUCH!
...OH!
N...NO PROBLEM...
AH!
Y-YOU'RE NOT... HURT?
UM ...!
WE MET TIMOTHY-SAN AT THE BEGINNING OF OUR JOURNEY HERE IN THE VIRTUAL WORLD...
...BUT HE SEEMS TO HAVE CHANGED SINCE THEN...
YOU AL-READY... MET HIM?

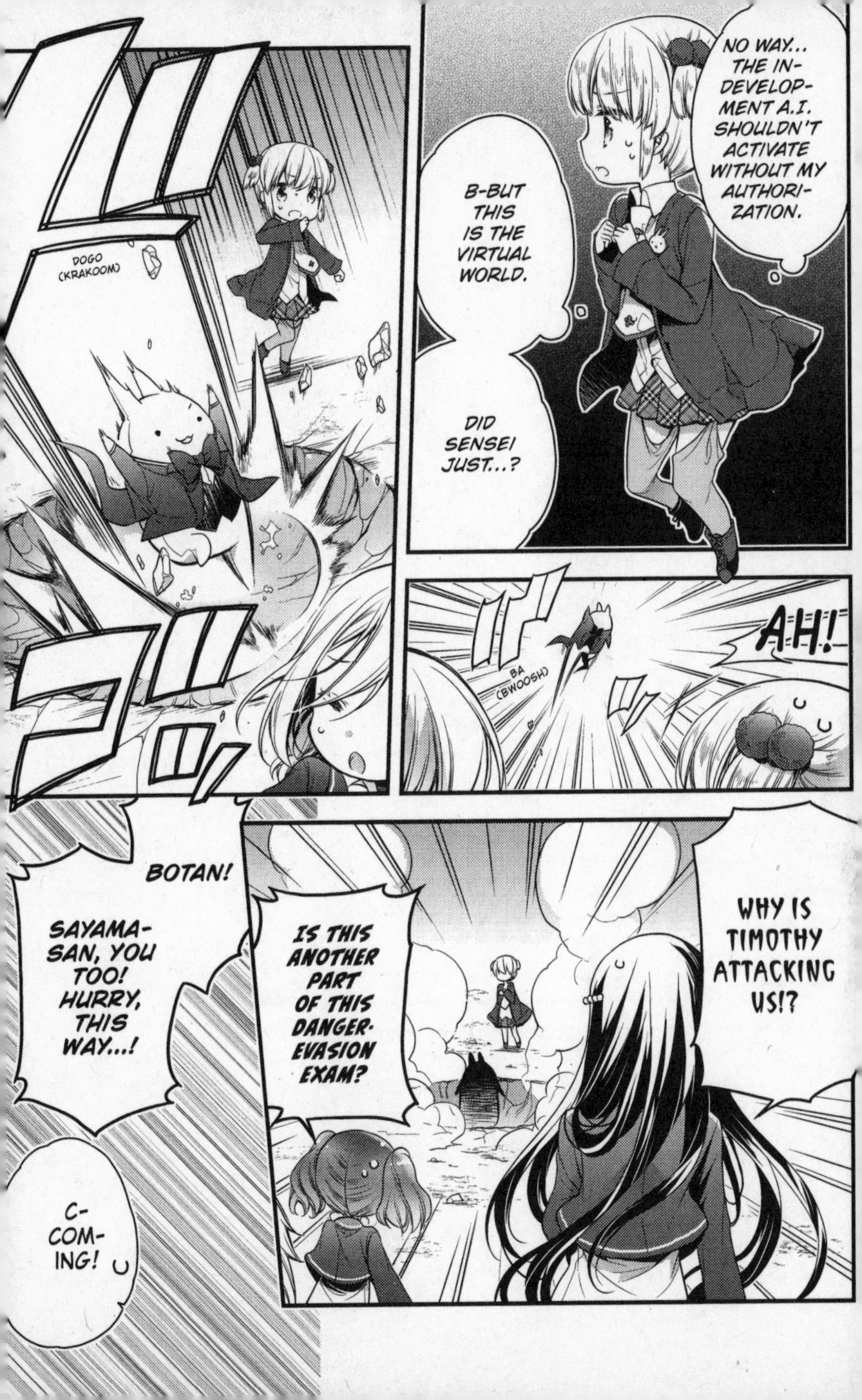
NO WAY... THE IN-DEVELOPMENT A.I. SHOULDN'T ACTIVATE WITHOUT MY AUTHORIZATION.
B-BUT THIS IS THE VIRTUAL WORLD.
DID SENSEI JUST...?
AH!
BA (BWOOSH)
DOGO (KRAKOOM)
WHY IS TIMOTHY ATTACKING US!?
IS THIS ANOTHER PART OF THIS DANGER-EVASION EXAM?
BOTAN!
SAYAMA-SAN, YOU TOO! HURRY, THIS WAY...!
C-COMING!

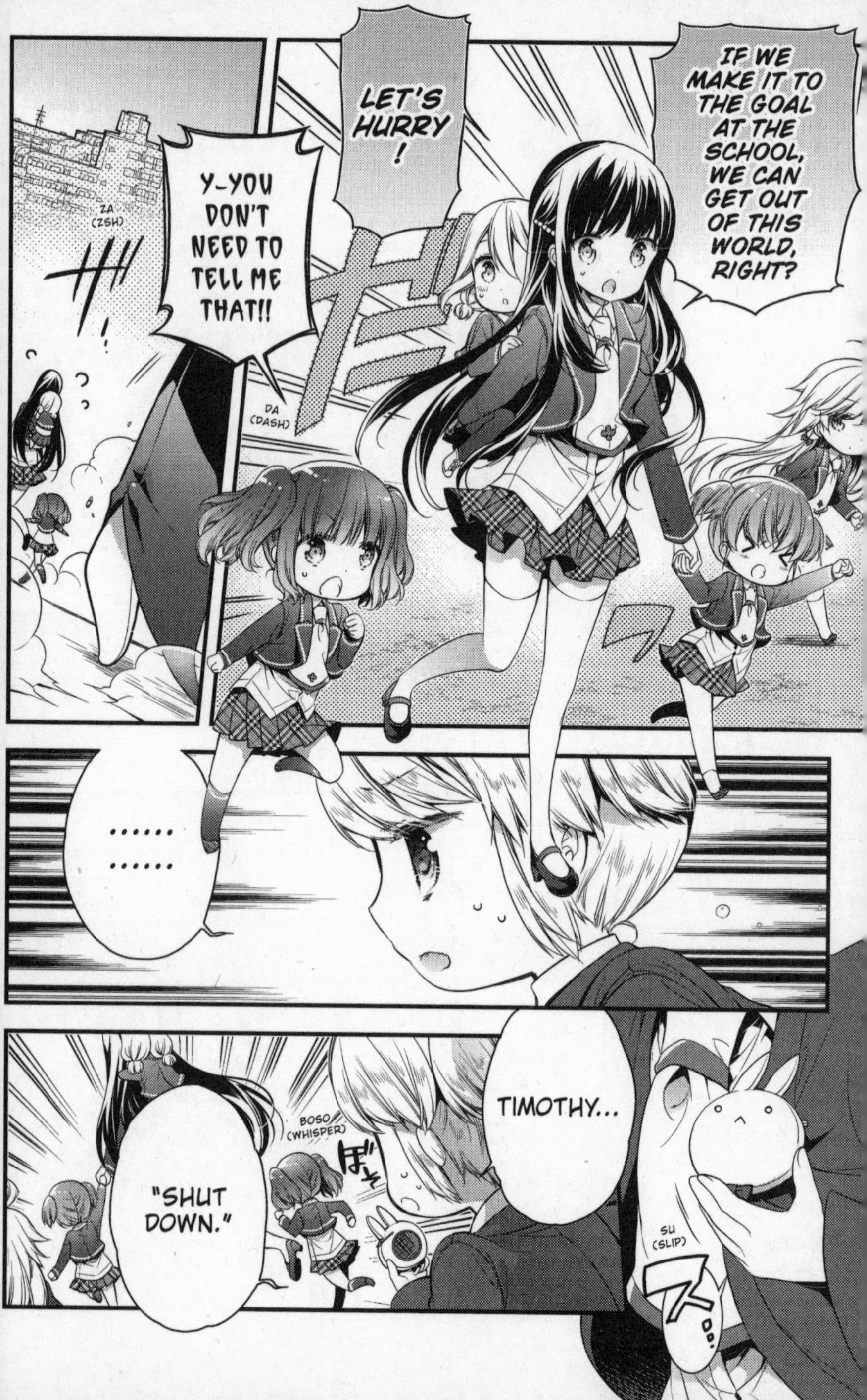
IF WE MAKE IT TO THE GOAL AT THE SCHOOL, WE CAN GET OUT OF THIS WORLD, RIGHT?
LET'S HURRY!
DA (DASH)
Y-YOU DON'T NEED TO TELL ME THAT!!
ZA (ZSH)
......
......
TIMOTHY...
SU (SLIP)
BOSO (WHISPER)
"SHUT DOWN."

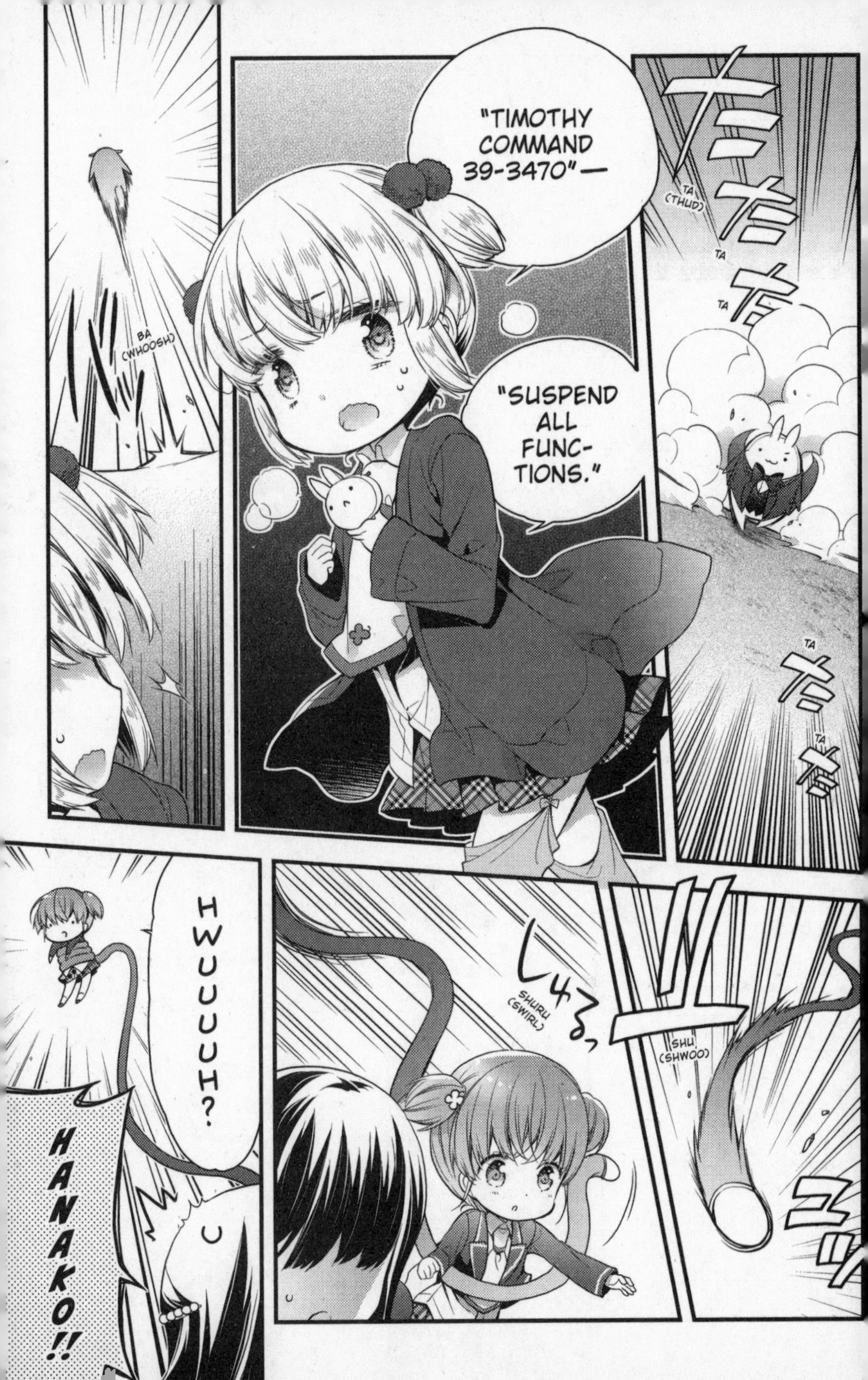

TA (THUD)
TA
TA
TA
TA
"TIMOTHY COMMAND 39-3470"—
"SUSPEND ALL FUNCTIONS."
BA (WHOOSH)
SHU (SHWOO)
SHURU (SWIRL)
HWUUUUUH?
HANAKO!!

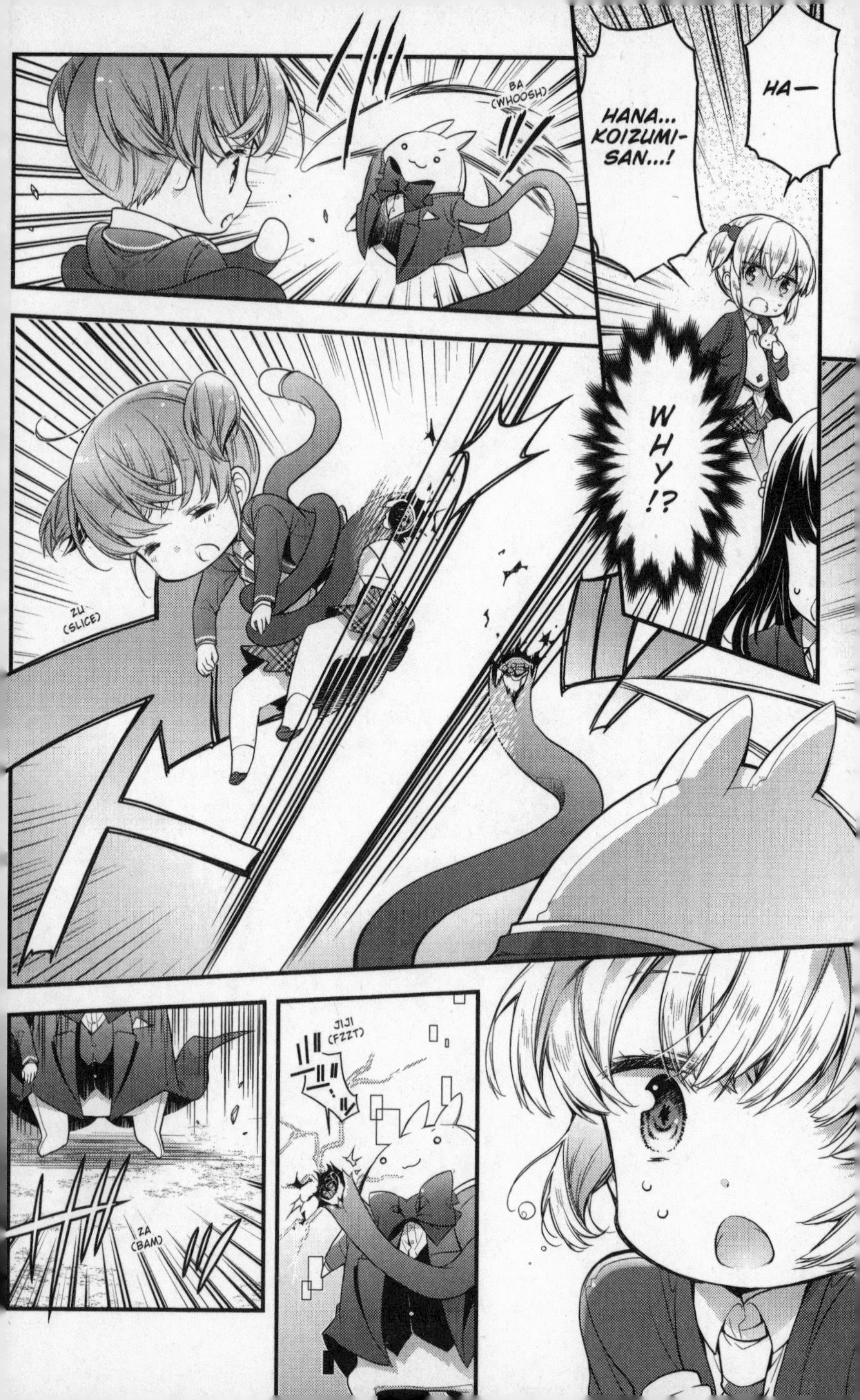
HA—
HANA... KOIZUMI-SAN...!
BA (WHOOSH)
WHY!?
ZU (SLICE)
JIJI (FZZT)
ZA (BAM)

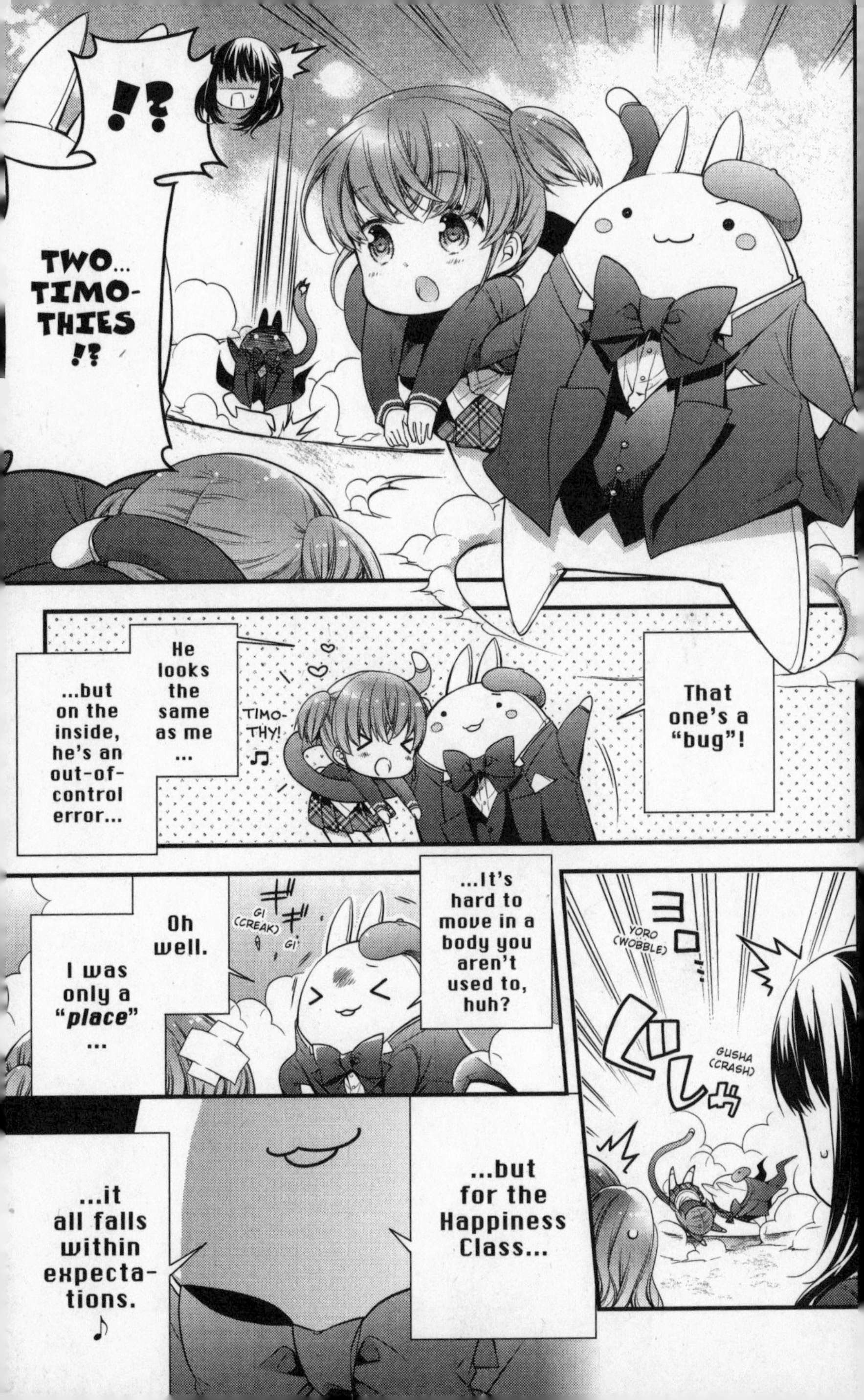
!?
TWO... TIMOTHIES!?
That one's a "bug"!
TIMOTHY! ♫
He looks the same as me...
...but on the inside, he's an out-of-control error...
YORO (WOBBLE)
GUSHA (CRASH)
...It's hard to move in a body you aren't used to, huh?
GI (CREAK) GI
Oh well.
I was only a "*place*"...
...but for the Happiness Class...
...it all falls within expectations. ♪

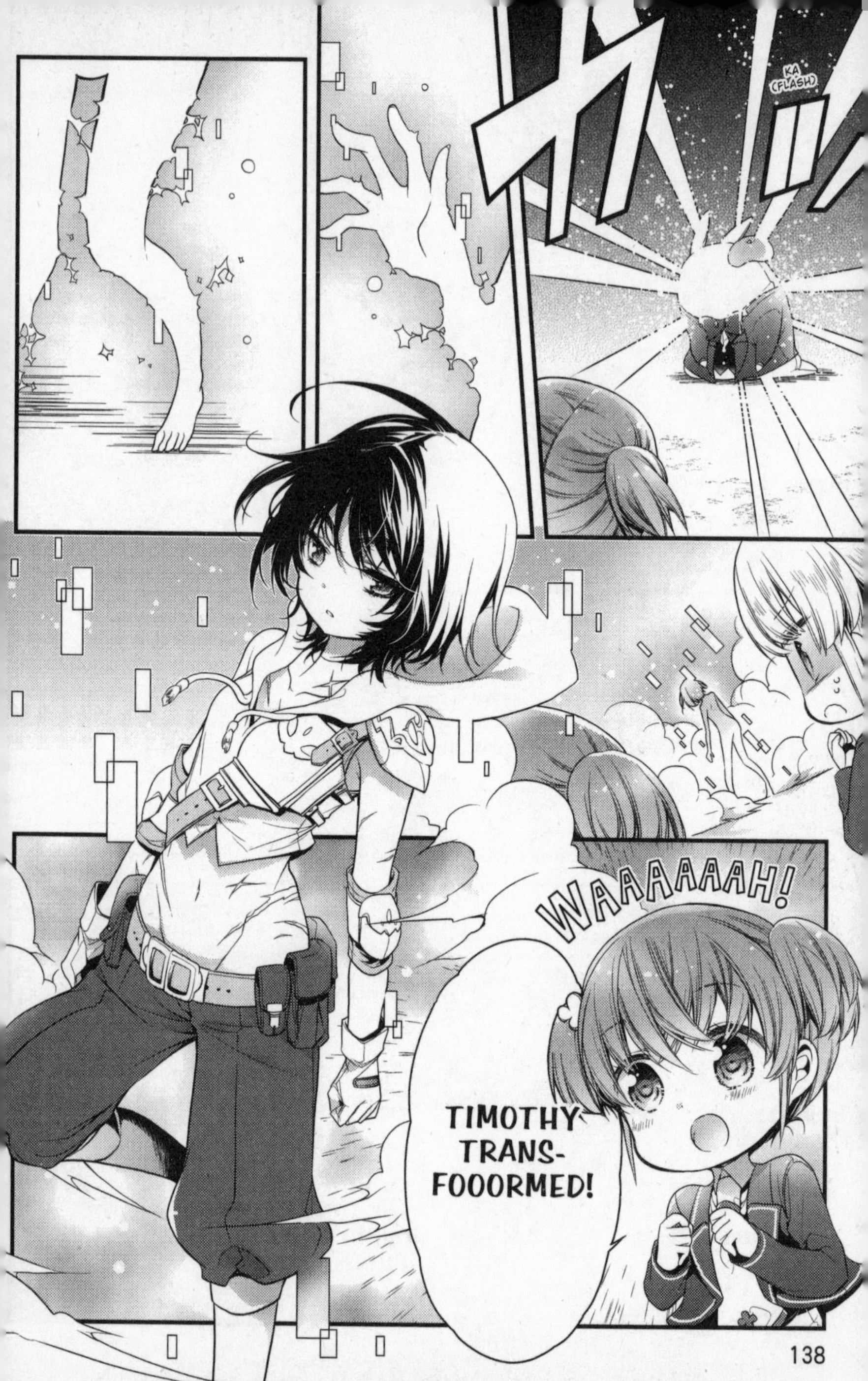
KA (FLASH)
WAAAAAAH!
TIMOTHY TRANS-FOOORMED!

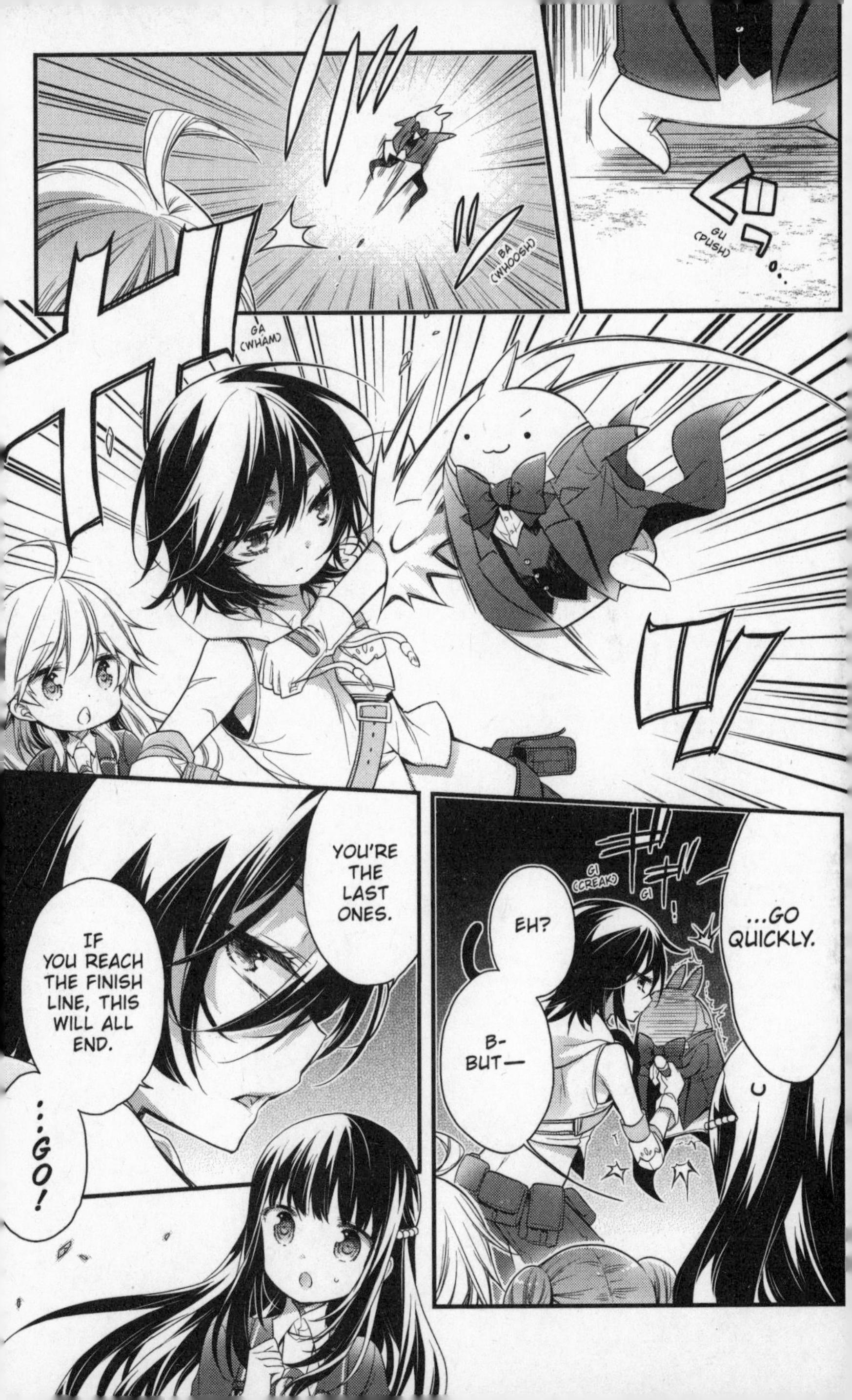
GU (PUSH)
BA (WHOOSH)
GA (WHAM)
GI (CREAK)
GI
...GO QUICKLY.
EH?
B-BUT—
YOU'RE THE LAST ONES.
IF YOU REACH THE FINISH LINE, THIS WILL ALL END.
...GO!

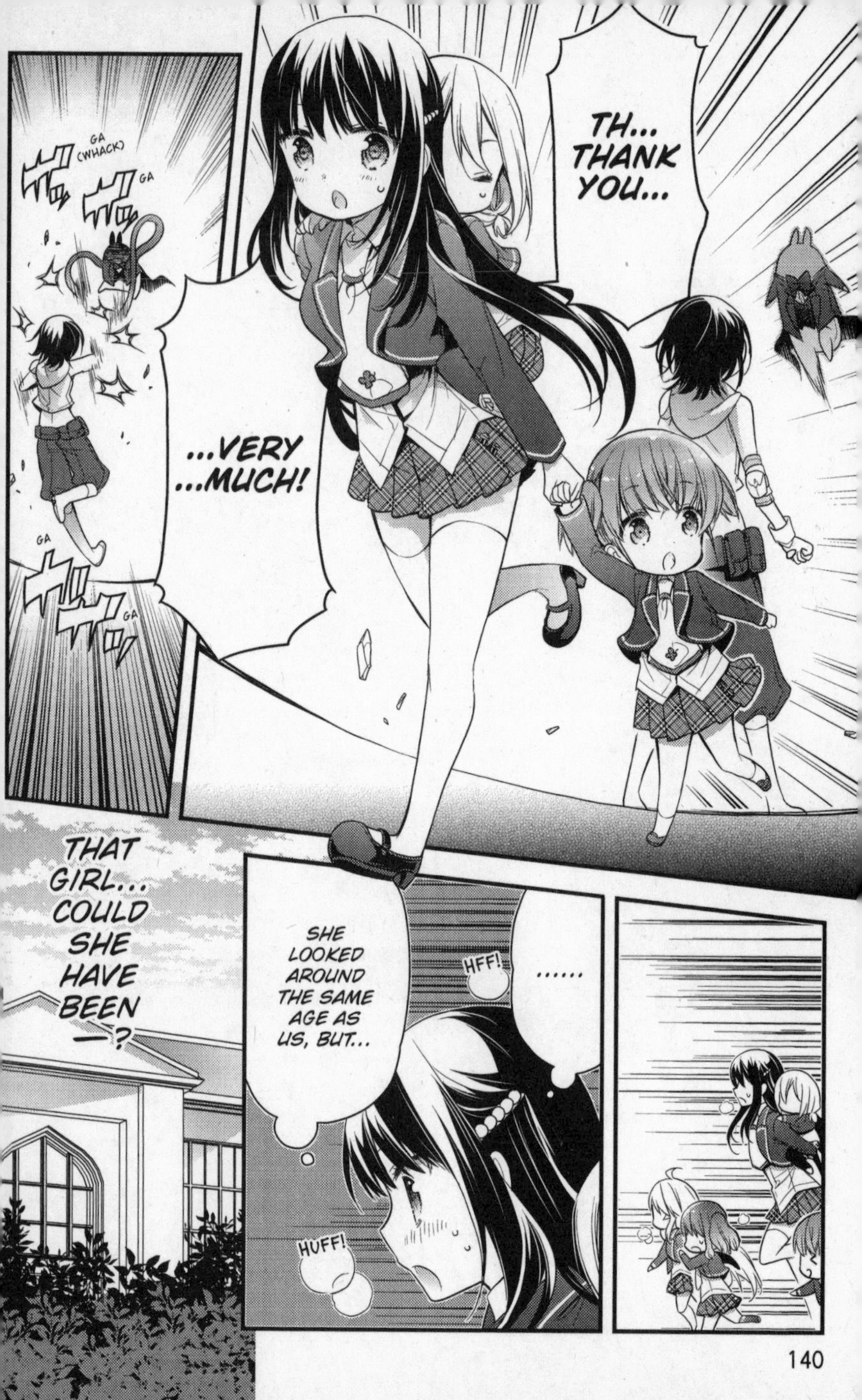
TH... THANK YOU...
...VERY ...MUCH!
GA (WHACK)
GA
GA
GA
......
HFF!
SHE LOOKED AROUND THE SAME AGE AS US, BUT...
HUFF!
THAT GIRL... COULD SHE HAVE BEEN—?

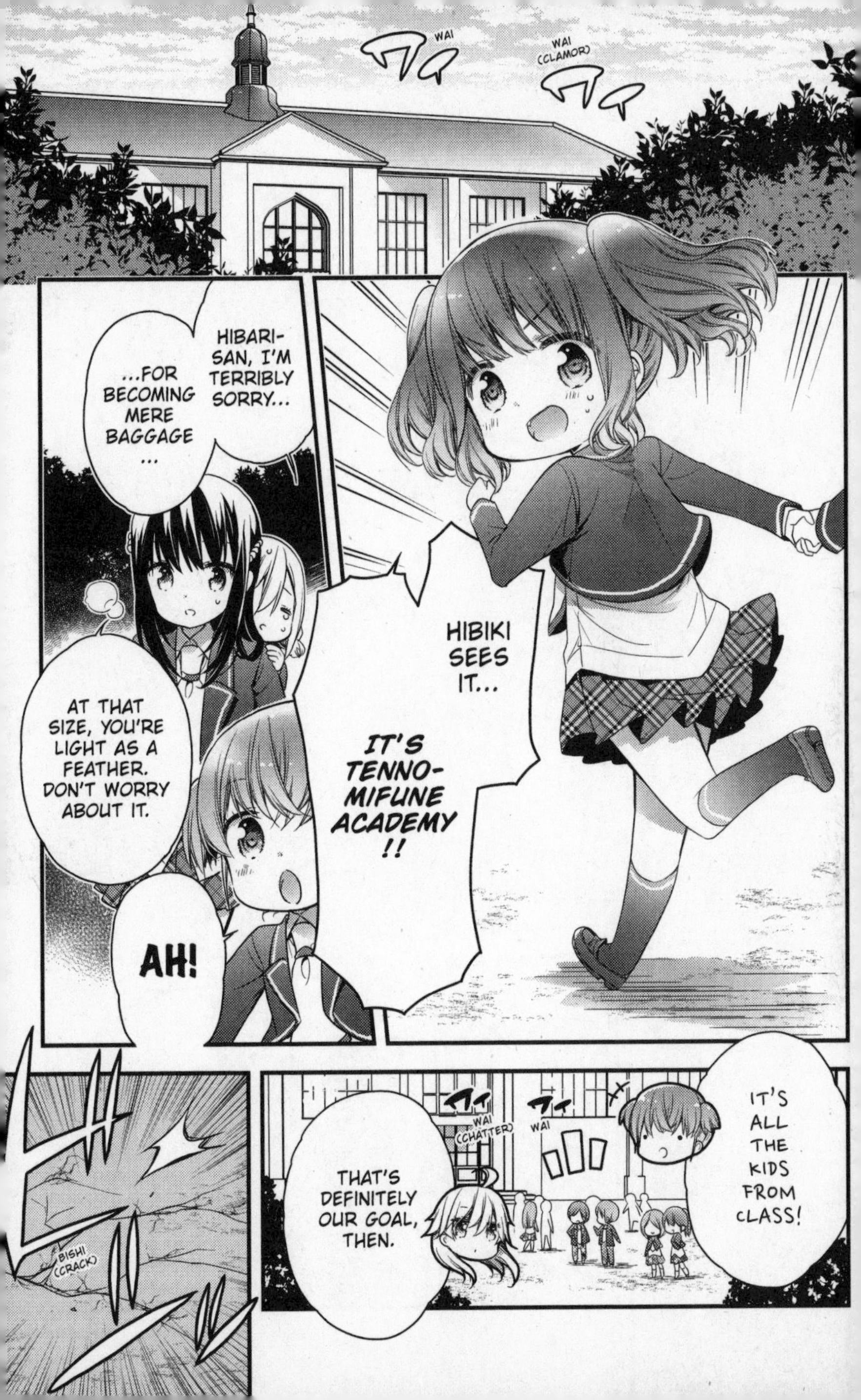
WAI (CLAMOR)
WAI
HIBIKI SEES IT...
IT'S TENNO-MIFUNE ACADEMY!!
HIBARI-SAN, I'M TERRIBLY SORRY...
...FOR BECOMING MERE BAGGAGE...
AT THAT SIZE, YOU'RE LIGHT AS A FEATHER. DON'T WORRY ABOUT IT.
AH!
IT'S ALL THE KIDS FROM CLASS!
WAI
WAI (CHATTER)
THAT'S DEFINITELY OUR GOAL, THEN.
BISHI (CRACK)

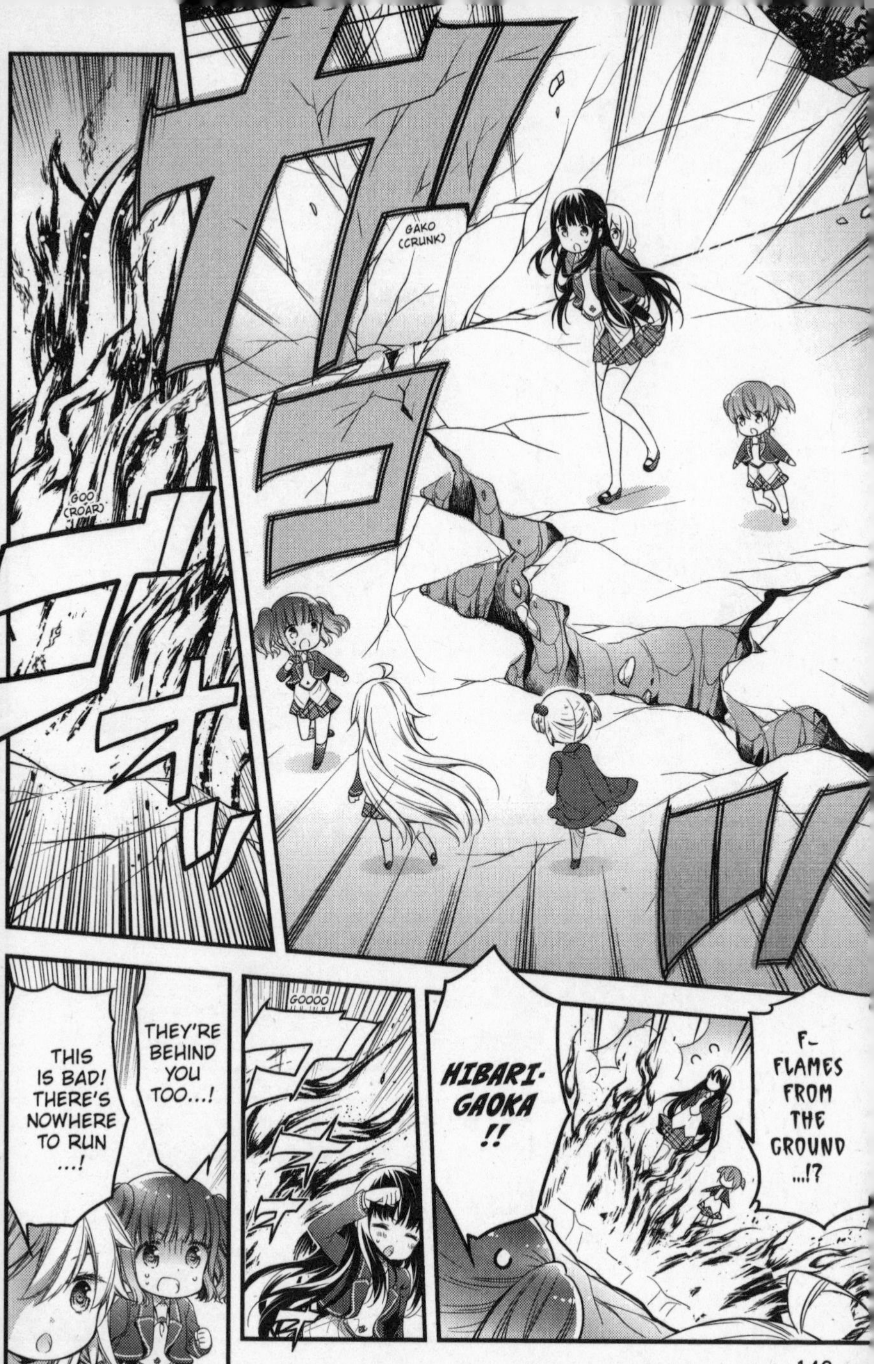
GAKO (CRUNK)
GOO (ROAR)
F–FLAMES FROM THE GROUND ...!?
HIBARI-GAOKA!!
GOOOO
THEY'RE BEHIND YOU TOO...!
THIS IS BAD! THERE'S NOWHERE TO RUN ...!

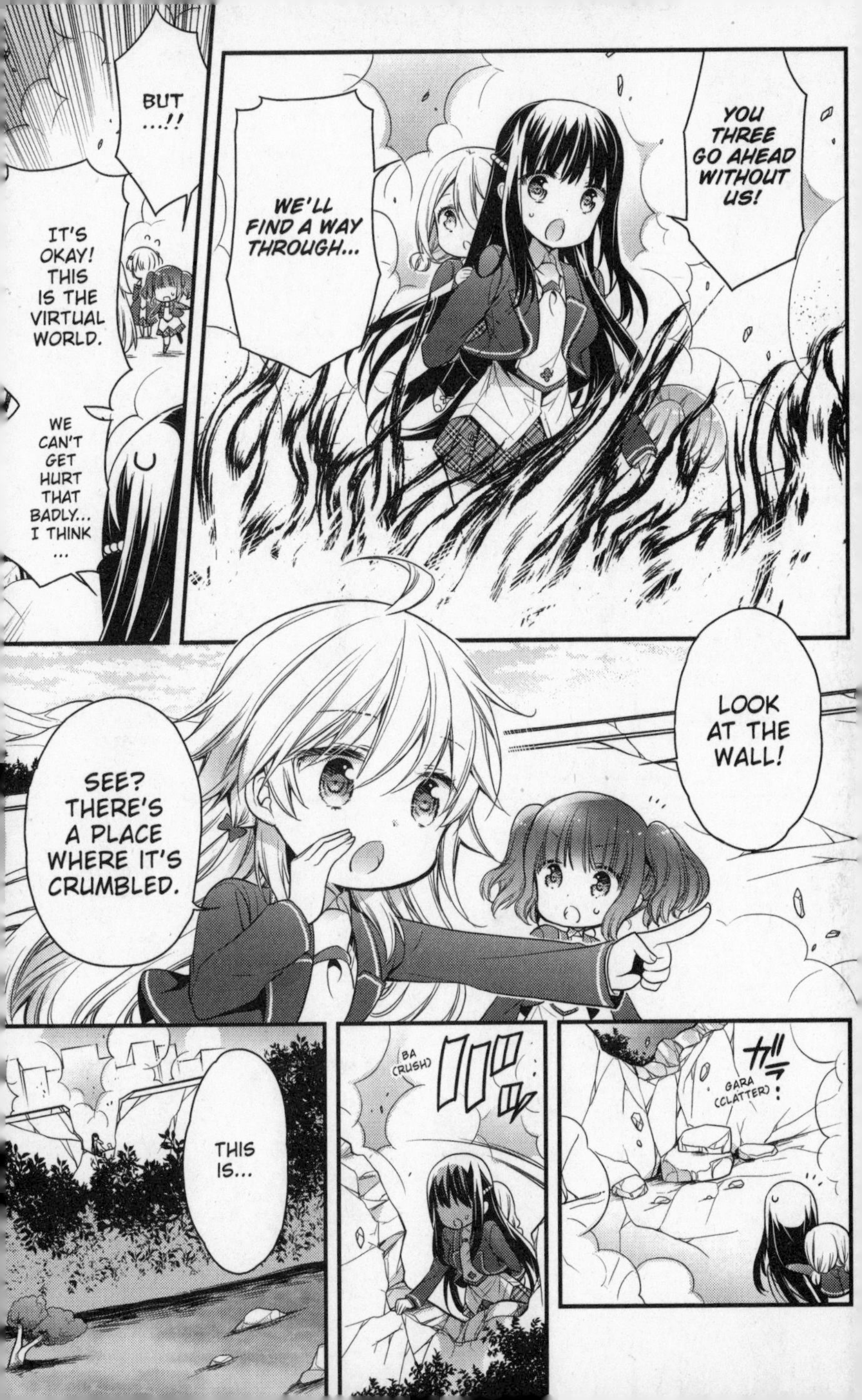

YOU THREE GO AHEAD WITHOUT US!
WE'LL FIND A WAY THROUGH...
BUT ...!!
IT'S OKAY! THIS IS THE VIRTUAL WORLD.
WE CAN'T GET HURT THAT BADLY... I THINK ...
LOOK AT THE WALL!
SEE? THERE'S A PLACE WHERE IT'S CRUMBLED.
GARA (CLATTER)
BA (CRUSH)
THIS IS...

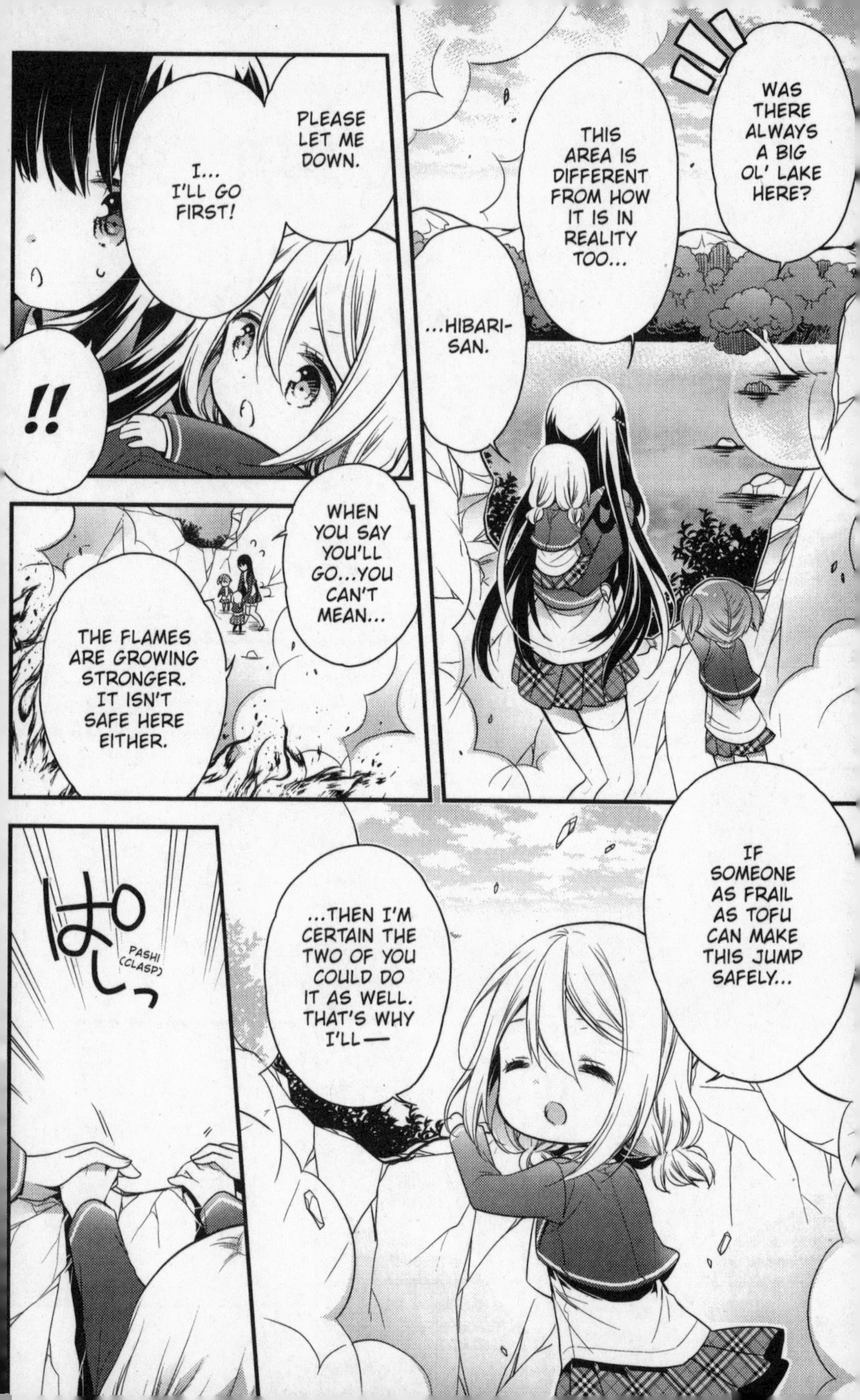
WAS THERE ALWAYS A BIG OL' LAKE HERE?
THIS AREA IS DIFFERENT FROM HOW IT IS IN REALITY TOO...
...HIBARI-SAN.
PLEASE LET ME DOWN.
I... I'LL GO FIRST!
!!
WHEN YOU SAY YOU'LL GO...YOU CAN'T MEAN...
THE FLAMES ARE GROWING STRONGER. IT ISN'T SAFE HERE EITHER.
IF SOMEONE AS FRAIL AS TOFU CAN MAKE THIS JUMP SAFELY...
...THEN I'M CERTAIN THE TWO OF YOU COULD DO IT AS WELL. THAT'S WHY I'LL—
ぱしっ
PASHI (CLASP)

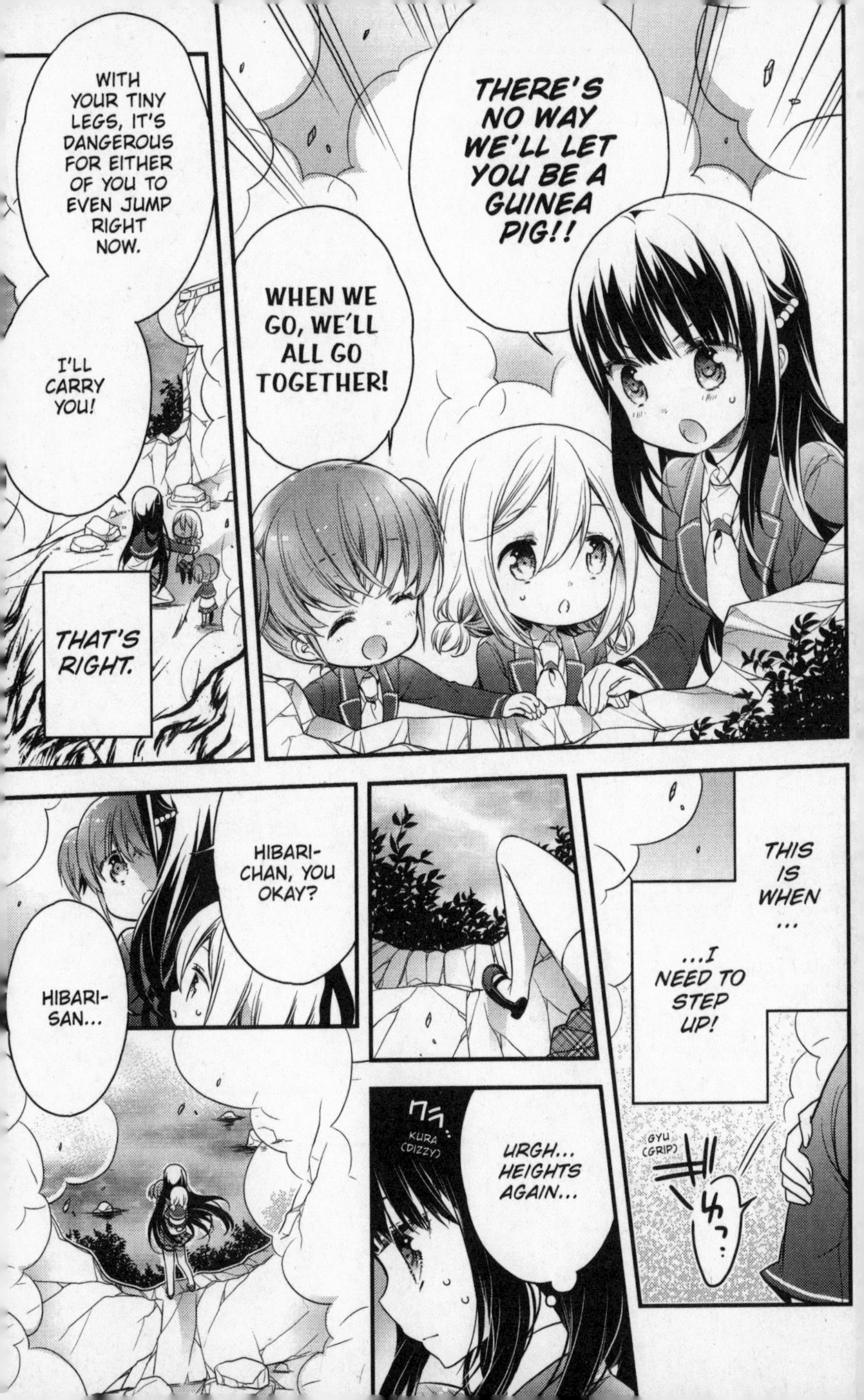
THERE'S NO WAY WE'LL LET YOU BE A GUINEA PIG!!
WHEN WE GO, WE'LL ALL GO TOGETHER!
WITH YOUR TINY LEGS, IT'S DANGEROUS FOR EITHER OF YOU TO EVEN JUMP RIGHT NOW.
I'LL CARRY YOU!
THAT'S RIGHT.
THIS IS WHEN ...
...I NEED TO STEP UP!
GYU (GRIP)
HIBARI-CHAN, YOU OKAY?
HIBARI-SAN...
KURA (DIZZY)
URGH... HEIGHTS AGAIN...

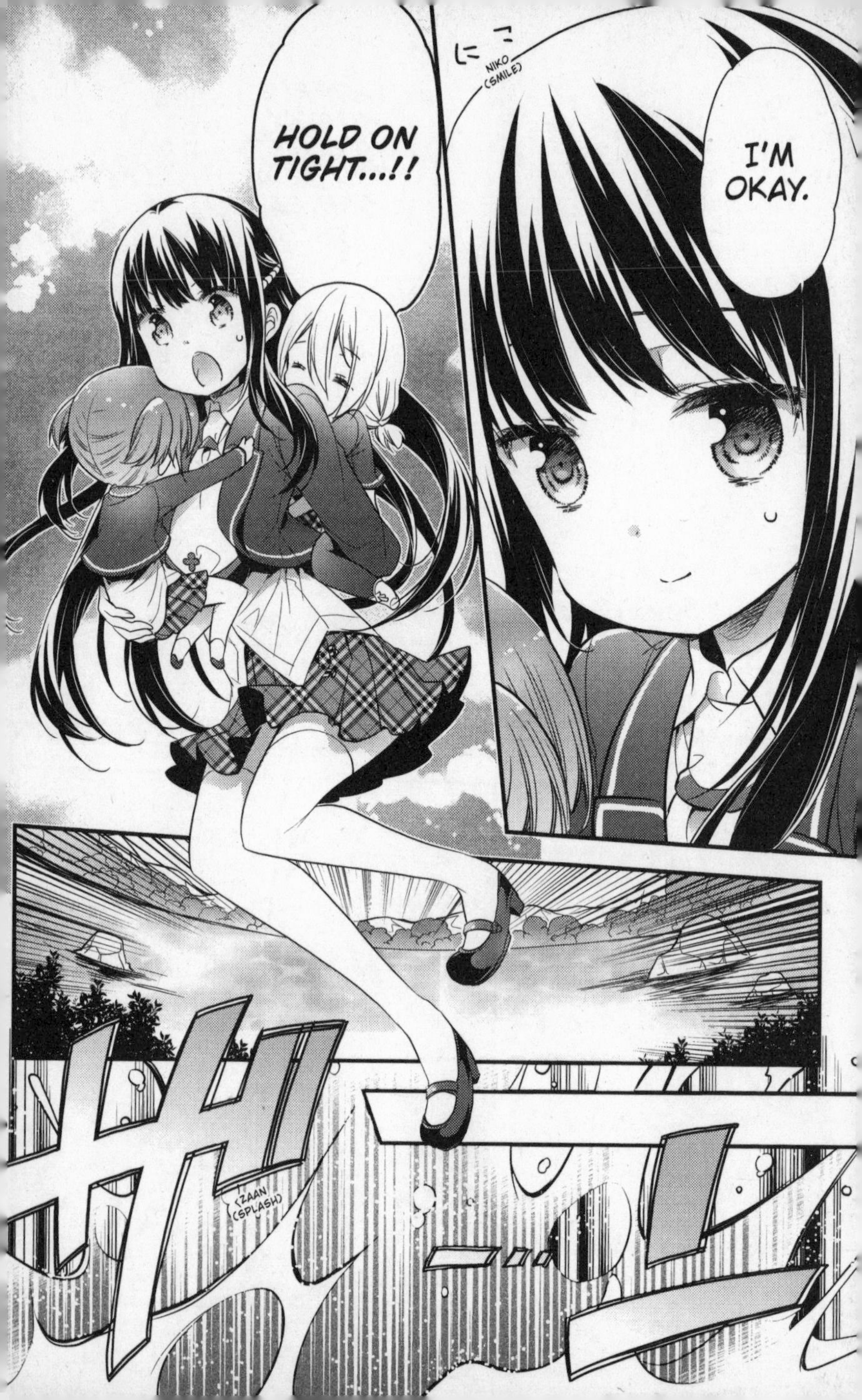
NIKO (SMILE)
I'M OKAY.
HOLD ON TIGHT...!!
ZAAN (SPLASH)

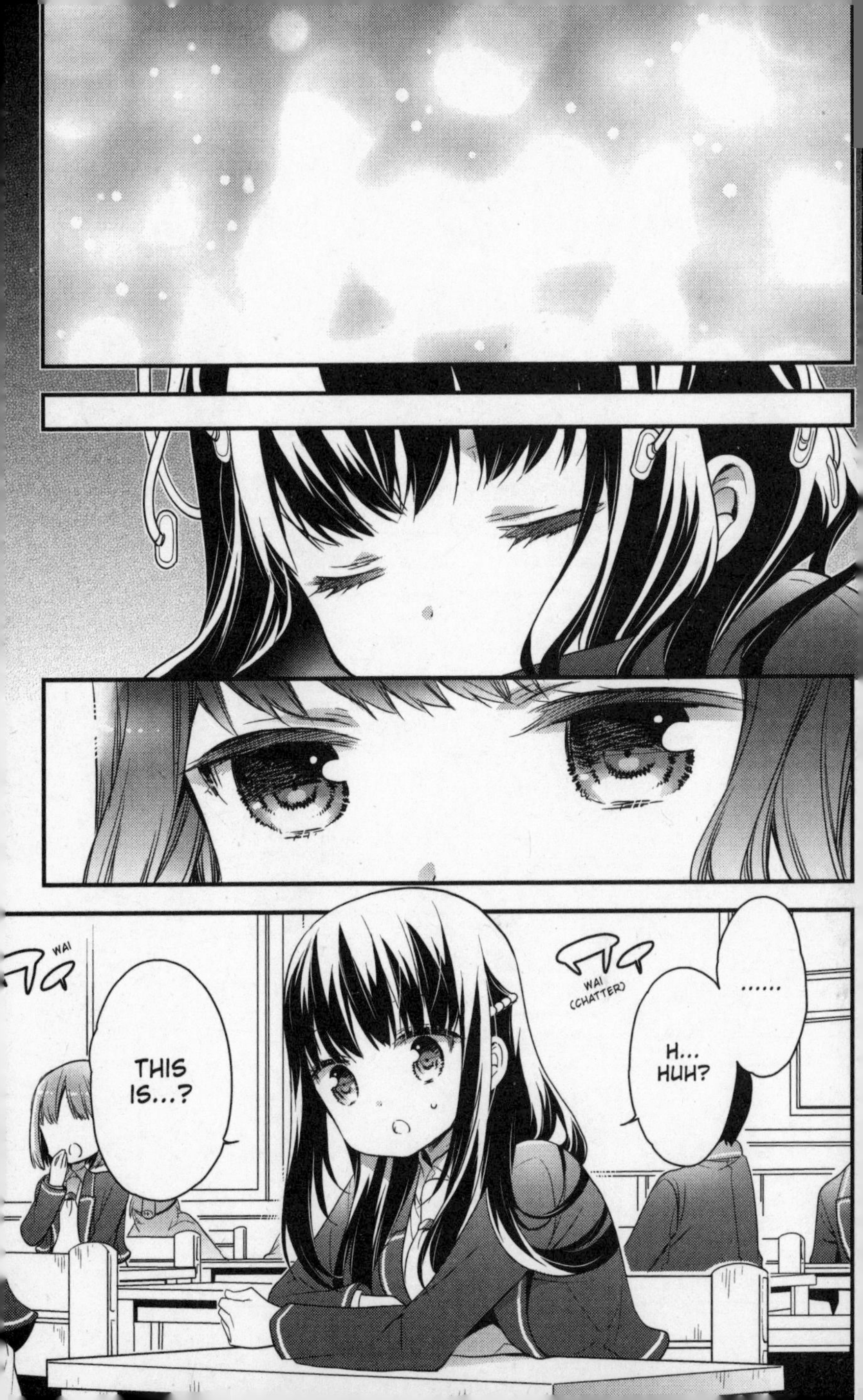
......
WAI (CHATTER)
H... HUH?
WAI
THIS IS...?

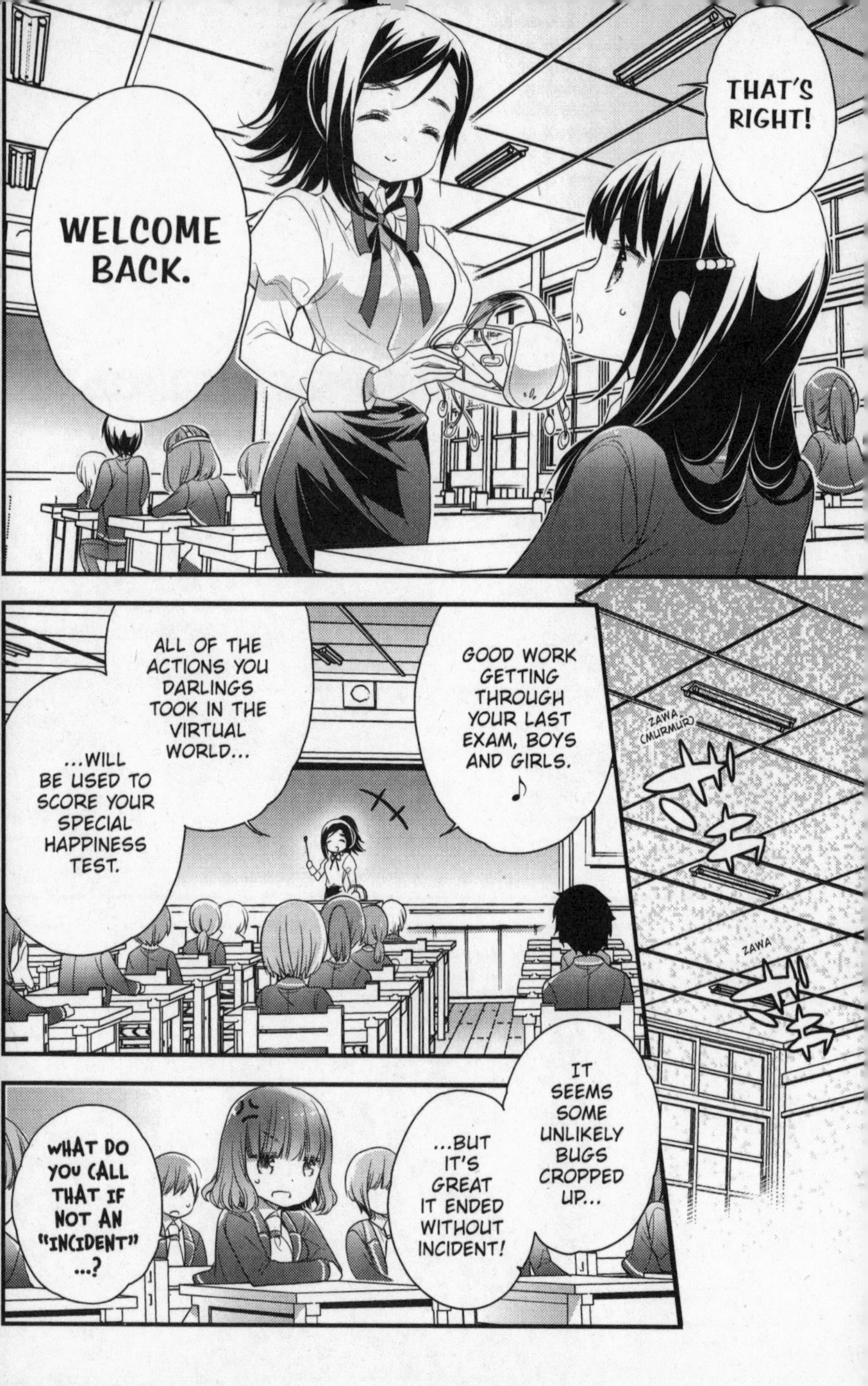
THAT'S RIGHT!
WELCOME BACK.
ZAWA (MURMUR)
ZAWA
GOOD WORK GETTING THROUGH YOUR LAST EXAM, BOYS AND GIRLS. ♪
ALL OF THE ACTIONS YOU DARLINGS TOOK IN THE VIRTUAL WORLD...
...WILL BE USED TO SCORE YOUR SPECIAL HAPPINESS TEST.
IT SEEMS SOME UNLIKELY BUGS CROPPED UP...
...BUT IT'S GREAT IT ENDED WITHOUT INCIDENT!
WHAT DO YOU CALL THAT IF NOT AN "INCIDENT" ...?

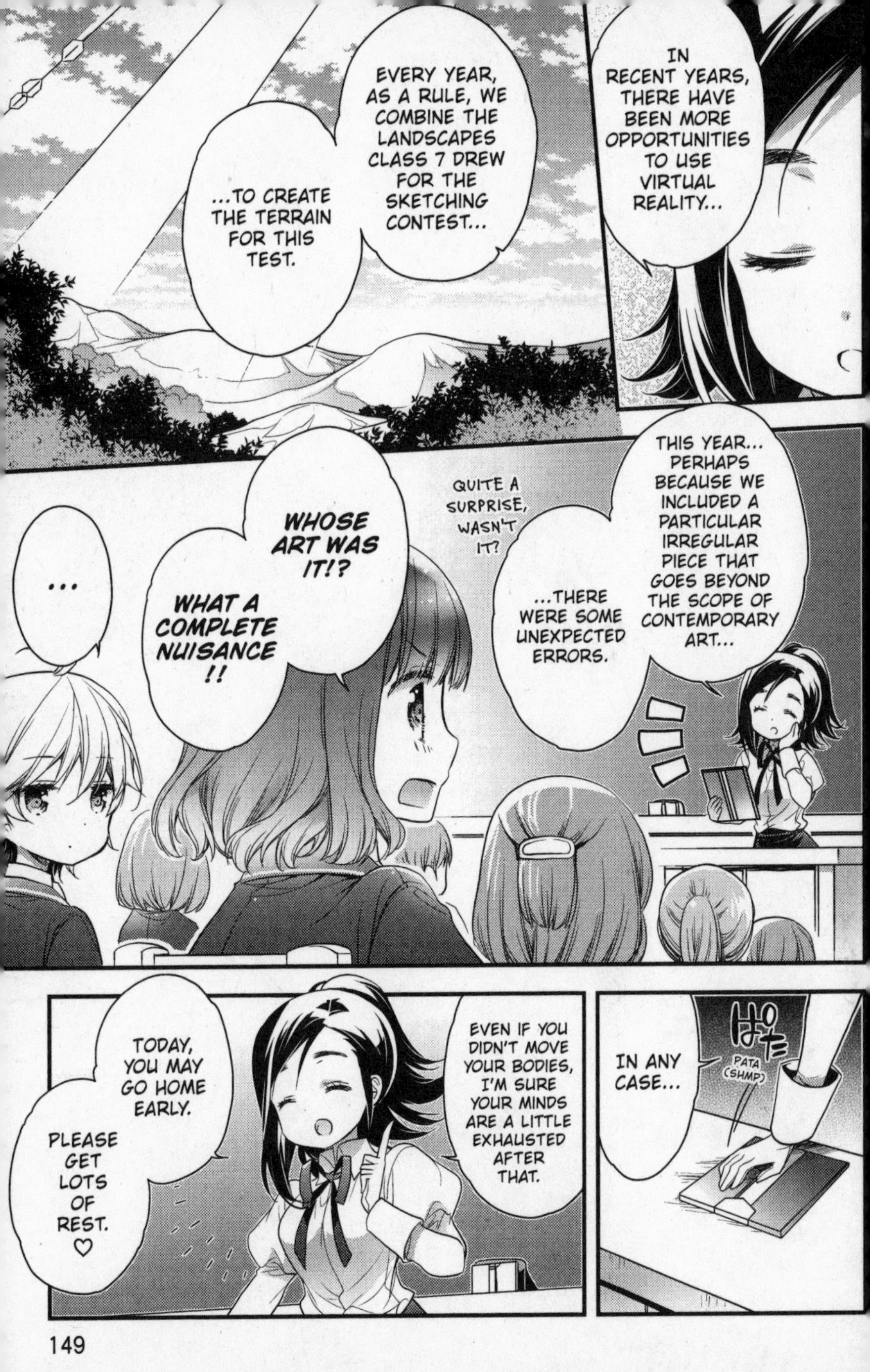
IN RECENT YEARS, THERE HAVE BEEN MORE OPPORTUNITIES TO USE VIRTUAL REALITY...
EVERY YEAR, AS A RULE, WE COMBINE THE LANDSCAPES CLASS 7 DREW FOR THE SKETCHING CONTEST...
...TO CREATE THE TERRAIN FOR THIS TEST.
THIS YEAR... PERHAPS BECAUSE WE INCLUDED A PARTICULAR IRREGULAR PIECE THAT GOES BEYOND THE SCOPE OF CONTEMPORARY ART...
...THERE WERE SOME UNEXPECTED ERRORS.
QUITE A SURPRISE, WASN'T IT?
WHOSE ART WAS IT!?
WHAT A COMPLETE NUISANCE!!
...
ぱた
PATA (SHMP)
IN ANY CASE...
EVEN IF YOU DIDN'T MOVE YOUR BODIES, I'M SURE YOUR MINDS ARE A LITTLE EXHAUSTED AFTER THAT.
TODAY, YOU MAY GO HOME EARLY.
PLEASE GET LOTS OF REST. ♡

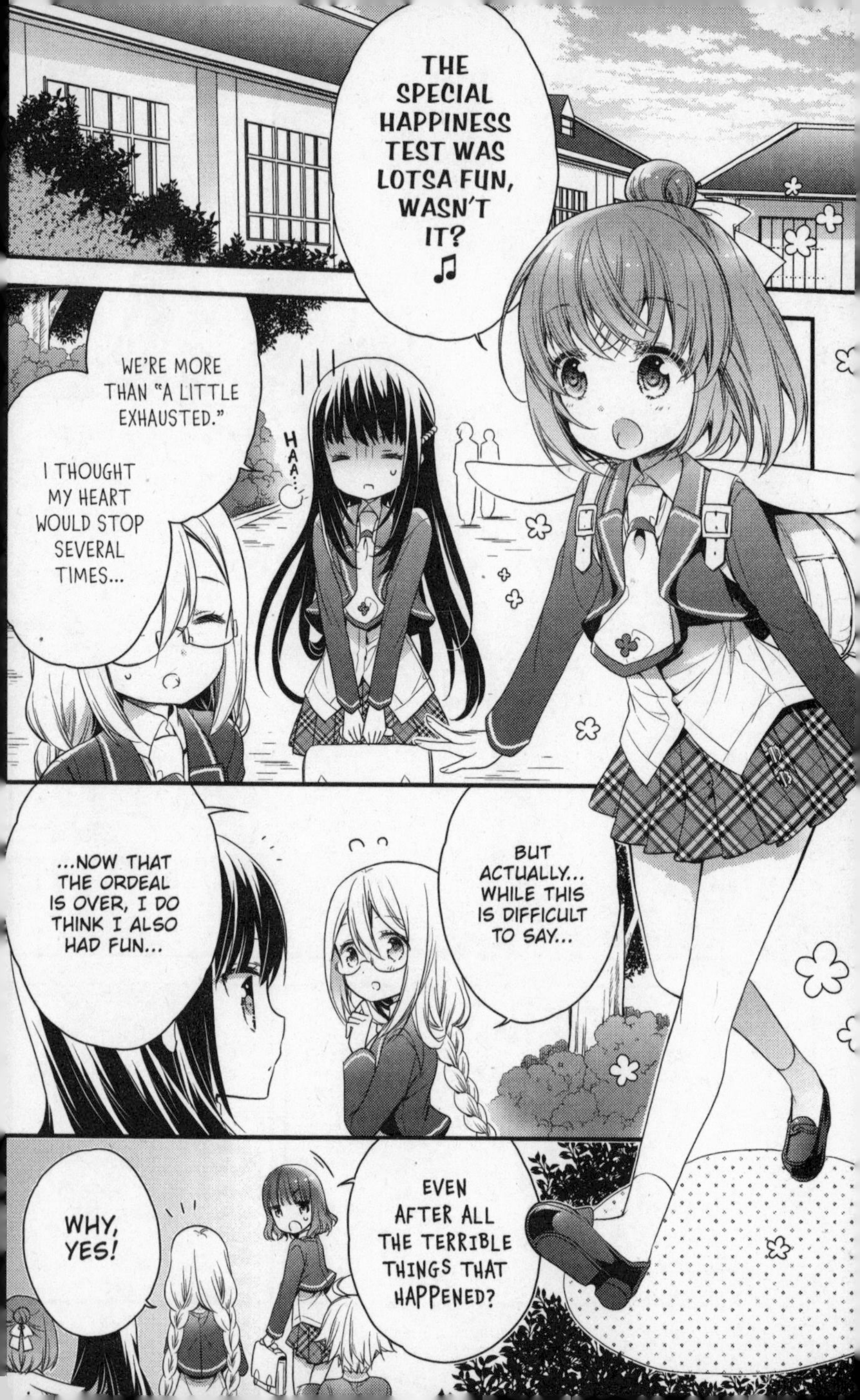
THE SPECIAL HAPPINESS TEST WAS LOTSA FUN, WASN'T IT? ♫
WE'RE MORE THAN "A LITTLE EXHAUSTED."
HAA...
I THOUGHT MY HEART WOULD STOP SEVERAL TIMES...
BUT ACTUALLY... WHILE THIS IS DIFFICULT TO SAY...
...NOW THAT THE ORDEAL IS OVER, I DO THINK I ALSO HAD FUN...
EVEN AFTER ALL THE TERRIBLE THINGS THAT HAPPENED?
WHY, YES!

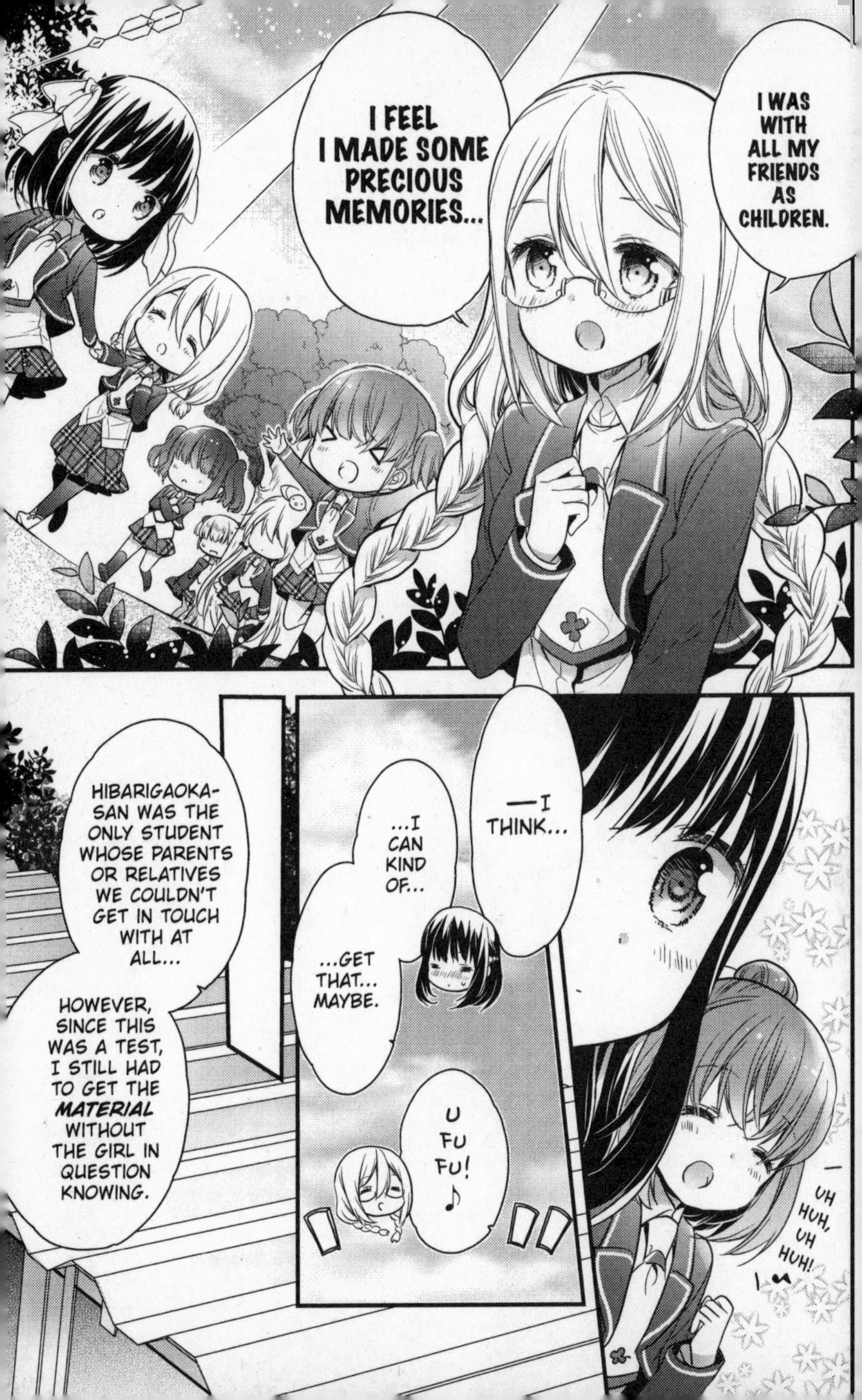
I WAS WITH ALL MY FRIENDS AS CHILDREN.
I FEEL I MADE SOME PRECIOUS MEMORIES...
—I THINK...
UH HUH, UH HUH!
...I CAN KIND OF...
...GET THAT... MAYBE.
U FU FU! ♪
HIBARIGAOKA-SAN WAS THE ONLY STUDENT WHOSE PARENTS OR RELATIVES WE COULDN'T GET IN TOUCH WITH AT ALL...
HOWEVER, SINCE THIS WAS A TEST, I STILL HAD TO GET THE *MATERIAL* WITHOUT THE GIRL IN QUESTION KNOWING.

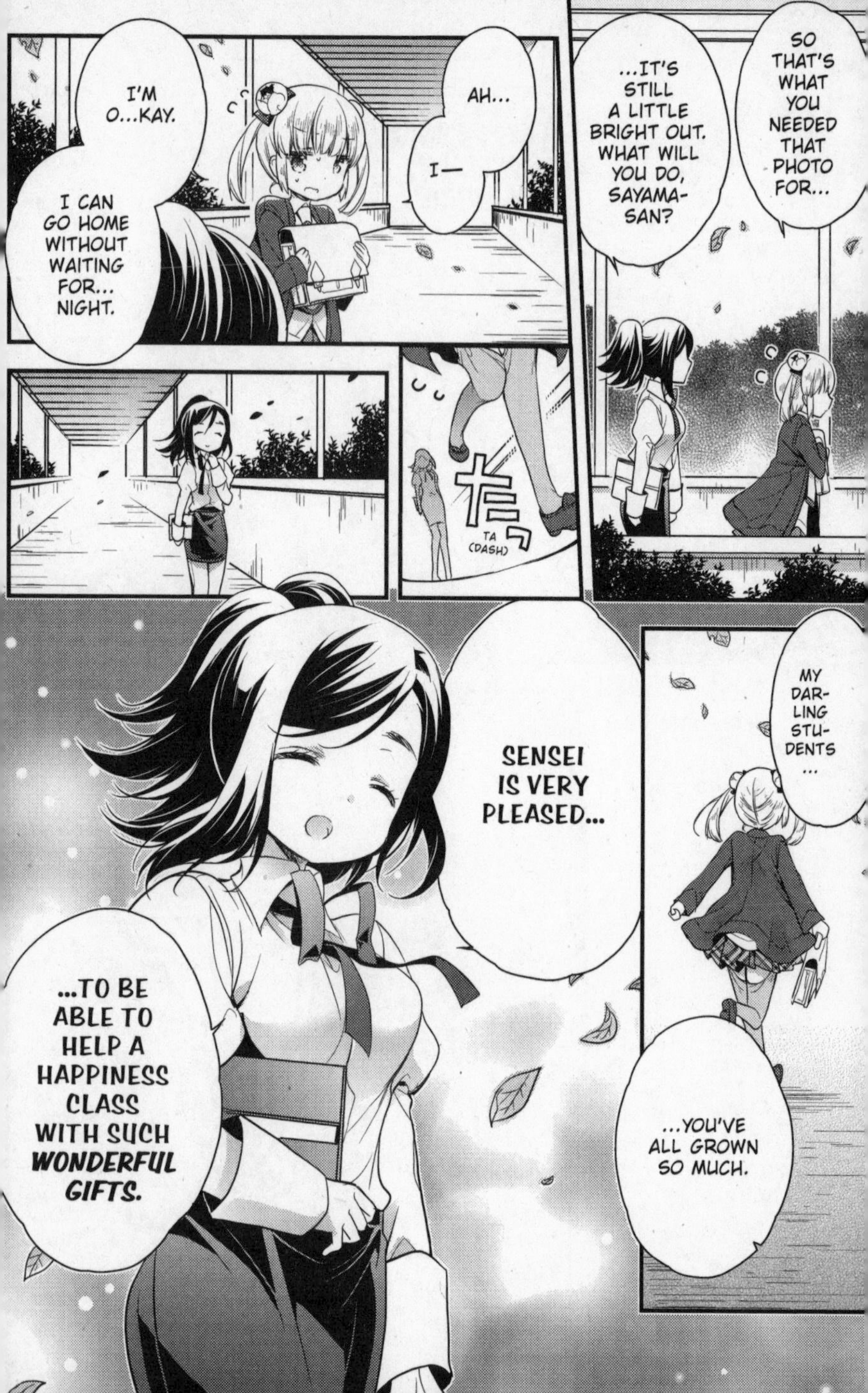
SO THAT'S WHAT YOU NEEDED THAT PHOTO FOR...
...IT'S STILL A LITTLE BRIGHT OUT. WHAT WILL YOU DO, SAYAMA-SAN?
AH...
I—
I'M O...KAY.
I CAN GO HOME WITHOUT WAITING FOR... NIGHT.
TA (DASH)
MY DARLING STUDENTS...
...YOU'VE ALL GROWN SO MUCH.
SENSEI IS VERY PLEASED...
...TO BE ABLE TO HELP A HAPPINESS CLASS WITH SUCH WONDERFUL GIFTS.

Anne Happy

unhappy go lucky!

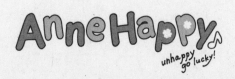

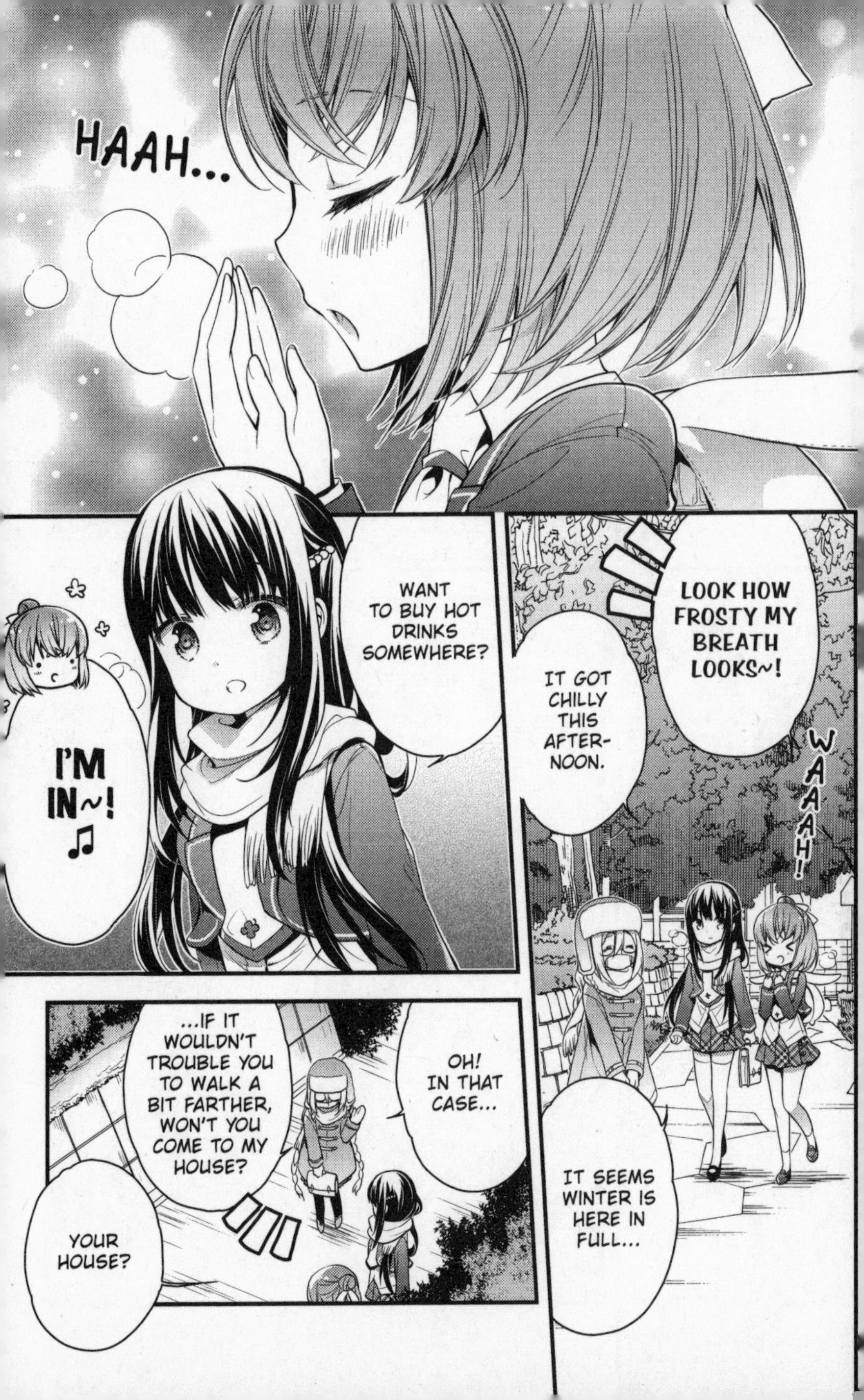
HAAH...
LOOK HOW FROSTY MY BREATH LOOKS~!
WAAAAH!
IT GOT CHILLY THIS AFTER-NOON.
IT SEEMS WINTER IS HERE IN FULL...
WANT TO BUY HOT DRINKS SOMEWHERE?
I'M IN~! ♫
OH! IN THAT CASE...
...IF IT WOULDN'T TROUBLE YOU TO WALK A BIT FARTHER, WON'T YOU COME TO MY HOUSE?
YOUR HOUSE?

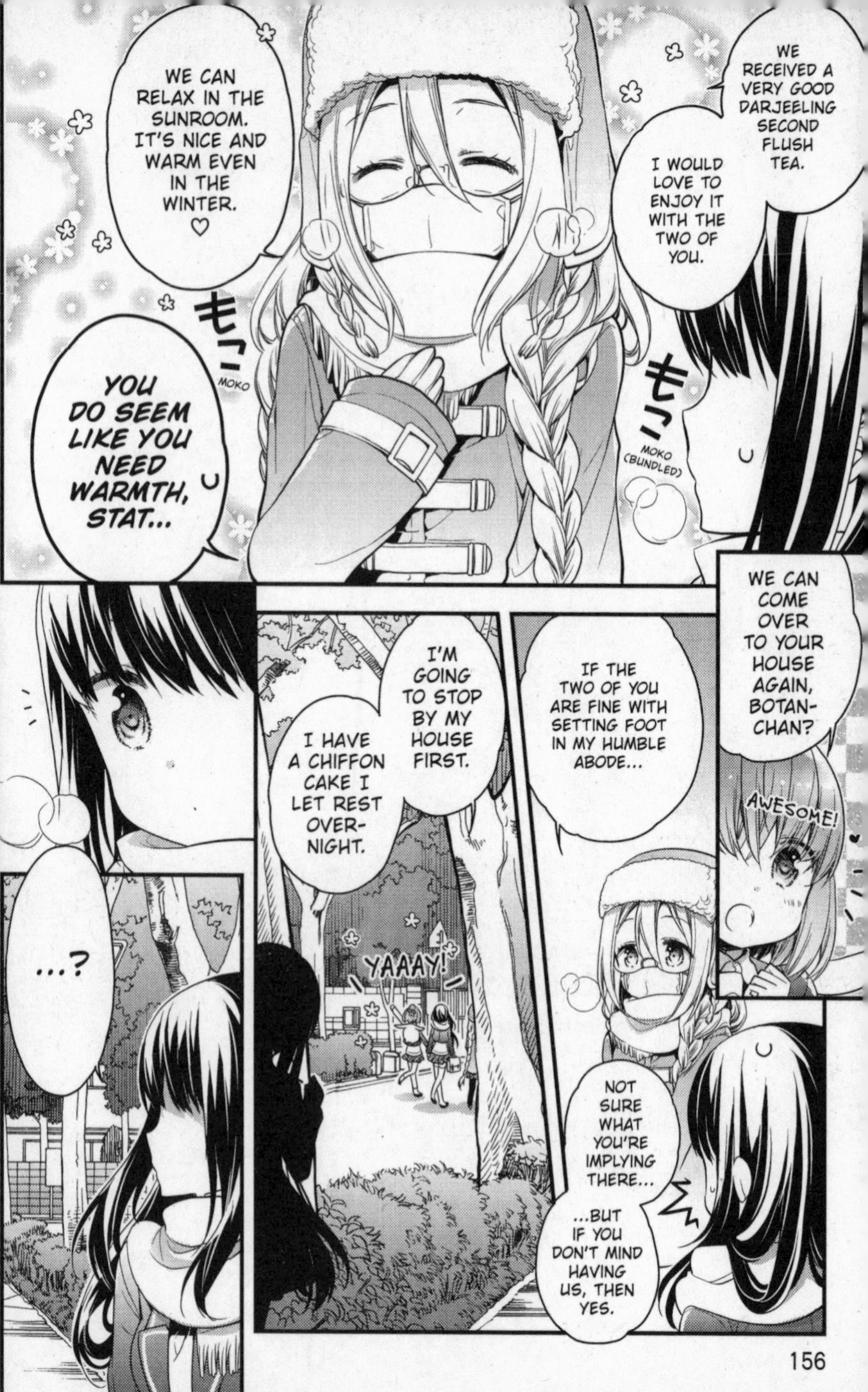
WE RECEIVED A VERY GOOD DARJEELING SECOND FLUSH TEA.
I WOULD LOVE TO ENJOY IT WITH THE TWO OF YOU.
WE CAN RELAX IN THE SUNROOM. IT'S NICE AND WARM EVEN IN THE WINTER. ♡
もこ
MOKO (BUNDLED)
もこ
MOKO
YOU DO SEEM LIKE YOU NEED WARMTH, STAT...
WE CAN COME OVER TO YOUR HOUSE AGAIN, BOTAN-CHAN?
AWESOME!
IF THE TWO OF YOU ARE FINE WITH SETTING FOOT IN MY HUMBLE ABODE...
NOT SURE WHAT YOU'RE IMPLYING THERE...
...BUT IF YOU DON'T MIND HAVING US, THEN YES.
I'M GOING TO STOP BY MY HOUSE FIRST.
I HAVE A CHIFFON CAKE I LET REST OVER-NIGHT.
YAAAY!
...?

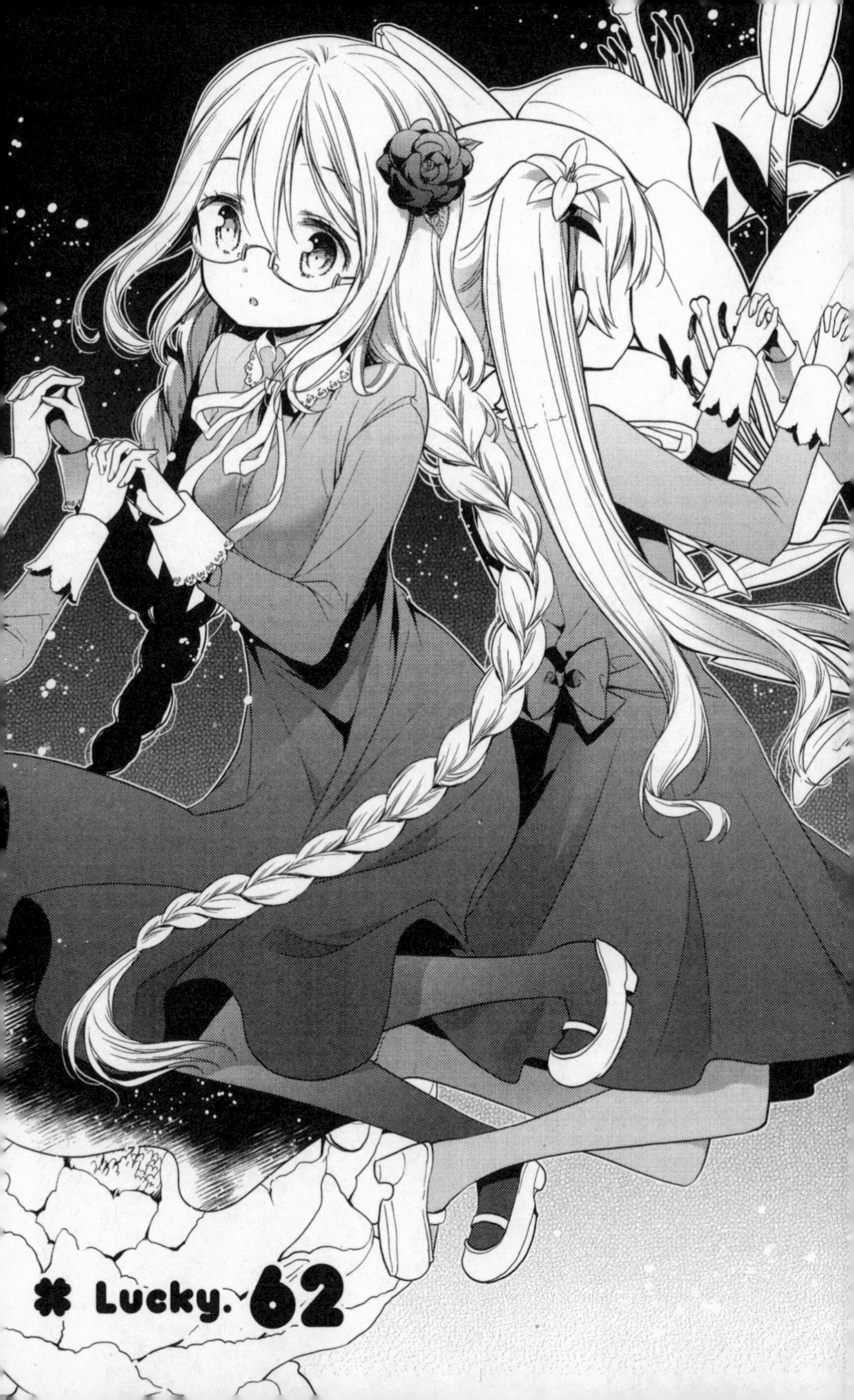
Lucky. 62

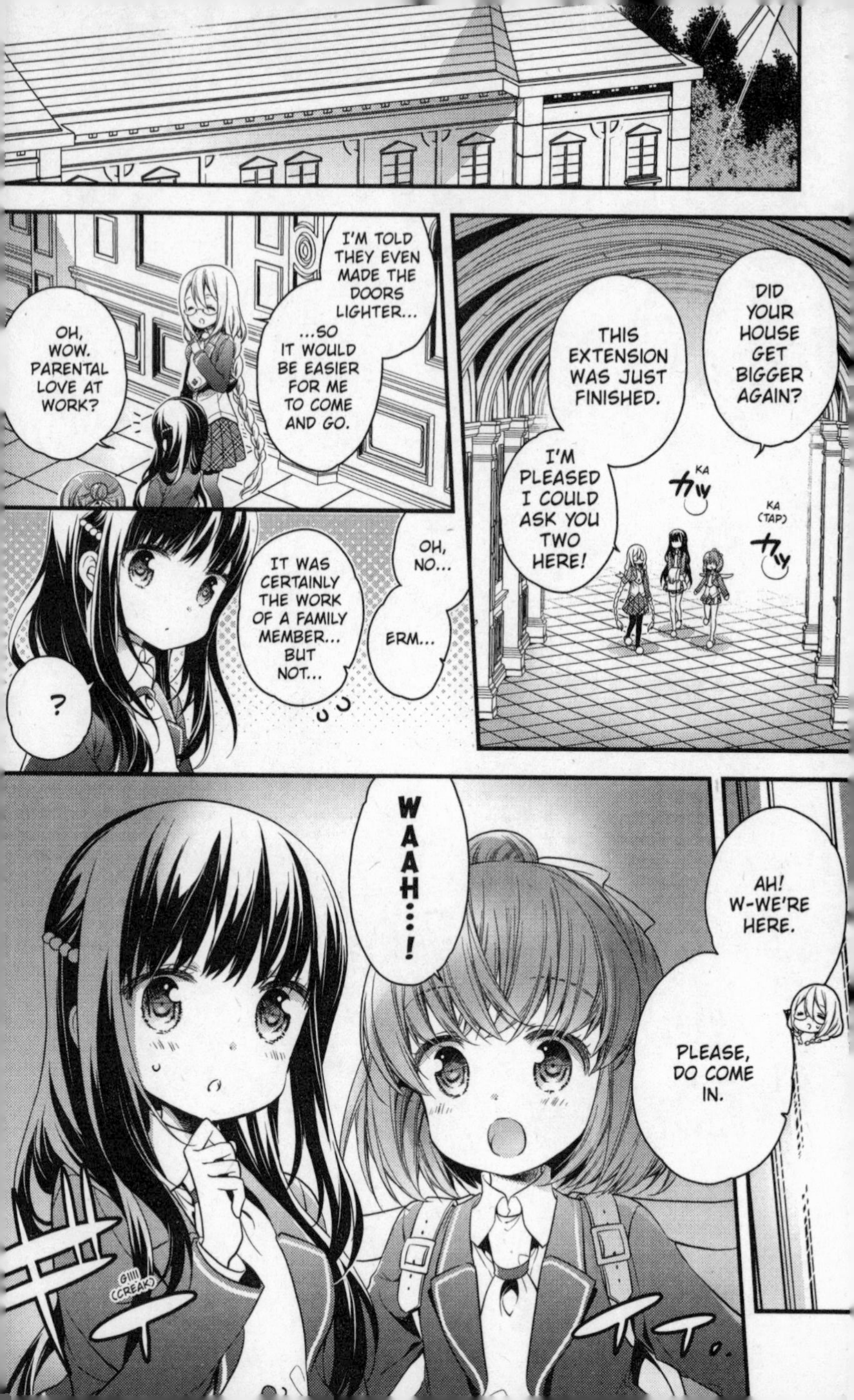
DID YOUR HOUSE GET BIGGER AGAIN?
THIS EXTENSION WAS JUST FINISHED.
I'M PLEASED I COULD ASK YOU TWO HERE!
KA
KA (TAP)
I'M TOLD THEY EVEN MADE THE DOORS LIGHTER...
...SO IT WOULD BE EASIER FOR ME TO COME AND GO.
OH, WOW. PARENTAL LOVE AT WORK?
OH, NO...
ERM...
IT WAS CERTAINLY THE WORK OF A FAMILY MEMBER... BUT NOT...
?
AH! W-WE'RE HERE.
PLEASE, DO COME IN.
WAAH...!
GIIII (CREAK)

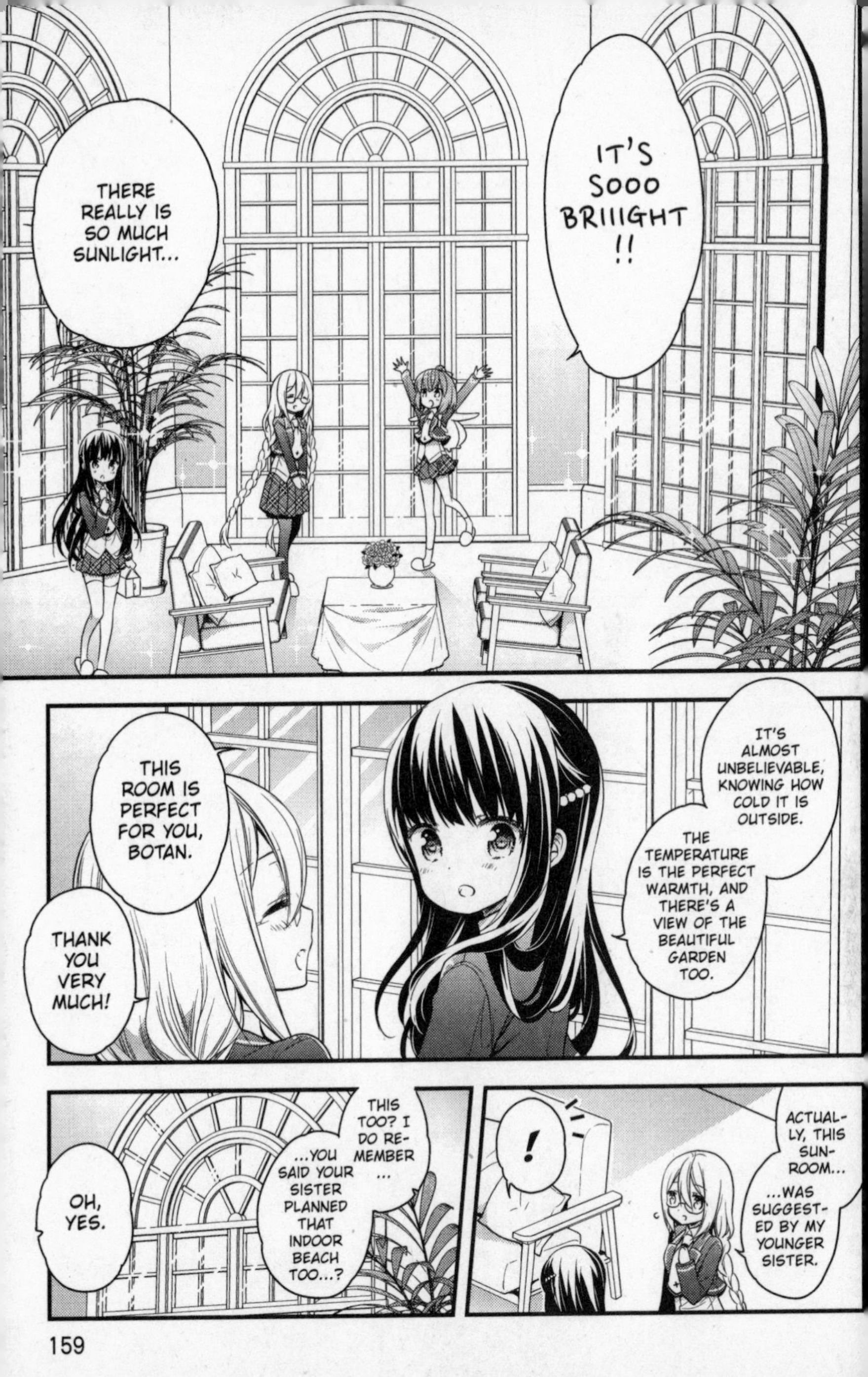
IT'S SOOO BRIIIGHT!!
THERE REALLY IS SO MUCH SUNLIGHT...
IT'S ALMOST UNBELIEVABLE, KNOWING HOW COLD IT IS OUTSIDE.
THE TEMPERATURE IS THE PERFECT WARMTH, AND THERE'S A VIEW OF THE BEAUTIFUL GARDEN TOO.
THIS ROOM IS PERFECT FOR YOU, BOTAN.
THANK YOU VERY MUCH!
ACTUALLY, THIS SUNROOM...
...WAS SUGGESTED BY MY YOUNGER SISTER.
!
THIS TOO? I DO REMEMBER...
...YOU SAID YOUR SISTER PLANNED THAT INDOOR BEACH TOO...?
OH, YES.

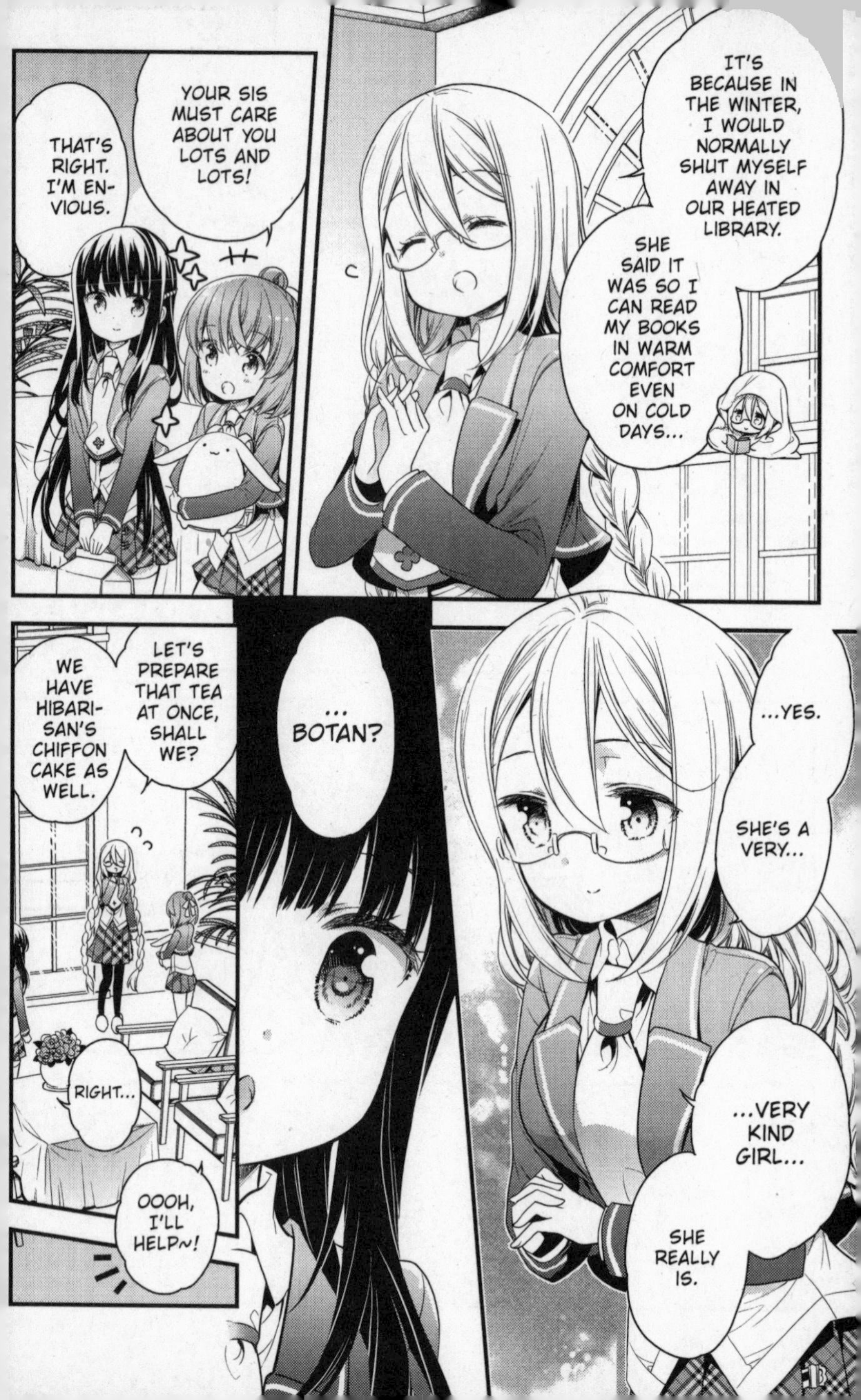
IT'S BECAUSE IN THE WINTER, I WOULD NORMALLY SHUT MYSELF AWAY IN OUR HEATED LIBRARY.
SHE SAID IT WAS SO I CAN READ MY BOOKS IN WARM COMFORT EVEN ON COLD DAYS...
YOUR SIS MUST CARE ABOUT YOU LOTS AND LOTS!
THAT'S RIGHT. I'M ENVIOUS.
...YES.
SHE'S A VERY...
...VERY KIND GIRL...
SHE REALLY IS.
...BOTAN?
LET'S PREPARE THAT TEA AT ONCE, SHALL WE?
WE HAVE HIBARI-SAN'S CHIFFON CAKE AS WELL.
RIGHT...
OOOH, I'LL HELP~!

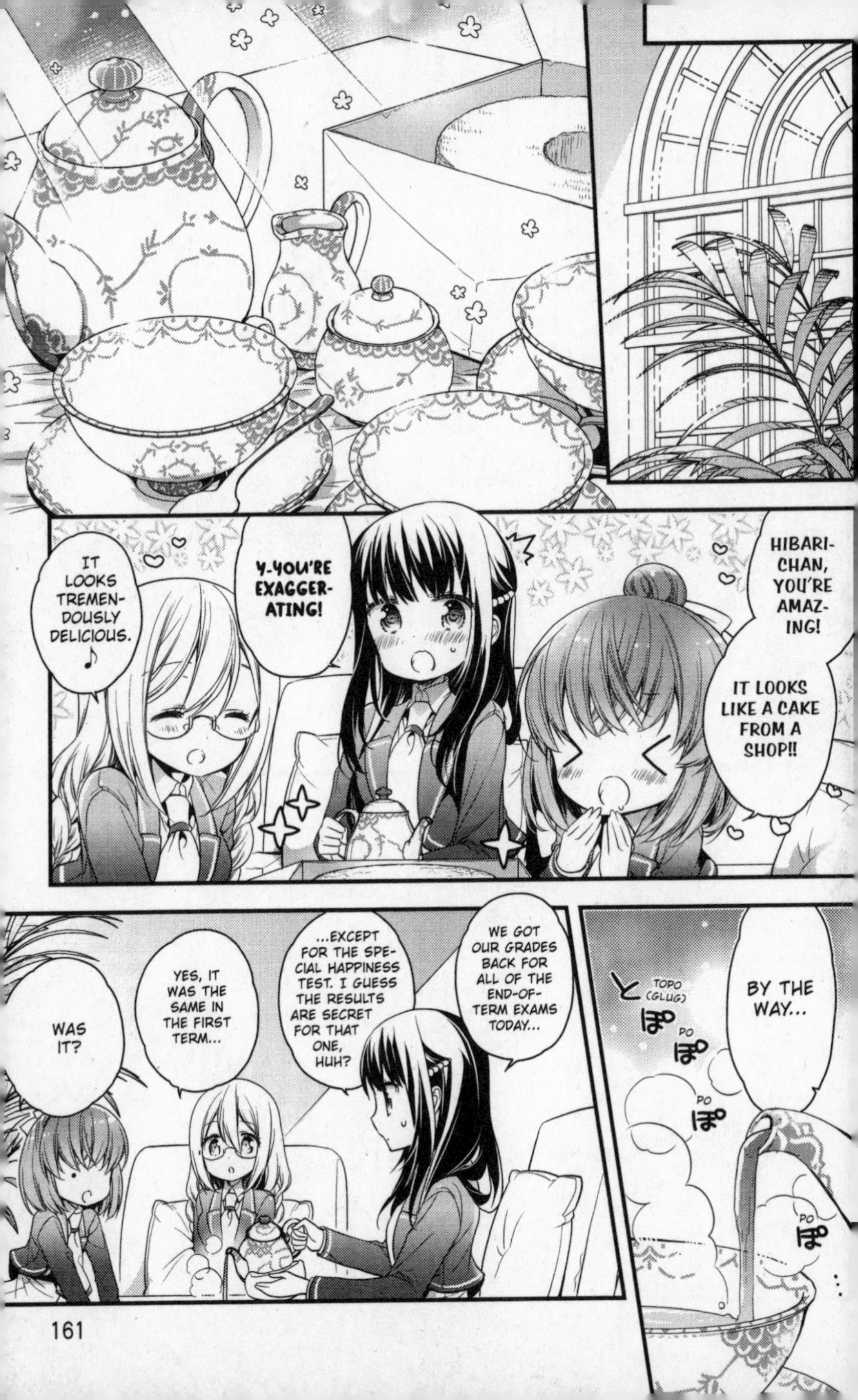
HIBARI-CHAN, YOU'RE AMAZING!
IT LOOKS LIKE A CAKE FROM A SHOP!!
Y-YOU'RE EXAGGERATING!
IT LOOKS TREMENDOUSLY DELICIOUS. ♪
BY THE WAY...
と TOPO (GLUG)
ぽ PO
ぽ PO
ぽ PO
ぽ PO
WE GOT OUR GRADES BACK FOR ALL OF THE END-OF-TERM EXAMS TODAY...
...EXCEPT FOR THE SPECIAL HAPPINESS TEST. I GUESS THE RESULTS ARE SECRET FOR THAT ONE, HUH?
YES, IT WAS THE SAME IN THE FIRST TERM...
WAS IT?

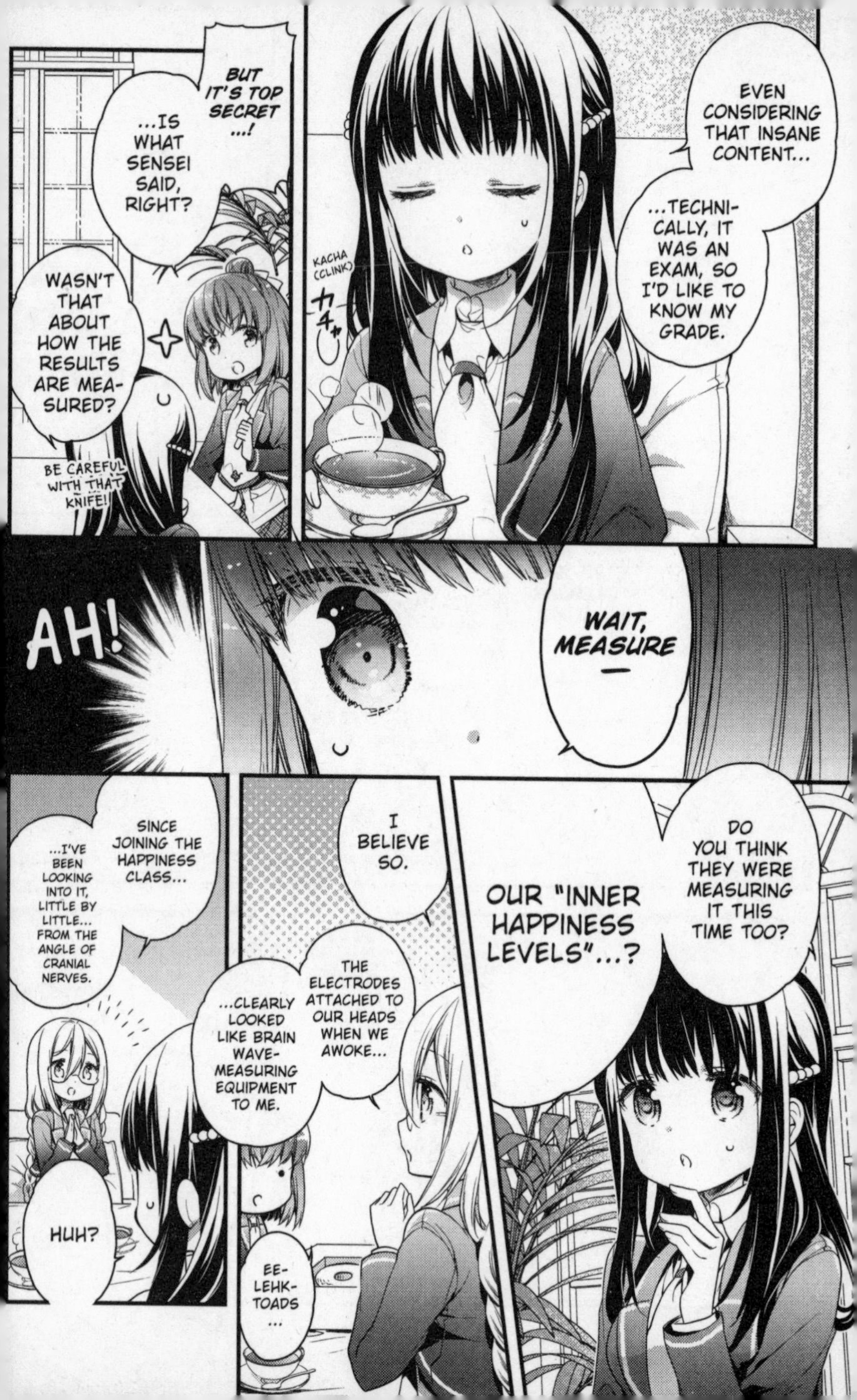
EVEN CONSIDERING THAT INSANE CONTENT...
...TECHNICALLY, IT WAS AN EXAM, SO I'D LIKE TO KNOW MY GRADE.
KACHA (CLINK)
カチャ
BUT IT'S TOP SECRET ...!
...IS WHAT SENSEI SAID, RIGHT?
WASN'T THAT ABOUT HOW THE RESULTS ARE MEASURED?
BE CAREFUL WITH THAT KNIFE!
WAIT, MEASURE—
AH!
DO YOU THINK THEY WERE MEASURING IT THIS TIME TOO?
OUR "INNER HAPPINESS LEVELS"...?
I BELIEVE SO.
SINCE JOINING THE HAPPINESS CLASS...
...I'VE BEEN LOOKING INTO IT, LITTLE BY LITTLE... FROM THE ANGLE OF CRANIAL NERVES.
THE ELECTRODES ATTACHED TO OUR HEADS WHEN WE AWOKE...
...CLEARLY LOOKED LIKE BRAIN WAVE-MEASURING EQUIPMENT TO ME.
EE-LEHK-TOADS...
HUH?

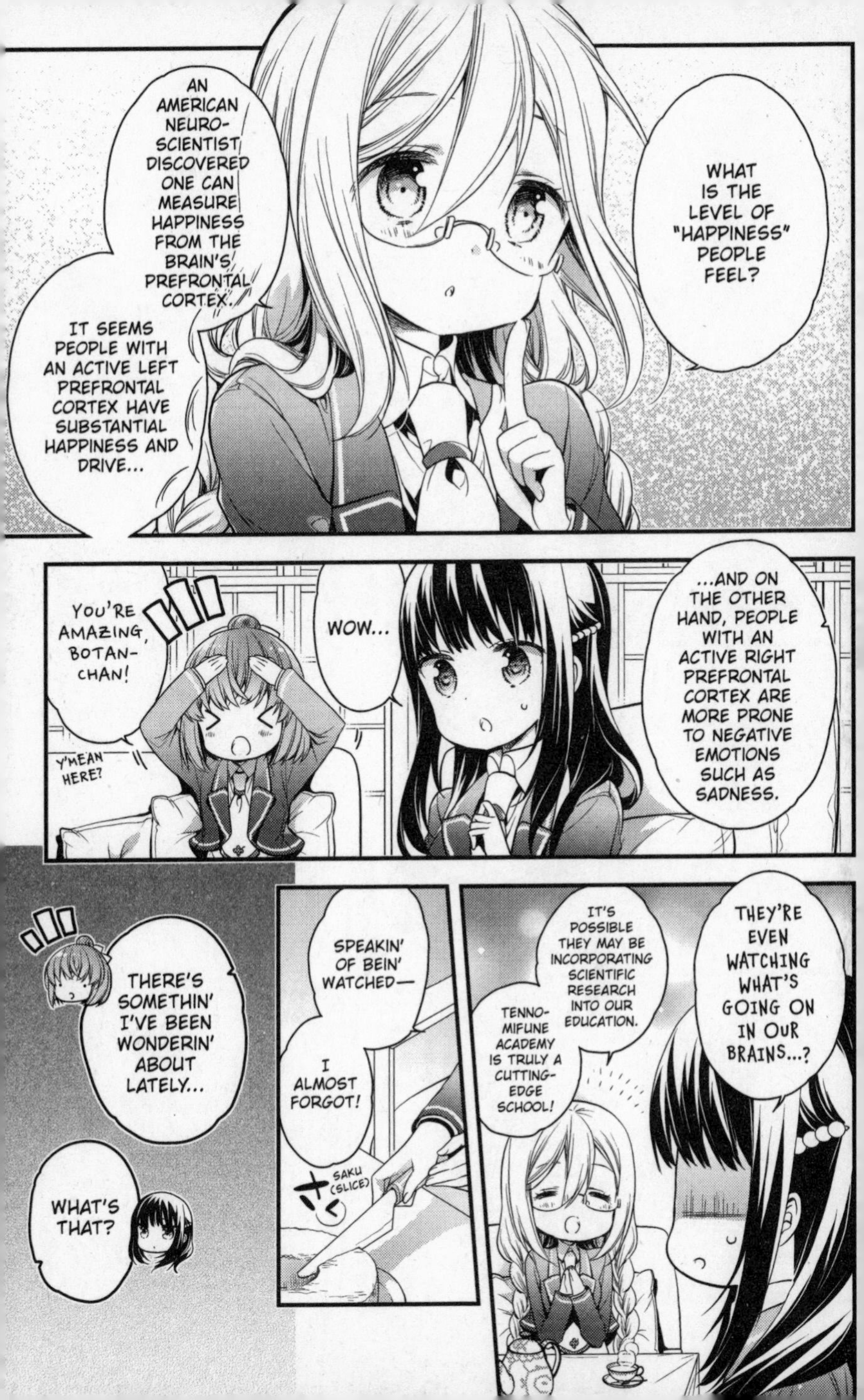
WHAT IS THE LEVEL OF "HAPPINESS" PEOPLE FEEL?
AN AMERICAN NEURO-SCIENTIST DISCOVERED ONE CAN MEASURE HAPPINESS FROM THE BRAIN'S PREFRONTAL CORTEX.
IT SEEMS PEOPLE WITH AN ACTIVE LEFT PREFRONTAL CORTEX HAVE SUBSTANTIAL HAPPINESS AND DRIVE...
...AND ON THE OTHER HAND, PEOPLE WITH AN ACTIVE RIGHT PREFRONTAL CORTEX ARE MORE PRONE TO NEGATIVE EMOTIONS SUCH AS SADNESS.
WOW...
YOU'RE AMAZING, BOTAN-CHAN!
Y'MEAN HERE?
THEY'RE EVEN WATCHING WHAT'S GOING ON IN OUR BRAINS...?
IT'S POSSIBLE THEY MAY BE INCORPORATING SCIENTIFIC RESEARCH INTO OUR EDUCATION.
TENNO-MIFUNE ACADEMY IS TRULY A CUTTING-EDGE SCHOOL!
SPEAKIN' OF BEIN' WATCHED—
I ALMOST FORGOT!
SAKU (SLICE)
THERE'S SOMETHIN' I'VE BEEN WONDERIN' ABOUT LATELY...
WHAT'S THAT?

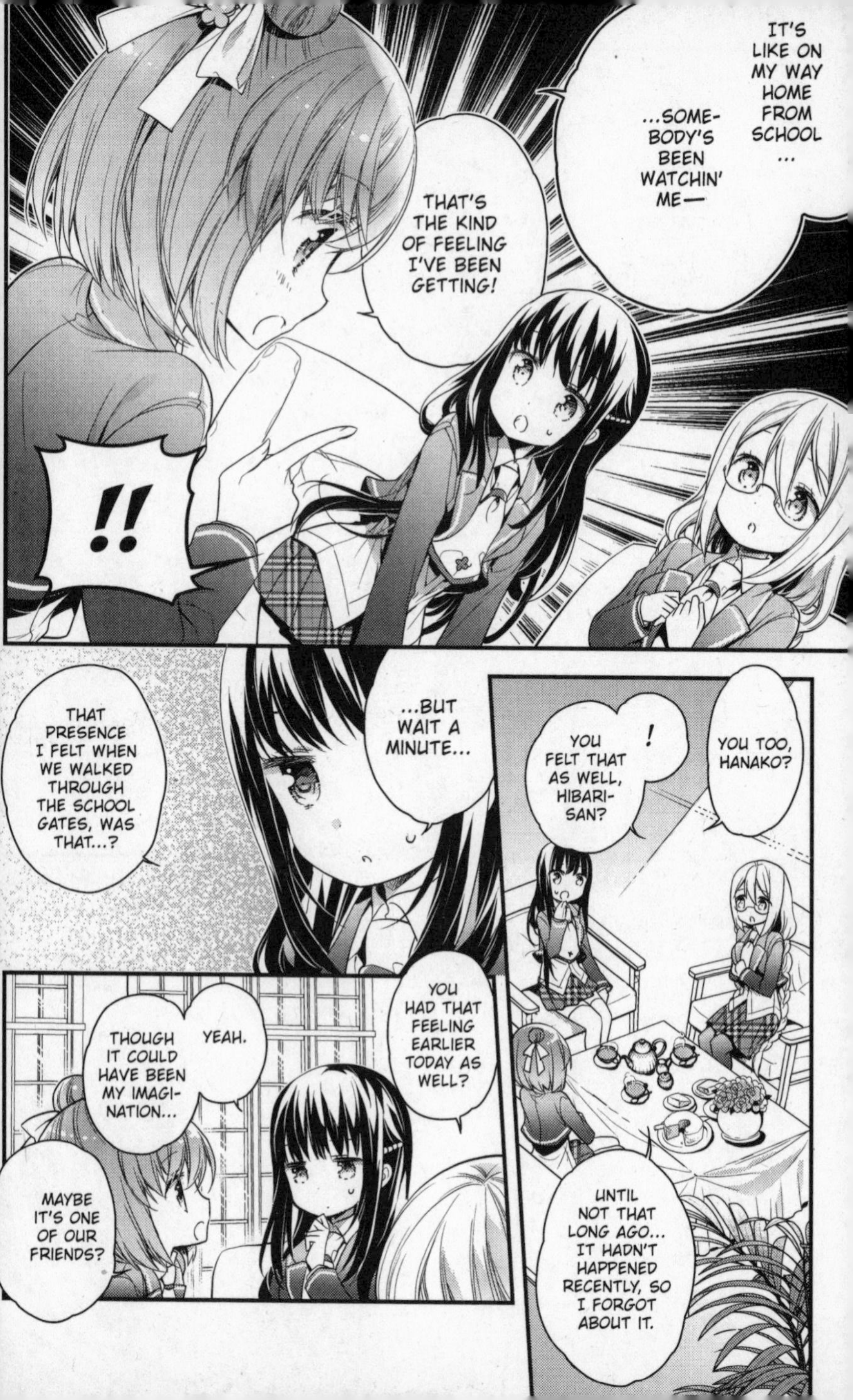
IT'S LIKE ON MY WAY HOME FROM SCHOOL ...
...SOME-BODY'S BEEN WATCHIN' ME—
THAT'S THE KIND OF FEELING I'VE BEEN GETTING!
!!
YOU TOO, HANAKO?
!
YOU FELT THAT AS WELL, HIBARI-SAN?
UNTIL NOT THAT LONG AGO... IT HADN'T HAPPENED RECENTLY, SO I FORGOT ABOUT IT.
...BUT WAIT A MINUTE...
THAT PRESENCE I FELT WHEN WE WALKED THROUGH THE SCHOOL GATES, WAS THAT...?
YOU HAD THAT FEELING EARLIER TODAY AS WELL?
YEAH.
THOUGH IT COULD HAVE BEEN MY IMAGI-NATION...
MAYBE IT'S ONE OF OUR FRIENDS?

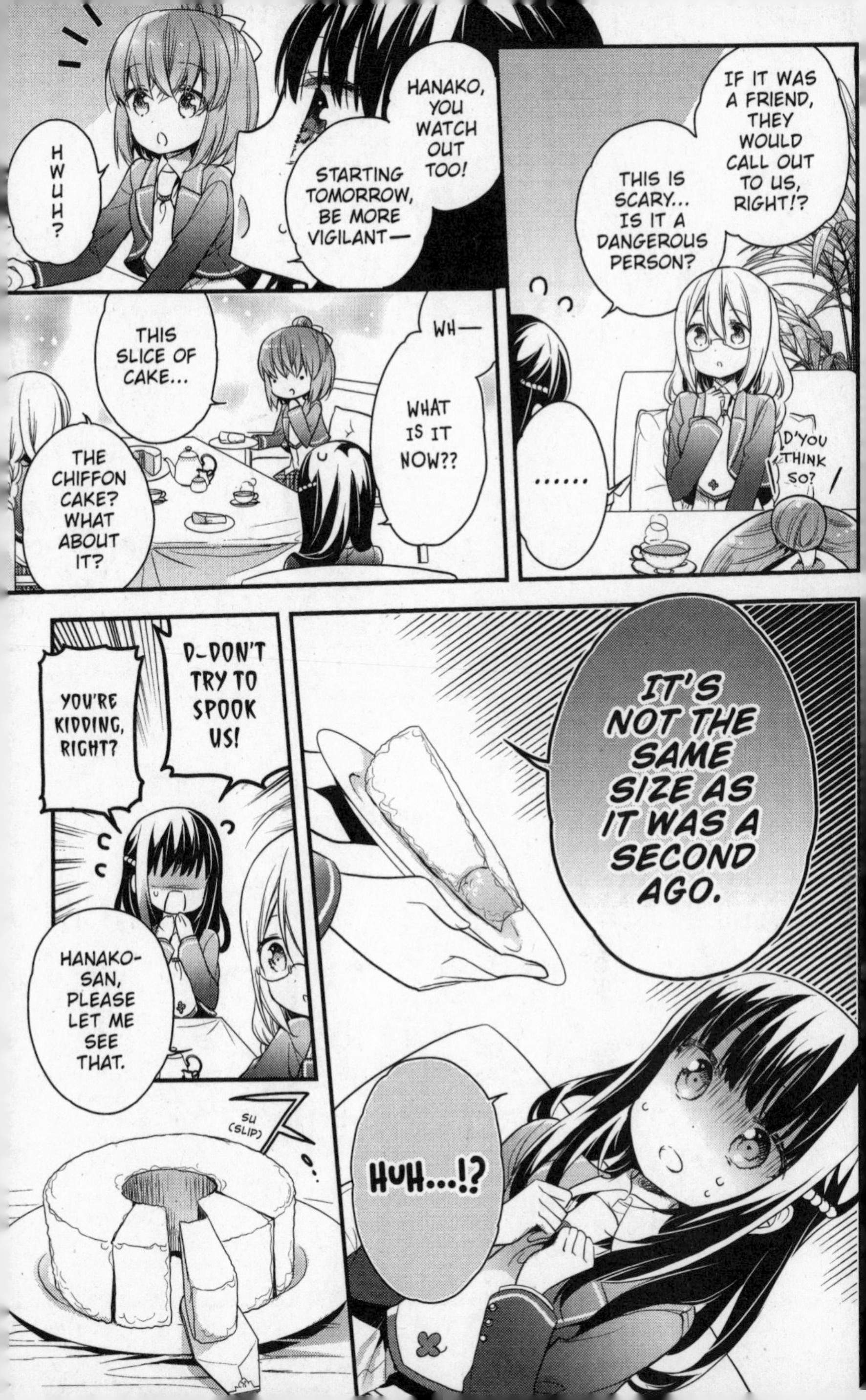
IF IT WAS A FRIEND, THEY WOULD CALL OUT TO US, RIGHT!?
THIS IS SCARY... IS IT A DANGEROUS PERSON?
HANAKO, YOU WATCH OUT TOO!
STARTING TOMORROW, BE MORE VIGILANT—
HWUH?
D'YOU THINK SO?
......
WH—
WHAT IS IT NOW??
THIS SLICE OF CAKE...
THE CHIFFON CAKE? WHAT ABOUT IT?
IT'S NOT THE SAME SIZE AS IT WAS A SECOND AGO.
D-DON'T TRY TO SPOOK US!
YOU'RE KIDDING, RIGHT?
HANAKO-SAN, PLEASE LET ME SEE THAT.
HUH...!?
SU (SLIP)

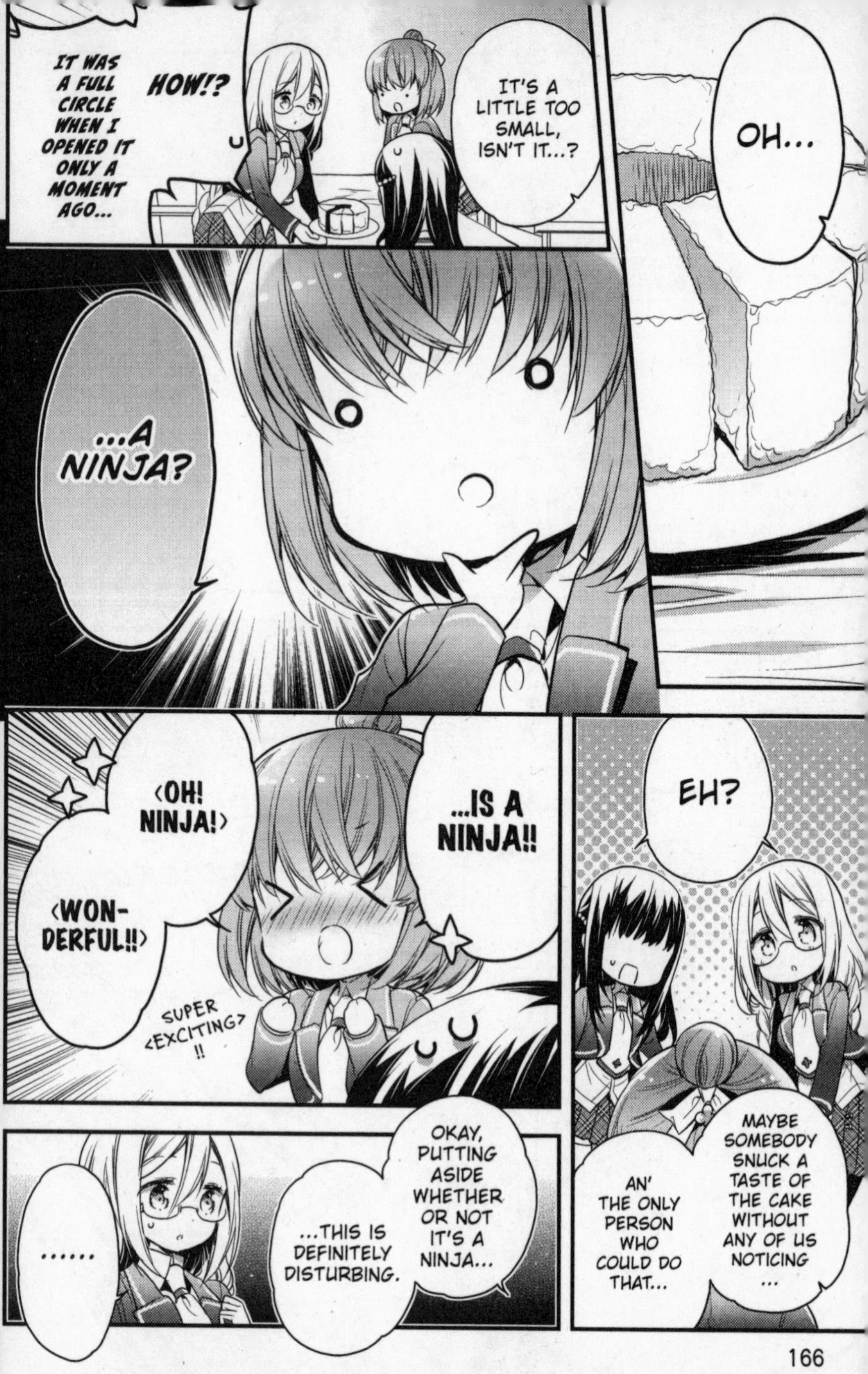
OH...
IT'S A LITTLE TOO SMALL, ISN'T IT...?
HOW!?
IT WAS A FULL CIRCLE WHEN I OPENED IT ONLY A MOMENT AGO...
...A NINJA?
EH?
...IS A NINJA!!
‹OH! NINJA!›
‹WON-DERFUL!!›
SUPER ‹EXCITING› !!
MAYBE SOMEBODY SNUCK A TASTE OF THE CAKE WITHOUT ANY OF US NOTICING ...
AN' THE ONLY PERSON WHO COULD DO THAT...
OKAY, PUTTING ASIDE WHETHER OR NOT IT'S A NINJA...
...THIS IS DEFINITELY DISTURBING.
......

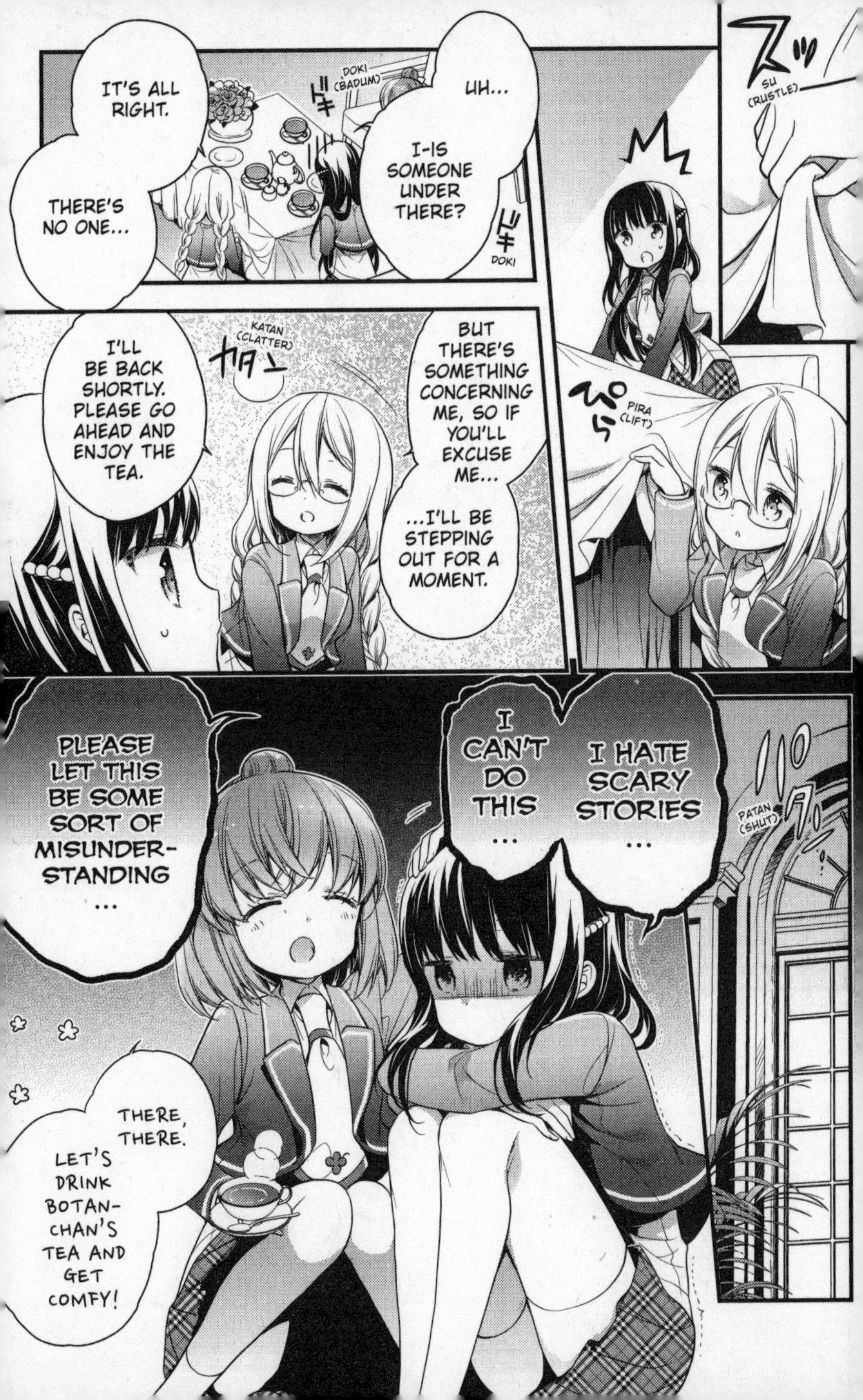
SU (RUSTLE)
PIRA (LIFT)
DOKI (BADUM)
UH...
I-IS SOMEONE UNDER THERE?
DOKI
IT'S ALL RIGHT.
THERE'S NO ONE...
BUT THERE'S SOMETHING CONCERNING ME, SO IF YOU'LL EXCUSE ME...
...I'LL BE STEPPING OUT FOR A MOMENT.
KATAN (CLATTER)
I'LL BE BACK SHORTLY. PLEASE GO AHEAD AND ENJOY THE TEA.
PATAN (SHUT)
I HATE SCARY STORIES...
I CAN'T DO THIS...
PLEASE LET THIS BE SOME SORT OF MISUNDER-STANDING...
THERE, THERE.
LET'S DRINK BOTAN-CHAN'S TEA AND GET COMFY!

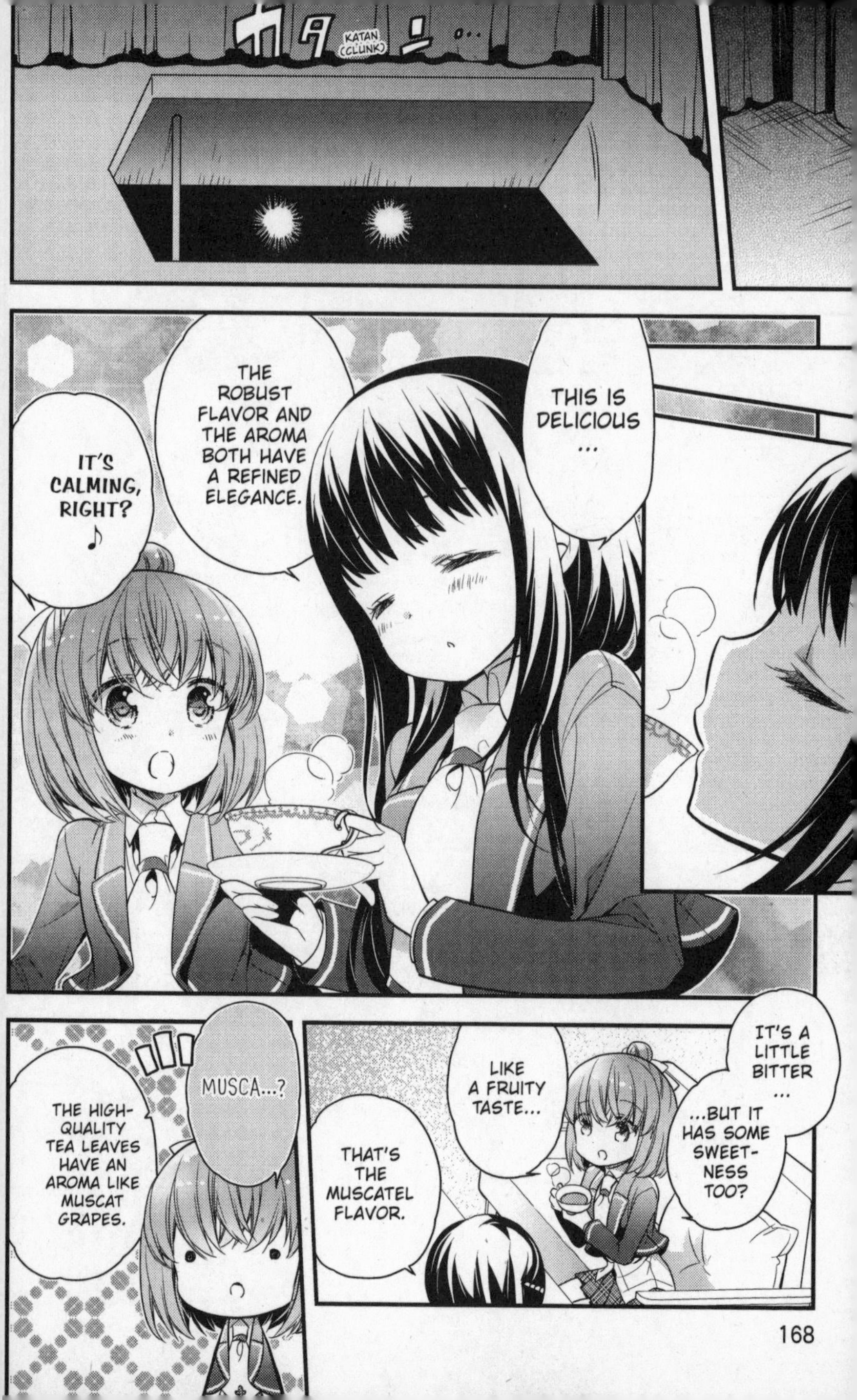
KATAN (CLUNK)
THIS IS DELICIOUS...
THE ROBUST FLAVOR AND THE AROMA BOTH HAVE A REFINED ELEGANCE.
IT'S CALMING, RIGHT? ♪
IT'S A LITTLE BITTER...
...BUT IT HAS SOME SWEET-NESS TOO?
LIKE A FRUITY TASTE...
THAT'S THE MUSCATEL FLAVOR.
MUSCA...?
THE HIGH-QUALITY TEA LEAVES HAVE AN AROMA LIKE MUSCAT GRAPES.

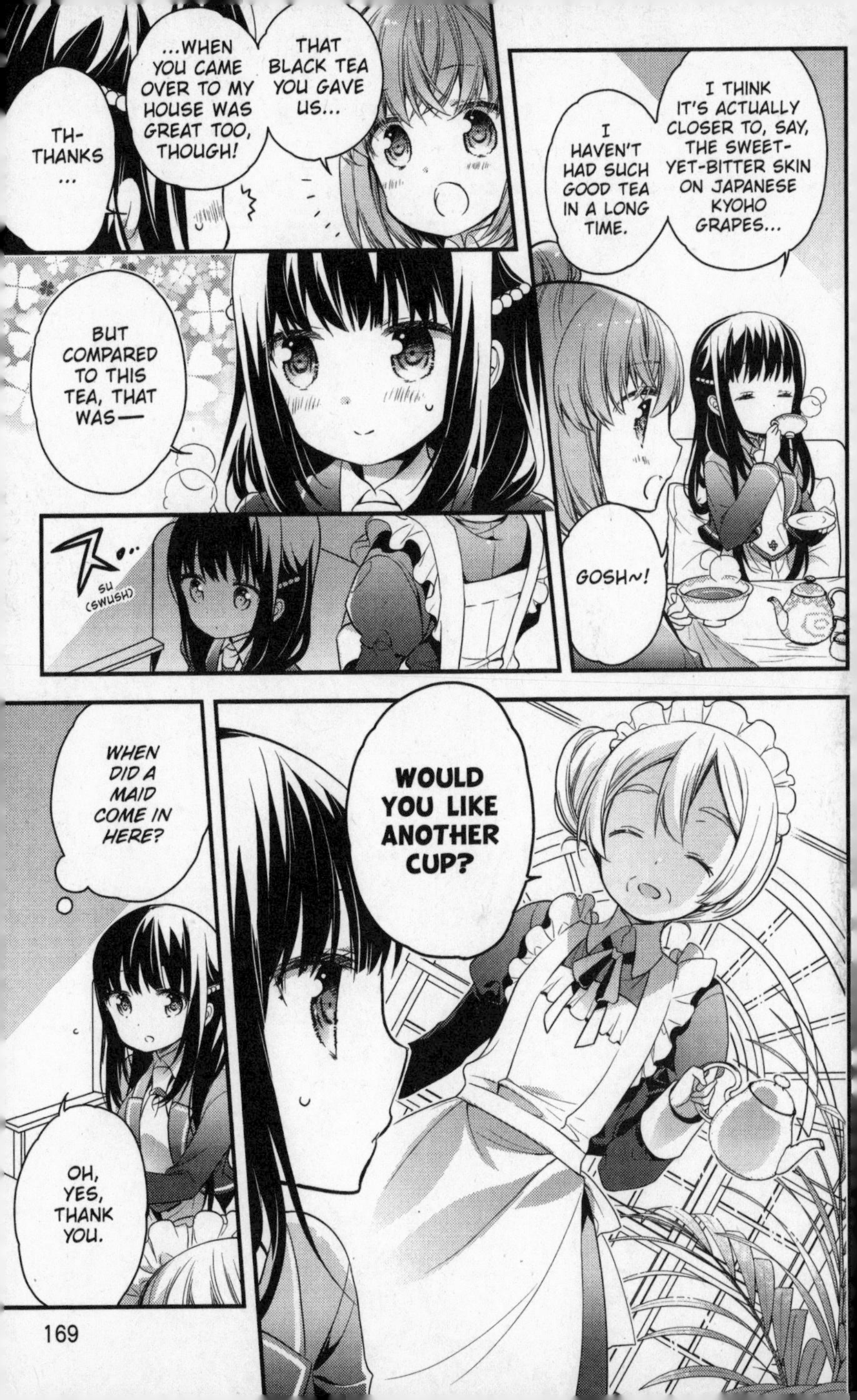
I THINK IT'S ACTUALLY CLOSER TO, SAY, THE SWEET-YET-BITTER SKIN ON JAPANESE KYOHO GRAPES...
I HAVEN'T HAD SUCH GOOD TEA IN A LONG TIME.
GOSH~!
THAT BLACK TEA YOU GAVE US...
...WHEN YOU CAME OVER TO MY HOUSE WAS GREAT TOO, THOUGH!
TH-THANKS...
BUT COMPARED TO THIS TEA, THAT WAS—
SU (SWUSH)
WOULD YOU LIKE ANOTHER CUP?
WHEN DID A MAID COME IN HERE?
OH, YES, THANK YOU.

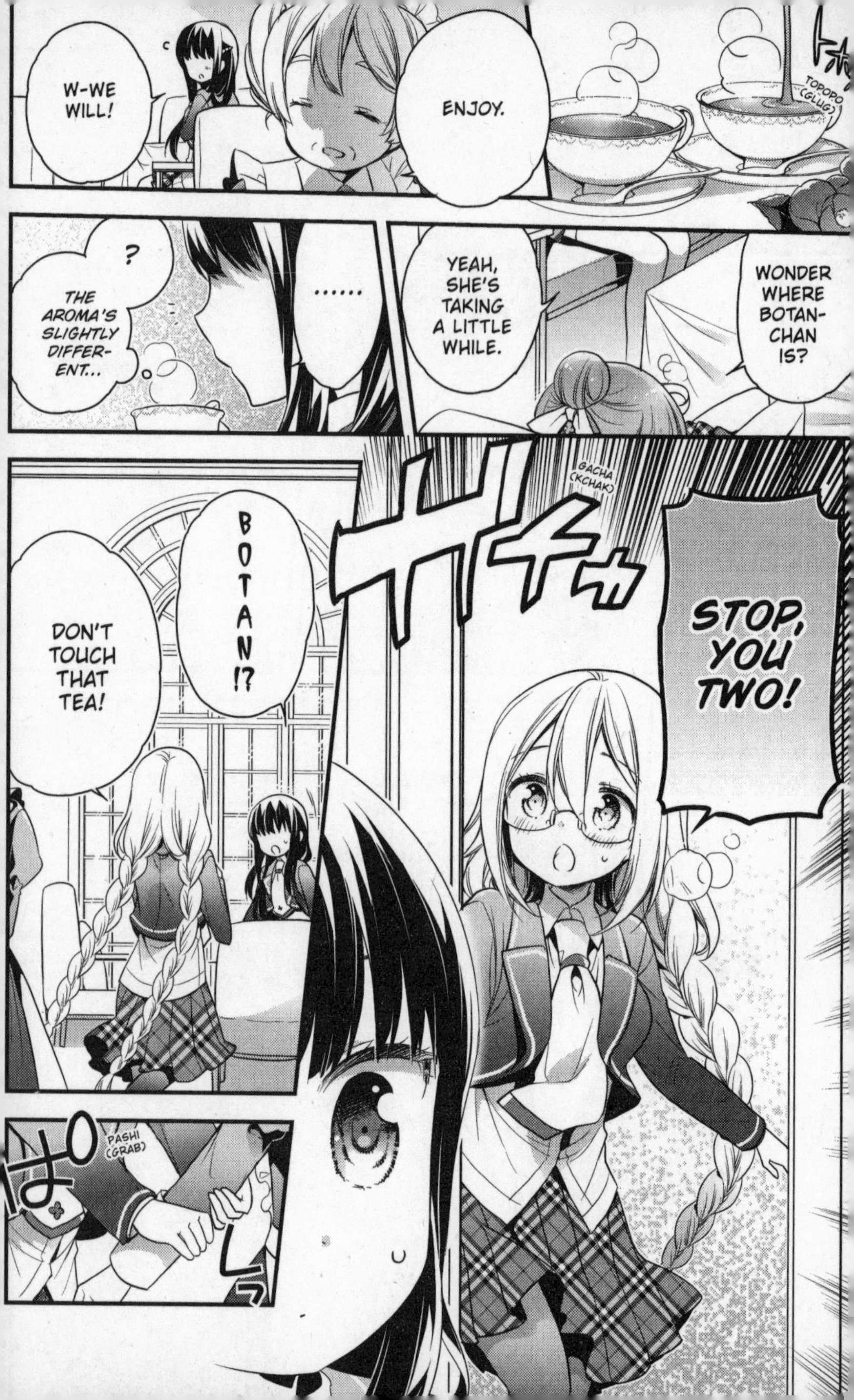
TOPOPO (GLUG)
ENJOY.
W-WE WILL!
WONDER WHERE BOTAN-CHAN IS?
YEAH, SHE'S TAKING A LITTLE WHILE.
......
?
THE AROMA'S SLIGHTLY DIFFER-ENT...
GACHA (KCHAK)
STOP, YOU TWO!
BOTAN!?
DON'T TOUCH THAT TEA!
PASHI (GRAB)

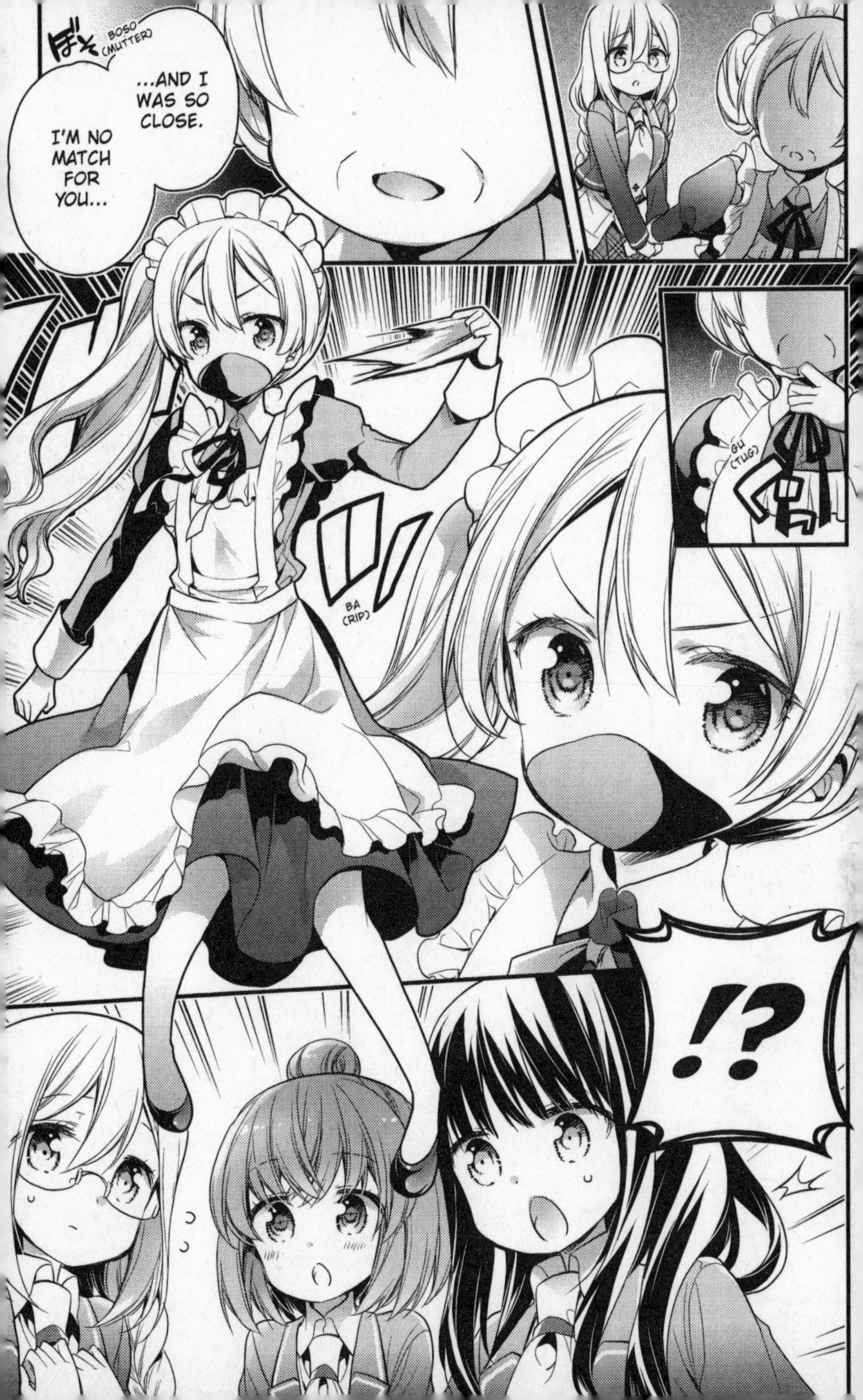
BOSO (MUTTER)
...AND I WAS SO CLOSE.
I'M NO MATCH FOR YOU...
GU (TUG)
BA (RIP)
!?

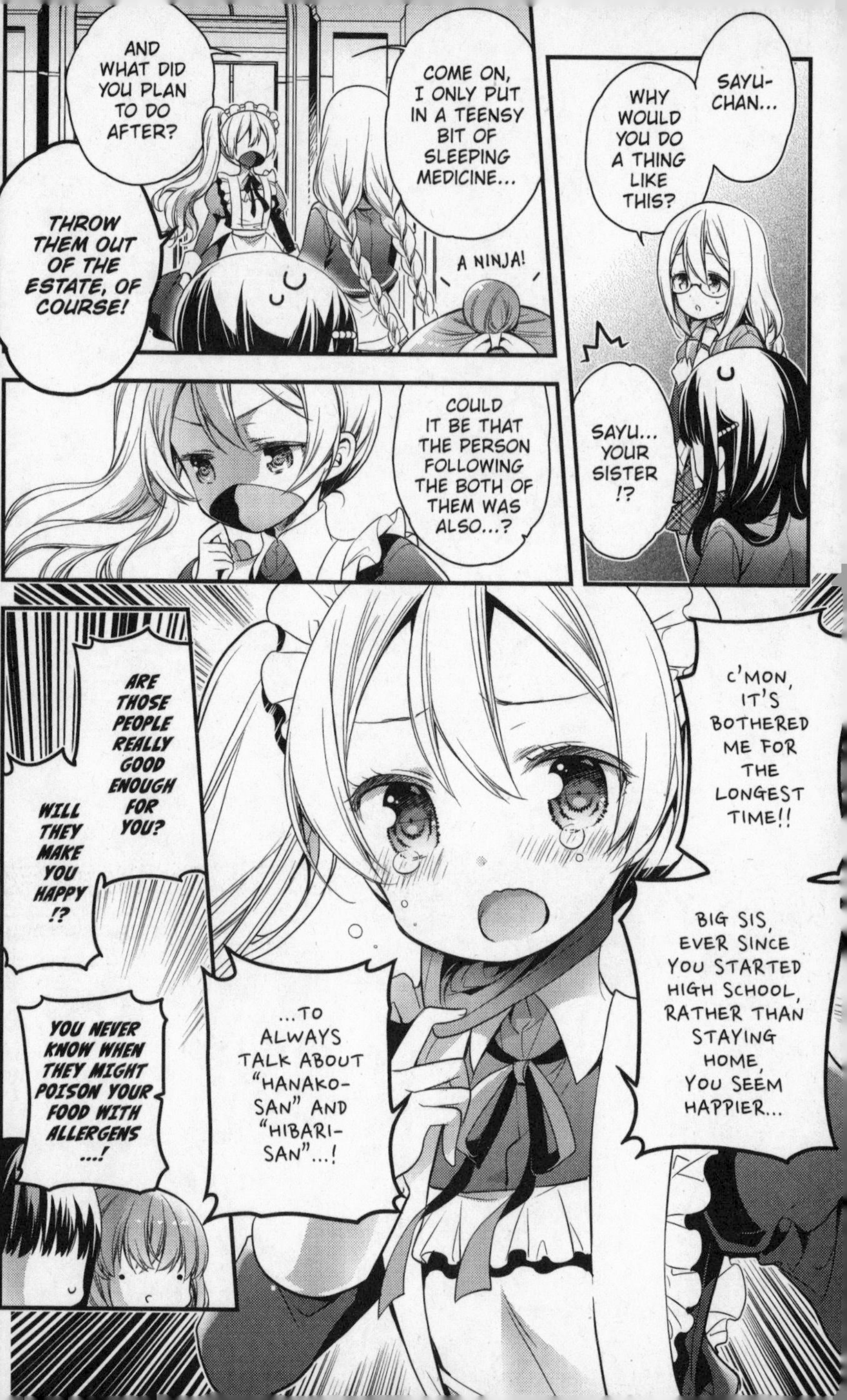
SAYU-CHAN...
WHY WOULD YOU DO A THING LIKE THIS?
SAYU... YOUR SISTER!?
COME ON, I ONLY PUT IN A TEENSY BIT OF SLEEPING MEDICINE...
A NINJA!
AND WHAT DID YOU PLAN TO DO AFTER?
THROW THEM OUT OF THE ESTATE, OF COURSE!
COULD IT BE THAT THE PERSON FOLLOWING THE BOTH OF THEM WAS ALSO...?
C'MON, IT'S BOTHERED ME FOR THE LONGEST TIME!!
BIG SIS, EVER SINCE YOU STARTED HIGH SCHOOL, RATHER THAN STAYING HOME, YOU SEEM HAPPIER...
...TO ALWAYS TALK ABOUT "HANAKO-SAN" AND "HIBARI-SAN"...!
ARE THOSE PEOPLE REALLY GOOD ENOUGH FOR YOU? WILL THEY MAKE YOU HAPPY!?
YOU NEVER KNOW WHEN THEY MIGHT POISON YOUR FOOD WITH ALLERGENS...!

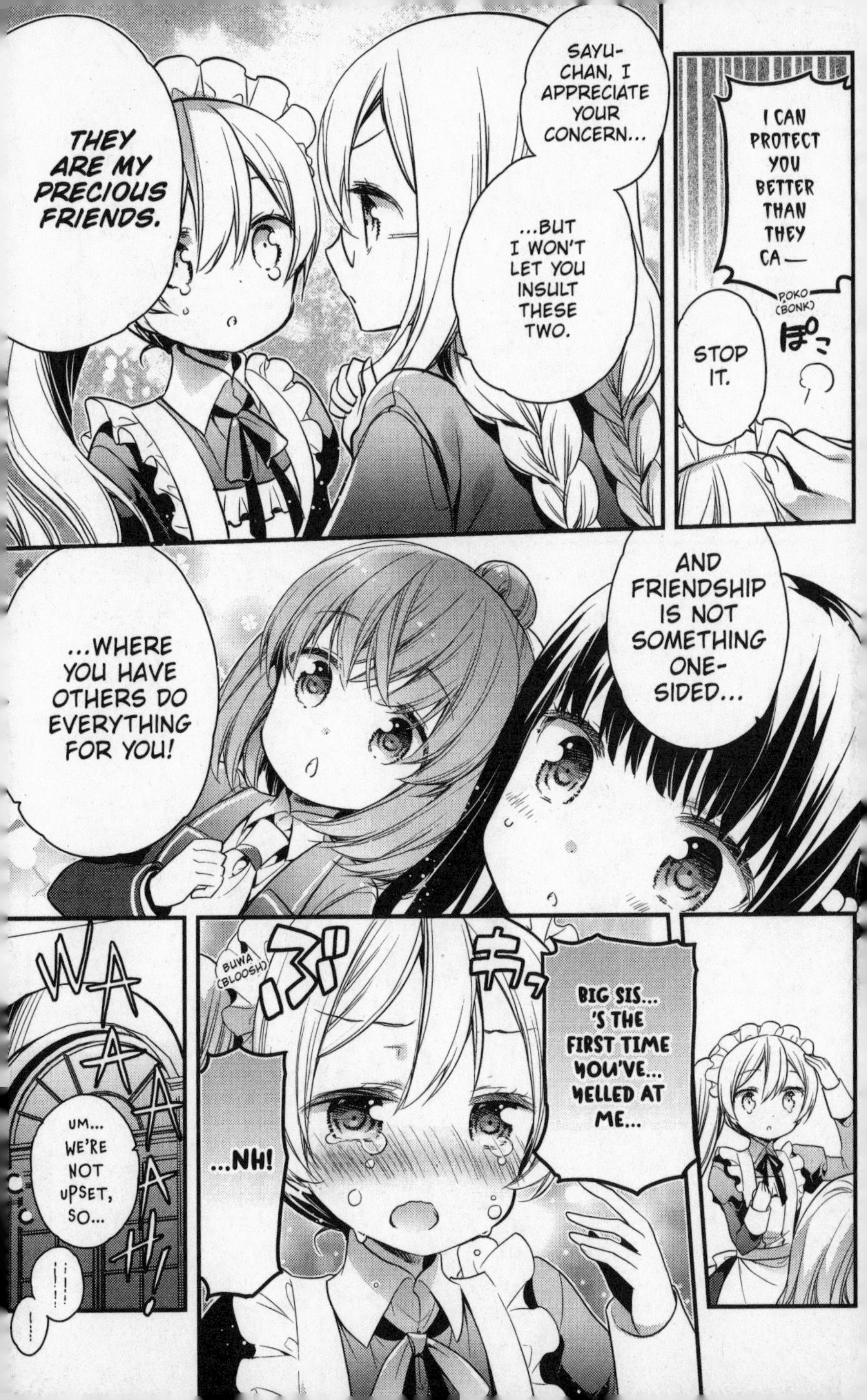
I CAN PROTECT YOU BETTER THAN THEY CA—
POKO (BONK)
ぽこ
STOP IT.
SAYU-CHAN, I APPRECIATE YOUR CONCERN...
...BUT I WON'T LET YOU INSULT THESE TWO.
THEY ARE MY PRECIOUS FRIENDS.
AND FRIENDSHIP IS NOT SOMETHING ONE-SIDED...
...WHERE YOU HAVE OTHERS DO EVERYTHING FOR YOU!
BIG SIS... 'S THE FIRST TIME YOU'VE... YELLED AT ME...
BUWA (BLOOSH)
...NH!
WAAAAH!
UM... WE'RE NOT UPSET, SO...
!!!

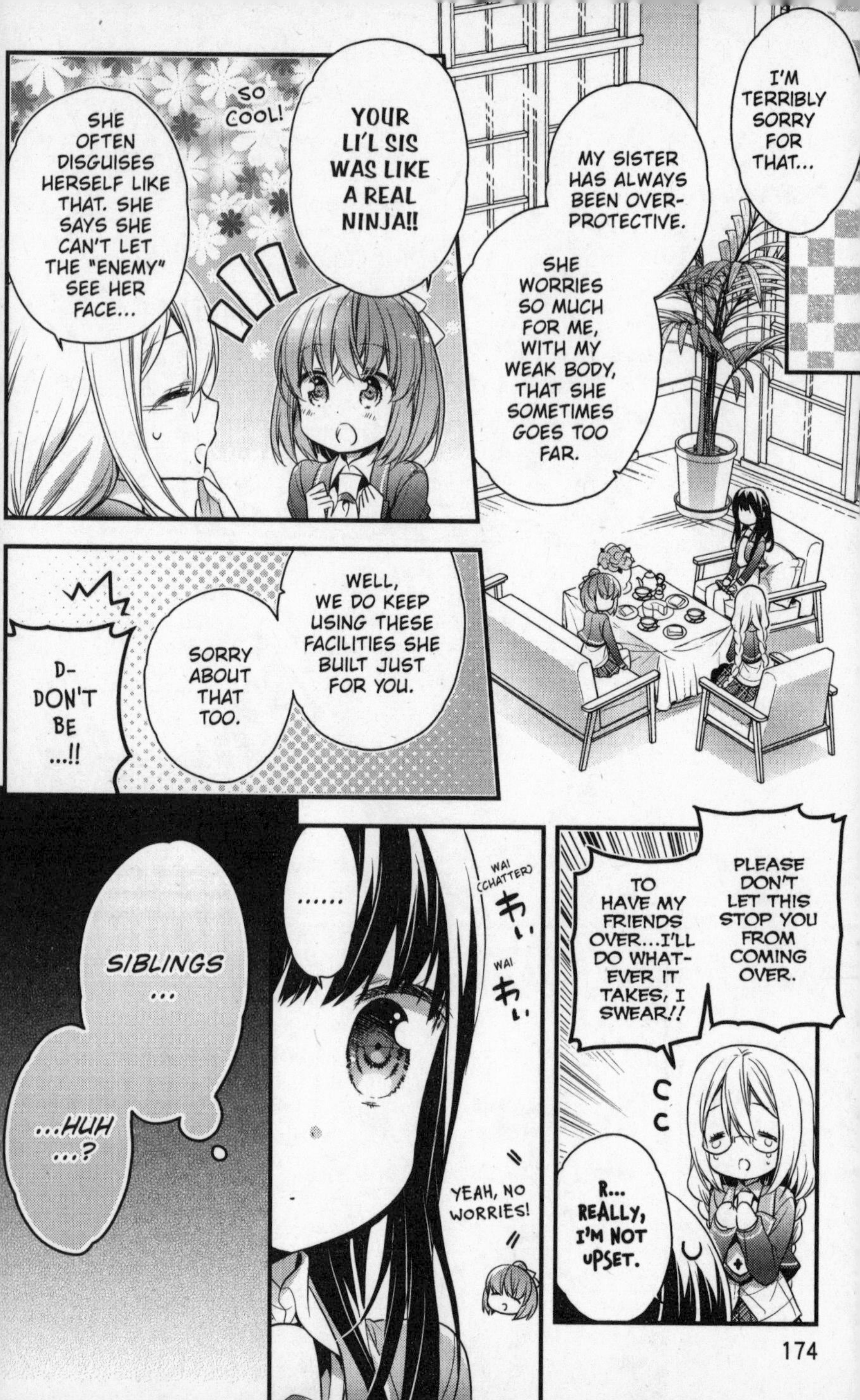
I'M TERRIBLY SORRY FOR THAT...
MY SISTER HAS ALWAYS BEEN OVER-PROTECTIVE.
SHE WORRIES SO MUCH FOR ME, WITH MY WEAK BODY, THAT SHE SOMETIMES GOES TOO FAR.
YOUR LI'L SIS WAS LIKE A REAL NINJA!!
SO COOL!
SHE OFTEN DISGUISES HERSELF LIKE THAT. SHE SAYS SHE CAN'T LET THE "ENEMY" SEE HER FACE...
WELL, WE DO KEEP USING THESE FACILITIES SHE BUILT JUST FOR YOU.
SORRY ABOUT THAT TOO.
D-DON'T BE...!!
PLEASE DON'T LET THIS STOP YOU FROM COMING OVER.
TO HAVE MY FRIENDS OVER...I'LL DO WHATEVER IT TAKES, I SWEAR!!
R... REALLY, I'M NOT UPSET.
......
WAI (CHATTER)
WAI
YEAH, NO WORRIES!
SIBLINGS...
...HUH...?

AnneHappy♪

unhappy
go lucky!

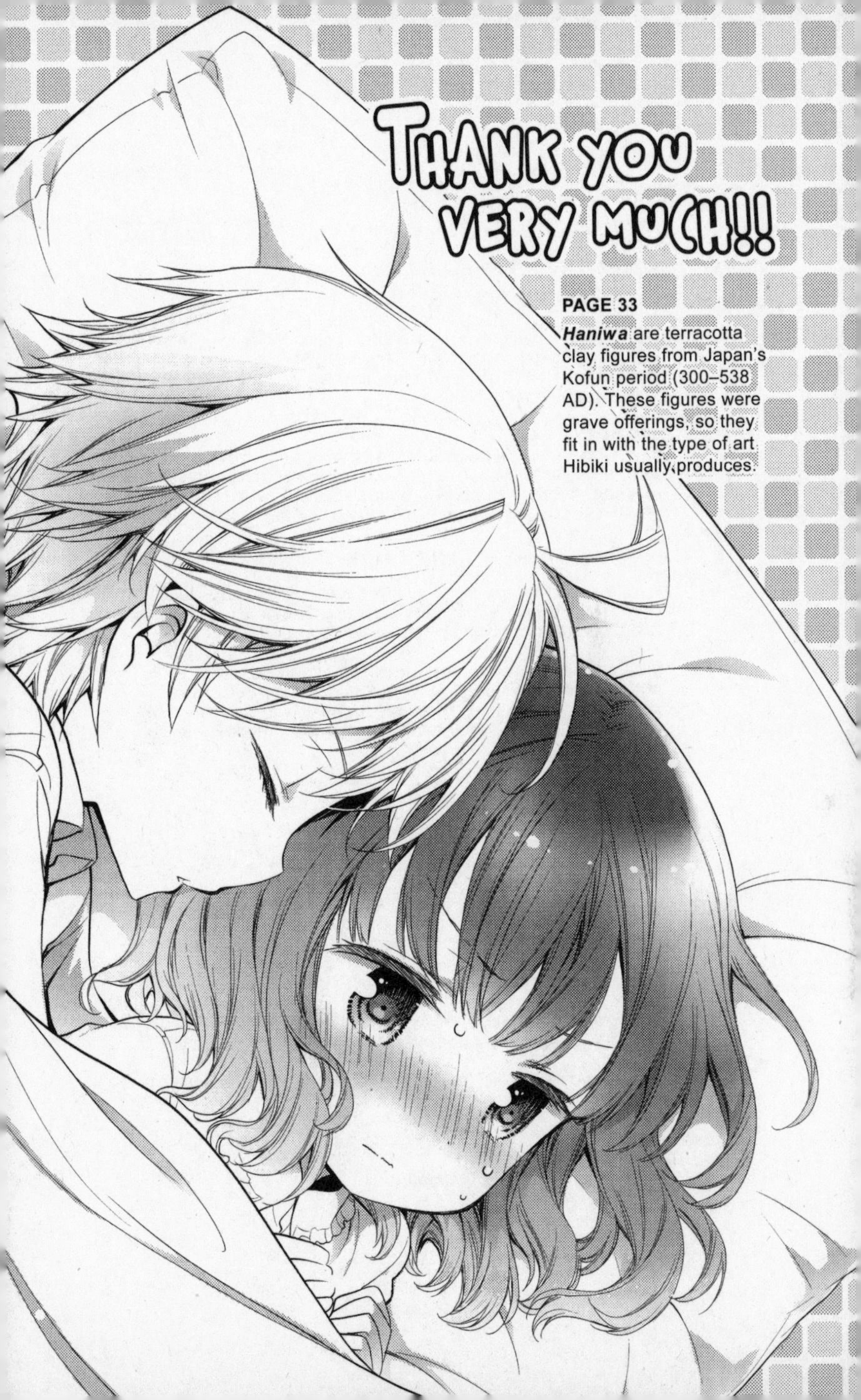
THANK YOU
VERY MUCH!!

PAGE 33

Haniwa are terracotta clay figures from Japan's Kofun period (300–538 AD). These figures were grave offerings, so they fit in with the type of art Hibiki usually produces.

COTOJI

Translation: Amanda Haley
Lettering: Rochelle Gancio

ANNE HAPPY ♪ VOL. 9
© 2018 Cotoji. All rights reserved. First published in Japan in 2018 by HOUBUNSHA CO., LTD., TOKYO. English translation rights in United States, Canada, and United Kingdom arranged with HOUBUNSHA CO., LTD. through Tuttle-Mori Agency, Inc., TOKYO.

English translation © 2019 by Yen Press, LLC

Yen Press
1290 Avenue of the Americas
New York, NY 10104

Visit us at yenpress.com
facebook.com/yenpress
twitter.com/yenpress
yenpress.tumblr.com
instagram.com/yenpress

First Yen Press Edition: May 2019

Yen Press is an imprint of Yen Press, LLC.
The Yen Press name and logo are trademarks of Yen Press, LLC.

The publisher is not responsible for websites (or their content) that are not owned by the publisher.

Library of Congress Control Number: 2016931012

ISBNs: 978-1-9753-5670-5 (paperback)
978-1-9753-5671-2 (ebook)

10 9 8 7 6 5 4 3 2 1

WOR

Printed in the United States of America